URBAN ECONOMICS

PERSPECTIVES IN URBAN GEOGRAPHY

VOLUME THIRTEEN

Concept's International Series in Geography

No. 1 Perspectives in Agricultural Geography (In Five Volumes)
Edited by NOOR MOHAMMAD

No. 2 Perspectives in Geomorphology (In Four Volumes)
Edited by H.S. SHARMA

No. 3 Perspectives in Urban Geography
Edited by C.S. YADAV

1. New Directions in Urban Geography
2. Comparative Urban Research
3. Comparative Urbanization : City Growth and Change
4.A Models in Urban Geography (Theoretical)
4.B Models in Urban Geography (Mathematical)
5. Urban Research Methods : Central Place, Hierarchical and City Size Models
6. Contemporary City Ecology
7. Slums, Urban Decline and Revitalization
8. Contemporary Urban Problems (Issues)
9. Rural-Urban Fringe
10. Morphology of Towns
11. Cities and Housing
12. Perceptual and Cognitive Image of the City
13. Urban Economics
14. City Planning : Problems and Prospects
15. City Planning : Administration and Participation
16.A Urban Planning and Policies : Reorientation of Policy Norms
16.B Urban Planning and Policies : Cross-Cultural Urban Policies

Concept's International Series in Geography No. 3

PERSPECTIVES IN URBAN GEOGRAPHY

VOLUME THIRTEEN

URBAN ECONOMICS

Edited by

C. S. YADAV

CONCEPT PUBLISHING COMPANY, NEW DELHI

First Published 1987

Published by

Naurang Rai
Concept Publishing Company
H-13, Bali Nagar
NEW DELHI-110015 (India)

Printed in India by

Printway India
at S. Narayan and Sons
7117/18, Pahari Dhiraj,
DELHI-110006

PREFACE

NATURE OF URBAN GEOGRAPHY

THERE are several studies on urban geography which reveal that, as a major sub-discipline, it has a long tail but a short body. However, the spectrum is so vast and broad that researchers are able to make general statements in defence of its conception, philosophy, nature and orientation. Urban geography today encompasses and interfaces with various disciplines which are interested in urban studies. As an introduction to this series, our task here is to make an attempt to briefly review the development of geographical interest in various aspects of cities.

There are several reviews of the early development of urban geography which have been dealt with by Berry and Harton (1970)[1] and Carter (1974).[2] Berry and Harton in their book, *Geographical Perspective on Urban System*, have made an attempt to introduce readers to its present-day status. They have clearly resolved that "the formative years of the social science in the late nineteenth century and early twentieth century were also the years in which urban studies first developed,"[3] thus providing the context for the geographer's emerging interest in cities. However, the emergence of urban studies dates back to the writing of Greek scholars, but as a sub-discipline, it has reached its present-day status only in the past 30 years.

In their historical perspective the works on urban geography show that the pre-20th century studies primarily concerned themselves with themes of location, size and shape of the cities. The initial findings were strongly subjective, descriptive and dependent more on observation such as the works of Hassert (1907)[4] and Blanchard (1911).[5] In the succeeding years the conceptual framework of site and situation was criticized by Aurousseau (1924)[6] and Crowe (1938)[7], their conception being that cities were not inanimate objects in landscape, but also organic elements which involved people and their movements. The morphologist, later in 1960, truly brought the indigenous line of evolution in the sphere of urban geography and studies on the build-up fabric of cities (Conzone, 1960).[8] Smails (1955)[9] constituted the prime base of urban geography, which remained articulated without any major conceptual change till early 1960s. The studies on the morphological aspects of the urban system were influenced by external forces, consequently the methodological frameworks got impetus within the discipline. At this juncture the evolution of concepts was not based on environment but took shelter under the umbrella of economics of location, and incorporated analysis of land values and rents, and the concept of nodality and accessibility. These concepts were derived from the economic theories of Cooley (1894)[10], Weber (1899),[11] and Hurd (1903).[12]

The Chicago School of Urban Ecology hastened the evolution of urban geography. In his monumental work Park (1925)[13] developed the idea of order and analysis of towns. Further, a powerful thrust and much of the rationale was provided to the studies of urban geography by the Central Place Theory of Christallar (1933).[14]

The impact of the statistical method was powerful and it brought rapid and enormous changes in the field of urban geography. It also brought new insights into the development and application of urban geography towards increased quantification. Brian J. Berry, a pioneer in the field, analysed the spatial order, size and location of towns and cities. There was widespread use of innovative techniques to explore the nature of urban problems, hypotheses were tested, new theories propounded and old theories remodelled. The statistical methods were put to a variety of uses. Smith (1965)[15] evaluated the classification of settlements ; Berry and Garrison (1956)[16] examined the utility of the rank-size rule for urban populations. The models of Park and Burgess (1925),[17] Harris and Ullman (1945)[18] and Homar Hoyt (1939)[19] were tested and re-examined by various geographers.

A new impetus to urban geography came from social area analysis which was initially propounded by Shevky and Bell (1955)[20] and later on this provided a basis for factorial ecology. The collaboration of this stream in urban geography was offered by Berry (1971),[21] Herbert (1972)[22] and Johnston (1971).[23] As a consequence of these thrusts in geography after 1960, the techniques of investigation were sharpened and this has provided the basis for a scientific explanation of cities. Attempts were made to introduce new theories and frame laws to make the explanation of events more rational and logical. Sophisticated models were propounded as urban geography entered a new era of rationalizing the subject matter of urban studies on the basis of new philosophies, new concepts, new theories, new methodologies and applications.

However, the status of contemporary urban geography has been elevated only recently by the behavioural approach. The studies of perception and cognition which have a long tradition in physiology were first introduced into the field of geography by Lynch (1960),[24] Dowson and Stea (1973)[25] Gould and White (1974).[26] At present there is a sudden spurt in the studies on the subject with a new paradigm. But the full impact of behavioural approaches upon urban geography has yet to be realized.

The aim of this series is to seek reorientation of the discipline strengthened by new philosophies, methodologies, subject matter or application. The series has been arranged in such a way that all contemporary viewpoints are covered comprehensively. Hopefully, this series will inspire researchers to appreciate the work already done by geographers in studying cities. Geography by nature seems to be a synthesizing field of inquiry. As such we have made an endeavour to combine some of the otherwise disparate facts garnered by other disciplines in such a manner that we can gain a better understanding of the urban system. The study of urban geography is essential if we are to analyse the human consequences of the settlements in which we live. It is useful to planners, decision makers in government and corporations and also to each one of us as citizens. Finally, it gives us a perspective on what may be happening to our cities and to the nature.

To achieve the above goal only those contributions with originality and contrasting viewpoints were selected for inclusion in this series. In doing so the editor does not wish to compete with the journals in the field in which innovative research and methodological aspects are presented. But he does wish to convey, and convey with conviction, that significant researches are being undertaken in the different branches of urban geography and in other allied disciplines. The present series is an attempt to provide a selective reappraisal and rigorous examination of the assumptions and the urge to disseminate new knowledge created by the mutual interaction. Emphasis is also placed on the conceptualization and theorization of the subject matter so that general laws may emerge. A conscious effort has been to organize the series in such a way that it reflects the philosophical approach parallel to that of the behavioural school. Finally, a vigorous attempt has been made to demonsrate throughout the series how geographers are basically involved in solving the urban problems.

C.S. YADAV

REFERENCES

1. Berry and Harton, *Geographic Perspectives on Urban Systems : With Integrated Readings*, New Jersey, Prentice Hall, Inc, Englewood Cliffs, 1970.
2. Carter, *The Study of Urban Geography*, Edward Arnold, London, 1974.
3. Berry and Harton, 1970.
4. Hassert, K., *Die Stadte Geographisch Betrachect*, Leipzig, 1907.
5. Blanchard, R., *Grenoble : Etude de Geographic Urbanine*, Paris, 1911.
6. Aurousseau, M., "Recent Contributions to Geography : A Review," *Geographical Review*, 1924, 14, p. 444.
7. Crowe, P. R., "On Progress in Geography", *Scottish Geographical Magazine*, 1938, 54, 1-19.
8. Conzone, M.R.G., "The Plan Analysis of an English City Centre", In Norkorg (Ed.), *Proceedings of I.G.U. Symposium on Urban Geography*, C.W.K. Gleerup, Lund, 1962.
9. Smails, A.E., "The Urban Mess of England and Wales", *Transactions and Papers*, Institute of British Geographers, 1946, 11, 85, p. 101.
10. Cooley, C.H., "The Theory of Transportation", *Publications of the American Economic Association*, 1894, 9, p. 5-7.
11. Weber, A.F., *The Growth of Cities in the Nineteenth Century : A Study of Statistics*, New York, 1899.
12. Hurd, R., *Principles of City Land Values : New York Record and Guide*, 1903, p. 19-21.
13. Park, R.E., "Suggestions for the Investigation of Human Behaviour in an Urban Environment", in R.E. Park, E.W. Burgess, R.D. Mackenzie (eds.), *The City*, University of Chicago Press, 1925.

14. Christallar, W., *Central Place in Southern Germany*, Gustar Fischer, Teno, 1933.
15. Smith, R.M.T., "Method and Purpose in Functional Town Classification", *Annals of Association of American Geographers*, 1965, 55, pp. 539-548.
16. Garrison, W.L., "Applicability of Statistical Inference to Geographical Research", *Geographical Review*, 1956, 46, 427, 429.
17. Burgess, E.W., "The Growth of City", in R.E. Park, E.W. Burgess and R.D. Mackenzie (eds.), *The City*, University of Chicago Press, 1925.
18. Ullman, E.L., "The Nature of Cities", *Annals, American Academy of Political and Social Science*, 1945, 242, 7-17.
19. Hoyt, H., *The Structure and Growth of Residential Neighbourhoods in American Cities*, Washington, Federal Housing Administration, 1939.
20. Shevky, E. and Bell, W., *Social Area Analysis*, Stanford University Press, Stanford, 1955.
21. Berry, B.J.L. (ed.), "Comparative Factorial Ecology", *Economic Geographic (Supplement)*, 1971, 47.
22. Herbert, D.T., *Urban Geography : A Social Perspective*, David and Charles, Newton Abbot, 1972.
23. Johnston, *Urban Residential Pattern*, Bell, London, 1971.
24. Lynch, *Image of the City*, Massachusetts, Cambridge, 1960.
25. Dowson and Stea, "Image and Environment", Chicago and London, 1973.
26. Gould and White, R., *Mental Maps*, London, 1974.

ACKNOWLEDGEMENT

We thank Editors Gerd-Michael Hellstern, Frithjof Spreer Hellmut Wollmann, *Heft 2, Vol. II* and *Vol. III*, for their permission to use material from "Applied Urban Research," Proceedings of the European Meeting on Applied Research, Essen, Oct. 2-4, 1981.

CONTENTS

SECTION THREE

SEGREGATION AND HOUSING MARKET

SECTION FOUR

INTRA-URBAN LOCATION OF ECONOMIC ACTIVITIES

LIST OF CONTRIBUTORS

Masatoshi A. Abe : Department of Economics, Marquette University, Milwaukee, Wisconsin

S. Banerjee : Department of Geography, University of Bombay, Vidyanagari, Bombay-400098

W. Patrick Beaton : Associate Research Professor, Centre for Urban Policy Research, Rutgers University, New Brunswick, New Jersey

Malcolin Fairweather : Associate Professor and Chairman, Department of Geography, State University of New York, Plattsburgh, New York, 12901, USA

Christine Furedy : Division of Social Science, York University, Toronto

Clifford M. Guy : University of Wales, Institute of Science and Technology, Cardiff

Rolf G. Heinze : University of Paderborn, FB 1 (Sociology) Warburger Str. 100, D-4790 Paderborn

Detlev Ipsen : University of Kassel, Department of City and Landscape Planning, Henschelstrasse 2, D-3500 Kassel, Federel Republic of Germany

George M. Johnston : Currently affiliated with Eastern Oregan State College, La Grande, Ozegon 97850

S.R. Joshi : Department of Geography, University of Bombay, Vidyanagari, Bombay 400098

Fabio Lando : Assistant Professor in Economic Geography, University of Vinice, Italy

C. John Langley, Jr. : Professor of Marketing and Transportation, Department of Marketing and Transportation, College of Business Administration, University of Tennessee, Knoxville-37916

Prof. Gilles Lavigne : Tele-Universite de l'Universite de Quebec, Montreal

Sharon G. Levin : Department of Economics, University of Missouri-St. Louis, St. Louis, Missouri-63121

John F. McDonald : Department of Economics, University of Illinois at Chicago Circle, Chicago, Illinois, 60680

Thomas Olk : University of Oldenburg, FB 1 (Education) Ammerlander Heerstr, 67-99, D-2900 Oldenburg

Tonu Puu : Ordinary Professor in Economy Chairman of the Department, University of Umea, S 901 87 Umea, Swedan

B. Merenne-Schoumaker : University de Liége 7 Place du Vingt-Aout 400 Liege, Belgium

Kumares C. Sinha : Department of Civil Engineering, Marquette University, Milwaukee, Wisconsin

Leonard B. Sossaman : Planning Director, City of Concord, Concord, N. C.

C.S. Yadav : Reader and Head, Department of Geography, Bhagat Singh College, Delhi University, New Delhi

ONE

C. S. YADAV

INTRODUCTION

CITIES exists where there is action. It is a focal point where more than any where else new knowledge, new products, new life styles, new art forms and new social institutions emerge (Werner 1984).[1] In this milieu of complex societies, there is a high degree of functional interdependence of economic and social services. Several urban theorists have advocated that a city play a dominant role to foster this interdependence which in turn increases economic efficiency and social advancement, contacts with diverse people, products, and points of view is seen as a source of cultural attainment where as for economist this interdependence creates a division of labour that develop the markets for commodities and services which provide subject matter of the discipline under consideration. There is no denying to this fact, in virtually any city, regardless of its population size, there exist any array of economic activities and functions in which much of the population is regularly engaged. The expansion of economic activities in a city usually facilitated because city provide superior transport facilities for the movement of goods and people, it also provides large and flexible pool of labour. Apart from these two basic facilities, cities also provide provisions of certain professional services, and new technological innovations. Thus cities not only provide a wider variety of goods and services, they also provide many commodities. Another important aspect which catches the eyes of economist is that city is the geographical location where the poorest member of the society are most likely find opportunities to improve their socio-economic status. Thus it will not be wrong to assert here that any plan for the improvement of urban scene whilst ignoring economic consideration would be to invite disaster (Goodal 1972).[2] Economic resources are limited in quantity and they also vary considerably in quality. Therefore, a rational decision to allocate these resources amongst competing uses must be taken so that a society may achieve the highest possible level of economic efficiency.

THE SCOPE OF URBAN ECONOMICS

Although economist have studied urban problems for a long time, the discipline of urban economics is the still in its infancy. It is so infant that very term one may not be appropriate. The reason is obvious, because there is not yet agreement on what constitutes the discipline of urban economics. As a matter of fact there is enormous body of knowledge available concerning cities, which is still expanding at a most impressive rate, however the development of urban economics has been uneven and upto date there is no agreement on what constitute the discipline of urban economics (Edel and Rothenberg 1972).[3] As a result its scope and limits, as well as its intellectual underpinnings, continue to be debated widely. Thus it is not surprising that urban economics is not well defined in the light of the relatively recent range of research in the field. Traditionally urban economics is defined in terms of urban problems that take place in an urban setting. If it is taken for granted that approximately three fourth's of economic activities are carried in urban areas and hence all economic problems are called urban problems. Therefore it is difinitely accepted that all economic activities occurring in the city is "urban economics". Thus this field of study has incredible proportions to claim that urban economics includes the problems of growth, unemployment, competition and monopoly and income distribution : But this does not state urban economics as a meaningful category of study, it must be defined in such a way that it would explore important relationships. In this context then the study of urban economics deals with how a city affects the economic welfare of its population "it investigates how cities function as a factor of production" (Rasmussen 1973).[4] This definition constitutes a wider perspective of the relationship of urban economics to regional economics. In essence, urban economics analyses how the city raises the welfare of its inhabitants given level of population, employment and per capita income.

The key role that urban economist can play is to analyse the essential character of urban areas in terms of concentration of various activities—economic, social and political—over space, which in turn generate capital earning so to an urban economic geographer it is the spatial concentration of activities that is the central fact. The analytical structure of urban economics begins with the queries—why activities cluster in an urban setting? Why these activities and what difference this clustering makes? It is a undeniable fact that the unique spatial relations between the character of many of the types of urban issues that have given this field its recent public relevance (Edel and Rothenberg 1972).[5] In this way urban economics can tackle a wide variety of urban problems by organizing the subject matter around the economics of spatial relations. By this one should not make conclusion that space is the only consideration to be emphasized. It only suggests the technique to approach a phenomenon and tests its validity how it fits into the spatial relationship that make up a city and then make an attempt to explore what special characteristics this spatial linkage imparts to the phenomenon. So these characteristics are only analytical tools with which to examine the complex phenomenon of economic activities in a particular city. Undoubtedly then this analytical framework provides a comprehensive account of inter- and intra-urban location patterns, the land market, the housing market, the economics of spatial segregation of racial and ethnic groups, the congestion and pollution, the urban transportation system and financial problems of local government.

The location theory and metropolitan growth

The urban economists consider it noteworthy to examine the location of economic activities, growth of cities and the origins of some urban problems in a market economy, so that economic conditions of cities may be investigated thoroughly. The economics of a city consists of overall economic activities, their growth and decline and the composition of their productive activity. As a matter of fact the location decisions of firms and households and the effect of these decisions on the patterns of land uses and spatial variations of these activities, is the domain of economic location theory. Regional scientists and economic geographers have made concerted efforts to explain the development of cities, growth of industries and the effect of principal exporting activities on production. So the urban economists are primarily concerned with the internal organization of a city, they follow the dictom of Brian J. Berry's phrase "systems within system of cities".[6] In a free market economy, an economic analysis of a city can describe the city as coming into existence because owners of various productive resources, various form of labour and capital, consider it to be profitable to use these resources in combination with land parcels located in close together. William Alonso[7] in this direction has made an attempt to review the theory of location of the firm. He found that individual decisions of firms are always governed by existing patterns of residential and business location. Alonso's analysis throws light on the processes in which firm locations lead to the creation of market areas with the producing firms at their centers, and the additional agglomerative forces that lead different producers to concentrate at a limited number of central places.

The external economics of agglomeration always leads firms to cluster together (Raymond Verman).[8] The need for close contract among firms, may not be as great in all industries as it is in the provision of office services. The rank size distribution of cities in world is largely effected by government spending decisions. All economic theorist believed that a theory of location of economic activities in cities advocates that a evolutionary process of market decisions and a market with instantaneous relocation of firms can yield an efficient allocation of activities in space. The theory of microeconomics propagates that in some perfect market decentralization decision of the location of firm lead to efficient allocation which is based on the principle, where no further advantage for one person can be had with out the disadvantage of another. In this respect decentralized allocation may lead to inefficiencies where a firm does not take into account the effect of its location on other firms. Koopmans and Beckman[9] postulated a model in which each firm has a fixed activity to perform, which it can perform with different degrees of profit in different locations. Moses

(1958)[10] in his analysis advocates that location can influence a firm's choice of, and changes in productive processes by affecting relative proximity of different inputs.

Intra-urban location and land use

The urban economist have largely concentrated on intra-urban location patterns of different functions which are rendered by the cities. Business districts, industrial parks, residential neighbourhoods represent a familiar functional separation of land uses within a city. As a matter of fact urban economist and ecologist have developed separate theories of land values and land use succession. Today the urban economist are trying to show how locational patterns in city affect the nature of many specific urban problems. Most of the urban economist have raised the issue of co-locational economies or the advantage of proximity to interrelated activities which help the survival of cities. The co-locational economies provide a rational explanation of the dustering of some activities into different districts, which depend on the economic specialization or the economic base of the city itself. It is an established fact that once in a city any clustering of activities located in any district, there are immediate advantages to others locating near them. The urban economist have postulated that it is less costly to commute to work in these districts from one's home or to carry business from one's office, shop or plant. They have advocated the principle that in a market economy land near a center of activity can command a higher price than more peripheral land. Therefore urban economist have constructed models of the demand for land based on the advantages of proximity. There is a tendency of firms and households to adopt a trade off principle in their location decisions and always try to locate near to the center because of advantages of proximity. It has been observed that major retail establishments always tend to seek central locations, where they would be convenient to access from the population of entire city. Some models of this process are presented by William Alonso (1960),[11] Edvin, S. Mills (1967),[12] Leon Moses, Harold F. Williamson Jr. (1967),[13] Mathew Edel (1972).[14]

Labour force and economic base of the city

From the previous section one can draw conclusion that in

virtually all cities, irrespective of their population size, there exist an array of economic activities and functions in which most of the population is regularly engaged who contribute to the city's economic support. It is an established fact that the wages and salaries earned by the employed labourforce contribute much of the economic support and taxable wealth of the city. The numerical size of the urban labour force is our aspect of the urban economy. Also significant is the output, character and structure of the urban labour force. Therefore urban economics analyses the demographic traits of population in terms of occupations in which people are engaged, income levels, degrees of unemployment, composition by race and sex. They stress more on the industrial composition of the labour force and kinds of economic activities in which the urban workers are engaged. There are various attempts made by urban economist to divide the urban labour force into industrial groups and into economic sector.

A major concern of urban economist is the reason why cities exist. The probable answer to this query is obtained when we consider that cities exist because within them are performed certain operations—industrial and commercial which facilitates the production, transfer and distribution of goods and services for the population of areas outside the city itself. The output of goods and services in an industry in the city is consumed by both residents of the city and by residents beyond the bounds of the city in the tributory area or service area. It reveals then the fact that in reality there exist two production sectors of the urban economy that have to do with the spatial relationship between location of the Producer (Northam 1979).[15] Therefore a situation arises where a portion of the economic activity of the city is to satisfy the needs of local residents, with the other portion going to satisfy demands of more distant, non-local consumer. Thus determination of the extent to which each of the urban functions serves the population outside the city, in contrast to the production of goods and services for consumption inside the city, is an important part of the urban economic base. Most studies of the urban economic base are concerned with economic activity and production destined to serve demands of consumers in two sectors—non local consumers in the basic sector and local consumer in the non-basic sector. There are various academicians who have evaluated the importance of basic and non basic activities in a city. They have provided methodology and procedures to be adopted to classify the cities on the basis of 'basic', 'non basic' functions rendered by different cities. The list includes Gunnar Alexander (1956),[16] John W. Alexander (1956),[17] Edward L. Ullman and Michael F. Dacey,[18] Richard T. Pratt (1968),[19] Craig L. Moor (1975).[20] The studies of economic base of a city appropriately explain the characteristics of the urban population and its economy. A thorough understanding of the economic base analysis leads to an understanding of the role of the specific city in its regional setting and of the interrelationships between the city and its tributory area. The value of economic base studies is to provide information of value in implementation of tax policy. They also help in the identification of the future economic structure and population of the city.

ABOUT THIS VOLUME

Scholars, who are engaged in analysing urbanization and its consequences must collect information and derive ideas from diverse fields : archaeology, economics, geography, law, mathematics, politics, administration, psychology, regional science, sociology, traffic engineering, urban and regional planning etc. This volume attempts an exploratory survey of one of these fields, namely economics and include those papers which emphasize the importance of economic consideration in the functioning of urban systems. The volume is designed to offer to the reader a survey of themes and analytical tools that have been used in the recent development of economic analysis of the city. We have collected here a series of articles which offer a variety of analysis and perspectives on some of the more notable urban problems, local finance, clustering of economic activities, commuter transportation, segregation of housing and property values.

This volume, however, is not merely a sample of methods and policy discussion, rather we have attempted in our selection to present a possible scheme of organization for urban economics as a sub-discipline of urban studies. As a matter of fact the readings provide some background in the application of economics to the study of cities for those in other disciplines as well as for the public at large. For convenience of reading the volume is divided into five sections : (i) sectors of economy and financial management of cities ; (ii) intra urban land values and rental values ; (iii) segregation and housing market ; (iv) intra urban location of economic activities and (v) urban transportation.

State and regional economic development has for many years focussed upon efforts to encourage the growth of jobs and the immigration of high wage industry into economically depressed areas. Essential intermediary activities such as market research, financing wholesaling and advertising, traditionally have exported their services out of a few major metropolitan centers instead of being spread like levening throughout the national economy. Now under the current redistribution of national economic activity, there seems to be an assumption that if goods producer can be induced to move into a new location, the problem of locating and servicing his consumer will resolve itself. In a relatively stable regional economy, it may be safely assumed that normal market pressures will ensure an adequate supply of the services of economic intermediaries. Marketing firms will know the locations of producers and consumers (both intermediate and final) : and lines of communications will be well established linking financing, advertising, shipping and inventory operations with the producer. The role of economic intermediaries in an economic system has gone largely unexplored to this date. The authors W. Patrick Beaton and Leonard B. Sossamon in their article "The Role of Economic Intermediaries in the Shifting National Economy : The Northeast Versus the Sunbelt" analyses the contribution of trade sector to the economic development. The analysis is an attempt to show more clearly the dramatic impact of trade and more specially, the effect of a lag, in the growth of this sector in developing economics. The examination in this paper involve the specification and estimation of the determinants of state wholesales, the locational shifts that have occurred in the interstate trade component of wholesale sales and lastly the role that wholesale activity quaeconomic intermediaries has upon the economic well-being of a states citizenry. The authors in this article explore the role of the economic intermediary which is to provide a bridge in line and over space between a producer and a consumer. According to the authors the nation is currently involved in a shift of economic activity and population out of the Northeast and into the states of the Sunbelt. This work argues that a key component to balanced economic growth and development : economic intermediaries, is lagging behind the growth of manufacturing and retail activity in the Sunbelt states. Based upon an analysis of the residual obtained from a determinants equation of state wholesale sales, the interstate component of wholesale sales is isolate, mapped, and used in turn as a determinant of state's family income structure. It is concluded that the presence of economic intermediaries, as represented by the interstate component of wholesale sales, is positively related to state income structure.

Thus, if an economic development strategy to improve a state's income level is being planned, it must include efforts to ease the entrance of economic intermediaries along with the commonly sought after manufacturing industries into the region or state.

When the economic and political situation in the FRG had consolidated at the beginning of the year 1960s, unemployment had become a marginal phenomenon. Not only official policy but also the social sciences considered large scale unemployment to be a period belonging to the past. Since the mid 1970s, however, this situation has changed fundamentally. The FRG is experiencing comparatively high unemployment levels for several years with a strongly increasing tendency during the past year, and there are many signs indicating a chronic under employment for the years to come. The authors Rolf. G. Heinze and Thomas Olk in their article "Informal and Peripheral Economics in Sociological Theory : The Two Faces of the Informal Sector" focus their attention on the future development of the Informal Sector in the Federal Republic of Germany. The authors identify that as a result of unemployment and financial crisis of the welfare state the informal economy which had been neglected for a long time is being brought again to the forefront. According to the authors the informal sector comprises any types of activities which are performed outside the formal economy and which do not show up in gross national product figures. The work within the domestic households as well as jobs not registered in the official economy and voluntary work for self help groups, unions and associations, constitute an essential part of the informal sector. The rediscovery and increasing importance of the informal economy which exists beyond market and state has an ambivalent character which the authors discuss in their paper. In the first section of the present paper the authors provide a general view of the actual labour market situation in the FRG. Then against the background of economic stagnation periods, selected strategies of flexibilization pursued by the capital are discussed more in detail. In the last the authors turn to the behaviour of those groups of workers who strive for a new combination of employment and informal work.

The term "informal sector" is the legacy of attempts of the late 1960s and the 1970s to characterise and explain the economic dualism of modernizing societies. The concept of 'formal' and 'informal' has taken root in academic studies and policy discussions and has served to focus attention on a number of problems of employment and the urban poor in developing countries. Undoubtedly the principal factor in the general acceptance of the term "informal sector" in the last decade was its use in studies sponsored by the ILO Under its World Employment Programme (WEP) which grew out of the ICO/UNDP mission report on Kenya, Employment, Income and Equality (1971). The ILO urbanization and employment research project has sponsored a series of case studies of selected cities, all making reference to the informal sector, with an ultimately comparative purpose. Two of these have been of Calcutta. However, international literature on employment and the formal sector contains few references to them. The author Christine Furedy in his article "The Informal Sector in Calcutta : Issues for Analysis" makes an attempt to examine the use of the informal sector concept in discussions of employment in Calcutta, considering the articulation of issues for this city in the light of current trends of research and discussion. The author emphatically demonstrates that this analysis should raise questions concerning the use of the concept as a basis for policy recommendations, and its applicability to a complex Indian city.

Local governments use a wide variety of financial inducements to influence the location of economic activity. These devices include property tax delusions industrial revenue bonus of various types and urban development. Local governments also provide assistance to businesses in the forms of land assembly and provision of these services seriously and the use of these inducements has grown rapidly. The local officials may be percieved as "doing nothing" about the problem. Nevertheless they are engaged in efforts which are ineffective but generate favourable political publicity. The contention of the author John F. Mc Donald in his paper "An Economic Analysis of Local Inducements for Business" is that there is a better explanation for local inducements to business which can be derived from the standard urban economic analysis of real estate and local real estate taxes. The analysis uses conventional micro economic theory to focus on the impacts of various subsidy programs on the intensity of landuse and related variables at a specific urban site.

Abstract

This paper presents a theoretical and preliminary empirical examination of various local real estate subsidies to business. Local governments can subsidize the structure capital, land, or both at a particular urban site. Standard micro-economic theory is used to investigate the effects of subsidy programmes on the structure-land ratio, the employment-land ratio, and the amount of real estate taxes collected at the site in question.

It is concluded that municipalities may benefit from subsidies to businesses even if those businesses would have located in the municipality without the subsidy. The plan of the paper is to present a fairly general model of local production and the demand for inputs in the next section. Section 3 contains an analysis of the effects of various subsidies on the nature of the real estate supplied at the site in question ; and Section 4 reviews the empirical evidence relevant to the determination of the signs and magnitudes of the effects on real estate tax collections derived in Section 3. Section 5 contains a brief examination of the impacts of various subsidy programs on employment at the site in question and a summary concludes the paper.

It is a truism to call present day industrial society on urban society, since the end of the 18th century Western cities have grown inordinately changing their appearance a number of times. The concept of expansion, development and redevelopment are all attemps to understand this phenomenon. Analysis of this growth has revealed some of its aspects : construction, financing, housing, and servicing.

Science offers two basic approaches to the question of a universal theory, packaged under the generic names of Functionalism and Marxism. Each one offers its own apparently original explanation, each one has its untouchable and irreducible general framework. As a result any reflection on urban questions —or the larger problem of the social relationship to space—is necessarily subordinated to wider theoretical conclusions about society as a whole, since it is compelled to fall within one or other of the two authorized versions of reality. As a matter of fact both perspectives marginalize certain objects of investigation, objects that might be considered, a priori, to be essential for an understanding of the urban environment. This alone justifies subjecting both the Functionalist and Marxist paradigms to the implicit critique posed by certain aspects of social reality that have been hidden, avoided, marginalized and ostracised. Rent is one of these aspects. The author Gilles Lavigne in his long version "Land Rent : Questions and Answers", reveals that land rent stands as the economic manifestation of the exercise of the right to private property of land. The author remarks that it is the symptom, on the economic level, of the nature and state of the political relation of appropriation a society maintains with space. Thus the author appropriately convinces that analyzing the phenomenon of rent means analyzing the economic effects of land ownership. The author identifies that Functionalism ignores rent on the theoretical level, although remarking on its practical importance, where as Marxism theorizes endlessly about rent but empties the question of any practical significance. Neither side resolves the question, however. The author in his conclusion remarks that at the end of this investigation, one gathers the impression that while every thing has not been said, neither has every thing been left out. A look back reveals the contradiction inherent in a study that has been carried through but which remains incomplete. So many problems, imprecisions and weaknesses remain that our patiently constructed edifice appears rather fragile.

The goal pursued throughout this article has been to examine the "profit and loss" of several years work on the question of rent. The aim has not been to convince any one or prove any thing, just to retrace the road taken. The author is confused and put the question, why has a question as crucial as rent never raised interest equivalent to its importance ? Why are obscure research assistants the only one's facinated by it.

The city we have been building for a hundred years now is the incarnation of our values, ideals and beliefs. In its contemporary form it clearly shows, the place that science, technology and reason occupy in our culture. But behind these obvious and official manifestations, city incarnates the power and omni science of money, that cultureless form, equivalent to every thing and nothing. Ultimately urban rent operates on this level of significance. On the scale of the enormous transactions involved, men are but bits of information, or less, since money is the only object of much transactions.

The land values in an urban setting are determined in a variety of forms: (1) the effects of changes on a particular location over time ; (2) comparison of different sites within a city at the same time ; (3) comparison of different location with inacity over time ; and (4) inter-urban comparisons of aggregate variables. The inter-urban land value research has concentrated on demand variables such as total population, median family income, percent change in population etc. The author George M. Johnston in his article "Survey and Critique of Empirical Studies of Inter-Urban Land Values" has made an attempt to review the literature on inter-urban land value research. The author found that most of the research work has concentrated on demand variables as total population etc., to explain a varied estimate of site price and for appreciation. The author concludes that in both the selection of explanatory demand variables and units of analysis, the final choice is arbitrary. Because of the complexity of the urban structure, many aspects of community characteristics are independent with other characteristics. The author further explores that while each listed variable is indicative of different trends of interest, selection of variables can only be made after an analysis of specific theoretical model to be tested. The author emphasises that pragmatic choice have to be made.

The author Tonu Puu in his article "On the Equilibrium Distribution of Population and Land Value in an Urban Region" tries to construct a model for the spatial equilibrium distribution of population with in some urban areas. The author identifies that there exists an equilibrium when all locations are considered as equivalent and no reason for migration exist. The author proposes that escape the complicated utility approach we simply state that there is equivalence of location when the sum of housing and communication costs for an individual balance so that more expensive accommodation is compensated by less expensive communication and vice-versa.

Land values in central business districts (CBD) of North American cities have long been studied by geographers for the purpose of assessing their spatial characteristics and further more to determine if common distributional pattern exist. The urban economist have postulated that in cities the economic rent of a piece of land is based on its locational characteristics and that the most accessible point in the city would have the highest land values. The author Malcolm Fairweather in his article "Land Values and Land Use Intensity in North American Central Business District : An appraisal" deals with the land values in the Central Business District of North American cities. The author evaluates the problem in its right perspective through a case study of Rochester. The author concludes that the CBD does represent the greatest clustering of highest land use for the city as a whole but that even this pattern may be changing with the establishment of suburban office and relating centres. Thus the CBDs of North American cities are complex areas undergoing changes in form and functions. Similarly the land use intensity pattern is being modified constantly as newer, taller structures are picking their way skyward.

The system of local property taxation has received substantial criticism in the area of the effects of the system on allocative efficiency with in urban housing markets. It is a truism that the property tax system discourages the up keep and upgrading of the existing housing stock and as a result largely contributes towards urban housing decay and abandonment. Increasing concern with this problem has led many states in U.S.A. to pass special legislation, enabling their cities to implement programmes providing property tax relief for rehabilitation activities. The author Sharon G. Levin in his article "Property Tax Incentives for Housing Rehabilitation : Theory and Evidence" makes an attempt to review the theory and design of local government property tax incentives for housing rehabilitation with the purpose of evaluating their effectiveness. With this objective in mind, Section I reviews the economic justifications for government activity in the urban housing market, Section II sets the scene for the ensuing analysis of the incentives by presenting as a simple model of the urban housing market. In Section III the design and expected effects of property tax relief measures for housing rehabilitation are examined. And finally, in Section IV reviews the design operations, and cost effectiveness of several programmes which had sufficient data for analysis.

The author in his conclusion states that local property tax incentives for housing rehabilitation alone cannot ensure that urban housing conditions will improve dramatically. However such local policy instruments, if properly designed and understood, could prove to be cost-effective tools in a multi-dimensional approach towards meeting the dual objectives of efficiency and equity : conserving and improving the existing housing stock and providing "decent" housing for "needy" citizens.

The housing market has been closely related to global and specific housing policies of the government since the end of the first world war. Thus the question of the structure and function of the housing market is always at the same time the question of direction and dimension of housing policy. Recently the voices calling for a strengthening of the market in housing supply have become numerous. The author Detlev Ipsen in his article "Segregation, Mobility and Opportunity on the Housing Market : An Empirical Study in Mannheim" provides a sociological analysis of the housing market.

The author in this article attempts to show, using empirical research, that the housing market is divided into market segments which offer varying opportunity to consumers of different social levels. Segregation mobility and bariers to mobility are the social process through which the specific market segments are formed and which lend a characteristic shape to the economic processes. Section III analyse several theoretical considerations on the sociological boundaries of these market segments. Section IV deals with factors determined on one hand by the intensity of mobility and on the other hand by the concentration of certain social classes in particular. Section V provides a representation of the results of empirical research on the various market opportunities of different social classes on the individual market segment. Section VI provides some empirical indicators of the barriers to mobility which forms the basis of in the creation of such segregated market segment. Finally in Section VII the author gives some indication of inconsequences of findings for housing policy.

Since 1950 there has been a marked change in the localization of many economic activities, although the process is specially typical of industrial enterprise, tertiary activities such as in retail trade or services to industry have also been effected. In spite of the numerous article written about this problem, exhaustive analyses are relatively rare and often limited to the most striking aspects, such as the creation of big industrial estates or activities, the opening up of new shopping centres or the development of large office areas. On the other hand nothing or hardly any thing, is known about changes in localization in the heart of an urban center or in a suburban district and often little is known about the changes of occupation in the pre-existent network. Keeping these deficiencies in mind the author B. Merenne-Schoumaker in his article "Analysis of the Mobility of Economic Activities in Urban Areas" attempts to show the interest of studies about the mobility of business organizations and tries to present some type of research that could be done in this field of investigation. The author in this article analyses the concept of mobility, spatial trend in mobility causes of mobility and spatial results of mobility. The author in his concluding remarks suggests that the mobility of businesses, major process of the evolution of cities and of the changes in urban spatial structures, appears to be one of the principal subjects to be explored when analysing cities.

A city which is not only at the service of its residents but pursue a number of different functions. Such a city is Venice, Which is a tourist and cultural centre of international value, plays a directorial role towards a large part of the region. These functions are intermingling and occupy various areas and render inextricable the various roles of the economic urban space. Moreover, the number of retail activities and the services offered is not only notable in respect to the limited space in Venice, but seems to be almost uniformally distributed along the various streets. The author Fabio Lando in his article "Functional Areas in the Town : The Example of Venice, Italy" makes an attempt to assign a number of functions to the Venice city and consider it tourist and cultural centre of international value. He postulates that it is a historic centre which render many economic activities. With the help of first principal component analysis, the author found that Venice city can be distinctly divided into different functional areas which play a specific role to make it a foci of attraction.

It may be assumed that individual types of retail commodity can be distinguished relatively unambiguously. The problem is to classify these commodities into distinctive groups : This is necessary not only for research purposes but often also for the clarification of policies in marketing or property development, or town planning. A logical basis for classification would be that each group or commodities implies a particular set of decision making rules on the part of retailers and/or consumers. These 'rules' might also imply certain-patterns in space of location and consumption respectively. The author M. Guy in his article "Classifications of Urban Retail Facilities" examines a topic of utmost importance to geographers and planners alike—the classification of retail facilities in urban areas. In order to devise a rational, logical and consistent detailed descriptive classification of shops the author find it necessary to review relevant existing practice in three areas of research which author has pursued independently in this paper. The author first demonstrates to analyse market research which seems to explain the shopping behaviour of consumers paying particular attention to the ways in which behaviour appears to be affected either in economic, social and psychological characteristics of consumers themselves, or by characteristics of retail commodities and of the methods in selling them. The second research area is concerned most with physical attributes (sizes, location and characteristics of shopping centres. Thirdly, some spatial analysts have examined the spatial distribution of shops of various types in cities. The paper proceeds as follows : In Section 2 summaries are made of the way in which retail commodities and outlets have been classified by market researchers, economists and geographers. The author made an attempt to discuss the locational implications of various classifications. In Section 3 the work of spatial analysts on patterns of retail location is briefly discussed. In Section 4 some results of research into retail location in Reading area carried out by the author from 1974 onwards.

Spatial arrangements of commercial activities in an urban area is far more important than the limited amount of space they cover. This is largely because their distribution on space reflects the aggregate demand conditions of a city. Their concentrated and deconcentrated patterns are related to the intra-urban mobility and the social status of the people. The number and size of the retail units on the other hand depict the economic characteristics of the population. The authors S. Banerjee and S.R. Joshi in their article "Spatial Structure of Retaining Activities in Pune City" reveals that spatial distribution of retail activities within an urban area is an expression of aggregate demand conditions, the latter being reflected through pattern of population distribution and the socio-economic status of the people. The number of size of retail units when observed together with the population figures, can signify the relationship between demand and supply sectors.

The present paper identifies (a) the areas of retail concentration in Pune in 1961 and 1981, (b) the relationship between demand and supply sectors and explains the related dynamics of retail structure of the city. Correlation coefficient and regression analysis have been carried out to show the relationship between population and shops—the demand and supply sectors.

Although food, clothing and shelter are the basic necessities of human beings, transport in fact commands a larger share of consumers budget than clothing in most of the cities. Mobility from homes and work places is essential for the functioning of a city. The economic models have evaluated that land uses and values with in cities depend crucially on the advantages of proximity between land uses.

Todays society has placed extremely high priority on the development of transportation system that will facilitate the movement of both goods and people in a swift and reliable fashion and with the greatest convenience, comfort and privacy. Although conflicts of interest are inevitable on the design and modification of alternative systems, transportation planners attempt to select those projects that will provide the greatest benefit to society. The author C. John Langley Jr. in his article "Highways and Property Values : The Washington Beltway Revisited" investigates the impacts of Washington Beltways on residential property value. According to the author this study proves conclusively that high way originated environmental externalities are the major cause of inverse relationship between yearly increases in North spring field property resale values and proximity. The analysis found significant differences among distance related property value index number in 12 of the 17 years under study. The author finds it appropriate to mention that the findings of this study are quite consistent with generally accepted theories of capital asset pricing.

The authors Masatoshi A. Abe and Kumares C. Sinha in their paper discuss and produce two reports on "Pricing in Urban Transportation—1. The Problem of Peak Local Pricing. 2. Pricing and Quality of Service in Mass Transportation." This report includes two parts. In the first part the peak load pricing problem in urban transportation is examined within a theoretical framework. A general social welfare function is used to show what the optimal price levels should be for peak and off-peak periods in order to maximize social welfare. The paper also shows that given current pricing practice of urban transportation a strict adherence to marginal cost pricing does not yield the maximum social welfare but that a systematic deviation from marginal cost pricing is required for attainment of maximum social welfare.

The second part of the report deals with the pricing problem in urban mass transportation. As an example, the operation of the private bus transit company in the Milwaukee area is examined. The investigation finds that a lowered bus fare, together with improved service, will substantially increase transit patronage, which will in turn reduce the cost of operating bus transit as a consequence of the existence of the economy of scale. In addition, the characteristics of mass transit users in this country are also reviewed, and it is concluded that the majority of the transit riders are captive riders in the sense that they do not have any choice in their mode of transportation. This finding substantiates the hypothesis that mass transit fare should be significantly reduced, not just for attracting automobile users to transit and thus to limit congestion, but also for increased social welfare resulting in improved equity.

The first part of the report has been prepared by Masatoshi A. Abe and the second part has been prepared jointly by Masatoshi A. Abe and Kumares C. Sinha.

FOOTNOTES

1. Werner, Z., Hinsch (1984) *Urban Economics*, Macmillan Publishing Co., New York.
2. Goodal, Brian (1972) *The Economics of Urban Areas*, Pergamon Press, New York.
3. Edel, Mathew and Jerome Rothenberg (1972), *Readings in Urban Economics*, The Macmillan Company, New York.
4. Rasmussen (1973), *Urban Economics*, Harper and Raw Publishers, New York.
5. *Ibid.*
6. Berry, Brian J. "Cities as Systems Within Systems of Cities" in Friedmann and W. Alonso, *Regional Development and Planning*, Cambridge, Mass, M.I.T. Press.
7. Alonso, William (1964) "Location Theory" in John Friedmann and William Alonso (Ed), *Regional Development and Planning, A Reader*, M.I.T. Press, Cambridge,
8. Verman, Raymond (1960), *Metropolis 1985*, Harvard University Press.
9. Koopmans, Illalling C. and Beckman, Martin, "Assignment Problems and The Location of Economic Activities" *Econometrica XXV*, I (January 1957), pp. 53-76.
10. Moses, Leon N. "Location and Theory of Production". *The Quarterly Journal of Economics*, May 1958.
11. Alonso, William, A Theory of Urban Land Market", *Papers and Proceedings Regional Science Association*, 6 (1960), pp. 149-157.
12. Mills, Edvin S., "An Aggregative Model of Resource Allocation in a Metropolitan Area" *American Economic Review*, Papers and Proceedings (May 1967), pp. 197-210.
13. Moses, Leon and Williamson, Harold F. Jr. (1967) "The Location of Economic Activity in Cities", *American Economic Review*, Papers and Proceedings (May 1967), pp. 211-222.
14. Edel, Mathew, "Planning Market or Warfare ? Recent Use Conflict in American Cities" in Mathew Edel and Jerome Pothenberg (Ed), *Readings in Urban Economics* 1972. The Macmillan Company, New York (1972).
15. Northam, Ray M., *Urban Geography*, John Wiley and Sons, New York, (1979), pp. 192,.
16. Alexander, Gunner, *The Industrial Structure of American Cities*", University of Narraska Press (1956).
17. Alexander, John W., "The Basic-Non Basic Concept of Urban Economic Function", *Economic Geography* XXX (July 1956), pp. 246-261.
18. Ullman, Edward L. and Dacey, Michael F., "The Minimum Requirements Approach to the Union Economic Base" *Papers and Proceedings of the Regional Science Association*, Vol. 6, (1975).
19. Pratt, Richard T., "An Appraisal of the Minimum Requirement

Technique" *Economic Geography*, Vol. 44, No. 2. (1968).

20. Moore, Craig L., "A New Look at the Minimum Requirements Approach to Regional Economic Analysis" *Economic Geography*, Vol. 51, No. 4 (1975).

SECTION ONE

SECTORS OF ECONOMY AND FINANCIAL MANAGEMENT OF CITIES

TWO

W. PATRICK BEATON AND LEONARD B. SOSSAMON

THE ROLE OF ECONOMIC INTERMEDIARIES IN THE SHIFTING NATIONAL ECONOMY
The Northeast Versus the Sunbelt

STATE and regional economic development has for many years focused upon efforts to encourage the growth of jobs and the immigration of high wage industry into economically depressed areas. Usually these efforts are designed to acquire manufacturing firms and research type operations. Seldom is the role and importance of the economic intermediary considered.

In the work that follows, it will be shown that a lag exists in the growth of economic intermediaries in those areas of the country currently undergoing rapid economic growth in the manufacturing sector. Second, it shall be demonstrated that the economic cost of this lag can in the long term be translated into lower worker incomes and hence lower local purchasing power and a lower tax capacity for state and local government.

Essential intermediary activities such as market research, financing, wholesaling and advertising, traditionally have exported their services out of a few major metropolitan centers instead of being spread like levening throughout the national economy (Vance, 1970, 41-47). Now, under the current redistribution of national economic activity, there seems to be an assumption that if a goods producer can be induced to move into a new location, the problem of locating and servicing his consumers will resolve itself.

In a relatively stable regional economy, it may be safely assumed that normal market pressures will ensure an adequate supply of the services of economic intermediaries. Marketing firms will know the locations of producers and consumers (both intermediate and final) ; and lines of communications will be well established linking financing, advertising, shipping and inventory operations with the producer. However, in a period of radical regional shifts, such as the recently recognized growth in the "Sunbelt" states (Sales, 1975), lines of product and information flow can become disrupted.[1]

The establishment of new business relationships involves a great deal of uncertainty regarding the abilities of the new business partners to hold up their respective sides of the economic transaction. Early recognition of any weakness within a developing economy should permit planners to suggest alternative ways to ease the path of regional economic growth and possibly to prevent a permanent deficiency from being incorporated into the regional economy.

Economic intermediaries

The role of economic intermediaries in an economic system has gone largely unexplored to this date. In the input-output mode of analysis initiated by Wassily Leontief, the supporting role of the intermediary as the mover of goods among the elements of the interindustry matrix is de-emphasized by treating it as a producing or purchasing industry ; that is, its status in the input-output table is, for example, the same as chemicals, apparel, or stone, clay and glass products (Leontief, 1966, 1-40).

Economic geography has similarly discounted the role of the intermediary. As noted by James Vance in his analysis of central-place theory, the theory tends to emphasize local self-sufficiency and internally induced change rather than local economic development derived from inter-regional interdependence (Vance, 1970, Chapt. 1, passim.).

Regional independence is not a characteristic common to modern industrial economies. However, a profitable interdependence resulting from a well developed intermediary function is a prerequisite to the capitalization of regional comparative advantages in transportation, labor or resource costs (Isard, 1956, Chapt. 9, passim.). Demands must be observed, producers informed, products made and shipped, consumers alerted to their availability, and a means of financing secured. Excluding actual production, these are the roles assumed by the economic intermediary. In essence, the intermediary is an "agent of trade" ; he is the means for facilitating interregional interdependence and hence the ability of a region to acquire the economic benefits accruing to its comparative advantage in one or more of the inputs to the production process (Beckman, 1965).

Theodore Beckman suggests that several factors account for the failure of economic development research to deal with intermediaries. These factors include the complexity of the sector's structure and the absence of adequate census data. Recent scholarly research further suggests that the dynamic nature of the trade environment limits the ability of researchers to adequately describe the structure of this sector of the economy (McKeon, 1972, 37-8).

Each of these explanations contributes to the overall neglect of the trade sector by scholars. However, an important additional factor may well be an inadequate appreciation of the importance of the trade sector to economic development. The following analysis is an attempt to show more clearly the dramatic impact of trade and, more specifically, the effect of a lag in the growth of this sector in developing economies.

The examination will involve the specification and estimation of the determinants of state wholesale sales, the locational shifts that have occurred in the interstate trade component of wholesale sales and lastly the role that wholesale activity *qua* economic intermediaries has upon the economic well-being of a state's citizenry.

Empirical analysis

As previously noted, the role of the economic intermediary is to provide a bridge in time and over space between a producer and a consumer. An intermediary sells two services : access to relevant market information and the collecting, sorting and dispersing of products (McKeon, 1972). The successful fulfilment of this role requires the use of marketing specialists and salesmen ; financial, advertising, legal and publishing firms ; shippers, warehouse operators and laborers.

No single measure of the total level of activities of economic intermediaries is readily available from a nationwide data source. Alternatives such as employment levels in the trade industries or wholesale sales exist. Neither of these indicators, however, encompasses the full range of activities of economic intermediaries.

Wholesale sales data make on distinction between labor intensive activities of merchant wholesalers and sales branches with the information processing activities of both the agent and broker as well as sales offices. On the other hand, employment level data crosscut both the type of firm and the levels of productivity within a given type of firm. Since the purpose of this analysis was to explore the importance of economic intermediaries from the point of view of family wealth and state tax potential, the value of wholesale sales was chosen to act as the surrogate of the total level of economic activity by economic intermediaries.

The causes of state wholesale activity

The internal driving force behind wholesale sales activity is the primary, secondary and tertiary components of a state's economy. The surrogates of the forces derived from the primary and the secondary economic sectors of the economy are mining, agriculture and manufacturing sales (value of shipments). As surrogates of the retail sector, population and average family income levels are used.

The unit of observation used throughout this work is the state. The use of the state as an economic region assumes that locally produced products and local consumption will use the services of local economic intermediaries.

Two sources of error are incurred in the use of this assumption. One error has to be accepted as a limitation to the analysis, the second is used as an index of the exportation or importation of the services of economic intermediaries. The first error will be observed where major economic centers (metropolitan areas) overlap state boundaries. So long as the various components of the economy are randomly distributed across state boundaries, this source of error will not bias our results.

The second source of error is more statistical than substantive. That is, the relationship between wholesale sales and the set of determinants in a cross sectional model is assumed to be stochastic. This situation occurs because state economic systems are not isolated. Interstate trade is a form of basic economic activity. It is this fact that permits researchers to partition wholesale sales into their interstate and intrastate components. In

Equation 1 we show a model of the causes of a state's level of wholesale sales activity.

Eq. 1. $Wholesale_i = Manufacturing_i + Retailing_i +$
$Agriculture_i + Mining_i + Interstate\ trade_i$

where : $Interstate\ trade_i = Wholesale\ exports_i - Wholesale\ imports_i$ i=state.[1]

This equation recognizes that a state's total wholesale sales are not solely derived from activities within its borders ; rather, the explanatory equation must include a term which identifies either the state's ability to export the services of its economic intermediaries or its necessity to import such services. It is a state's interstate trade activity that is the index of the strength of that state's economic intermediaries.

Analysis of gross and interstate wholesale sales

The total volume of wholesale sales is, as would be expected, strongly associated with the size of a state's population (r_0=.90 for 1970).* Table 2.1** shows that as of 1972, the states leading in wholesale sales were New York, California, and Illinois. Similarly, these same states were the top dollar gainers for wholesale sales from 1967 to 1972.

However, between 1967 and 1972, the significant shifts occurred within the national economy. Based upon the model of the determinants of wholesale sales, it is concluded that the interstate wholesale sales of both California and New York experienced the heaviest losses. Table 2.2 shows that New York has fallen from its preeminent position in 1967 where it had a surplus of over 33 billion dollars in wholesale sales to a still leading but reduced position having 22 plus billion dollars of interstate trade. Strong gainers over that same time period include Illinois, New Jersey, and Georgia.

A graphic presentation of these patterns is provided in Figures 2.1 and 2.2. Figure 2.1 is a map of the distribution of interstate wholesale sales for 1972. Figure 2.2 is the map of the change in interstate wholesale sales between 1967 and 1972.[2]

*The Symbol r_0 represents a zero order Pearson Correlation Coefficient.

**Tables are grouped together following the text.

TABLE 2.1 : **Wholesale sales by State for United States, 1967—1972**

State Name	1972 Wholesale Sales (Million $)	1967 Wholesale Sales (Million $)	% Change in Wholsale Sales 1967-1972
New York	100,414	77,957	28.8
California	68,562	44,254	54.9
Illinois	52,804	39,538	33.6
Texas	42,188	23,910	76.4
Ohio	33,680	23,466	43.5
Pennsylvania	32,374	23,479	37.9
New Jersey	31,840	17,931	77.6
Michigan	26,545	18,800	41.2
Missouri	20,703	14,758	40.3
Florida	19,983	10,302	94.0
Georgia	19,789	11,459	72.7
Massachusetts	19,303	13,157	46.7
North Carolina	15,911	9,530	67.0
Minnesota	15,053	10,507	43.3
Tennessee	14,836	8,628	72.0
Indiana	13,417	8,348	60.7
Wisconsin	10,838	7,299	48.5
Virginia	10,267	6,043	69.9
Maryland	10,212	5,957	71.4
Washington	10,007	6,696	49.4
Iowa	9,969	5,949	67.6
Louisiana	9,805	6,642	47.6
Oregon	9,289	5,873	58.2
Connecticut	8,828	4,672	89.0
Kansas	8,214	4,405	86.5
Colorado	8,030	4,385	83.1
Alabama	7,538	4,437	70.0
Kentucky	7,020	3,988	76.0
Oklahoma	6,809	4,262	59.8
Nebraska	6,391	4,384	45.8
South Carolina	4,696	2,745	71.1
Arkansas	4,438	1,955	127.0
Arizona	4,389	2,143	104.8
Mississippi	3,942	2,309	70.7
Utah	2,925	1,661	76.1
Delaware	2,482	1,429	73.7
West Virginia	2,394	1,690	41.7
North Dakota	2,222	1,491	49.0
Rhode Island	2,072	1,475	40.5

South Dakota	1,966	1,250	57.3
Maine	1,886	1,233	53.0
Idaho	1,738	911	90.8
District of Columbia	1,731	2,376	—27.1
Montana	1,573	1,081	45.5
Hawaii	1,561	1,013	54.1
New Mexico	1,515	909	66.7
New Hampshire	1,144	689	66.0
Nevada	917	461	99.0
Wyoming	717	287	150.0
Vermont	669	382	75.1
Alaska	604	286	111.2

Source : U.S. Department of Commerce, Bureau of the Census.

TABLE 2.2 : **Wholesale trade surplus (+) or deficit (—) for : (1) states with above average wholesale sales and (2) states with below average wholesale sales ; 1967, 1972***

	States with above average total wholesale sales		
	1972 Interstate Wholesale Sales (Million $)	1967 Interstate Wholesale Sales (Million $)	Difference 1972—1967 (Million $)
California	—12,169	— 2,857	— 9,312
Florida	— 9,825	5,134	—14,959
Georgia	4,427	2,286	2,141
Illinois	14,432	787	13,645
Massachusetts	— 4,532	— 73	— 4,459
Michigan	— 5,649	—15,191	9,542
Minnesota	7,010	591	6,419
Missouri	3,435	2,590	845
New Jersey	4,272	— 4,318	8,590
New York	22,558	33,261	—10,703
North Carolina	— 3,533	— 2,511	— 1,022
Ohio	— 9,262	—14,630	5,368
Pennsylvania	—15,129	—10,180	— 4,949
Tennessee	617	2,125	— 1,508
Texas	3,347	2,985	362
Alabama	— 945	763	— 1,708
Alaska	84	— 1,374	1,458
Arizona	— 719	— 84	— 635
Arkansas	— 1,137	— 632	— 505
Colorado	1,512	1,505	7
Connecticut	1,874	— 944	2,818

TABLE 2.2 : (*Contd.*)

Delaware	1,253	– 541	1,794
District of Columbia	610	1,126	– 516
Hawaii	– 408	– 703	295
Idaho	– 569	– 644	75
Indiana	– 33	– 1,596	1,563
Iowa	– 498	– 1,049	551
Kansas	1,257	80	1,177
Kentucky	– 1,061	– 110	– 951
Louisiana	778	41	737
Maine	– 311	– 264	– 47
Maryland	1,103	1,634	– 531
Mississippi	– 1,813	– 102	– 1,711
Montana	– 371	– 378	7
Nebraska	754	866	– 112
Nevada	– 242	– 708	466
New Hampshire	– 348	– 724	376
New Mexico	– 1,074	– 550	– 524
North Dakota	374	171	203
Oklahoma	– 53	1,149	– 1,202
Oregon	3,755	2,959	796
Rhode Island	448	– 249	697
South Carolina	– 1,713	– 268	– 1,445
South Dakota	– 218	– 145	– 73
Utah	359	9	350
Vermont	– 375	– 778	403
Virginia	– 1,059	1,586	– 2,527
Washington	1,605	1,993	– 388
West Virginia	– 1,701	– 660	– 1,041
Wisconsin	– 904	– 354	– 550
Wyoming	– 209	– 1,022	813

* The wholesale trade surplus or deficit values are the residuals from the regression equations displayed in Table 2.4.

The causes for these shifts in wholesale sales come from at least two sources : The national redistribution of the population (Barabba, 1975), part of which has been termed the "Sunbelt" phenomenon, and the corresponding shift in manufacturing activity (Thompson, 1975).

An examination of the relationship between changes in manufacturing and gross wholesale levels for the various states shows that in both 1967 and 1972 a strong positive correlation exists between these two components of the economy (r_0=0.89).

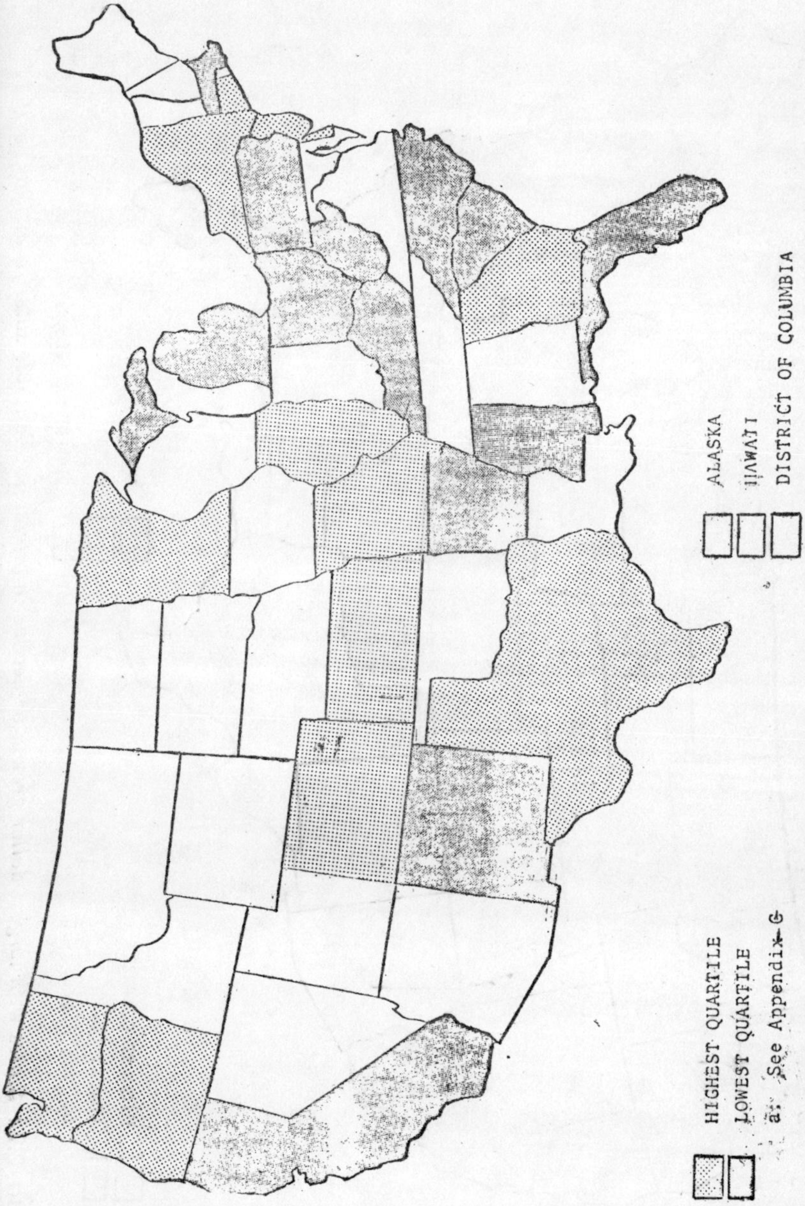

FIG. 2.1 : *States with the highest and lowest levels[a] of interstate wholesale sales for 1972*

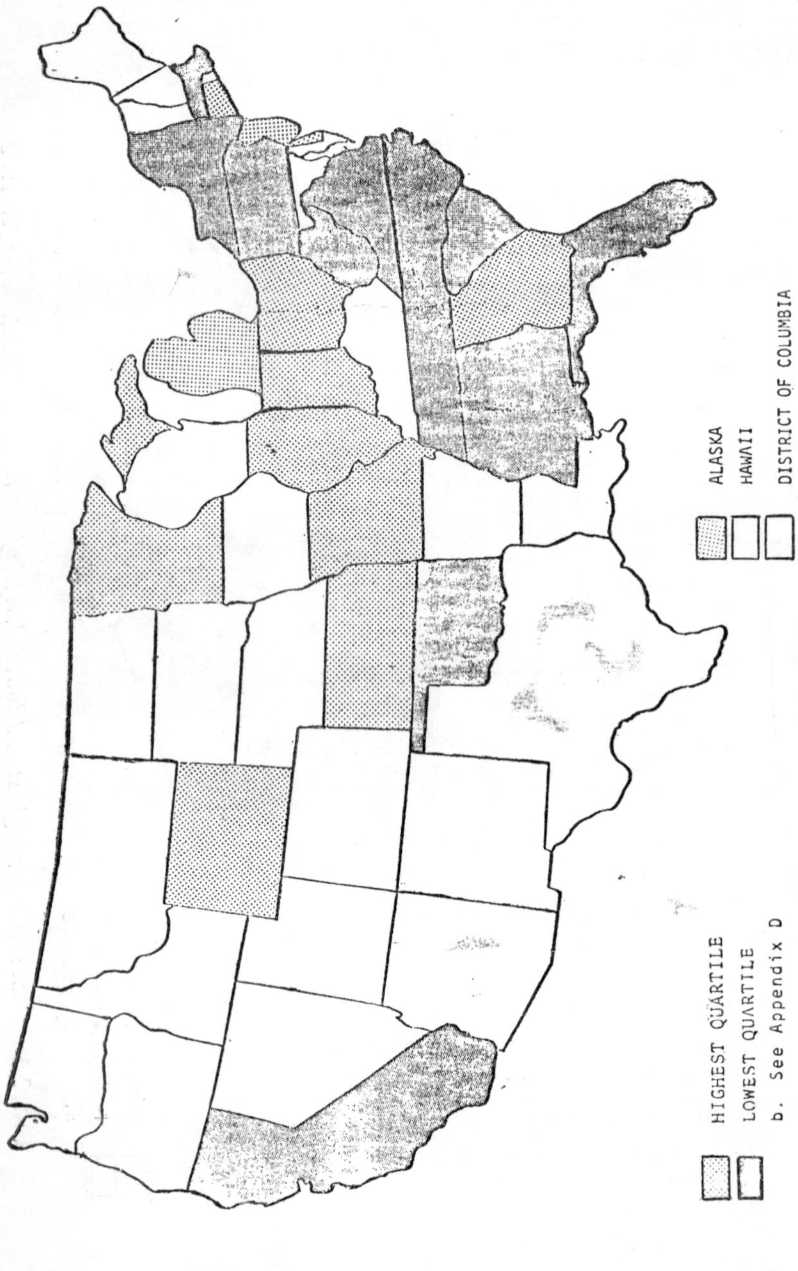

FIG. 2.2 : *States with largest dollar growth or decline in interstate wholesale sales from 1969 to 1972*

However, it does not necessarily follow that the trade sector and the manufacturing sector change at the same relative rates required for balanced growth. Nationally, the correlation between the percentage change in manufacturing value added and wholesale sales was only 0.42. In order to study this phenomenon, the determinants of wholesale sales for 1967 and 1972 were examined.

Determinants of wholesale sales

This research examines the lag in the growth of economic intermediaries. It will be shown that after statistically controlling for changes in a state's population growth and manufacturing activity, reliance upon imported wholesale services occurs in those states growing most rapidly in population and manufacturing activity.

Two models have been developed for this analysis. The models identify and produce estimates of the various determinants of wholesale sales variation across the states for 1967 and 1972 respectively. The lag phenomenon is observed by identifying, for each of the states, the direction and degree of change from 1967 and 1972 of the residuals from the two determinants equations.

The experimental identification of these models was conducted through the use of cross-sectional multiple regression analysis. Data for each state and the District of Columbia for the years 1967 and 1972 were used to construct models. When using the full set of 51 economic units as observations for a single regression equation, a clear case of heteroscedastic residuals occurred.[3] To minimize this problem, the data were partitioned into two subsets : those states that had above average wholesale sales in 1967 and those states that had below average wholesale sales for 1967.[4]

The regression equations for these two subsets of states are displayed in Table 2.3. In each of the four equations, the combined explanatory power for the full set of independent variables is significantly different than zero at the 0.05 level. While the central focus of the analysis is the residuals from the regression equations, a drastic shift must be noted in the specific variables showing up as significant determinants in 1967 as opposed to 1972. In both the 1967 subsets of states, the variation in manufacturing sales significantly explains variation in wholesale sales while the

TABLE 2.3 : **Regression equations explaining cross-state variation in wholesale sales ; 1967, 1972 for states with below and above average levels of wholesale sales**

	1967		1972	
	Low Wholesale Sales	High Wholesale Sales	Low Wholesale Sales	High Wholesale Sales
Manufacturing	.34 (.04)*	.88 (.30)*	.02 (.14)	—.11 (.37)
Population		—.019 (.13)	21.60 (.14)*	48.44 (14.3)*
Income	.20 (.12)[a]	.69 (3.6)	—.0037 (.06)	.07 (.15)
Agriculture	1.27 (.43)*	2.24 (5.5)	1.19 (.06)*	—2.6 (4.7)
Mining	.80 (.28)*	—.81 (3.6)	.09 (.06)	—0.6 (2.6)
Mean Wholesale Sales[b]	$3,086.00	$23,178.00	$5,061.00	$34,265.00
Std. Deviation Wholesale Sales[b]	(2,337.)	(18,502.)	(3,781.)	(23,803.)
R^2	.81	.63	.90	.81
F	33.2*	3.1*	58.8*	8.0*
N	36	15	36	15

a. Values in parentheses are standard errors of the net regression coefficients.

b. Mean and standard deviation statistics are expressed in millions of dollars.

* Coefficient is significantly different than zero at .01 level.

variation in state populations has no explanatory power. Now in 1972 the complete reversal is the case. The index of intrastate manufacturing activity requiring wholesale services has no significant explanatory power while population size has a significant positive effect.

Turning to an analysis of the residuals, each state's wholesale sales were partitioned into two subsets. The first partition represents the level of wholesale sales derived from its ability to meet its within-state requirements from manufacturing, retailing, agriculture and mining activities. The second partition represents its interstate wholesale activity. This value represents either the surplus or deficiency in wholesale sales after the average wholesale dollars per unit of manufacturing, retailing, etc., activity has been removed from the total wholesale sales level.

In the case of a positive residual, the state is an exporter of wholesale services ; on the other hand, if the state has a negative residual, it must import wholesale services from outside its borders. Based upon this logic, the explained portion of a state's wholesale sales level represents or is a surrogate for the intrastate activity of economic intermediaries. It follows that the residual portion of a state's wholesale sales is a surrogate for its interstate activities.

Table 2.2 displays the residual or interstate component of the state's economic intermediaries. Two spatial patterns are worth noting. First, the Northeastern tier of states appears to be anchored around New York. This state has suffered the most severe loss in its level of interstate commerce. Surrounding New York are two states which have registered strong gains in this activity : Connecticut and New Jersey.

The second case focuses upon the "Sunbelt" states of the Southeast and Southcentral regions of the country. For the most part these are the states which compose the Southern Industrial Development Council (SIDC). The pattern within these states is the opposite to that which is occurring within the states of the Northeast. One state, Georgia, dominates the region in terms of its relative growth in interstate commerce. Most of the remaining southern states are observed to be lagging or to increasingly lag in the development of their capacity to trade their manufactured goods. While Georgia can be termed the jobber and shipper of the new South, it has not filled all of the needs of these states. Table 2.4 focuses upon the 16 states comprising the SIDC. Summing the column of residuals, it is concluded that as a region, the growth of economic intermediaries has lagged behind its growth in manufacturing. In 1972, the analysis suggests that an over 9 billion dollar shortfall in interstate wholesale sales exists.

What are the consequences of this state of affairs ? For simplicity's sake, two alternatives present themselves. First, the lag can be viewed as a transient phenomenon. In this case it would be assumed that over time the natural operation of the free enterprise economy would respond with the optimal spatial solution to the problem of the location of economic intermediaries. Second, the lag can be viewed as an unanticipated consequence of policies developed by state departments of economic development and encouraged by local

TABLE 2.4 : **Interstate wholesale trade surplus (+) or deficiency (—)* for 16 states of the Southern Industrial Development Council ranked according to their 1972 wholesale trade (all values in millions of dollars)**

State	1972 Interstate Wholesale Trade	1967 Interstate Wholesale Trade	1972-1967 Difference in Interstate Wholesale Trade
Georgia	4,427	2,286	2,141
Missouri	3,435	2,590	845
Texas	3,347	2,985	362
Maryland	1,103	1,634	— 531
Louisiana	778	41	737
Tennessee	617	2,125	—1,508
Oklahoma	— 53	1,149	—1,202
Alabama	— 945	763	—1,708
Virginia	—1,059	1,586	—2,645
Kentucky	—1,061	— 110	— 951
Arkansas	—1,137	— 632	— 505
West Virginia	—1,701	— 660	—1,041
South Carolina	—1,713	— 268	—1,445
Mississippi	—1,813	— 102	—1,711
North Carolina	—3,533	—2,511	—1,022
Florida	—9,825	5,134	—14,959
Regional Total	—9,133	16,010	—25,143

* Interstate wholesale trade surplus (+) or deficiency (—) is derived from the residuls of a regression equation relating a state's gross wholesale sales to its manufacturing, agricultural and mining activity as well as its population and family income. See Table 2.3.

chambers of commerce.

If the former view is held, only the self optimizing activities of business within the market economy need to be supported. On the other hand, if business, government and the academy have a collective role in guiding and determining regional economic development, two additional issues present themselves. First, what are the consequences of policies involving varying levels of action or inaction ? Second, if an action oriented alternative is selected, what can be done to facilitate a condition of more balanced economic growth ?

The consequences of continued unbalanced development

If the analytical models posited in this paper are valid representatives of economic reality, economic development in the South is becoming increasingly out of balance. If this pattern were to continue, what might be some of the consequences for the people of the region ? One measure of the influence of economic structure upon economic well-being is family income.

For analytical purposes, the index that is used to measure the impact of a state's economic structure upon its income levels is the difference between its mean and median family incomes. The values for the mean, median and difference scores are displayed in Table 2.5. Besides indicating the relative concentration of higher income families and correspondingly their higher purchasing power, this index corresponds positively with the income level of the median or fiftieth percentile family. Table 2.6

TABLE 2.5 : **Mean, median and the difference between the mean and median family income for all states, those with above average wholesale sales, and those with below average wholesale sales, 1970**

	All States	Above Average Wholesale Sales	Below Average Wholesale Sales
Mean Income	10,490	11,027	10,266
Median Income	9,177	9,629	8,989
Difference	1,312	1,398	1,277

Source : U.S. Census of Population, 1970.

displays the zero order correlation coefficients among these various measures of family income. The set of positive correlations between median family income and the difference between the mean and median family incomes suggests that there is a process whereby a broader mix of family income levels within a state promotes a rise in the income levels of the poorer families as well as those of greater wealth.

To return now to the basic issue, how does the structure of a state's economy contribute to the income levels of its citizenry ? It is hypothesized that an economy rich in economic intermediaries should have a stronger family income structure. That is, a state that has developed urban areas that have succeeded

TABLE 2.6 : **Zero order correlation coefficients among the mean, median and the difference between the mean and median family incomes for all states, those with above average wholesale sales and those with below average wholesale sales, 1970**

	All States DIFAM70[a]	Above Average Wholesale Sales DIFAM70	Below Average Wholesale Sales DIFAM70
Mean Income	.53	.40	.54
Median Income	.38	.25	.37

Source : U.S. Census of Population.

a. Difference between the average family income, 1970, and the median family income, 1970.

through the stages of export specialization, export complexity, economic maturation, etc., will attract and hold new, growing industries as well as the income benefits accruing from the same (Thompson, 1965, Chapt. 1, passim.).

To test this hypothesis, four regression equations were identified and estimated. A cross-section regression model was set up with the dependent variable being the difference between the mean and median family income levels of the state. Independent variables are represented by statewide aggregates of manufacturing, mining, agriculture, intrastate and interstate wholesale activities. The residuals from the equations determining variations in wholesale sales were used as the surrogate for interstate commerce while the difference between a state's actual wholesale sales and the residual score was used as the surrogate for intrastate trade activity. Table 2.7 displays the results of these regression analyses.

The results show that three of the four equations explain a statistically significant portion of the variation in the income difference index. Correspondingly, in those three equations, only the index of interstate wholesale activity was found to be a significant determinant of variation in the income index. In each case, the impact of interstate trade was to increase the value of the index of family income strength.

TABLE 2.7 : **Regression equations relating a state's economic structure to the difference between a state's mean family income and its median family income**

	1967		1972	
	States with above average wholesale sales	States with below average wholesale sales	States with above average wholesale sales	States with below average wholesale sales
Interstate wholesale trade	.013*[a] (.005)[b]	.099* (.047)	.013* (.004)	.02 (.04)
Intrastate wholesale trade	—.022 (.043)		.015 (.026)	.03 (.13)
Manufacturing	.051 (.086)		—.038 (.052)	—.08 (.13)
Agriculture		—.15 (.10)		—.09 (.22)
Mining	.016 (.047)	—.02 (.07)	.009 (.052)	
Constant	1266.1[c.]	1361.0	1897.2	1989.2
R^2	.43	.17	.57	.11
F	1.8*	2.3*	3.4*	.93
N	15	36	15	36

a. This can be interpreted as : for a one million dollar increase in interstate wholesale sales, the difference between mean and median family income will increase by .013 dollars.

b. Values in parentheses are the standard errors of the net regression coefficients.

c. Constant is in terms of millions of dollars.

* Coefficient is significantly different than zero at .01 level.

CONCLUSION

Given the extensive internal changes within the U.S. economy, this research has examined the shifts that have occurred within several of the more volatile sectors of that economy. The results show that during the period 1967 to 1972, economic intermediaries have not shifted to the "Sunbelt" states at the same rate as has manufacturing activity. To the extent that this lag in development among jobbers, shippers, marketing specialists, financial firms, etc., is capitalized into the permanent structure of the "Sunbelt" states, this analysis suggests that low family incomes, reduced purchasing power, and a lower tax capacity will result or be perpetuated.

Public policy may or may not be effective in changing this course of events. However, in order to give public and private decision makers workable alternatives to this future, further research must be mounted. The dynamic model suggested by McKeon shows that each class of producing firms develops different needs for intermediaries. Some of these needs may be developed within the region. Others may well have to reside at the final demand end of the production-consumption process. Such research that is mounted must therefore examine the behavior and needs of each class of new firms *vis a vis* the roles of economic intermediaries.

FOOTNOTES

1. The "Sunbelt" states form the southern tier of states which are currently receiving a large volume of immigration from Northeastern and Northcentral businesses and families. While several alternative listings of these states may be compiled we have chosen to remain with Sale's listing (Sale, 1975). The "Sunbelt" states include all or parts of : Florida, Georgia, North and South Carolina, Tennessee, Alabama, Mississippi, Louisiana, Arkansas, Texas, Oklahoma, New Mexico, Arizona, Nevada and California.
2. For further work in this mapping of residuals from regression, see Leslie King's 1969 work (King, 1969, 148-49).
3. This problem is examined by means of the Goldfeld-Quandt Test in Appendix B.
4. With but one exception, the same states were found to exist in the 1972 subsets of states. For simplicity, the 1967 based partition was used throughout the analysis.

REFERENCES

Barabba, Vincent P. 1975. "The National Setting : Regional Shifts, Metropolitan Decline and Urban Decay". In *Post Industrial America : Metropolitan Decline and Inter-Regional Job Shifts*. Edited by George Sternlieb and James W. Hughes. New Brunswick, N.J. : Center for Urban Policy Research, Rutgers University.

Beaton, W. Patrick. 1974. "The Determinants of Police Protection Expenditures". *National Tax Journal*, Vol. XXVII, June, 335-49.

Beckman, Theodore N. 1965. "Changes in Wholesaling Structure and

Performance". In *Marketing and Economic Development*, Chicago, III : American Marketing Asso.

Goldfeld, S.M. and Quandt, 1965. "Some Tests for Homoscedasticity". *Journal of the American Statistical Association*. Vol. 60, 539-47.

Isard, Walter. 1956. *Location and Space-Economy*, Cambridge, Mass. : The M.I.T. Press.

King, Leslie J. 1969. *Statistical Analysis in Geography*, Englewood Cliffs, N.J. : Prentice-Hall, Inc.

Leontief, Wassily. 1966. *Input-Output Economics*, New York : Oxford University Press.

McKeon, James C. 1972. "Conflicting Patterns of Structural Change in Wholesaling", *Economics and Business Bulletin*, Vol. 24, No. 2.

Sale, Kirkpatrick. 1975. *Power Shift*, New York : Random House.

Thompson, Wilbur R. 1967. *A Preface to Urban Economics*, Baltimore, Md. : Johns Hopkins Press.

Thompson, Wilbur R. 1975. "Economic Processes and Employment Problems in Declining Metropolitan Areas". In *Post Industrial America : Metropolitan Decline and Inter-Regional Job Shifts*. Edited by George Sternlieb and James W. Hughes. New Brunswick, N.J. : Center for Urban Policy Research, Rutgers University.

U.S. Department of Commerce. Bureau of the Census, 1972, *Census of Wholesale Trade*, Washington, D.C. ; U.S. Government Printing Office.

Vance, James E. Jr. 1970. *The Merchant's World : The Geography of Wholesaling*. Englewood Cliffs, N.J. : Prentice-Hall, Inc.

GLOSSARY OF TERMS

Agricultural sales

The *market value of all agriculture products sold* represents the market value, before taxes and expenses, of all agricultural products sold in the census year, including livestock and poultry and their products ; crops, including nursery products and hay ; forest products, and all miscellaneous products. The figures include landlord's and contractor's shares.

Wholesale sales

This includes merchandise sold and receipts from repairs and other services to customers, whether or not payment was received in 1972. Sales are net after deductions for refunds and allowances for merchandise returned by customers. Total sales exclude amounts other than those received from customers, such as income from investment, rental of real estate, etc. They include local and state sales taxes and federal excise taxes collected by the wholesale establishment directly from customers and paid directly by the wholesale establishment to a local, state, or federal tax agency. Gasoline, liquor, tobacco, and other excise taxes paid by the manufacturer and passed along to the wholesaler are also included.

Sales do not include wholesale sales made by manufacturers, retailers, service establishments, or other businesses whose primary activity is other than wholesale trade. They do, however, include receipts other than from the sale of merchandise at wholesale (e.g., service receipts, retail sales, etc.) by establishments primarily engaged in wholesale trade.

Manufacturing value added

Value added by manufacture is derived by subtracting the total cost of materials (including materials, supplies, fuel, electric energy, cost of resales, and miscellaneous receipts) from the value of shipments (including resales) and other receipts, and adjusting the resulting amount by the net change in finished products and work-in-process inventories between the beginning and end of the year.

Value added avoids the duplication in the value of shipments figure which results from the inclusion of the shipments of establishments producing materials and components along with the shipments of establishments producing finished products. It does not exclude purchased services. Nevertheless, it is considered to be the best value measure now available for comparing the relative economic importance of manufacturing among industries and geographic areas.

Mining value added

Value added in mining since the 1954 census, this measure has been computed by subtracting the cost of supplies, etc., and purchased machinery from the value of shipments and receipts plus capital expenditures.

Value added avoids the duplication in the value of shipments figure which results from the use of products of some establishments as supplies, energy sources, or materials by others. Moreover, it provides a measure, not only of value added in mineral production, but also in the development of mineral properties. For these reasons, it is considered to be the best value measure available for comparing the relative economic importance of mining among industries and geographic areas.

Manufacturing—Value of shipments

Net selling values, f. o. b. plant after discount and allowances and excluding freight charges and excise taxes (delivery prices acceptable if delivery was included as integral part of plant operations as in milk and bakery industries). Includes products made in the establishment as well as under contract from materials owned by the establishment. Included were contract work performed for others, resales, receipts for sale of scrap and refuse, and value of installation and repair work performed by plant employees.

Since the index of wholesale sales used in this analysis reflects intrastate transactions and processing of goods the value of manufacturing shipments and net value added is used as the determinant of wholesale sales activity.

Listing of the definitions of the variables used in the study of wholesale activity for the years 1967 and 1972.

Variable	*Definition*
Manufacturing	Value of manufacturing shipments, by state, 1967 and 1972 (in millions).
Population	1970 state population, 1974 state population estimates (in thousands).
Income	Mean family income, 1970.
Agriculture	Agricultural sales, 1964, 1969 (in millions).
Mining	Mining sales, by state, 1967 and 1972 (in millions).
Wholesale Sales	Wholesale sales, by state, 1967, 1972 (in millions).
AVINC 70	Mean family income, by state, 1970.
MEDINC 70	Median family income, by state, 1970.
DIFAM 70	Difference between the average and median family incomes, 1970.

THE PROBLEM OF HETEROSCEDASTICALLY DISTRIBUTED RESIDUALS

In a cross-sectional determinants analysis, the cases selected for inclusion in the regression model must produce a vector of residuals which are homoscedastically distributed (Johnston, 1972). This is usually not a safe assumption to make for analyses of sets of states or for that matter intrastate systems of cities (Beaton, 1974). Tests must be performed to insure that homoscedasticity holds for the analysis. The test used for this purpose has been devised by Goldfeld and Quandt (Goldfeld and Quandt, 1965).

Heteroscedasticity is detected by first ordering the cases within the desired partition by the increasing value of the dependent variable ; second, omitting a number of central observations in order to obtain residuals characteristic of either end of the size range ; third, fitting separate regression equations to the first and last set of observations, and lastly, using an F distribution to test the ratio of the residual sum of squares from the former regression equation with those of the latter.

The test ratio is :

$$R=S_2/S_1,$$

where R has an F distribution with (n-k-2m2/2, n-k-2m-2/2) degrees of freedom, and

- S_1 is the smaller value of the residual sum of squares,
- S_2 is the larger value of the residual sum of squares,
- n is the number of cases present within the original pooled sample,
- k is the number of central cases omitted, and
- m is the number of independent variables used to specify the model.

If S_2 and S_1 come from the same linearly homoscedastic population, then in all probability, the R ratio should be a number close to unity. However, if the population represented by one or the other end of the size range is characterized by differing structural conditions, the ratio will most likely generate a value above unity. If the size of this deviation is highly improbable, the assumption of homoscedasticity with the pooled system of states will be rejected and the pooled set of states will not be used as the model of the determinants of state wholesale sales.

Table B1 shows that the residuals obtained from the pooled system of states is probably not homoscedastically distributed. As a consequence, at least two regression equations must be fitted. One for states with above average wholesale sales, the other for states with below average wholesale sales.

TABLE B1 : Application of the Goldfeld-Quandt Test to the problem of the distribution of residuals from a wholesale sales determinants equation using the pooled set of states as observations

$$S_1 = 336,285,576$$
$$S_2 = 35,529,225$$
$$n = 51$$
$$k = 5$$
$$m = 5$$
$$R = 94.7$$
$$F\ (17, 17) = 94.7$$
$$F\ (0.01) = 3.3$$

APPENDIX-C

Interstate wholesale trade levels inferred from the residuals of the 1972 regression analysis and displayed on Table 2.4. Highest level scores represent states where residual score is above the third quartile ; while the lowest level scores are those below the first quartile score.

APPENDIX-D

Changes in interstate wholesale sales as inferred from the differences in the residuals from the 1967 and 1972 regression equations respectively. Higher level scores represent states whose differences in residuals are above the third quartile score ; while the lowest level scores are those below the first quartile score.

THREE

ROLF G. HEINZE AND THOMAS OLK

THE TWO FACES OF THE INFORMAL SECTOR

PRELIMINARY REMARKS

THE present paper focuses on the future development of the informal sector in the Federal Republic of Germany. As a result of various problems that have arisen, especially the employment and financial crises of the welfare state, the informal economy which had been neglected for a long time, is being brought again to the forefront of discussion. The informal sector comprises any types of activities which are performed outside the formal economy and which do not show up in gross national product figures. The work within the domestic household as well as jobs not registered in the official economy (especially moonlighting) and voluntary work for self-help groups, unions, associations, and so forth, constitute an essential part of the informal sector (cf. Berger and Offe, 1982 ; Heinze and Olk, 1982 ; Matzner, 1982, 164ff.).

The rediscovery and the increasing importance of the informal economy which exists beyond market and state has an ambivalent character which we will discuss in the following with a view to some aspects. On the one hand, considering the lasting period of economic stagnation, the firms pursue changed strategies of flexibilization designed to lower the cost of labor as well as to adapt the assignment of work to the fluctuating demand for labor, by circumventing the employment protection legislation and by impeding the collective organization of interests on the side of the workers. In the FRG, the new forms of reaction practised by the firms show themselves less in an expansion of homework as it is the case, for example, in Italy (cf. Mingione, 1981), but rather, for instance, in a flexibilization of working hours and the resort to subcontracting. While this strategy proves to be cost-saving for the firms, certain groups of workers merely take such unprotected employments because they have no other possibilities of officially participating in the labor market as a result of limited options (e.g. women, young people, older and disabled people which are early excluded from waged employment, illegal immigrants, etc.)

On the other hand, there are signs that a re-direction is taking place as to the labor force behavior of certain groups. For example, there is the increasing wish for shorter and more flexible working hours in order to have time for extra-professional activities (various forms of leisure work such as home maintenance, repair of cars and other technical equipment, neighborhood help, etc.).

In the first section of the present paper we will give a general view of the actual labor market situation in the FRG. Against the background of the economic stagnation period, selected strategies of flexibilization pursued by the capital are discussed more in detail. Then we will turn to the behavior of those groups of workers which strive for a new combination of employment and informal work.

WORK AND EMPLOYMENT IN THE 1980S

An end to full-employment ?

When the economic and political situation in the FRG had consolidated at the beginning of 1960s, unemployment had become a marginal phenomenon. Not only official policy, but also the social sciences considered large-scale unemployment to be a period belonging to the past. Since the mid-1970s, however, this situation has changed fundamentally. The FRG is experiencing comparatively high unemployment levels for several years (on the annual average about 1 million persons), with a strongly increasing tendency during the past year, and there are many signs indicating a *chronic underemployment* for the years to come. In winter 1981-82, the number of those unemployed nearly climbed up to 2 million and thus reached the highest level since almost 30 years.

Up until now the political system has relatively well coped with the relatively high levels of unemployment. Political crises have failed to come on the ground of the continuing underemployment. One rather has the impression that the general public has got used to the high unemployment figures and regards the monthly rates of increase as inevitable fate. A view to the other European countries even adds to this passive attitude : the 'model Germany' could reach a relatively good position compared to other countries. While unemployment rates of over 8 per cent became a permanent condition in Belgium, Great Britain, Italy, and Ireland, the unemployment rates of the FRG were relatively favorable up until early in 1981. During the last months, however, the situation likewise has changed for the worse. It is true that the number of those unemployed which amounted to 5.6 per cent in November 1981 was distinctly lower than that of most other EEC countries ; in Great Britain, the unemployment rate was 11.3 per cent, in Belgium 12.8 per cent, and in Italy 9.5 per cent, only in Luxemburg and in Greece it was noticeably lower. But the FRG, however, has experienced the relatively highest increase in unemployment rates. In the EEC alone, the number of those unemployed has surpassed the 10 million mark in December 1981 so that quantitative comparisons with the world depression occurring towards the end of the 1920s and the beginning of the 1930s and the mass unemployment which was attached to it in several regions cannot be denied.

As to the development prospects on the labor market, both the supply of labor and the overall growth rates (demand) are two central factors which must be taken into account. In contrast to the 1970s, labor potential will increase relatively strongly in the years to come. From 1975 through 1990, the German labor potential alone will raise by over 1 million. Certainly, the total number of the German resident population will steadily decrease till 1990, but in return the age classes with high birth rates push on the labor market, seeking employment possibilities, whilst, at the same time, the age classes of pensioners decimated by war vacate only very fewpositions.

It is difficult to establish exact figures with respect to the concrete labor potential, since not only the total number of the age-eligible population, but also the extent of labor force participation is important. On the basis of the hitherto existing labor force participation rates, it can be assumed that the labor force participation of retired persons will continue to slightly decrease, while female labor force participation did not decrease in spite of the economic crisis, but rather adapted to the fluctuations of the market and increased and will continue to increase if the present trend carries on. Of course, it cannot be excluded that in the case of constantly high unemployment levels, the female labor force participation rate will cease to increase. But it is likely that a possible withdrawal from the labor force will be accompanied by more conflicts than it was the case in the 1960s, when women flexibly adapted to the course of the business cycle. As a result it can be derived from the forecasts that an increasing labor potential is pushing on the labor market. Alone in order to counteract the demographic shifts as well as the increasing tendency of women to take an employment, it would be necessary to create at least over 1 million new jobs.

Whether the imbalances of the labor market will continue to increase depends to a large degree on the extent of the demand for labor. In contrast to the relatively reliable forecasts as to the demographic development, estimations with respect to the development of demand and growth rates are more difficult to establish and therefore differ more strongly. However, there is agreement on the fact that a real annual growth rate of more than 6 per cent is necessary in order to gradually diminish the actual unemployment. Let alone the question as to whether such growth rates would not create new environmental and natural resource exhaustion problems, all forecasts agree that such growth expectations are unrealistic. The factors accounting for that which are mentioned in the literature can only be touched upon very briefly here. On the one hand, the enormous rise of the energy and raw material prices has led to a decline in demand in the past few years which cannot be compensated even by additional orders of the oil producing countries. Furthermore, there are signs that the market for conventional manufactured goods, especially for durable consumer goods such as cars, electrical appliances, household equipment, and so forth, has reached saturation point. The new conditions on the world market also add to the existing stagnation. On account of the changed international distribution of work, involving the transfer of industrial production from the traditional industrial countries to the so-called low-wage or threshold countries, and the increasing import competition, a great number of jobs is being destroyed in the FRG.

A bottleneck in growth thus appears in outlines which takes the place of the postwar period of prosperity with high growth rates. As far since the 1950s, there is to be noted a decline in growth rates : whilst the average annual growth rate of production increased by 7.2 per cent during the decade 1950-60, the increase merely was 4.6 per cent in 1960-70, and even only 3.4 per cent in 1968-78.

Most forecasts relating to the economic development in the 1980s are based on the assumption that the growth rate will amount to 3-4 per cent, but that it will probably be lower. Some authors even predict a long period of economic stagnation and rapidly increasing unemployment levels. To explain the lasting accumulation crisis, recently it is often referred to the theorem of long waves in order to point to the enduring character of the economic stagnation on the one hand, and to the historic return of depression periods on the other hand.

Up until now, the Federal Republic of Germany experienced no acute political crisis. An important mechanism to reduce social tensions is the uneven incidence of employment. Latent employment conflicts were controlled by the fact that the 'marginal groups' on the labor market were first affected by the crisis, whilst the 'core' of the workers is still relatively safe from being hit by unemployment. Both the risk to be thrown out of work and to remain unemployed for a relatively long period mainly hits upon the vulnerable groups on the labor market. The 'problem' groups of the labor market comprise the disabled, older people, young people, and foreigners.

THE INFORMALIZATION OF WORK RELATIONSHIPS THROUGH FLEXIBILIZATION STRATEGIES OF THE FIRMS

Without considering here carefully the details of branch specific characteristics and business structures, new strategies of employment of the firms can be observed which modify the traditional principle to keep the permanent workforce and to employ additional personnel as the case may be, depending on the economic situation. Under the conditions of intensified competition and trends on the market which are difficult to predict, the firms increasingly turn to the practice to level out fluctuations in their demand for labor by flexibly using the permanent labor force and to manage as far as possible without having recourse to external labor markets. By this means the firms try to evade the rigidities ensuing from the legal and collective agreement provisions of labor protection (e.g. protection against arbitrary dismissal, etc.).

Evidence for the firms' strategies of shielding from the external labor force and flexibly using the internal labor force are the increased deviations from the standard working hours. These deviations include both overtime and short-time work which even can occur simultaneously within the same firm, but also part-time work and subcontracting. Thus the number of hours spent on working overtime and on additional shifts has constantly increased since 1960 ; even in the crisis year 1975, the total amount of this additional work exceeded unemployment (cf. Mendius, 1979). Such deviations from nominal working hours are admitted to a large extent by the legislation on working hours and the working-time regulations dating from 1938 which are still binding. Thus it is possible to extend the 8-hour day to approximately 10 hours, if there is an 'urgent need' (e.g. economic interests of the firm).

As an effective control of extra working hours through collective agreement provisions has not been achieved up to now, the works council or the staff and the management clash in the bargaining of extra hours and extra shifts. From a comparative study of an automobile concern and dock workers conducted by Dombois (1980) results that such regulations are always negotiated on an informal basis when the type of work and the existing technologies impede generalization and standardization.

Aside from extra work, part-time work is playing an important role within the scope of the flexibilization strategies adopted by employers. The proportion of part-time workers of the total labor force has increased from 2.6 per cent in 1960 to 8.5 per cent in 1978 ; these are not quite 2 million wage and salary earners, from which the most are women (over 90 %). Added to this must be the number of part-time employees working only seasonally or fewer than 15 hours per week (statutory limits where social security contributions are not compulsory) ; they are estimated to amount to another 900,000 (cf. Bacher, 1981). Part-time work which has been done up to now mainly by married women with children of school age, will further expand in the near future. There is, however, a relatively large gap between the supply of and the demand for labor on this specific labor market. The vast majority of part-time workers has a job in the service sector, such as vendor, office worker or charwoman. Although part-time work occurs on all levels of qualification, it is mostly to be found with respect to unskilled activities involving high psychic and physical strain.

The expansion of part-time work is due to the firms' flexibilization strategies which are designed to harmonize the volume of work with the supply of labor, to achieve increases in productivity through shortening individual working hours as well as to recruit groups of workers (especially women with children) which can only dispose of a limited amount of time. The implementation of this strategy can be observed above all in the retail trade. Here, full-time jobs are, in some cases, divided up into part-time jobs in order to manage the varying volume of work with a minimum of costs. In this context, the 'capacity-oriented variable working hours' (KAPOVAZ, i.e. German abbreviation) have become especially known. The purpose of this variant of working hours which has been introduced above all by department stores and supermarkets, is to make an optimal use of the body of workers in relation to customers' attendance. The capacity-oriented variable working hours can be seen as a consequent realization of flexible labor force use which enables all firms confronted with fluctuating demand for labor (especially in trade and other service sectors) to keep their permanent labor force the smallest possible and to manage peak hours by means of part-time workers which can be employed in case of need. The considerable gain in flexibility resulting from all variants of part-time work on the side of the firms contrasts with a legally undefined status on the side of the workers (cf. Engfer, 1982 ; Gabriel, 1982). The workers are thus more at risk of losing their jobs as the employer has, in case of dismissals, to pay regard to the importance the job has for the individual. In addition, there are larger margins as to the admissibility of contracts of employment concluded for a limited period.

However, many of the women in part-time employment do not come up to a certain number of working hours and a certain amount of earnings : they perform a so-called 'minor job'. This is why they do not fall under the provisions of the law governing health, social and unemployment insurances. Thus part-time employees working not more than 10 hours per week are not eligible for rights relating to continuance of pay during sickness. Likewise, part-time employees working fewer than 15 hours per week and earning not more than 390 marks per week are not covered by the social insurance regulations. At the same time, they are not required to pay contributions to the Federal Agency for the Placement of Labor and Unemployment Insurance and are more likely to be dismissed. The number of women affected by this tendency towards the suspension of the protective labor legislation can be calculated for 1977 : according to the Micro Census, 2.18 million female blue and white collar workers hold a part-time job, but only 1.32 million paid compulsory contributions to the social and unemployment insurances ; the remainder of 800,000 hence does 'minor jobs' which are not covered by the protective labor legislation.

Parallel to the increasing importance of flexible working hours, subcontracting has also increased in the last several years. Especially within branches experiencing relatively great cyclical and seasonal fluctuations (construction industry, shipbuilding, etc.) employers are turning more and more to the practice of managing variations in their demand for labor with a minimum of permanent labor force and additional workers hired at short notice if required. Though there is likewise not always a clear definition of legal status in the case of subcontracting, encroachments upon the protective labor legislation can nevertheless be stated. A higher risk of losing the job must be added. "They have different hours of work, contracts of employment on a temporary basis, no claims to hold certain positions. Central conditions of work are regulated on an individual basis, and not by collective agreement as it is the case for the permanent labor force. The minimum standards and protective regulations which are guaranteed to the permanent labor force through the collective bargaining contract, do not apply to the subcontract and part-time workers, although they are employed in the same firm and possibly carry out the same work. Their marginal status which confers to them the function of an institutional buffer group, is reinforced by the fact that they are not participating in institutionalized forms of collective organization" (Dombois and

Osterland, 1981, 20).

Since the beginning of the 1974-75 recession, the sub-contracting branch has developed by leaps and bounds. In 1980, there were already about 1,400 lawful subcontractors, whereas their number amounted not quite to 770 in 1977 ; the number of the legally employed subcontract workers increased likewise from about 9,000 in 1975 through 21,000 in 1977 to 47,000 in 1980 (cf. Sozialpolitische Umschau, 10-4-1980). However, reliable data are available only with a view to lawful subcontracting which has got its legal basis in 1972 by the "Law Governing Professional Subcontracting".

Experts estimate, however, that a by far larger extent of illegal subcontract workers must be taken into account. Its size varies depending on the specific branches, often there are 6 through 10 illegally employed persons to one legally employed subcontract worker. Illegal subcontract work occurs primarily in the construction industry, but also in the case of assembly work in the metal-working industry and as to dockwork. Subcontracting is concentrated in large towns and overcrowded areas. Often the illegal work is carried out by work immigrants ; in 1979 alone, 27,600 foreigners were picked up which did a job without a work permit, and in 29,000 cases firms had employed foreigners having no work permit. These figures might even be higher in 1980 and 1981.

As no detailed studies on illegal subcontracting are available, a brief outline will be given of the situation in Bavaria which has been investigated more in detail by the Bavarian association of the German Federation of Trade Unions. According to the figures supplied by the German Federation, in Bavaria alone there are about 300 lawful and 500 illegal subcontractors. Approximately 50,000 persons, among them 30,000 alone in the district of Munich, are working in these firms which are often co-managed by foreigners. The majority of the illegal subcontract workers comes from Yugoslavia and Turkey, but increasingly also from Great Britain and the Benelux countries. Protective labor regulations of the firms and collective agreement provisions are being evaded particularly through this form of subcontracting. Thus the protective function of collective labor agreements and the tariff uniformity is impaired to a considerable extent. At the same time, this 'slave trade' causes substantial losses in income taxation and social security contributions. In the case of the illegal subcontract work we unmistakably confront processes of deprivation of rights, whereas the legal subcontract workers certainly hold a special, however disadvantaged status in comparison with the permanent labor force, but after all, they are not legally discriminated.

In the light of the variable working hours which are increasingly spreading in the past few years and the prospering branch of subcontracting, we have tried to point out that the new flexibilization strategies adopted by employers are gaining in importance on the demand side of the labor market. It surely would be possible to find further examples, for instance the increase of homework in Italy and other countries (cf. Rubery and Wilkinson, 1980 ; Mingione, 1978, 1981), which also show the tendency to evade the protective labor legislation and limit the potential for collective action through internal division and fragmentation of the workers. The dividing up of the workforce raises considerable unification problems for trade union policy (cf. Heinze et al., 1981b).

In the following we turn to the supply side of the labor market in order to examine the question as to whether the workers also tend to deviate from the model of the 'full-time worker'.

THE CHANGING VALUE AND THE DIMINISHING IMPORTANCE OF EMPLOYMENT

The respective labor force participation depends on the concurrence of a great number of 'subjective' and 'objective' factors. As far as the type and the extent of the desired employment were concerned, central variables such as age, sex, place within the life cycle, and value patterns on the one hand, and labor market policy, wage levels, and tax load on the other hand have been investigated. Recently, however, more attention has been paid to the fact that the domestic household itself constitutes a productive unit within which goods form the formal economy and time are being combined in order to produce commodities (cf. the contributions in Ostner and Pieper, 1980 ; Fenstermaker and Berk, 1980). This change in perspective brings into view that the level of reproduction of the household members depends not exclusively on the earnings from paid employment, but also on the income from the home economy. The domestic household is developing more and more into a capital- and technology-intensive productive sector, rather than being just a center for consumption. Capital investment in the average household (durable consumer goods, cars, mechanical gadgets) is higher today than the average commercial firm needed a hundred years ago (cf. Joerges, 1981). Consequently, according to Gershuny (1981), new consumer needs are satisfied less by services than by goods in conjunction with 'do-it-yourself'. Thus a so-called domestic 'do-it-yourself sector' is emerging within the domestic household.

Individual deviations from the 'normal full-time worker' holding a 'stable position' occur in various forms and have—as we are assuming—acquired another signification in the past few years. Several empirical studies suggest that the attitudes towards employment are changing. Evidence for this change is the increasing attraction of employment opportunities outside 'constant employment', the direction towards diversified and autonomous activities, the reduced effectiveness of the wage incentive as well as the higher demands concerning the conditions of work (cf. with respect to the FRG Kmieciak, 1976 ; Olk and Otto, 1981). This change in value patterns coincides with a simultaneous change as to the importance attributed to the life spheres within which the respective values, shall or can be realized : the subjective importance attributed to the work sphere decreases whereas the importance of the leisure sphere is increasing. This change in direction is not *limited to younger workers* : symptoms of decline as to the traditional work ethic have been repeatedly identified (cf. Strumpel, 1977). From the comparison of survey data collected during the 1950s and 1970s follows that the importance employment has for the individual has strongly decreased, especially among the male occupied population (under 30s age group), whereas women as a unit show a greater interest in paid employment. It seems that housework and nonmarket activities increase in attraction especially for younger men. Furthermore, several studies conducted on working hours preferences suggest that an ever increasing number of workers would in certain cases make use of flexible hours of work remaining under the normal 40-hour week (cf. Mertens, 1979 ; Gorz, 1980, 136ff.).

The changed attitudes towards work have led to a re-direction in labor force behavior. Informal, non-contractual kinds of work gain increasingly in attraction as compared to waged labor. Such nonmarket activities include not only alternative forms of work within craft cooperatives or self-help groups, but also various forms of leisure activities such as house-building, repair of cars and technical appliances, home-decorating, gardening as well as the development of the do-it-yourself-movement (cf. Dahrendorf, 1980 ; Berger, 1982 ; Vonderach, 1982).

This change in labor force behavior finds a particularly prominent expression in the activities of *alternative projects* which are increasingly spreading in the FRG (cf. Huber, 1980 ; Hollstein and Penth, 1980). On account of the limited possibilities of access to the formal labor market, it is mainly young people which are turning to look for and create alternative job opportunities such as, for example, small craft trades, rural communes, shops, and the like. The relatively unskilled youngsters which are coming mainly from the working classes, are joined by students and graduates who reject the alienation of paid work and therefore rather try themselves as 'new self-employed' (Vonderach, 1980).

Another kind of non-contractual work is the expanding moonlighting. In other Western European countries, for example in Italy and Great Britain, but also in the USA ('black' or 'secret' economy), moonlighting which is very difficult to control, has an estimated share varying from 7 to more than 10 per cent of GNP, showing an increasing tendency (cf. Gershuny and Pahl, 1980 ; Shankland, 1980). As to the FRG, an increase in moonlighting is likewise to be registered : according to the figures supplied by the Central German Trade Association, 1980 was a 'record year' for 'moonlighters', especially for bricklayers, roofers, painters, joiners, and heating plant constructors. The annual turnover of moonlighting varied between 30 and 40 billion marks (cf. Gretschmann and Ulrich, 1980). Recently, governmental authorities are again increasing their efforts to control these activities. Doing so, they are supported by the Central German Trade Association for whom moonlighters constitute unwelcomed competitors for its own clientele. In spite of various measures that have been taken (e.g. extension and redefinition of the notion of illegal work and increase of penalties), it is not to be expected that the size of moonlighting will noticeably decrease, as it constitutes in many respects a 'response' to the malfunctioning of the formal economy. On the side of the workers, moonlighting is gaining increasingly in attraction as the levels of income taxation rise ; and the demand for moonlighting corresponds with the lack of quick and cheap professional services.

A further kind of informal work which is only very difficult to distinguish from moonlighting, is neighborhood help. Individual work undertaken in the neighborhood which does not enter into national accounts statistics, comprises activities such as repair of cars, home maintenance, help in gardening, shopping and messenger services. The reasons for this kind of neighborhood help are roughly the same as in the case of moonlighting: on the one hand, neighborhood help can be seen as a response to craftsmen and repair services which are too dear and too slow, on the other hand, it forms part of the strategies for reducing reproduction costs in view of the relative income losses resulting from inflation, short-time work and unemployment.

Added to this must be the element of immediate job satisfaction resulting from the autonomous organization of work (not only the goods and services produced, but already the very process of work offers possibilities of job satisfaction). Furthermore, neighborhood help includes also services oriented towards the person which act as a substitute for the public provision of services. These services comprise care of persons in need of nursing, raising and looking after children, care for sick persons, and so forth. This kind of neighborhood help can be viewed as a response to tendencies of state failure. The lessening quality and the dismantling of social services in face of the increasing costs in the service sector as well as the lacking orientation of governmental and local bureaucracies towards the needs of consumers favor the development of independent forms of need satisfaction. In the course of industrialization and urbanization, however, the performance potential of the neighborhood has been largely reduced to residual functions. According to the evidence furnished by empirical studies, neighborhood is being conceived of at best as a subsidiary help institution which steps in when government and family relations fail (cf. Hamm, 1973 ; Schubert, 1977).

THE SOCIO-POLITICAL PROSPECTS OF THE INFORMAL SECTOR

In view of the fact that strategies for increased flexibility of work are being followed not only by the employers, but also by the workers, it could be concluded that these developments produce no negative effects. Consequently, the restrained scope of application and the reduced effectiveness of the employment protection legislation could be regarded as a result of the voluntary preferences of those involved.

On closer examination, however, this view proves to be false : those groups of workers which are primarily affected by the flexibilization strategies of the firms are not identical with those groups of workers which are practising a 'deviant' labor force behavior on their own account. Thus, for example, part-time work is one of the strategies of employers to improve their access to labor reserves hitherto unused. Female workers which dispose only of a limited amount of time on account of their family obligations are in a particularly marked state of dependence vis-a-vis the firms offering part-time jobs. That is why they have to accept particularly monotonous and degraded work as well as low wages and lacking promotional opportunities if they are to find a job at all. A similar state of dependence often exists in the case of subcontract work. This applies first quite obviously to the legal forms of subcontracting, where, for example, the 'distress' of the immigrants is being taken largely advantage of. But it applies also to those workers which, on account of their personal situation, seek only a temporary employment. Deviating from 'normal constant employment' implies for them likewise a discrimination as to legal status.

The situation is quite different in the case of those groups of workers which prefer shorter and more flexible working hours on account of their material saturation and changed value patterns. There are no negative effects resulting for them from reduced protection by collective regulations : their material security and their specific skills confer to them a stronger position in relation to the firms. Also without benefiting from employment protection legislation, they are able to give weight to their work-related interests. Workers on whose skills the firms depend to a high degree, are more likely in a position to succeed with special demands concerning the conditions of work as well as to successfully resist to an unconditional subordination of their own interests to the goals of the firm.

The firms' strategies for increasing the flexibility of labor amount to stabilize the formal capitalist economy at the expense of the development potential of the informal sector. This 'colonization' of the informal sector could be avoided in our opinion by implementing the strategy of the 'complementary network'. It is based on the recognition of the efficiency and effectiveness and the specific productive capacity of informal activities and on an acceptance of the principle that these should be given the chance to develop. In our view, the informal sector could be especially productive in areas where a flexible, personally oriented supply with non-standardized and non-professional goods and services is desirable. In addition, not only the goods and services produced, but also the autonomous method of production would create job satisfaction and thus could revitalize underused skills and abilities for self-help. Wherever informal activities prove to be able to more adequately satisfy needs as state or private market provision, these private initiatives must be especially encouraged. Accordingly, private market and state activities should be limited to those areas where informal activities would be likely to fail. Whereas there can be little chance for expansion of the informal sector in areas of economic production which require high capital or skill input, it is to be expected that considerable development potential exists in particularly labor-intensive areas. It must in any case be dependent on an adequate material security of those working within the informal sector and a voluntary decision as to whether or not join the informal sector. This must include *flexible* transitions from one sector to another without loss of rights and protection. Shorter and more flexible working hours as well as liberal regulations on part-time working, longer holidays, flexible retirement ages, etc. would help to establish a permanent exchange between work spheres. Shorter and 'fluid' working hours would greatly increase the possibility for individuals to combine formal employment with some individual private activities. With that, the combination of formal and informal work would not only be realizable—as was stated above—for a small group of privileged workers, but would be potentially achievable for all suppliers of labor. The most significant area of expansion of informal activity has been the *social services* which were previously controlled by professionals and bureaucrats. The old, the sick, the children can be cared for by community groups or self-help groups, alternative educational and day-care centers can be organized and alternative therapy, refuge and youth centers can be set up.

The *future of work* accordingly lies not exclusively in waged employment, but more and more in activities which are not oriented towards money-making. Individual social and professional skills would face new challenges. Individuals would need skills such as creativity, craftsmanship, organizing genius and they would need to be more gregarious—i.e. they would need skills which are not used in our present system. Added to that, the informal sector's operations depend on the existence of functioning social relationships, for example on the community or neighborhood levels or among like-minded people.

A considerable proportion of economic output, however, can only be produced in a capital- and technology-intensive system. If higher productivity in these areas could reduce the number of man-hours needed, then there would be more freedom for manoeuvre for privately organized activities. Indeed, it is only possible to protect the informal sector from being assimilated into the capitalist modernization process, if the radical political reformers start pressing the case for autonomy and industrial democracy, i.e. for humanization of work. An extreme strategy to liberate us *from* work—such as it is brought forward by prominent proponents of socialist ecology (cf. especially Gorz, 1980)—surrenders the very core of the 'work-oriented society' without a struggle, without even considering the possibility of a productive co-existence of humanized wage-earning and autonomous private work. To discourage unrealistic expectations, i.e. illusions as to an 'empire of freedom', it must always be remembered that the political protagonists of such a concept seem at present to be diverse and beset with internal and external conflicts which prevent the realization of their model of society. Their major opponents are all the institutions and social forces whose existence depends on the present system of production, distribution and consumption. Among these central representatives of the waning 'work-oriented society' rank last but not least the trade unions which cannot do other than draw their own conclusions—about the consequences for their own organization of the future development of work. For example, besides the immediately employment-related interests, they could also promote the interests of those which have been placed out of the system of waged labor and which are developing—more or less voluntarily—informal economy activities (cf. Heinze et al., 1981b). A strategy for transforming society must proceed cautiously and must first of all break down the restrictions to the expansion of the informal sector. For example, the tight connection between the wage and welfare systems must be broken and the imperative need for flexible working hours and organizational structures must be put into action.

REFERENCES

Backer, G., 1981 : Teilzeitarbeit und individuelle Arbeitszeitflexibilisierung, in : WSI-Mitteilungen 34 (H. 4), 194ff

Berger, J., 1982 : Zur Zukunft der Dualwirtschaft, in : Benseler, F./Heinze, R.G./Klonne, A. (eds.), Zukunft der Arbeit, Hamburg, S. 97ff

Berger. J./Offe, C., 1982 : Die Zukunft des Arbeitsmarktes, MS (erscheint in : G. Schmidt u.a. (eds.), Sonderheft "Industriesoziologie" der KZfSS)

Dahrendorf, R., 1980 : Im Entschwinden der Arbeitsgesellschaft, in MERKUR XXXIV, 749ff

Dombois, R., 1980 : Informelle Norm und Interessenvertretung, in : Leviathan 8, 375ff

Dombois, R./Osterland, M., 1981 : Neue Formen des flexiblen Arbeitskrafteeinsatzes : Teilzeitarbeit und Leiharbeit, MS (Bremen)

Engfer, U., 1982 : Arbeitszeitflexibilisierung als Rationalisierungsstrategie im Dienstleistungssektor, in : Offe, C./Hinrichs, K./Wiesenthal, H. (eds.), Arbeitszeitpolitik, Frankfurt/New York, S. 106ff

Fenstermaker Berk, S. (ed.), 1980 : Women and Household Labour, Beverly Hills/London

Gabriel, J., 1982 : "Neue Arbeitszeitpolitik" als Resultat unternehmerischer Interessen in der okonomischen Krise, in : Prokla H. 46 (12. Jhg.), S. 134ff

Gershuny, J., 1982 : Die Okonomie der nachindustriellen Gesellschaft, Frankfurt/New York

Gershuny, J.I./Pahl, R.E., 1980 : Britain in the decade of the three economies, in : New Society, 3, 7ff

Gorz, A., 1980 : Abschied vom Proletariat, Frankfurt

Gretschmann, K/Ulrich, W., 1980 : Wirtschaft im Untergrund, in : Wirtschaftsdienst 60, 444ff

Hamm, B., 1973 : Betrifft : Nachbarschaft. Verstandigung uber Inhalt und Gebrauch eines Begriffs, Dusseldorf

Heinze, R.G./Olk, Th., 1982 : Selbsthilfe, Eigenarbeit, Schattenwirtschaft. Entwicklungstendenzen des informellen Sektors, in : Benseler, F./Heinze, R.G./Klonne, A. (eds.), Zukunft der Arbeit, a.a.O., S. 13ff

Heinze, R.G./Hinrichs, K./Hohn, H.-W./Olk, Th., 1981a : Armut und Arbeitsmarkt : Zum Zusammenhang von Klassenlagen und Verarmungsrisiken im Sozialstaat, in : Zeitschrift fur Soziologie 10, S. 219ff

Heinze, R.G./Hinrichs, K./Offe, C./Olk, Th., 1981b : Interessendifferenzierung und Gewerkschaftseinheit, in : Gewerkschaftliche Monatshefte 32, 336ff

Heinze, R.G./Hinrichs, K./Olk, Th., 1982 ; Produktion und Regulierung defizitarer Soziallagen. Zur Situation von Behinderten und Leistungsgeminderten im Sozialstaat, in : Heinze, R.G./Runde, P. (eds.), Lebensbedingungen Behinderter im Sozialstaat, Opladen. S. 79ff

Hollstein, W./Penth, B., 1980 : Alternativ-Projekte, Reinbek

Huber, J., 1980 : Wer soll das alles andern, Berlin

Kmieciak, P., 1976 : Wertstrukturen und Wertwandel in der Bundesrepublik Deutschland, Gottingen

Matzner, E., 1982 ; Der Wohlfahrtsstaat von morgen, Frankfurt/New York

Mendius, H.-G., 1978 : Arbeitszeit und Arbeitsmarkt—Zu Voraussetzungen und Moglichkeiten beschaftigungswirksamer Interessenvertretung, in : WSI-Mitteilungen 31, 202ff

Mertens, D., 1979 : Neue Arbeitszeitpolitik und Arbeitsmarkt, in MittAB 12, 263ff

Mingione, E., 1978 : Capitalist crisis, neodualism and marginalization, in : IJURR Vol. II, No. 2, S. 213ff

Mingione, E., 1981 : Perspectives on the Spatial Division of Labour under the recent productive Restructuring and Informalization of the Economy, MS

Olk, Th./Otto, H.-U., 1981 : Wertewandel und Sozialarbeit. Entwicklungsperspektiven kommunaler Sozialarbeitspolitik, in : Neue Praxis 11, S. 99 ff

Ostner, I./Pieper, B. (eds.), 1980 : Arbeitsbereich Familie, Frankfurt/New York

Rubery, J./Wilkinson, F., 1980 : Outwork and Segmented Labour Markets, MS

Schubert, H.A., 1977 : Soziologie stadtischer Wohnquartiere, Frankfurt/New York

Shankland, G., 1980 : Our Secret Economy, London/Bonn

Strumpel, B., 1977 : Die Krise des Wohlstandes, Stuttgart u.a.

Vonderach, G., 1980 : Die "neuen Selbstandigen", in : MittAB 13, S. 153ff

Vonderach, G., 1982 : Eigeninitiativen— Beginn einer "kulturellen Mutation" ?, in ; Benseler, F./Heinze, R.G./Klonne, A. (eds.), Zukunft der Arbeit, a.a.O., S. 31ff.

FOUR

CHRISTINE FUREDY

THE INFORMAL SECTOR IN CALCUTTA
Issues for Analysis

THE term "informal sector" is the legacy of attempts of the late 1960s and the 1970s to characterize and explain the economic dualism of modernizing societies, in the context of concern about income-earning opportunities. It is one in an evolving series of terms whose origin stretches back ten or fifteen years at least. Like its predecessor twin terms—modern/traditional, firm-centred/bazaar-type, upper and lower circuits, regulated/unregulated—the formal/informal set has come in for a good deal of scrutiny and criticism.[1] There have been several types of critique and differing levels of criticism, ranging from those that accept the basic referent of the concepts (i.e., accept some kind of dualism in economic structures) but that object to the terms "formal" and "informal", through those that seek to modify unduly dichotomous or static analysis based on the concepts, to those that have argued that a "sectorial" framework, however labelled and however elaborated, is fundamentally flawed.[2] In spite of this onslaught, the concept has taken root in academic studies and policy discussions and has served to focus attention on a number of problems of employment and the urban poor in developing countries.

Undoubtedly the principal factor in the general acceptance of the term "informal sector" in the last decade was its use in studies sponsored by the ILO under its World Employment Programme (WEP), which grew out of the ILO/UNDP mission report on Kenya, *Employment, Incomes and Equality* (1971).[3]

The ILO urbanization and employment research project has sponsored a series of case studies of selected cities,[4] all making reference to the informal sector, with an ultimately comparative purpose. Two of these have been of Calcutta. However, the international literature on employment and the informal sector contains few references to them. Indeed, the multifaceted debate about employment problems and urban economies rarely includes Indian data. The aim of this paper is to examine the use of the informal-sector concept in discussions of employment in Calcutta, considering the articulation of issues for this city in the light of current trends of research and discussion. This analysis should raise questions concerning the use of the concept as a basis for policy recommendations, and its applicability to a complex Indian city. I will limit my discussion to the two WEP case studies of Calcutta's employment characteristics and problems : *Urban Development and Employment : The Prospects for Calcutta*, by Harold Lubell (1976) and *Calcutta and Rural Bengal : Small Sector Symbiosis*, by A.N. Bose (1978).[5]

Terminological debate

For the present purpose I do not wish to elaborate upon the terminological debate, nor to examine in any detail the position of scholars who have argued that current trends of analysis are seriously in error. With respect to the former let me simply say that the terms themselves are problematical if taken too literally or if used to simplify or restrict the examination of a very complex reality. It would seem that, regardless of what terms are used for socio-economic structures, our analysis require as a *starting point* some means of denoting when important contrasts exist within a society in terms of employment, earnings, and economic and social organization. One may start by describing these contrasts in a dichotomous framework, but, inevitably, detailed analysis will reveal intermediate cases. Our initial organizing concepts must not be set in stone so that alternative modes of analysis are overlooked and data are artificially fitted into an inflexible framework. The formal/informal distinction may well prove more applicable to some societies than to others, and it may be more relevant to certain types of discussion than to others.

In accepting the terms "formal" and "informal" sectors for

the purpose of this discussion, I assume that we must look behind the facade of the labels to examine the assumptions underlying their use. This is particularly important when the concepts are used as a starting point for policy recommendations for complex urban economies.

Blockages or linkages

When the terms "formal" and "informal" are accepted, there is still a difference among scholars according to whether the emphasis is placed upon the distinctions between the two broad sectors which are assumed to exist in the economy, or upon the linkages between them. This has been the main thrust of the theoretical (or quasi-theoretical) discussion in the last few years. Some scholars see the informal sector as operating with a good deal of independence from the formal sector, an independence which results, on the one hand, from the lack of enumeration or regulation of certain activities and, on the other, from the urban poor's lack of ready access to formal institutions. They emphasize "blockages" in labour mobility, resources, markets, and information. Thus an influential paper published by a World Bank team in 1976 argued that dualism, in the form of contrasting technologies, was not *per se* a sign of a disfunctional economy, but :

> The problem in countries with restricted labour markets is that it becomes a discontinuous form of dualism. The two segments of the economy are isolated from one another, the possibility of stepwise adjustments and of movement of labour, capital and innovations between sectors is blocked, both are made more inefficient than they would otherwise be.[6]

This position is very different from the argument of neo-Marxist scholars who interpret the informal sector in terms of the dynamics of international capitalist penetration of third world economics. These scholars wish to define the informal sector more in terms of its "structural" relations to the formal sector than its contrasts with that sector. They emphasize the dependence of the informal sector upon the formal, in line with their understanding of underdevelopment. Hence they would interpret linkages between formal and informal sector enterprises not as entrepreneurial outreaches but as the result of capitalist corporations seeking to marginalize petty capitalists or to coopt informal sector workers.[7]

The former position has as its corollary the assumption that the dynamism of the informal sector (which many see as the hope for its positive contribution to the economy) resides mainly in its unregulated, unlinked characteristics. In contrast, Portes has argued that "its existence and dynamism are dependent upon the formal sector."[8] A less ideological statement come from Gerry : "it is *the relations between these different systems or subsystems of production* which determine those phenomena which will characterise each of the elements of the ensemble"[9] (emphasis added).

The orientation to "blockages," on the one hand, or to "linkages", on the other, is important because it can lead to quite different policies for intervention in the economy.

Productive enterprises and services

There is one further aspect of the evolving discussion of the last decade which should be noted. When attention was first given to employment problems in the developing countries, the feature considered to be most prominent in the informal sector (it was not usually so labelled in the early 1960s) was the multiplication of petty trading and services, which was considered a mark of underemployment.[10] The "lower" levels of urban economies were viewed predominantly as unproductive. Subsequently, largely as a result of the combined effect of the Kenya mission report and independent research elsewhere, researchers pointed to the "productive enterprises" of shantytowners, migrants and untrained urban dwellers. There was a desire to counteract the negative conceptions current in commentaries and policy documents. Once these small-scale enterprises were seen as holding hope for employment generation the earlier corrective point became a predominant emphasis. Reading many of the discussions of the last few years, one might easily conclude that the informal sector consisted largely of productive undertakings : the "unproductive" service occupations (including retailing) and other aspects which do not appear to be amenable to intervention are practically lift out of account. Preoccupied with policy making, the WEP studies have reinforced this tendency.

Relevance of international discussion to India

How relevant are the issues being debated in African and Latin American countries for the understanding of Indian cities? Certain aspects have not become points of controversy in Indian research. One need not bother to ask for India whether the informal/formal division is too simple and whether intermediate sectors must be distinguished. Nor can it be said that the nonformal parts of the economy have been overlooked, as was in for Kenya.[11] Analysis of the Indian economy has incorporated understanding of "cottage industries" in urban areas and distinctions have been made between the small-scale productive sector and the larger scale. India has recognized the differences even further in defining a "tiny" sector, with its distinct problems.[12] Since independence, the needs of these sectors have been included in policy discussions. (Whether they have received the support which some advisors now call for is another matter.) The main point is that the "productive enterprises" of the informal sector have been seen as having a distinct role in industrial strategy. (The service occupations have not, however received so much attention.)

Hence it is not surprising that Indian analysts have not thought it necessary to enter the international discussion about the formal/informal dichotomy. The great diversity of the national economy and the size of each distinguishable category of enterprise or occupation for India as a whole (and for large cities in particular) has left no doubt that the country possesses a continuum of enterprises. Again, the issues raised regarding petty producers, the self-employed and the "coopted" workers take on a different import in a complex economy : simplistic characterizations of informal-sector employment will not hold. The more important task becomes to distinguish significant categories and relationships in such a way as to understand the roles of different occupations and styles of enterprise within the economy.

In summary, one does not find in large Indian cities the sharp contrasts which have been emphasized for smaller African cities. With respect to complex cities one might expect to find greater attention paid to the dynamics of interaction between different types of enterprises and occupational groups, both within definable sectors and between them. This concern is emerging as an important one for research in Calcutta.

Harold Lubell's study

The study which was published as *Urban Development and Employment : the Prospects for Calcutta* was undertaken as one of the first of the city case studies of the urbanization and employment project of the WEP. The stated aims were to suggest practical policies for improving the employment situation by drawing upon the research and knowledge of local institutions, and to suggest future research orientations and lines of policy discussion. Each of the ILO case studies published so far has given some consideration to the city's relation to the national economy, the role of migration in employment pressures, the characteristics of the labour force and the 'economic effect of urban infrastructure development." In a recent explanation of the research series, S.V. Sethuraman suggests that the informal sector was the principal concern in each case.[13] The intention was to make comparisons among cities possible. Thus while the studies have policy recommendations as a priority, analytical frameworks and research directions were to be developed as a basis for further research.

In the light of these goals one would have expected that the Calcutta study would devote considerable attention to the informal sector, both because Calcutta is regarded as having one of the largest and most complex informal sectors among world cities and because at the time of the writing of the monograph the Kenya mission report was being widely discussed. Surprisingly, Lubell devotes only three or four pages to the informal sector, much of that consisting of fairly casual remarks. Lack of data was one constraint : Lubell did not consider that any direct information existed about the city's informal sector.[14] But this cannot have been significant in his decision since at least as much information existed as was available for Kenya. More important must have been Lubell's attitude that the informal sector in Calcutta was not a "problem" for employment analysis : he did not identify the migrant families whose income depends upon informal sector employment as a "target group" for an employment policy. On the contrary, Lubell identified Calcutta's most urgent problems as lying with the long-urbanized Bengali residents, in particular the educated unemployed of Bengali middle-class families. Lubell explicitly linked this preoccupation to his dismissal of the problems of migrants (who form a considerable portion of the informal sector and whom he expects to increase in numbers in the future):

> In the near future, the target group of employment policy for Metropolitan Calcutta need not be the new arrivals, or potential arrivals, of unskilled manpower from the countryside. As in the past, either they will fit into the lower productivity and lower paid employment opportunities that Calcutta has to offer, particularly if the industrial economy expands at a reasonable rate, or they will drift away.
> The main target group must be the young people who are already in the Calcutta Metropolitan environment in which they have grown up and to whose ways, both good and bad, they are accustomed.[15]

Lubell goes on to make it clear that these young people are those of Bengali middle-class families.

The careless attitude (in the literal sense of that term) embodied in the statement quoted above must surely be without parallel in the literature of employment problems in developing countries. One could spend some time examining the assumptions underlying this policy recommendation ; however, the present purpose is to consider what Lubell has to say about the informal sector in general. This is not easy since there is no coherence in Lubell's scattered references to the informal sector. He does not define the sector directly, but simply refers to the Kenya study definition.[16] He apparently includes in the sector all cottage industries, most of the casual manual workers of the city, the small-scale family enterprises which come under the Shops and Establishments Act, small workshops and the "unorganized" services. His remarks reflect a number of orientations current in the literature of the early 1970s and he seems unaware that there are a number of implicit contradictions in his various statements. For instance he characterizes the informal sector as a "labour market of last resort"[17] but refers to ethnic, language group and caste stratification in employment and surmises that rural migrants have "a rather effective network of information on the Calcutta labour market."[18] Further, the emphasis on the "last resort" concept seems to be inconsistent with his later stress on the informal sector as "an enormous reservoir of productive skills."[19] Lubell discounts his perception of the great variety of the informal sector by such blanket characterizations.

Systematic development of the informal sector

Although Lubell does not identify the participants in the informal sector as a target group for employment policy his chapter on "the employment problem and its solution" contains a recommendation for the "systematic development of the informal sector."[20] Here he brings together his two perceptions of the informal sector as a labour market of last resort and a reservoir of productive skills by suggesting a variety of ways in which unskilled jobs and productive enterprises can be increased. With optimistic sweeps of the brush he envisages the transformation of an ever-deteriorating urban economy by agricultural modernization which will generate demand for agricultural equipment and investment in urban infrastructure. This will increase jobs and generally stimulate consumer demand in the metropolitan area. Once the agricultural sector is "reorganized", he sees the smaller workshops of Calcutta and Howrah contributing to the market for agricultural products (with "proper organization", a repair industry would develop).[21] A passing reference is made to retailing and to cottage industries in the suggestion that a small-scale commercial and handicraft centre could be encouraged to grow around a planned trucking terminal on the edge of the metropolitan district.[22] As for the "unorganized services", which he recognizes to be one of the largest users of urban manpower, Lubell thinks that the best guarantee of continuing jobs is "a multiplicity of household incomes that are too small for the purchase of mechanical household appliances but large enough to command the services of sweepers, laundrymen and tailors."[23] He predicts an unchanging persistence of this part of the informal sector : "As long as a large labour surplus exists, all these unorganized services in the metropolis will continue to absorb large numbers of the unskilled at low rates of remuneration."[24]

Impact of Lubell's study

From the perspective of a decade of research and discussion of the informal sectors of third-world cities, Lubell's study of Calcutta seems to contribute little to the general international debate. Preoccupied with the problems of formal sector industry and of the educated unemployed, Lubell essentially dismissed the informal sector as a matter for real concern. Consequently he felt little need to identify a concept of the informal sector appropriate for the city or to apply an analytic framework to the variety of nonformal occupations. Although he recognizes linkages between the rural and urban economies (in his discussion of in-migration), his lack of a clear framework does not lead him to explore these in any detail. His observations on the informal sector in Calcutta cannot readily be used to compare this sector in Calcutta with other cities in the ILO case study series.

Furthermore, his recommendations for improvement of the informal sector are piecemeal : some are short-term and limited, others depend upon substantial economic revival in the whole region, a revival which his analysis of West Bengal's economic situation does not suggest is imminent. The lack of examination of ways in which the informal sector relates to the formal raises questions regarding some of his other recommendations. For instance, since the way in which small engineering workshops relate to formal-sector production is hardly touched upon, it is not easy to envisage how the desired encouragement of small-scale engineering and repair industries could be achieved. There is a suggestion that this would be accomplished by subcontracting by formal sector firms,[25] without any consideration of the problems which such subcontracting might entail for small firms. In general, the policy recommendations for the informal sector have a quality of unreality, since no reference is made to current policies towards the informal sector and one can gain no sense of how likely it is that any of his recommendations would be implemented.

Perhaps it is unfair to criticize Lubell for the many weaknesses in his treatment of the informal sector in Calcutta, since he did not see his main purpose as a consideration of the characteristics of that sector. The value of his study thus lies not in his treatment of the informal sector as such but in his laying out of the multiple problems of industry, commerce and employment in Calcutta. His general analysis has power, whatever one might conclude about his policy recommendations and his decisions on appropriate target groups for employment policy.

A.N. Bose, Calcutta and rural Bengal : Small sector symbiosis

This study, prepared "within the framework of the WEP" but published independently in Calcutta rather than by the ILO in Geneva, was designed as a follow-up to Lubell's. Specifically it was to implement his recommendation that a study be done of the production possibilities of workshops in Calcutta slums in order to see which lines of production could be developed to contribute to the anticipated need for modern agricultural equipment. The monograph is predominantly a summary, with comment, upon past surveys of small-scale industrial units in metropolitan Calcutta together with the results of a small survey undertaken in conjunction with the study. Bose presents these data with an interpretation of Calcutta's economic problems and a programme for development.

If Lubell's study suffered from lack of a consistent framework of analysis, Bose's is burdened by repetitive dogma and heavy rhetoric. Tracing the ills of Calcutta's system to the persistence of take up colonially-established relationships, Bose states a neo-Marxist dependency position in stark and simplistic terms. His discussion is replete with references to "economic necessity", "historic role", overall domination (of the formal sector over the whole economy), excessive profits for metropolitan "oligopolies" and other catch phrases of dependency theory.[26] There can be no doubt that Bose's orientation to the informal/formal sector distinction is in terms of structural linkages.

Thus Bose resolves the problem of the relations between the formal and informal sectors by asserting that they operate in separate markets[27] but are inexorably linked by dependency relations, the informal sector being "at the mercy of" a few large houses controlling modern industry and especially the marketing system.[28] The persistent poverty of the informal sector is explained in terms of this domination. These assumptions lead Bose to interpret aspects of the small-scale production process in Calcutta very differently from Lubell. For instance, Bose regards subcontracting not as a modernizing lifeline which may uplift part of the informal sector but a mechanism used by formal sector units for the exploitation and further marginalization of small units.[29]

Ultimately, Bose's repetitive rhetoric dulls the interest, yet there is much in his discussion of surveys of small-scale units in

Calcutta which is opposite. To have summarized the scattered and inaccessible survey and census material on small-scale units in Calcutta's industry is an important contribution to understanding a portion of the informal sector. Between the bracketing rhetoric one can piece together a very thorough analysis of the characteristics and problems of small-scale units. Bose convincingly points to the intertwining of factors such as access to capital, acquiring of orders, the use of capital, space and equipment, of marketing and transportation.[30] He underlines the extreme vulnerability of small units and their dependency upon the general condition of the economy. He sets the informal manufacturing sector in the context of the informal sector of West Bengal, asserting that, despite the fact that small units in the city deliver their proprietors and workers very low returns, they produce nevertheless significantly higher incomes than units elsewhere in the state and certainly produce a net surplus.[31] It is this surplus that Bose sees as the most distinctive feature of the small units, holding hope for improvement through intervention.[32]

Bose's analysis of the data is often perceptive. He suggests the importance of factors which are rarely mentioned in more general discussions. For instance, pointing to the relatively higher rents and the higher capitalized value of land and buildings of the small units, he draws attention to the pressing reasons why these enterprises seek to locate as near as possible to the "centre of demand". Among these is the fact that because the units do not produce enough to regularly hire modern transport, they must depend upon informal transport. Further inefficiencies in production and marketing occur if this transportation must be used to cover considerable distances.[33]

Bose stresses the constraints faced by small units in operating at full capacity as a major factor in limitations on income, productivity, and employment for small units. He concludes that for the metropolitan district as a whole, the capital productivity is not a great deal lower than for medium and large units, in spite of the multiple difficulties faced by them.[34] This challenges common assumptions about the use of capital by small units and their general productivity.

Perhaps the most valuable contribution of the descriptive chapters is a summary of some of the results of a survey of some slum industries in Calcutta, conducted as part of the study in 1974. Although Bose was unable to generate adequate statistical information from the survey of 649 units in Calcutta and Howrah covering 56 types of industries, the study can be used to suggest significant variables as a basis for further research. The immediate interest lies in some of the thumbnail sketches of small-scale enterprises. Bose includes brief details on sophisticated small engineering units, an electrical goods producer subcontracting-known company, and a "cottage" type footwear-making family.[35] Some surveys were designed to show the structure and functioning of a number of units within the same area. For instance, there is a discussion of garment-making units in a northern fringe bustee in which data from 78 families are used to demonstrate the differences among medium traders, small traders, and piece workers within the slum industry.[36] Makers of rubber goods, carpenters, and the image-makers of Kumartully are also included.

These brief sketches are sufficient to suggest how complex is the structure of relationships among different types of traditionally skilled workers and modern units within slum areas. In his "modern" case studies Bose suggests the demands which subcontracting to formal units make upon smaller enterprises.

Bose's dominant theme is the financial problems of the small units, their high insecurity and the probable reasons for the high mortality rates of small firms. He points to factors in the established structures which order many of the more traditional occupations and to the high volatility obtaining in the little-scrutinized fringe world of the subcontracting "modern" unit. It is through these sketches that one gains a sense of the dynamics of informal-sector industry in Calcutta, rather than from the survey statistical data of this and earlier studies. There is scope for a great deal more discussion of these data. Unfortunately Bose does not make the most of his material ; the chapter ends abruptly with little effort to relate his findings to the earlier government-conducted surveys.

Recommendations

What are Bose's recommendations and how do they compare to Lubell's ? He presents several levels of recommendation for improving the productive potential of informal-sector units. An economic "relief programme" for small units should aim to ensure that they would be able to raise capital at the same rate as formal-sector enterprises, thus removing financial discrimination against small units. In certain selected areas (he does not specify which) Bose believes economic relief would imbue operators with hope and the will to organize for larger benefits.[37] Bose does not attach much importance to such measures for they "will certainly not bring about a basic change in the livelihood pattern of the urban poor in general and the slum poor in particular."[38]

But the relief programme suggestion is essentially at variance with his main argument that policy must aim at "a basic reorientation and restructuring of the present metropolitan industrial commercial base . . . rather than a further strengthening of the existing base and its structure."[39] For the reorientation Bose turns to the same mechanism as Lubell: technological change in the rural economy. He too looks to a "green revolution" in West Bengal but argues that it will be counter productive unless accompanied by a thoroughgoing reform of rural socio-economic institutions (equitable land distribution, abolition of share cropping, full credit to agricultural producers at low rates of interest, state controlled or cooperative marketing systems, etc.).[40] A rejuvenated rural economy will create a higher volume of demand for industrial goods which will generate "massive new employment in the non-agricultural sector."[41] Thus it would be possible to accomplish a reordering of the entire "industry mix" in the metropolitan area, reorienting it towards the needs of the rural economy. Here we discover the meaning of the book's title.

But how is this radical change to be accomplished ? On this crucial point Bose is silent, except to say : "This can be achieved only by a self-reliant, militant organization of the rural and urban poor."[42]

Thus Bose and Lubell share the assumption that development of the informal sector is dependent upon change in Calcutta's industrial economy and, specifically, on an adaptation of several lines of industry to the production of agricultural equipment. Lubell sees agricultural modernization as a technological precondition for urban changes. In a direct although implicit criticism of Lubell's position and his reluctance to look beyond the goal of employment generation in Calcutta, Bose rejects mere technological modernization without radical socio-economic change. Neither scholar is able to suggest in detail the means by which the troubled small-scale industry units could participate in an expanded agricultural production system without being tied more closely to subcontracting relationships with formal sector-firms. (of course, since Lubell regards subcontracting positively, he feels no need to address this issue.)

CONCLUSION

Many detailed criticisms could be made of both ILO WEP reports on Calcutta on account of their analytic frameworks, fundamental assumptions, their incompleteness and their inconsistencies. But it is important to focus upon the substantial weaknesses. These lie in the conception of the informal sector and the context of policy recommendation.

In the final analysis, whatever their general remarks about the nature of the informal sector, both scholars narrow their vision to concentrate on a partial and perhaps exceptional part of the informal sector : small-scale productive units which are "modern" or capable of conversion to modern production. They do this because it is only in the productive enterprises that they see any prospect for long-term employment generation which can be linked to general economic development. The majority of informal-sector undertakings—the many and miscellaneous services, retailing and petty trading, and casual work of all kinds—receive scarcely any mention. We can understand why the manufacturing units were selected for attention. However, we might have expected that both scholars would have pointed out the limited scope of their interest and would have qualified their concluding references to "systematic development of the informal sector." In neglecting to do this Lubell and Bose have added to what is becoming a serious distortion in recent discussions of the informal sector : the emphasis upon "productive enterprises" as though these constituted the majority of the sector's employment possibilities. Then, work within a manufacturing unit is usually part of primary employment, so that the secondary-employment aspect of the informal sector, and in particular the activities of women and children, are overlooked. These distortions do not serve the purpose of broad understanding of employment problems in urban areas.

The small-manufacturing focus also reinforces the tendency to separate employment from its social context and to analyse it largely in terms of economic variables. Thus the very benefits of the term "informal sector," which, being derived from sociology and social anthropology, suggested the connections between employment, social structures, behaviour and values, that is, employment in a social and residential context, are reduced.

These analytical failings are the result of the pressure to articulate practical policies for intervention in urban economies. Both practitioners and researchers are sympathetic to these needs, but how much confidence is to be placed in policies formulated on the basis of a distorted framework and piecemeal data ?

Perhaps we can live with imperfect conceptualizations and models. Policies may work without us really understanding why. However, the chances of the WEP recommendations for effecting employment improvement in Calcutta are jeopardized by naivety. The policy recommendations of both studies are offered without references to either the past history of policy towards the informal sector, and small-scale industry in particular, or to the present structure of decision-making for the state, the metropolitan area, and the city. There being no discussion of the constraints—financial, political, administrative, technical—which might impede measures designed to influence the informal sector, one is unable to assess the ultimate practicability of the recommendations. The Calcutta studies are thus subject to the same "political" criticism as were made of the Kenya recommendations of the informal sector.[43] Furthermore the suggested "systematic development" of the informal sector, if implemented successfully, might merely formalize the sector, or a part of it. This, some have argued, would merely extend the structures of privilege "without any real attack on inequality."[44]

FOOTNOTES

1. Two of the most thorough discussions are contained in Stuart W. Sinclair, *Urbanization and Labour Markets in Developing Countries* (London : Croom Helm, 1978) and Joan M. Nelson, *Access to Power*

(Princeton : Princeton U.P., 1979).

2. See, for instance, J. Bremen, "A dualistic labour system ? A critique of the 'informal sector' concept." *Economic and Political Weekly*, 27 Nov., 4 Dec., 11 Dec., 1976.
3. Report of an interagency team financed by the United Nations Development Programme and organized by the ILO (Geneva : ILO, 1972).
4. Among them are Jakarta, Manila, Colombo, Cordoba, Lagos, Kumasi, Freetown, Abidjam, Bogota and Sao Paulo in addition to Calcutta.
5. The former was published in Geneva by the ILO and the latter in Calcutta by Minerva Associates (Publications) Pvt. Ltd.
6. George Beier, Anthony Churchill, Michael Cohen and Bertrand Renaud, "The task ahead for the cities of the developing countries." *World Development*, vol. 4, no. 5 (May 1976), p. 390. Also available as World Bank Reprint Series No. 97.
7. Alejandro Portes, "The informal sector and the world economy : notes on the structure of subsidised labour." *IDS Bulletin*, vol. 9, no. 4 (June 1978), pp. 35-39.
8. *Ibid.*, p. 39.
9. Chris Gerry, "Underemployment, petty production and government promotion schemes in Senegal." *IDS Bulletin*, vol. 9, no. 3 (Feb. 1978) p. 11.
10. See John Friedmann and Robert Wulff, *The Urban Transition* (London : Edward Arnold, 1976), pp. 50-51.
11. *Employment, Incomes and Equality*, p. 226.
12. C.T. Kurien, "Small sector in the new industrial policy," *Economic and Political Weekly*, March 4, 1978, pp. 455-56.
13. S.V. Sethuraman, "The urban informal sector : Concept, measurement and policy," *International Labour Review*, vol. 114, no. 1 (July-Aug., 1976) p. 75.
14. p. 25.
15. p. 64.
16. p. 46.
17. p. 88.
18. p. 34.
19. p. 88.
20. p. 96.
21. p 89
22. *Loc cit.*
23. p. 90.
24. *Loc. cit.*
25. Lubell elaborates this point in a later article, "Migration and employment : the case of Calcutta." *Social Action*, vol. 27 (July-Sept., 1977), p. 290.
26. pp. 2-5, 85, 97 and passim.
27. pp. 35, 38, 48.

28. p. 97.
29. p. 105.
30. p. 51.
31. pp. 48-53.
32. pp. 54, 57, 121-22.
33. p. 51.
34. pp. 53-54.
35. Chapt. IV.
36. pp. 106-110.
37. p. 121.
38. *Loc cit.*
39. p. 127.
40. pp. 142-44.
41. p. 156.
42. *Op. cit.*
43. See Paul Mosley, "Implicit models and policy recommendations : policy towards the 'informal sector' in Kenya," *IDS Bulletin*, vol. 9, no. 3 (Feb. 1978), pp. 3-10.
44. *Ibid.*, p. 6.

FIVE

JOHN F. MCDONALD

AN ECONOMIC ANALYSIS OF LOCAL INDUCEMENTS FOR BUSINESS

INTRODUCTION

LOCAL governments use a wide variety of financial inducements to influence the location of economic activity. These devices include property tax reductions, industrial revenue bonds of various types, and Urban Development Action Grants (UDAG) provided by the U.S. Department of Housing and Urban Development. Local governments also provide assistance to businesses in the forms of land assembly and provision of public services. Clearly local governmental officials take the provision of these services seriously, and the use of these inducements has grown rapidly. In contrast, as Wasylenko (25, p. 155) states in his recent survey article on the subject,

> Economists have concluded that taxes and fiscal inducements have very little, if any, effect on industry locational decisions. Thus, state and local policies designed to attract business are generally wasted governmental resources, since businesses that ultimately locate in a jurisdiction would have made the same decision with or without the fiscal incentive.

Wasylenko[25] notes that most of the empirical evidence supports this conclusion, but that there is some recent evidence to suggest that local taxes do influence intrametropolitan locational decisions to a limited extent.[1] We seem to have an anomaly : local officials are devoting a great deal of effort to policies most of which are judged by economists to be ineffective.

The apparent anomaly may be explained by the notion that local officials do not wish to be perceived as "doing nothing" about a problem. Thus they engage in efforts which are ineffective but generate favorable political publicity. The contention in this paper is that there is a better explanation for local inducements to business which can be derived from the standard urban economic analysis of real estate and local real estate taxes as presented by Muth[19, 20], Grieson [12], Mieszkowski[17] and many others. The results in this paper show that there can be benefits derived by a municipal government from the use of financial inducements to business *even if* the business that locates in that jurisdiction would have done so *without* the inducement. Furthermore, the type of inducement chosen critically influences the magnitudes of those benefits. The analysis uses conventional microeconomic theory to focus on the impacts of various subsidy programs on the intensity of land use and related variables at a specific urban site.

The plan of the paper is to present a fairly general model of local production and the demand for inputs in the next section. Section 3 contains an analysis of the effects of various subsidies on the nature of the real estate supplied at the site in question ; and Section 4 reviews the empirical evidence relevant to the determination of the signs and magnitudes of the effects on real estate tax collections derived in Section 3. Section 5 contains a brief examination of the impacts of various subsidy programs on employment at the site in question, and a summary concludes the paper.

A MODEL OF PRODUCTION ON AN URBAN SITE

The general problem considered in this paper is the impact of inducements for business on the demand for inputs at the single urban site in question. In order to accomplish this task, it is necessary to consider first the nature of the inputs involved and the structure of production technology. The model that has been most fully developed and the only one that has been subjected to much empirical testing in the urban context is the two-input model. However, it is argued here that the number of inputs assumed in the model must be expanded in order to investigate questions of interest. The theoretical development of the two-input model is provided by Muth,[19, 20] Clapp,[5,6] Couch,[7] Henderson,[13] Goldberg,[11] Fallis,[9] Mills,[18] Niedercorn [22] and Orr.[23] Muth [21] has assumed in the urban housing sector that capital and land produce an intermediate output called real estate, which is an input (along with another input current expenditures) into the production of housing services. Here it is assumed that the marginal rate of substitution of capital for land is not influenced by the quantity of the current expenditures input. Muth's model[21] implies that the Allen partial elasticities of substitution of capital for current expenditures and land for current expenditures are equal, but that these elasticities are not necessarily equal to the elasticity of substitution of capital for land.

In some instances it may be necessary to separate the capital input into two components : floor space and other capital such as machinery and equipment, etc. This assumption of four inputs seems particularly appropriate for urban manufacturing activity, for example. Indeed, now we can imagine more easily that land and floor space are nested together and produce the intermediate output called real estate. A simplifying assumption that greatly facilitates the empirical analysis is the assumption of weak separability in the sense that the marginal rate of substitution of land for floor space is independent of the amounts of labor and machinery. If such is the case, then the market for urban real estate can be examined separately. In fact, this is what most of the empirical work in the field amounts to. In order for a study of the market for real estate to have implications for the demand for labor, more assumptions about the form of the production function must be introduced. One possibility is discussed in Section 5.

EFFECTS OF SUBSIDIES ON THE REAL ESTATE MARKET

In this section I consider the effects of various subsidy programs on the level of real estate investment and the amount of real estate taxes collected on the site in question. Consider a unit of land which a municipality makes available for private real estate development. Assume that this unit of land has been zoned for a category of land use (housing, commercial, etc.), but that the intensity of land use will be determined by the private developer. The problem facing the municipality involves determining, from its viewpoint, the best type of subsidy to offer the developer of the site. The municipality may provide a reduction in real estate taxes for some period of time on both land and structures or on only land or structures. A low interest loan may be provided, or the municipality may issue an industrial revenue bond for the construction of a structure for lease to a private firm. The implications of these various plans are examined here using the standard model of the urban firm as presented by Muth.[19, 20]

The basic model assumes that perfect competition prevails in the input and output markets and that the input commodity real estate is separable from the other input decisions as discussed above. Thus the model considers a real estate development firm that produces an output called real estate R, which is the capacity to produce real estate services, by combining stocks of land L and structure capital S. All actual or potential real estate developers of the site in question have identical constant elasticity of substitution (CES) production functions with constant returns to scale, written :

$$R=R\,(L,\,S)=[aL^{-\rho}+(1-a)\,S^{-\rho}],^{-1/\rho} \tag{1}$$

where a is the distribution parameter and $\sigma=1/(+1\rho)$ is the elasticity of substitution. Further assume that the price of a unit of real estate, p, and the price of a unit of S, i, are exogenous to the site in question. The market value of the real estate on the site is subject to the real estate tax at rate t. The price of the unit of land is denoted by v.

The analysis of the introduction of the real estate tax can be developed in much the same way that Mieszkowski[17] accomplished the task. As Mieszkowski[17] pointed out, the introduction of a uniform real estate tax across all jurisdictions will have no effect on the allocation of resources. The output price and input prices faced by the developer do not change in this case. Rather, it is real estate tax differentials which alter the intensity of land use. The issue then is the effect on land value and land-use intensity at the site in question of variations in the real estate tax rate from the rate prevailing elsewhere.

Assuming that the site in question would be developed

without subsidy, and assuming the same real estate tax rate prevails there as elsewhere, the ratio of structure capital to land is

$$S/L=\left(\frac{a}{1-a}\right)\left(\frac{V}{i}\right)^{\sigma}, \tag{2}$$

where v is the price of the unit of land, and i is the exogenous price of structure capital. The output-land ratio is

$$R/L=(1-a)^{-\sigma}\,(v/p)^{\sigma}. \tag{3}$$

Here, because the uniform real estate tax is fully shifted backwards, p is the before *and* after-tax price, and v and i include the tax.

As Brueckner[4] points out, the annual real estate tax is levied on both land and structures and can be expressed as a percentage of the value of real estate property. If it is assumed that the property tax rate will never change, then the present value of a hypothetical infinite stream of property tax payments on a dollar of real estate is t/r, where t is the percentage tax rate and r is the real rate of discount. The fundamental equation for the analysis of the present value of tax collections is :

$$T=\frac{t}{r}\,pR=\frac{t}{r}(\,v+iS), \tag{4}$$

where T is the present value of tax collections.

Consider first a reduction in the real estate tax applied only to structure capital. From (4),

$$-\frac{dT}{d(t/r)_s}=-iS-\frac{t}{r}\,\frac{dlni}{d(t/r)_s}\left[V\,\frac{dlnv}{dlni}+iS\,\frac{dlnS}{dlni}\right], \tag{5}$$

where $d(t/r)_s$ is a marginal change in the tax applied only to structure capital. A reduction in the tax on structure capital is not shifted to suppliers of such capital because the supply is perfectly elastic to the site in question. However, because the purchaser of the real estate will benefit from the tax reduction, the real estate developer sees an increase in the value of the marginal product of structure capital according to $dlni=d(t/r)_s$ and adjusts accordingly. Furthermore, it is demonstrated in the appendix [following Muth[19]] that $dlnS/dlni=-\sigma/\gamma L$, where $\gamma L=v/pR$, the share of land. Also, it is shown in the appendix that $dlnv/dlni=-\gamma s/\gamma L$, where $\gamma s=iS/pR$, the share of structure capital. These results are derived assuming a fixed supply of land, a perfectly elastic demand for R, and a perfectly elastic supply of S. Substitution of these results into (5) produces

$$-\frac{dT}{d(t/r)_S} = -iS - \frac{t}{r}\left[-\frac{\gamma_S}{\gamma_L} v - iS\frac{\sigma}{\gamma_L}\right], \tag{6}$$

or
$$-\frac{dT}{d(t/r)_S} = pR\left[\frac{t}{r}\frac{\gamma_S}{\gamma_L}\sigma + \gamma_S\left(\frac{t}{r} - 1\right)\right] \tag{7}$$

It is an important to note that the impact of a tax cut on tax collections consists of three effects ; the direct negative effect of taxing iS at a lower rate, the positive effect on the value of land, and the positive effect on the intensity of land use.

Consider next a reduction in the real estate tax applied only to land. From (4),

$$-\frac{dT}{d(t/r)_L} = -v - \frac{t}{r} v \frac{d\ln v}{d(t/r)_L}. \tag{8}$$

A reduction in the tax on land will be fully capitalized into the land value, so $d\ln v/d(t/r)_L = -1$. Since the land input is fixed at one unit, a change in the fixed cost land value has no impact on the intensity of land use. These results imply

$$-\frac{dT}{d(t/r)_L} = -v\left(1 - \frac{t}{r}\right) = pR\left(\frac{t}{r}\gamma_L - \gamma_L\right). \tag{9}$$

A reduction in the tax on land has an ambiguous effect on tax collections because of the direct negative effect of taxing v at a lower rate and the positive impact on land value itself. The sign of the sum of these two effects is positive (negative) if $\frac{t}{r}$ is greater than (less than) unity. Since the tax rate t is usually below the real rate of interest (t is 1% to 2%, for example), the presumption is that the sign of (9) is negative.

A reduction in the real estate tax on both structure capital and land will have an impact on tax collections that is simply the sum of (7) and (9), or

$$-\frac{dT}{dt/r} = pR\left[\frac{t}{r}\frac{\gamma_S}{\gamma_L}\sigma + \frac{t}{r} - 1\right]. \tag{10}$$

This same result can be found by noting that a redction in the tax on both structure capital and land is, in effect, an increase in the (after-tax) price of real estate to the developer. Because real estate supplied on a small unit of land is elastically demanded, a marginal reduction in the tax rate below the level that prevails elsewhere will be capitalized into the property value by competition among the buyers of real estate according to $dt/r+dlnp=0$, where $dlnp$ represents a shift in a perfectly elastic demand curve. From (4),

$$-\frac{dT}{dt/r}=-pR-\frac{t}{r}pR\left(\frac{dlnp}{dt/r}+\frac{dlnR}{dlnp}\frac{dlnp}{dt/r}\right). \qquad (11)$$

It is shown in the appendix (following Muth[19]) that $dlnR/dlnp = \gamma_S\sigma/\gamma_L$. Substitution for $dlnp/dt/r$ and $dlnR/dlnp$ in (11) produces (10).

The subsidy to the real estate developer may involve the acquisition of federal funds for the purpose. For example, the program operated by the U.S. Department of H.U.D. of Urban Development Action Grants (UDAG) permits the municipality to subsidize land clearance, new construction, rehabilitation, loans, loan guarantees, lease guarantees, etc. The nature of the UDAG is very flexible, and all possibilities will not be examined here. However, one simple example is to assume that the real estate developer is subsidized in all aspects of the project at no cost to the municipality. This case is equivalent to the reduction in the real estate tax on both land and structures, except that no real estate tax revenue is lost from the site in question. From equation (8) above, the change in the present value of tax collections can be written

$$\frac{dT}{dlnp}=pR\left[\frac{t}{r}\frac{\gamma_S}{\gamma_L}\sigma+\frac{t}{r}\right]>0, \qquad (12)$$

where $dlnp$ is the size of the subsidy. Also, a subsidy to structure capital may be accomplished through a UDAG or by the granting of a low-interest loan that is obtained by the power of the municipality to issue bonds that are free from federal income taxation. The previous analysis of the effects of a change in the tax on structure capital applies, except that no loss of real estate tax revenue can occur. The subsidy is assumed to take the form of annual payments to cover part of the real estate tax due. In this case,

$$-\frac{dT}{d(t/r)s}=pR\left[\frac{t}{r}\frac{\gamma_S}{\gamma_L}\sigma+\frac{t}{r}\gamma_s\right]>0. \qquad (13)$$

A similar subsidy only to land generates additional tax revenue according to

$$-\frac{d\Gamma}{d(t/r)_L} = pR\ \frac{t}{r}\gamma_L. \qquad (14)$$

In other words, a subsidy to land increases the value of the land and increases tax collections accordingly. Note that (13) and (14) sum to (12).

A final suggestion is the use of industrial revenue bonds in the original meaning of the term [Bridges[3]]. Municipalities issue bonds that are used to construct facilities that are publicly owned and leased to firms. The firms pay rent to cover the principal and interest on the bonds and maintenance costs. No real estate taxes are collected. Obviously the municipality has forfeited the entire real estate tax that could have been collected had the site in question been developed privately. However, the industrial revenue bond has an interesting impact on the intensity of land use. Structure capital is purchased by the municipality given that it will not be taxed. The municipality can thus "buy" structure capital for a lower price than i because i reflects the existence of the general real estate tax. The intensity of land will thus be increased according to

$$d\ln\,(S/L) = -\sigma d\ln i. \qquad (15)$$

SUBSIDIES IN THE REAL ESTATE MARKET : EMPIRICAL EVIDENCE

Some preliminary estimates of the magnitudes of the effects of the various subsidy programs in Section 3 on real estate tax collections can be found by using the available estimates of the relevant parameters. This section contains a brief review of the relevant empirical studies for the office, manufacturing, commercial, and housing sectors. Then a set of calculations is presented to illustrate the possible ranges for the effects of alternative subsidy programs. However, first it is necessary to examine the method used to estimate the elasticity of substitution of structures for land in urban real estate.

All of the studies examined below use some variant of the equation

$$d\ln\,(S/L) = \sigma \ln(v/i) \qquad (16)$$

to estimate σ, the elasticity of substitution. All of the studies have ignored the existence of the general real estate tax as well as variations in that tax. Does this omission produce biased estimates of σ? Consider the case that corresponds to the analysis in Section 3. It was concluded that the general real estate tax with the same rate at all sites is fully shifted backwards to the owners of land and structures. The real estate developer faces p, the given price of real estate output, and i and v, the after-tax input prices. If i and v are measured without error, then no bias will occur. Now add the assumption that the real estate tax rate varies across sites, and assume that the units of observation are "small" sites in relationship to the total real estate market. The analysis in Section 3 demonstrated that a tax break for structure capital will alter the intensity of land use without changing the market price of structure capital. Thus, all empirical studies of σ are potentially biased by the failure to control for variations in the tax applied to structures. The nature and extent of this bias is the topic to further research.

Clapp [5,6] has estimated σ in the office sector in Los Angeles for 1963-1973 through a variety of techniques. His basic conclusion is that the Cobb-Douglass form ($\sigma=1$) cannot be rejected. The best estimates from Clapp (5, p. 132) appear to be $\sigma=.95$ and $\gamma S=.79$, although his estimates of σ vary from .54 to 1.67. McDonald[15] has also estimated σ for the office sector in Melbourne in 1969. These estimates vary from .89 to 1.21, but the best estimate is 1.21 because an instrumental variable is used to correct for measurement error bias. McDonald's estimate of γS is .76. Thus in the office sector, it appears that σ is at least 1.0 and γS is .75 to .80. Values of 1.0 for σ and .8 for γs will be used here.

There is a paucity of estimates of σ for the manufacturing and commercial real estate sectors. McDonald[15] produces estimates of σ in manufacturing in Melbourne for 1969 that range from .59 to .77. The best estimate is .77 because, once again, an instrumental variable is used to correct for measurement error bias. These estimates are very close to the estimate reported by Fallis[9] of .69. McDonald's data indicate that $\gamma S=.78$ in manufacturing real estate. In the commercial sector (retailing, service sector, hotels, wholesaling, etc.), McDonald's[15] estimate of σ ranges from .28 to .50. However, these estimates are not statistically significantly different from zero. Fallis[9] reports that $\sigma=.68$ in the commercial sector. McDonald[15] provides an estimate of $\gamma S=.81$ in commercial sector real estate.

The substantial empirical literature on σ in urban housing has been reviewed by McDonald.[16] The reported estimates range from .36 to 1.13, although some of these estimates are biased downward by measurement error. It appears that σ is not significantly different from unity in some urban areas such as Chicago and Santa Clara County, but that σ is less than unity in some other locations. Estimates of γS in housing from the .88 reported by Muth[19] for FHA housing in 1946 to .63 reported by Berry[2] for single-family housing in Melbourne in 1969. A value of .8 will be assumed.

The value of one additional parameter, t/r, is needed. The Advisory Commission on Intergovernmental Relations[26] reports that the average property tax on FHA single-family homes in the U.S. in 1979 (1971) was 1.34% (1.98%) of market value. Assuming $r=12\%$ or 6%, the range for t/i used here is .11 to .33. A summary of all of the assumed parameter values is provided in Table 5.1. Finally, note that equations (7), (9), (10), (12), (13) and (14) contain pR on the right-hand side. For purposes of the calculations below, pR is moved to the left-hand side of these equations so that the calculations are of the elasticity of tax collections with respect to a real estate tax rate. To see this, write

$$E=\frac{dT/T}{d(t/r)/(t/r)},$$

where E is the elasticity of T with respect to t/r. Now $T=\frac{t}{r}pR$,

so

$$E=\frac{dT/pr}{d(t/r)}\,. \tag{18}$$

Table 5.2 shows the calculations of E from equations (7), (9), (10), (12), (13) and (14) using the parameter values in Table 5.1.

The results in Table 5.2 can be summarized easily. As shown in column 1, a tax cut applied to structure capital increases tax collections if t/r is .33, but decreases tax collections if t/r is only .11. The only exception to this result in Table 5.2 occurs in the housing sector if σ=.36. With this relatively low value for σ and t/r=.33, the elasticity of tax collections with respect to the tax rate on structures is —.06. Given the parameter values in Table 5.1, column 2 in Table 5.2 shows that a tax cut on land always reduces tax collections. A tax cut applied to both structures and land produces a result that is the sum of the figures in columns 1 and 2. These elasticities (shown in column 3) are all smaller than those produced by a tax cut only on structures.

A subsidy for business provided by a higher level of government will always increase local real estate tax collections. As shown in column 4 of Table 5.2, the subsidy for structures produces a greater elasticity of tax collections the larger is t/r or σ. As shown in column 5, a subsidy for land produces a small positive elasticity of tax collections, and a subsidy for both structures and land (column 6) produces an elasticity of tax collections that is the sum of the figures in columns 4 and 5.

EMPLOYMENT EFFECTS OF SUBSIDY PROGRAMS

Often the use of local inducements for business of the types examined above is partly justified on the grounds that an expansion of employment opportunities at the site in question will result. The purposes of this section are to examine this proposition theoretically and to provide some necessarily sketchy empirical estimates. The basic question to be answered is whether the policies which increase the structure capital-land ratio will also increase (and by how much) the ratio of employment to land.

Underlying the analysis is the four-input production function from Section 2, written

$$Q=Q\,(E,M,S,\bar{L}), \tag{19}$$

where Q is output, E is employment, M is machinery and equipment, S is structure capital, and $\bar{L}$ is the fixed amount of land. No estimates of the parameters of this production function exist,[2] so to make some progress it is necessary to assume weak separability of the form

$$Q=Q\,(E,\,M,\,R\,(S,\,\bar{L})\,), \tag{20}$$

where R is the intermediate good real estate. Assume that the prices of E and M are constant. If the production function is homogeneous of degree one (or just homothetic) E and M increase by the same percentage that R increases. From the appendix, $dln\ (R/L)/dlnp = \frac{\gamma S}{\gamma L}\ \sigma$. For the case of a subsidy to structure capital only, Muth (19, p. 228) has shown that, for a shift in the supply of S along the i axis (where e_L is the elasticity of supply of land),

$$-dln\ \ (R/L)/dlni = \frac{\gamma_S\ (\sigma + e_L)}{\gamma_L}, \tag{21}$$

which also reduces to $\frac{\gamma S}{\gamma_L}\ \sigma$ when $e_L = 0$. Table 5.3 shows the range of $\frac{\gamma S}{\gamma_L}\sigma$ for three sectors (excluding housing) based upon the parameter estimates shown in Table 5.1. All of the elasticities

TABLE 5.1 : **Assumed parameter values by sector**

	σ	γ^s	t/r
Office Sector	1.00	.80	.11 or .33
Manufacturing Sector	.77	.78	.11 or .33
Commercial Sector	.68	.81	.11 or .33
Housing Sector	.36 or 1.13	.80	.11 or .33

exceed 2.0, and the elasticity of employment in the office sector may be as great as 4.0. A subsidy to land does not change R/L, so employment does not change.

Thus, if it can be assumed that the elasticity of demand for the final product and for real estate are infinite, and the elasticities of supply of the inputs other than land are also infinite, the subsidy programs for structure capital or both structures and land discussed in this paper will generate increases in employment. Furthermore, the choice of subsidy program (subsidy to R in general or only to S) does not matter from the standpoint of employment effects.

SUMMARY AND CONCLUSIONS

This paper has applied the standard theory of the urban real estate firm and the "new" view of the real estate tax to the

TABLE 5.2 : **Impacts of local inducements on real estate tax collections (elasticity of tax collections with respect to the tax rate)**

	Tax Cut on Structures Eq. (7)	Tax Cut on Land Eq. (9)	Tax Cut on Both Eq. (10)	Subsidy for Structures Eq. (13)	Subsidy for Land Eq. (14)	Subsidy for Both Eq. (12)
Office Sector						
$t/r=.11$	—.27	—.18	—.45	.53	.02	.55
$t/r=.33$	.78	—.13	.65	1.58	.07	1.65
Manufacturing Sector						
$t/r=.11$	—.39	—.20	—.59	.39	.02	.41
$t/r=.33$	.38	—.15	.23	1.16	.07	1.23
Commercial Sector						
$t/r=.11$	—.40	—.17	—.57	.41	.02	.43
$t/r=.33$	.41	—.13	.28	1.67	.06	1.73
Housing Sector						
$\sigma=.36, t/r=.11$	—.55	—.18	—.73	.25	.02	.27
$\sigma=.36, t/r=.33$	—.06	—.13	—.19	.74	.07	.81
$\sigma=1.13, t/r=.11$	—.21	—.18	—.39	.59	.02	.61
$\sigma=1.13, t/r=.33$	.96	—.13	.83	1.76	.07	1.83

analysis of the effects of various subsidy programs to that firm. It was assumed that the firm in question occupies a site that is "small" in relationship to the real estate market. Input supplies (except for land) and output demands are infinitely elastic. It was found that programs which subsidize real estate in general or just structure capital will increase the intensity of land use (the structure-land ratio) and will thus tend to increase employment at the site in question. However, real estate tax collections may rise or fall depending upon the nature of the subsidy program, the tax rate, the real discount rate, and the parameters of the production function for real estate. The best option from the viewpoint of the municipality in which the site is located is to get some other level of government (state or federal) to pay for a subsidy to both structure capital and land.

The "new" view of the real estate tax [Mieszhowski [17]] has been employed in the sense that subsidy programs have an impact

TABLE 5.3 : **Effects of subsidy programs on employment (elasticity of employment with respect to p or i)**

Office Sector	
$\gamma S=.80,\ \sigma=1.0$	4.00[a]
Manufacturing Sector	
$\gamma S=.78,\ \sigma=.77$	2.73
Commercial Sector	
$\gamma S=.81,\ \sigma=.68$	2.90

[a]The calculation is $\frac{\gamma S}{\gamma L}\ \sigma$.

to the extent that they represent subsidies relative to the options that are available elsewhere. The "elsewhere" must be defined as an area that is large enough to justify the assumption of infinite elasticities of supply and demand mentioned above. The model used in this paper implies that subsidy programs which are in widespread use will have no effect on the spatial allocation of resources. Indeed, a municipality that does not provide a subsidy when all other in the relevant market area do will feel the effects discussed in this paper in the opposite direction.

FOOTNOTES

1. These studies include Fox(10) and Wasylenko(24). Fox's study examines the demand for industrial land across municipalities in the Cleveland SMSA, and Wasylenko(24) reexamines the data on the site selection of firms relocating from the city of Milwaukee to a suburban municipality. Erickson and Wasylenko(8) had previously examined these data and concluded that fiscal variables were not important factors. Wasylenko(24) achieved a different result (for manufacturing and wholesaling firms) by excluding from the choice set municipalities that provide no land zoned for the industry in question.
2. See Berndt and Christensen (1) for a study of manufacturing production functions assuming three inputs : equipment, structures, and labor.

REFERENCES

Berndt, E. and L. Christensen, The translog function and the substitution of equipment, structures and labor in U.S. manufacturing 1929-68, *Journal of Econometrics*, 1, 81-114 (1973).

Berry, B. The economics of land-use intensities in Melbourne, Australia, *Geographical Review*, 64, 479-497 (1974).

Bridges, B. State and local inducements for industry, parts I and II, *National Tax Journal*, 18, 1-14 and 175-192 (1965).

Brueckner, J. Labor mobility and the incidence of the residential property tax, *Journal of Urban Economics*, 10, 173-182 (1981).

Clapp, J. The substitution of land for other inputs, *Journal of Urban Economics*, 6, 122-134 (1979).

Clapp, J. Production with land and nonland factors : Which functional form ? *Journal of Urban Economics*, 8, 32-46 (1980).

Couch, J. Employment density functions : A theory for E.S. Mills' conundra, *Journal of Regional Science*, 18, 293-301 (1978).

Erickson, R. and M. Wasylenko, Firm relocation and site selection in suburban communities, *Journal of Urban Economics*, 8, 69-85 (1980).

Fallis, G. Factor substitution, employment density and suburbanization, *Journal of Urban Economics*, 6, 156-175 (1979).

Fox, W. Fiscal differentials and industrial location : Some empirical evidence, *Urban Studies*, 18, 105-111 (1981).

Goldberg, M. An economic model of intrametropolitan industrial location, *Journal of Regional Science*, 10, 75-79 (1970).

Grieson, R. The economics of property taxes and land values : The elasticity of supply of structures, *Journal of Urban Economics*, 1, 367-381 (1974).

Henderson, J. "Economic Theory and the Cities," Academic Press, New York, 1977.

Hicks, J. "The Theory of Wages (2nd Ed.)," Macmillan, London (1963).

McDonald, J. The substitution of land for other inputs in urban areas, *Papers, Regional Science Assoc.*, 47 (1981).

McDonald, J. Capital-land substitution in urban housing : A survey of empirical estimates, *Journal of Urban Economics*, 9, 190-211 (1981).

Mieszkowski, P. The property tax : An excise tax or a profit tax ? *Journal of Public Economics*, 1, 73-96 (1972).

Mills, E. An aggregative model of resource allocation in a metropolitan area, *American Economic Review, Papers and Proceedings*, 57, 197-210 (1967).

Muth, R. The derived demand for a productive factor and the industry supply curve, *Oxford Economic Papers, New Series*, 16, 221-234 (1964).

Muth, R. "Cities and Housing", University of Chicago Press, Chicago, 1969.

APPENDIX

The derivations of the basic results of the paper in equations (7), (9), and (10) require three standard results from the theory of derived demand for an input and industry supply. These results can be easily derived from the results found in Hicks (14, pp. 373-5) and present extensions of the standard Hicksian theory of derived demand. In each case here it is assumed that the supply of structure capital is perfectly elastic, the demand for the output real estate is perfectly elastic, and the supply of land is fixed.

The first result needed to obtain equation (7) is the own-price elasticity of demand for an input. Muth's (19, p. 226) generalization of the Hicksian formula is

$$\frac{dlnS}{dlni}=\frac{\sigma\eta-\gamma L\sigma-\gamma s\eta)eL}{\gamma s\sigma-\gamma L\eta+eL}, \tag{A-1}$$

where η is the elasticity of demand for the output, ei is the elasticity of supply of the ith input, and the other notation is the same as in equation (7). Assume that $eL=0$, so (A-1) reduces to

$$\frac{dlnS}{dlni}=\frac{\sigma}{\dfrac{\gamma s\sigma}{\eta}-\gamma L} \tag{A-2}$$

and $dlnS/dlni=-\sigma/\gamma L$ if $n=-\infty$.

Next, the effect of changes in the price of structure capital on the value of land must be found. This effect can be written

$$\frac{dlnv}{dlni}=\frac{dlnv}{dlnS}\frac{dlnS}{dlni}. \tag{A-3}$$

The formula from Hicks (14, p. 375) for the inverse of the cross-elasticity of derived demand with the supply of land fixed is

$$\frac{dlnv}{dlnS}=\frac{\gamma s\,(\eta\text{-}\sigma)}{\sigma\eta}=\gamma s\left(\frac{1}{\sigma}+\frac{1}{\eta}\right). \tag{A-4}$$

This reduces to $dlnv/dlnS=\gamma s/\sigma$ if $\eta=-\infty$. Thus, from (A-2), (A-3) and (A-4) with $\eta=-\infty$,

$$\frac{dlnv}{dlni} = \gamma_S/\gamma_L. \tag{A-5}$$

Finally, the derivation of equation (11) requires the expression for supply elasticity. Muth (19, p. 227) shows that

$$\frac{dlnR}{dlnp} = \frac{\sigma(\gamma_L e_L + \gamma_S e_S) + e_L e_S}{\sigma + \gamma_S e_L + \gamma_L e_S}.$$

with $e_S = \infty$, this reduces to

$$\frac{dlnR}{dlnp} = \frac{\sigma\gamma_S + e_L}{\gamma_L}. \tag{A-6}$$

which reduces to $dlnR/dlnp = \sigma\gamma_S/\gamma_L$ when $e_L = 0$.

SECTION TWO

INTRA URBAN LAND VALUES AND RENTAL VALUES

SIX

PROFESSOR GILLES LAVIGNE

LAND RENT
Questions and Answers

It is a truism to call present-day industrial society an "urban" society. Since the end of the 18th century, Western cities have grown inordinately, changing their appearance a number of times. The concepts of expansion, development and redevelopment are all attempts to understand this phenomenon. Analysis of this growth has revealed some of its aspects : construction, financing, housing, services and so on. The various theories these analyses have given rise to have tended to go beyond the particular aspect in question, examining related facts and integrating their explanations of them into a more general conceptual framework, one which goes beyond the urban question as such to examine social reality in its totality.

Science offers two basic approaches to this question of a universal theory, packaged under the generic names of Functionalism and Marxism. Each one offers its own apparently original explanation, each one has its untouchable and irreducible general framework. As a result, any reflection on urban questions—or the larger problem of the social relationship to space—is necessarily subordinated to wider theoretical conclusions about society as a whole, since it is compelled to fall within one or other of the two authorized versions of reality. But does

This paper is a translation of "La rente en question", originally published in a preliminary edition by CRAD, 1' Universite Laval, Quebec. It was translated by Simon Horn.

the difference between Functionalism and Marxism truly represent an alternative between two scientific approaches or is it simply an opposition between obscurantisms ? Both perspectives marginalize certain objects of investigation, objects that might be considered, *a priori*, to be essential for an understanding of the urban phenomenon. This alone justifies subjecting both the functionalist and Marxist paradigms to the implicit critique posed by certain aspects of social reality that have been hidden, avoided, marginalized and ostracized. Rent is one of these aspects.

Land rent stands as the economic manifestation of the exercise of the right to private property of land. It is the symptom, on the economic level, of the nature and state of the political relation of appropriation a society maintains with space. Thus, analyzing the phenomenon of rent means analyzing the economic effects of land ownership. One might expect that the full importance of such a question would be recognized in any discussion of urbanization, but this is not the case. Functionalism ignores rent on the theoretical level, although remarking on its practical importance. Marxism theorizes endlessly about rent but empties the question of any practical significance. Neither side resolves the question, however.

IN SEARCH OF AN OBJECT

Functionalism explains events through to a general analytic framework that can only be qualified as lax. Its underlying premises are Von Thunen's theory of centrality, Max Weber's culturo-functionalist sociology, Keynes's liberal economics, and so on. But these various foundations do not form a rigorous body of theory along the lines of historical materialism. The fragmentation into disciplines breaks up functionalist propositions, separating and compartmentalizing them. Certainly it is easy to see a family resemblance among the many theoretical models proposed by Christaller, Park, Burgess, A. Weber, Samuelson and the rest, but it is virtually impossible, and in a sense useless, to attempt to submit them all to the criticism of close scientific scrutiny. A grasp of functionalism must be global. If not, one soon gets lost in a labyrinth of jealously protected closed systems.

Functionalism begins by treating space as an independent variable, since it is seen to be differentiated into areas possessing intrinsic natural characteristics (climatic, topographical, pedological, etc.) which imply that certain sites are better suited than others for particular activities. In other words, the location of functions is subject to natural conditions. But since, on the epistemological level, functionalist axioms also maintain that structures are determined by functions, space is necessarily seen as a quasi-determinant intermediary variable.

As for the dynamic of social development, functionalism sees a differentiation of functions arising out of a systemic process (a specialization of functions and increasing complexity of structures) that is driven by two antagonistic forces. The first is of an economic character and is derived from Nature itself, since it is a consequence of fundamental needs that are conditioned by the animal component of man. The second is of a cultural character, or derived from Culture, because it follows from fundamental values that are conditioned by the moral component of man. The functionalist discourse carries with it a teleonomy, since the end explains the process : in the final analysis, the antagonism between economic and cultural forces is resolved in a state of perfect equilibrium and social harmony. It follows from this that the role of social organization, particularly political organization (and with it the management of space), is to reduce to a minimum disfunctions resulting from functional modifications in society, such disfunctions being the inevitable but not inescapable cause of disequilibrium.

The functionalist conception of the urban question can be summed up as follows : a direct interaction between man and nature, evolution towards harmonious simplicity, and so on. Functionalism proposes a four-part argument. 1) Urbanization results from demographic growth, both natural and through migration, that is brought on by industrialization, which is itself stimulated by economic growth. 2) The localization of functions is determined by four types of factors : geo-physical (topographic, capacity of the soil. . .), systemic (functional relations. . .), economic (wealth. . .), and cultural ethnicity. . .). 3) The organization of urban space follows a radial-concentric, sectorial model structured in relation to a central point, where are localized the dominant functions, according to its accessibility, which is determined by the effectiveness of transport and communications, in turn dependent on technological development. 4) Modification of urban structures is systemic. On the one hand, obsolete functions disappear as they are replaced by new functions generated by systemic differentiation. On the other hand, the population moves from one area to another (the principle of succession) according to their social mobility (principle of filtering up.)

In brief, then, these are the main components of the functionalist discourse on the urban question. American scholars have been the principal contributors to this approach, in particular R.E. Park, E.W. Burgess, H. Hoyt and L. Wirth, who can be considered its founders.* The model is so dominant in the field that it encompasses much European work, the best known being that by Sorre (1952), Blumenfeld (1955), P. Chombart de Lauwe (1963), and P. Clavel (1973, 1980). Even the work of Manuel Castells (1968, 1969, 1972) can be interpreted from a functionalist perspective, but that is another matter.

It is'nt hard to see that any search for a theoretical approach to urban questions will sooner or later find itself confronted by the immense functionalist edifice, with its uncertain limits. This paper is no exception.

The functionalist model leaves no place for the financial component of urbanization. The capital investment involved in the development of an urban agglomeration of several million inhabitants is considered to fall in the domain of economics. Now economics has its own set of laws, as shown by the framework of supply and demand, with its corollaries, the notions of competition, the market, elasticity, and so on. Hence everything that makes up a part of the city must be considered a commodity, from the fire hydrant to the skyscraper, via the sewers and the streets. From this it follows that the price of urbanization tends to equal its

* The work of the following authors give a fairly complete idea of the functionalist treatment of the urban question : Park and Burgess (1924) ; Park (1925, 1926, 1929, 1936) ; Burgess (1925) ; Wirth (1938, 1945, 1964) ; Hoyt (1939) ; Shevky and Williams (1949) ; Bogue (1949) ; Shevky and Bell (1955) ; Hauser (1958) ; Berry and Garrison (1958) ; Burgess and Bogue (1964) ; Alonso (1960, 1964) ; Chapin (1962, 1979) ; Hill (1965) ; Berry (1964, 1965) ; Harris (1966, 1968) ; Shnore (1965) ; Lowry (1965) ; Murphy (1966).

cost of production, dependent on the size and vitality of the market for this type of "product."

Hence the functionalist model excludes the financial component from its explanations, since it is a consequence, not a cause, the development of cities being above all the business of economic agents of production. Park states this explicitly. Nonetheless, this marginalization of the financial component in no way prevents the examination of real estate investment in itself. On the contrary, American studies on this subject are extremely diverse, whether dealing with questions of circulation of capital, construction and the mortgage market (C.D. Long, 1940 ; G. Rosenbluth, 1958 ; J.M. Guttentag, 1961 ; W. Alberts, 1962) or seen from the point of view of investors (H. Jenson, 1967, 1971 ; K. Pearson, 1971 ; R. Starr, 1975 ; A. Downs, 1975, 1976). These specialized studies show that urban development requires enormous amounts of capital, but also, and above all, that this capital investment must satisfy the criteria of competitive profitability vis-a-vis other sectors of investment. Capital is mobile, after all, moving from one sector of activity to another according to its fundamental *raison d'etre* : to bring in dividends and to continue to accumulate.

Urbanization is profitable for those who carry it out, hardly surprising in a market economy. Lenders receive interest. Construction companies make profits. Property owners collect rent. But while interest and company profits are open to a "relatively simple" process of analysis (in fact it is difficult to apply the model of supply and demand to the production of goods such as housing), rent poses a problem.

Within the framework of liberal economics, land is presented as a pricing factor whose value in each particular case is determined by the demand for space. Apart from its circular character, this conception introduces the referent "land use", itself problematical on another level. The demand for space is not undifferentiated, rather it varies sectorially according to land use categories. Technically speaking, land use categories are the spacial derivation of functions, and their positioning in space follows from the model of structuration presented earlier. Thus each site is predestined, we might say, to serve only certain uses depending on its physical characteristics and its location in the systemic grid. Zoning by urban planners is an attempt to "prove" this predestination. It is easy to see that the supply of space for a particular utilization lacks elasticity, especially in the centre. The replacement of one land use by another would in fact imply the obsolescence of the original function and possibly its differentiation into two or more derivative functions. Thus liberal land economics is characterized by a general increase in the price of land from the periphery to the centre. This overall gradation can, however, be disturbed by questions of accessibility, inheritance, and so on. In practice, land economics is characterized by "terminal" speculation.

Liberal land economics places the question of rent within the realm of dependent variables. As a result, rent has no place in the explanatory model of urbanization. According to the same logic, rent is just one impact of urbanization among others. Any intervention in the urban sphere requires that payment be made in return for the alienation of the right of land ownership. What's more, according to the model the value of this right can only grow over time due to the pressure of economic development, in the same way that it rises spatially from the periphery to the centre. This rent, or landed "surplus value", provides a marvellous field for speculation, which becomes both the accelerator of urbanization and a brake on it. This parasitic enrichment—virtually certain, and certainly important—both drains off capital and limits its circulation towards and within the sphere of urban development.

Thus, like liberal economics, the functionalist approach recognizes that land rent plays a considerable role within a limited sphere : the market economy. But this amounts to saying that theoretically the question is out of bounds. Since the functionalist theoretical framework places the determination of rent outside of social practice, all one can do is recognize the effect of rent. Each site is unique, possessing an intrinsic potential value. The functional rationality of the urban system distinguishes between sites in such a way as to allow the realization of the potential value of each site ; the mechanical rationality of the market in land constantly increases the differential value of each site. But despite all this argumentation, rent is created neither by Nature nor by Function, but by the existence of the right to private property of land. And this is a crucial observation. Although by definition a condition is invariable, nevertheless, only by acting on this condition of private property of land can social action, obviously of a political nature, be exercised with the aim of countering the disfunctional effects of rent on the process of urbanization. The right put in question here is linked to fundamental values, the ideology, and any intervention concerning it must involve a debate among social classes ("Public interest requires......", for example).

Within the functionalist perspective, the problem of rent is both clear and obscure, relegated to the least of theoretical preoccupations because of its categorization as a derivative phenomenon. A reexamination of this theory is in order : an effect can reveal a form and not simply result from a function.

PORTRAIT OF (RE)DEVELOPMENT : MONTREAL

Globally, the functionalist framework at first appears coherent. But looked at concretely, in relation to a particular object of analysis—the formation of an ethnic neighbourhood, for example (Lavigne, 1979)—the functionalist system crumbles in the face of reality. This fragility necessarily makes its appearance if one examines a particular event, pinpointed according to various indices, in the light of the general conceptual framework. Thus the example of Montreal allows an understanding of the weakness of a number of fundamental functionalist concepts. The case of Montreal also allows an evaluation of (re)development in terms of its hidden side, rent.

Demographic upheaval

The development of the Montreal metropolitan area from the end of the 1950s to today is a perfect illustration of the boom that affected most North American cities.* In many ways the upheaval has resembled the aftermath of war : destruction, displacement of population, reconstruction. In demographic terms, the population of the metropolitan area has doubled, going

* On the occasion of the bicentennial of the United States, J. McMahan wrote a series of articles on the history of American urbanization (1976a, b, c). Although descriptive, they take on their full interest when compared to D. Harvey's 1977 article on the political economy of urbanization.

from 1.5 to three million in 20 years. Where did these people come from ? No one is certain, but we have a good idea. Although Quebec was already highly urbanized, another wave of rural population moved into its cities. The level of urbanization rose from 74.3% in 1961 to 77.6% today, showing the continued migration from countryside to city, including Montreal. During the same period Quebec has changed from being a source of emigrants* into the destination of numerous immigrants from Europe (Italy, Greece, Portugal) and the third world, particularly the Caribbean. Most of these immigrants have established themselves in Montreal. These two migratory forces combined with natural growth, still high in the late' 50s, to concentrate close to half of Quebec's population in the Montreal area.

This migratory influx coincided with a general shakeup of the Montreal population. Many who lived in neighbourhoods built before the Great Depression moved out to the suburbs in the late '50s, thus satisfying the ideology of the period (Pelletier, 1980). This movement was accentuated by the establishment of young households on the periphery (Foggin and Polese, 1975). The ethnic colonies, already long established, also moved out from the centre into new areas that they had apparently developed themselves (Legare, 1965). The phenomenon was literally an exodus, draining the centre of its youngest and most active elements.

Where did the new immigrants establish themselves, whether rural or foreign ? Certainly they occupied many of the neighbourhoods abandoned in the rush to the suburbs, though not the oldest of them. Recently arrived foreigners created new ethnic neighbourhoods by purchasing a part of the land that had belonged to earlier immigrants (Lavigne, 1979). This crystallization into ethnic areas was neither spontaneous nor generalized. Some ethnic groups dispersed. As well, the phenomenon involved only a certain proportion of immigrants, since a number went straight to the suburbs (Foggin and Polese, 1975).

Finally, after the high tide came the ebb. As early as 1971 it was possible to identify statistically the beginnings of a return

* From 1961 to 1981, rural immigration involved 200,000 people ; from 1968 to 1975, international immigration brought more than 200,000 people to Quebec.

to the city by some of those living in the suburbs. Today, in 1982, this movement has made the headlines, and is occurring even in some areas up till now occupied by ethnic communities.

So one cannot help but agree that the urbanization of Montreal was not a simple expansion based solely on demographic growth. Montreal's development involved and continues to involve qualitative transformations of population distribution in the urban landscape, and not simply quantitative change. The ideas of "succession" and "filtering up" are insufficient, even inadequate, to explain the exodus to the periphery, and they are totally incapable of explaining the return to the city. Even the idea of a "transition zone", put forward by Burgess and developed by Rex (1968) to explain the initial localization of immigrants, is inoperative due to the diversity of locations existing in practice. As for the determinant influence of ecocomic growth on Montreal's urban development, this remains to be demonstrated, especially as concerns industrialization. The first expressway was built in 1957 ; the first new generation skyscraper was begun in 1958. Those were recession years. Growth came later and affected other regions as well as Montreal.

Itinerant centrality

The example of Montreal challenges the functionalist schema on another level as well. The redevelopment of Montreal's downtown presents evidence that supports a critique of the notion of "centrality".

In 1944 the Montreal city planning department published a preliminary report for a master plan. It situated Montreal's downtown on St-Jacques Street, "where are found the headquarters of several banks and very important industrial and commercial companies" (p. 26. Our translation from French). At that time the planning department expected an extension of the centre towards the east, into extremely old urban spaces that by then were already more or less abandoned. Despite these predictions, the downtown moved west. In 1974 the same city planning department had to situate the centre approximately one kilometre from its previous position and two kilometres from its predicted position, without commenting on the fact that previous predictions had turned out to be wrong. In fact in the last 150 years the centre of Montreal has moved almost two kilometres.

Growth alone cannot explain this migration of central functions. In practice one can observe discontinuities in the urban network, in particular those caused by the construction of the Ville-Marie expressway.

While the redevelopment of Montreal's centre cannot be posed in terms of expansion, it can very well be understood as new construction. Between 1960 and 1976 some 150 new buildings were constructed to house offices, hotels, highrise apartments and businesses. In same period another 150 sites were "freed" of buildings in order to serve as parking lots. The work of demolition and construction was carried out by about 15 extremely enterprising developers (Barker, 1973).

In Montreal the "centre" cannot be understood as a stable geographic point around which the city was constructed. And why should this be a surprise ? Not only was the movement of the centre predictable, it was observable ! It began long ago. As early as the end of the 19th century the big commercial companies had relocated their Notre-Dame Street operations on Ste-Catherine Street. The Catholic archdiocese had also climbed the hill to set up on Dominion Square, along the route of Dorchester Boulevard. The stations of the two railway companies were also there, and Montreal's first skyscraper—completed in 1931, in the same period as the Empire State Building—had already been located on the very site of the future new centre. Why did the functionalist analysts of 1944 not notice the fact ? Why do today's talk as if the centre has always been in its present location ?

The development of Montreal's new centre cannot decently be considered the result of functional differentiation, no matter how complex. In planning terms nothing can justify the location of the present centre, not even the route of the subway. The change cannot be considered pure chance either. Must we not conclude, therefore, that the silence of the specialists shows both the fragility of their conceptual framework and their dogmatism, not to call it intellectual terrorism.

Property and rent

The (re)development of Montreal involved other transformations that were not easily visible ; in particular, the ownership of land changed hands. In the new centre, land ownership has come under the sway of capital that is difficult to trace, with international ramifications (Aubin, 1977). On the periphery, the urbanization of the countryside has transfered land ownership from the farmers to the suburbanites via middlemen. While the development of the city centre was the fruit of large real estate developers, the development of the suburbs, though just as phonomenal a process, appears to have been equally divided between a multitude of small entrepreneurs and the same powerful developers that were at work in the centre. The big developers in fact began and grew thanks to the boom in urbanization. Changes in land ownership resulting from this development took two forms. On the periphery ownership became scattered among tens of thousands of owner-occupiers, irremediably indebted for the rest of their lives. In the centre it fell into the hands of anonymous corporations, henceforth forming a significant proportion of their capital.

A transformation on this scale obviously required money. Easily accessible official statistics do not allow the extraction of figures directly relating to the (re)development of Montreal. At most one can find figures referring to Canada as a whole and to the province of Quebec. Given the importance of the Montreal area, these figures are nonetheless a good indicator of the order of capital involved. The sums are impressive, especially if one remembers that they perhaps do not include all the capital investments linked to urban development. Thus in Canada* from 1961 to 1976, $131,991,000,000.00 were invested in construction and $40,434,000,000.00 in maintenance and repairs, for a total of $172 billion. During the same period, the financing of real estate transactions led lenders to put $65 billion into circulation in the form of mortgages. This implies the circulation of at least an equivalent sum to cover interest payments. If we estimate Montreal's share of all this to be 10 per cent, then some $20 billion has been invested in the (re)development of the metropolis over 15 years.

These amounts include only the value of investments and mortgages, providing no information on profits, the increase in value of property, the fiscal advantages of this type of investment

* According to statistics from the Canada Mortgage and Housing Corporation and the government of Canada.

or the positive effects of financing. Evidently, no global studies exist concerning this particularly striking and uncertain aspect of urban development. One is forced to estimate. If one accepts that the $20 billion invested over this 15-year period be considered as an accumulated investment averaging $1.33 billion per year, and if one also accepts a minimum average annual rate of return, all effects accumulated, of 10 per cent, then it follows that investments in the urbanization of Montreal brought in, in various forms, an additional capital on the order of $16 billion over the same period (in current dollars, of course). This must be considered a minimum estimate. The significance of this amount is obvious, and no one can claim that this financial component of urban development is of negligeable proportions. Rent was part and parcel of this whole process, yet it is not part of functionalist research.

A NAIL IN THE COFFIN

In practice the functionalist framework is a poor instrument for the work of examining, analyzing and synthesizing the constituent elements of the urban reality. Either these elements go beyond the framework, or the framework focuses only on certain questions, obscuring the rest. The systemic mechanism of functional differentiation is too basic and simplistic to explain real changes. The mechanism adapts to the appearance of new needs with the aim of satisfying them. The origin of these needs is complex, and obscure as well. On the one hand they may result from more or less fortuitous events. On the other hand, they may arise out of fundamental needs, the existence of which is not subject to discussion because they are natural phenomena. "Nature" is either the product of spontaneous generation or a creation of God ; in any case, it is not discussed. Each new need, therefore, must be considered either as a derivation of a fundamental need or as a suitable response to a given contingency. The rhetoric may be subtle, but it isn't much use for describing and understanding facts arising from analysis such as those mentioned earlier. This powerlessness forces one to question the scientific character and the theoretical value of functionalism, to the point of accusing it of fraud. Such a indictment can made even of the most coherent of functionalist argument, that of Bronislaw

Malinowski.

The Malinowskian corpus is ruled by the notion of function, but its practical starting point is the examination of apparent forms, which are considered significative of structures. Culture, incorporating social reality, is made up of objects, activities and attitudes that are related to one another according to a given structure, considered a system. Ordinary scientific thought induces the existence of forces on the basis of structures, or vice versa, but functionalism departs from this understanding. Instead it induces functions on the basis of needs, or vice versa. This reduction justifies a principle of equivalence between forms and structures to the profit of an inevitable typology of needs.

This principle of equivalence lastly postulates that structure is indistinguishable from function : structure=form (cf. supra), or form=function (cf. infra), therefore structure=function, and everything falls back on the idea of need : " . . . in such an objective presentation of the sociological dimension, no line of demarcation can be drawn between form and function" (Malinowski, 1944, p. 152). Structure is thus subordinated to function and, on the basis of this principle, eliminated from the purview of theoretical or scientific knowledge : " . . . form is always determined by function, and . . . in so far as we cannot establish such a determinism, elements of form cannot be used in a scientific argument" (Malinowski, 1944, p. 149). As for the idea of needs, it is substituted for the concept of forces thanks to a double axiom and a profession of faith : " . . . every culture must satisfy the biological system of needs . . . every cultural achievement that implies the use of artifacts and symbolism is an instrumental enhancement of human anatomy, and refers directly or indirectly to the satisfaction of a bodily need" (Malinowski, 1944, p. 171). Underlying this revelation is the idea that only natural forces exist, derived from the universal law of gravity or the authority of God, no matter, and that every follows from them. "As we shall see, such a definition is provided by showing that human institutions, as well as partial activities within these, are related to primary, that is, biological, or derived, that is, cultural needs. Function means, therefore always the satisfaction of a need, from the simplest act of eating to the sacremental performance in which the talking of the communion is related to a whole system of beliefs determined by a cultural necessity to be at one with the living God" (Malinowski, 1944, p. 159). By associating need with Nature, functionalism's axioms (or revelations) circumvent the question of forces. Since needs are the manifestation of Nature—for some the emanation of the "big bang", for others the creation of God—they are determined by the blind forces of the physical world.

Now, since Nature is regulated according to positive teleonomic forces that are beyond the province of social understanding, the social dynamic is reduced to the single problem of functional differentiation, itself a systemic mechanism regulated by the function/need relationship. Once it has been substituted for the form/force relationship that was at the origin of the movement, this function/need relationship becomes the main, if not the only, subject of theoretical debate, since it represents the weakest link : "This type of functional analysis is easily exposed to the accusation of tautology and platitude, as well as to the criticism that it implies a logical circle, for, obviously, if we define function as the satisfaction of a need, it is easy to suspect that the need to be satisfied has been introduced in order to satisfy the need of satisfying a function" (Malinowski, 1944, p. 169). The critique of the concept of need has been made elsewhere (Baudrillard,1972) ; no "need" to restate it.

From the functionalist point of view, the sin against reason that is circular reasoning is no sin at all, and criticism is simply slander spread by paranoid opponents. The circle is complete. After all, the idea of need is not introduced by the functionalists, but by Nature itself. Hence in the final analysis it is on this precise point that the crucial question of the scientific nature of the functionalist discourse must be posed. Is functionalism a theory, a truth (or revelation) or a dogma ? In scientific terms a proposition is theoretical when its proof remains falsifiable, that is, open to contradiction. A proposition is true, or "revealed", when it is considered irrefutable and not subject to contradiction. A dogma takes a revelation yet further, often to absurdity. For example, a conclusion is unprovable and hence irrefutable. In this sense the proposition that considers needs to be determined by nature is irrefutable, since the concept of Nature is global and all-inclusive. The proposition nonetheless remains unproven. In other words, since this proposition cannot be taken as a premise because of the contradiction within it, it cannot be considered as more than a hypothesis. Yet it is presented as an axiom, an undemonstrable truth, one that is generally accepted by anyone capable of understanding it because, after all, it is self-evident. From this only one conclusion is possible : functionalism is either a truth or a dogma, but certainly not a theory. The fraud is blatantly obvious.

Now complete, our accusation sheds light on the two main tendencies apparently followed by the "scientific" practices of functionalist observers. On the one hand, they constantly collect data meant to prove their positions, carrying out endless empirical studies while taking care never to enter the domain of theoretical criticism (the choice and above all the delimitation of objects of study is crucial here). On the other hand, they bend over backwards to discredit those who would question the functionalist edifice, declaring them "unscientific"—this not being difficult if the critics are Marxists. In other words, the functionalists aren't taking any chances ; they accumulate the privileges of the priests and inquisitors of their scientistic church. Their dominant position in the institutionalized organization of the production and distribution of scientific knowledge assures their total mastery of the battlefield. Much is relegated to obscurity ; much is eliminated. With little risk of contradiction, one can lay at their doorstep the responsibility for the chaotic, and dogmatic, state of knowledge in the social sciences. One can also ask whether their presence and their power are not based on the desire to remove social questions from the field of knowledge altogether. It should be remembered that the "theory" of functionalism was developed in reaction to the "doctrine" of historical materialism, which was essentially oriented to the analysis of social forces. Under functionalist tutelage, the anthropological and social sciences are "useless", and hence threaten no one.

WHAT ABOUT RENT ?

This descent into the underpinnings of the functionalist discourse was intended to better establish why the question of land rent is reduced to its most simple expression in the functionalist analysis and literally ostracized by functionalist "theory". The reason should by now be clear. Rent poses a problem. Its very existence carries with it a potential critique, since it represents a relation between forces that are not in the least "natural" and a structuration of the urban morphology that that has nothing functional about it. And rent represents nothing more than that. The recognition of this relation puts into question the form-function unity along with the axiomatic relationship of needs and forces. It thus constitutes the beginnings of a refutation of functionalism at a particular level and so threatens to shake the entire functionalist edifice, contributing to its overthrow. But such an overthrow is presently impossible, since it requires that the forces which maintain the functionalist fraud be defeated on another level than that of science, since science is their "private preserve". What is this level to be ?

INVESTIGATION OF A CONCEPT

The doctrine of historical materialism—"Marxism"—by definition marginalizes two categories of social phenomena, those related to culture and those related to the organization of space.* Both are conceived of as simple consequences of underlying social structures. Nonetheless, Marxism examines these marginal questions on the basis of what may be called metaconcepts—bridges linking these peripheral questions to the central preoccupations of the doctrine. These metaconcepts are "ideology" in the case of culture and "land rent" in the case of space. So while the question of rent is not totally excluded by Marxism, theoretically it is of only secondary interest. Given the extremely coherent nature of the Marxist discourse—and its hierarchal organization—this marginality carries with it the risk that rent will be analyzed, not on the basis of practical reality, but according to theoretical necessity, that is, according to an orthodoxy dictated by the needs of the doctrine. At the risk of appearing didactic, if not iconoclastic, a rapid overview of the Marxist conceptual framework is indispensable to properly understand the marginal place of land rent relative to the main

* Translator's note : In the original the term used is *l'amenagement de l'espace*. No single English term provides a satisfactory translation of this term, which can cover concepts ranging from land policy planning to development, organization and so on.

body of the theory. Such an overview will in turn allow us to question the reasons for this marginality.

A thorn in the lion's foot

Despite its complexities, it is relatively simple to summarize the Marxist approach. The dynamic of social structures is determined by the relation between those social forces that constitute classes : in other words, by the class struggle. Classes are distinguished from one another according to their differing and contradictory relations with the production and distribution of wealth : these are the relations of production. Everything else simply clarifies, particularizes, qualifies, enriches and develops these two fundamental ideas.

The contradictory nature of the relations of production is enough in itself to ensure the social dynamic. Classes may be in contradiction and conflict, but at the same time they cooperate in the production of social wealth within a given, global social formation. This conflict/cooperation relation is seen as the motive force behind the overcoming of present contradictions. In practice, of course, new contradictions arise—showing perhaps the essentially contradictory character of all social practice ? While in itself this conception implies no teleonomy, the dynamic of social forces being cyclical, Marxism tacks one on. The relations of production within a given social formation are always characterized by a fundamental contradiction that "gives the tone" to all social relations. This contradiction applies not just to production but to social organization as a whole, hence the theoretical notion of mode of production, which synthesizes and globalizes juridical, political and cultural factors by linking them to the fundamental contradiction.

A mode of production tends to reproduce itself, reproducing those conditions necessary to maintain unchanged the relations of production. Over time, this stability strengthens the fundamental contradiction by retarding its resolution until the inevitable rupture finally occurs. This rupture is apparent as a revolution in the relations of production. History shows that the succession of pre-capitalist modes of production "leads" to capitalism. The overcoming of the contradictions inherent in earlier modes of production in turn generated new, increasingly paradoxical contradictions, finally reaching a breaking point in capitalism. The resolution of the fundamental contradiction of capitalism can only be a definitive break with this cycle, resulting in a society based on relations of equality—communism.

This promise—perfectly comparable to the teleonomy of functionalism—would be of little interest on a theoretical level were it not for the fact that, because of its implications, it dogmatizes the Marxist theoretical framework. Within the structure Marxism proposes for understanding the social dynamic, a force is at work that acts on three, sequential levels, with the passage from one level to another expressing a qualitative change induced by a quantitative, material "pressure". Thus the course of History is like a spiral, returning on itself, from primitive communism to scientific communism. Firstly the class struggle acts on the social formation, secondly it acts on the mode of production, thirdly it lays the groundwork for communism. One can draw a parallel between this dynamic and that of evolution in biology, based on the relation between ontogeny and phylogeny. But the teleonomy of the social dynamic is meant to subordinate not chance (blind forces) but human activity (that has become conscious). By posing the question in this way, Marxism evidently places a historical mission in the hands of the proletariat in its relations with the bourgeoisie, since only the proletariat through its struggle can engender the transformation to communism.

The teleonomy of the Marxist conception of materialism has three effects : it marginalizes classes other than those directly involved in the main contradiction ; it subordinates all of social reality to the question of the organization of production ; and it focuses research on the "debugging" of the theory, since all efforts must strengthen the theoretical analysis of the fundamental contradiction in order to support revolutionary praxis. This theoretical imperialism is inevitable the moment that Marxism closes the debate on future history—as does functionalism—by giving a moral content to its development towards a just and inevitable Second Coming. What is, in principle, an open conception of historical development, is forclosed to the profit of the perfect future. Anything and everything, from being to the void, must fit the mold. Marxism justifies this with its analysis of capitalism, the ultimate mode of production that engenders revolutionary praxis. Are we once again in the presence of a revelation or a dogma ?

While functionalism turns a hypothetical premise into an axiom, Marxism does the opposite, making an axiom out of the conclusion of its analysis. We should note that the finality proposed by Marxism is not an indispensible part of its conceptual framework. It is an analytical deduction, but doubtful all the same. If we ignore the end point of History—communism—the basic conceptual structure of Marxism is a perfectly acceptable postulate. On the other hand, while accepting the postulated existence of an inherent contradiction within the relations of production, the idea that this contradiction is essential and determinant can only be considered as a hypothesis, one whose refutation would forbid the imputation of any final end to history. Does this mean, on the other hand, that the verification of this hypothesis would allow one to declare a goal for history ? Not in the least. Even if this verification were both necessary and possible, it would not be sufficient. One would still have to show that the continuity of humanity's future would win out over discontinuity . . . Can this be done ?

Given this starting point, Marxism's efforts are invariably bent in the following directions : 1) maintenance of the orthodox definition of the relations of production ; 2) demonstration of the universality of the concept that "in the final analysis" the relations of production are determinant ; and 3) systematic demolition of all criticism, as Marx did so well vis-a-vis Proudhon and other contemporaries. Marxism's recourse to the idea of a single determining factor, and its inescapable finality, is extremely paradoxical and illogical compared to a dialectical conception of the nature of social reality (i.e. its contradictory nature). It is an inexhaustible source of confusion, and lends itself to the most low-level rhetoric. Given the history of our time, Marxism can readily be taxed with the ultimate insult, that of being a bourgeois ideology.

The definition of capitalist relations of production remains the centre of any proof or refutation of Marxism. The capitalist mode of production is built : 1) on the separation of the means of production and labour power, although their unity is required for all production ; and 2) on the generalization of the commodity form and, above all, its application to labour power. But labour power is a commodity with curious properties : the capitalist—owner of the means of production—purchases labour power to use in the production process, and comes out of the process with more capital than he originally invested. Marx defines the notion of surplus value to denounce this trickery at its source ; the notion takes on the function of a parametric variable. Without it the Marxist analysis of society and production is incomprehensible and inconsistent. The notion has no explanatory power outside of a theoretical framework that considers living, human labour as the only source of value. It follows that only products that incorporate living labour have a value, based precisely on the amount of this labour. Yet the land, the soil, has taken on value although not produced by man. Here we touch the question of land rent.

For what can be understood as material and, finally, regrettable, reasons, Marx did not have the time to finish his analysis of rent, which was relegated to the last sections of the last volume of *Capital*. The relegation of the question to the "end", "after" and "outside" the question of production, underlines the resistance that the nature of rent poses to its integration into Marx's theory of value. When he states that all he must do is demonstrate one fact, "the possibility of absolute rent, without violating the law of value" (Selected Correspondence, p. 164), Marx explicitly recognizes the contradiction inherent here. Did he succeed in his demonstration ? Did he not prejudice it from the start by analyzing a type of rent that was, perhaps, specific to agricultural production and/or to the 19th century ?

Some Marxists refuse to consider reopening the question of the labour theory of value, and are astonished that one can discuss on the basis of a notion, value, that Marx supposedly showed throughout his work to be nothing more than instrumental, operational. This fallacious argument, served up as needed and under cover, proceeds from an *ex cathedra* judgement, making perfectly clear that "leftist" discourse is just as repressive in the West as in the East, and that it is just as ideological as that of the "liberal" elites. Do the abuses of the one justify those of the other ?

Despite the intimidating architecture and thickness of this wall of bad faith, one may still hope that a theoretical reexamination of land rent may seriously shake the Marxist understanding of value, and more. In fact, if the analysis is followed through to its limit, it becomes clear that only one kind of rent functions at all times and in all circumstances. This observation implies that, at least in relative terms, political relations can have a determining effect on relations of production. It is thus the beginning of a refutation of the idea that in the final analysis the relations of production are universally the determining factor.

MARX ON RENT

The concept of land rent has been amply discussed since Marx analyzed it. During the 1970s in particular it was the subject of reflection related to the urban problem because of the upheaval in the cities at the time. All of this work was done on the basis of propositions advanced by Marx a century before, and this is what makes it indispensable to return to Mark. It is imperative to note, firstly, that all contemporary discussions of rent postulate the generality and universality of "absolute rent", the cornerstone of Marx's analysis, and, secondly, that the debate concerns the concrete social foundations of the necessity of absolute rent. So, our return to Marx begins with his definition of absolute rent.

The trials and tribulations of a concept

The term "rent" has been used in the French and English languages since the 12th century. Its etymology goes back to the idea of "to render". Originally the term concerned two types of transaction, either the sums paid to the owner of an asset by the person to whom that asset had been alienated, or the fee paid to a landowner for land leased out. In both cases the idea of rent signifies total passivity on the part of the owner of the asset, whether money or land, as far as increasing its value is concerned. Classic political economy kept the term rent in its second acceptation, that linked to land ownership. On top of this, theorists of the 18th and 19th centuries, from the Physiocrats to Marx, developed a theory of rent on the sole basis of an analysis of the process of agricultural production as it existed in their time.

The Physiocrate considered agricultural production to be the only activity capable of creating value, hence, logically enough, considered agricultural land rent to be the only form of surplus value. Adam Smith broke definitively with this "naturalist" approach when he defined labour as the basis of enrichment. At the same time, however, he marginalized the question of rent and turned it into a problem. The payment of rent became an aberration, a contradiction, an anachronistic leftover of the feudal period.

Smith did not grasp the incongruity posed by the obligation to pay rent in a productivist society driven by the antagonistic relation between capital and labour. For Smith rent was just one of the factors that determined the cost of production, like wages or profit (1974, pp. 152, 247-249). Its value depended on the market price of products, with the landowner taking all of the surplus once wages and the average profit had been paid. Since Smith considered that market prices were determined solely by demand, he is consistent when he classes landowners according to whether they always or only occasionally bring in rent. Smith includes a number of incident factors affecting the amount of rent : fertility of the soil, geographic proximity to the market, and the landowner's ability to "evaluate the value" of his land. And this is where the problem arises. If labour is the sole source of value, the land, not being producible, can have no value and hence can be neither a determining factor in the value of products nor a source of value. So how can one explain the payment of rent ? And why is rent paid ?

David Ricardo, considered the founder of the theory of rent, quite simply eludes the problem, strange as that may seem. To explain the existence of rent he refers to the "free gifts of nature", non-producible but belonging in fact and in right to landowners (1973, pp. 33-47, 219-226 and 272-292). Thus rent is necessarily differential. It is based on the differences in the costs of production incurred in the agricultural exploitation of the land. Since on the one hand, these costs vary according to the fertility of the soil, its location and the fixed capital invested in the improvement of the land, and on the other hand, the market price is determined by those units of land whose exploitation incurs the highest cost of production, those units whose exploitation incurs lower costs (that is, the most fertile, the best located, and the most improved land) bring in a rent. And, of course, the least productive units do not. As Marx points out, Ricardo's analysis is concerned only with the conditions of existence of surplus profits in agriculture, those which would exist even if landed property was abolished. Hence Ricardo eliminates the problem of rent, and his reasoning brings up a question that is also asked by Marx : Why would landowners lease out land that brought in no rent ?

Almost one hundred years passed after the publication of Adam Smith's work before Marx in turn looked at the question of rent. At this point in time the question remained totally unanswered, and elements of a solution were rare. While the problem of differential rent seemed fairly clear, it remained independent of landed property, and this was not acceptable. Rent began where the average profit ended, but the explanation for this excess was lacking. What is more, rent could not play a role in the determination of the value of commodities without invalidating all economic thought since Smith, who was the first to base value on labour. Marx was conscious of the danger rent posed for the labour theory of value. In fact Marx treated the question of rent on two levels. First he made an in-depth analysis of agricultural rent, showing the possibility of the existence of absolute rent (Volume III, Part VI, 1967 : pp. 614-814). Secondly he placed rent back into the more global context of the redistribution of society's surplus value (Volume III, Part VII, Chapter XLVIII, 1967, pp. 814-831).

Absolute rent

Marx's essential contribution to the question of agricultural rent is his definition of the concept of absolute rent. He could not endorse Ricardo's point of view as it stood, nor could he conceive of landowners as philanthropists. For Marx the market price of agricultural commodities equals the cost of production, plus the average profit, plus absolute rent. But this implies that rent is a factor of valorization, since the market price is more or less equal to the value of the product. Now from a Marxist point of view this interpretation is erroneous, since it contradicts the theory of value, eroding the cornerstone of classical economic theory and of Marxism itself. Of course the neo-classical economists have made sure to remark on this weakness with great fanfare. Samuelson peremptorily states :

> The simple theory of value, which said that the price ratios of goods can be predicted from labour costs alone, independently of the utilities which bring out a demand for the goods, has thus been refuted. Costs of production include

rent as well as payments" (1966, pp. 778-779).

But the neoclassicists do not have any alternative explanation for the value of rent. For all practical purposes it remains indefinable. Supply being inelastic by definition, the price of land, and with it rent, varies solely according to demand ; Samuelson is categorical on this point (1966, pp. 587-592). But a question must be posed here : if the value of rent is determined by the demand for land, which is in turn determined by the demand for commodities, wheat, for example, how can rent play a role in determining the price of wheat ? The reasoning is tautological, and Samuelson knows it :

> To conclude : whether rent is or is not a price-determining cost depends on the level of the viewpoint : firm, industry, or whole economy (1966, p. 584).

His "solution" is a weak one. In fact, neoclassical economics is incapable of explaining rent. Only Marx offers a relatively coherent theoretical argument, hence the interest in returning to it.

For Marx, then, absolute rent is based on the difference between the value of the product and the general price of production, while differential rent results from differences between general and particular prices of production. Differential rent is thus derived from disparities among costs of production, while absolute rent is "born" of the difference between the average rate of profit and the surplus value extracted. Now given an equal rate of exploitation, this difference can exist only if the organic composition of agricultural capital is lower than that of social capital as a whole. This difference cannot be maintained unless the principle of equalization of the rate of profit is not operative in the agricultural sector. This last condition can only occur if capital is not allowed to circulate freely, and this is precisely the role played by landed property. Thus landed property is well and truly the basis of rent. The abolition of landed property, and thus the equalization of the organic composition of capital, would eliminate absolute rent. Marx is very precise on this point (1967, p. 765). This definition of rent can be expressed by the following conditional equation : for

$i=1$ (i.e. the agricultural sector) and $j=.$ (i.e. all units of production) :

$V_{1}.>P_{1}.$ *if* $q_{1}.<q.\,.$ (1)

where $V_{1}.$=value of agricultural products
$P_{1}.$=general price of agricultural production
$q_{1}.$=organic composition of agricultural production
$q.$=organic composition of total social capital

By transforming (1) to take account of rotation time, we obtain a new equation.

As $V_{1}.=C_{1}.+Pl_{1}.$ (2)

As $P_{1}.=C_{1}.+PR_{1}.$ (3)

where $C_{1}.$=advanced agricultural capital
$Pl_{1}.$=agricultural surplus value
$PR_{1}.$=average agricultural profit

Knowing that :

$PR_{1}.=pr'.\,.K_{1}.$ (4)

where $pr'.\,.$=average rate of profit
$K_{1}.$=invested agricultural capital

It follows that :

$C_{1}.+Pl_{1}.>C_{1}.+pr'\,.\,.\,K_{1}.$ (5)

Hence $\frac{Pl_{1}.}{K_{1}.}>pr'.\,.$ (6)

If we suppose that $K_{1}.=C_{1}.$ (7)

Then $pr'_{1}=\frac{Pl_{1}.}{C_{1}.}>pr'\,.\,.$ (8)

where $pr'_{1}.$=agricultural rate of profit

Since $pr'=\frac{Pl}{C}$ (9)

And $C=c+v$ (10)

where c=constant capital
v=variable capital

It follows that :

$$pr'=\frac{\frac{P_{1}}{v}}{\frac{c+v}{v}}=\frac{Pl'}{q+1} \qquad (11)$$

Since

$pl'=\frac{Pl}{v}$, by definition (12)

And $q=\frac{c}{v}$, by definition (13)

where pl'=rate of surplus value

If we take into account the rotation time of capital (t), as suggested by Engels, it follows that :

$$pr'=\frac{pl'}{t\,(q+1)} \quad (14)$$

As a result equation (8) becomes :

$$\frac{pl'_1}{t_1\,.\,(q_1.+1)}>\frac{pl'\,.\,.}{t.\,.\,(q.\,+1)} \quad (15)$$

Where :

$$\frac{(pl'_1.)\,(t.\,.)\,(q.\,.+1)}{(pl'\,.\,.)\,(t_1.\,)\,(q1.+1)}>1 \quad (16)$$

Marx's thesis would appear admissible. Value will be higher than the price of production if the organic composition of social capital as a whole is greater than that of agricultural capital, insofar as :

1° $Pl'_1.\geqslant Pl'\,.\,.$ (17)

And 2° $t\,.\,.\geqslant t_1.$ (18)

Or 3° $(pl'_1.)\,(t\,.\,.)\geqslant(pl'\,.\,.)(t_1\,.)$ (19)

But alongside the relation between organic compositions are other, equally important conditions : the relation between rates of exploitation and the relation between rotation times. What were these relations in the 19th century ? What are they today ? Only a quantitative analysis of agricultural production, comparing it to conditions of production in the economy as a whole, can provide adequate information concerning these relations. Marx recognized this :

> As to the *existence* of absolute ground rent, that is a question which would have to be solved *statistically* in each country (Selected Correspondence, p. 164).

As first glance, Marx's general definition would appear to reconcile rent and value. But to properly understand the complexity of this definition, and its fragility, we must continue our examination of a number of variables that may come into it. In fact the problem is deciding what is included in invested capital and what is not. The schema on the following page should facilitate understanding the path taken by the various forms of capital.

While Marx's process of analysis clearly shows theoretically the possible existence of absolute rent, two problems remain. First we must note that while the market price of commodities is generally more or less equal to their average value, in the case of agricultural products the market price must be "fixed" according to the maximum value rather than the average. Otherwise one is forced to admit that less productive land might possibly bring in no rent at all, since everything depends on the difference between extracted surplus value and average profits.

The second point at issue concerns the calculation of average profit. The cost of production equals capital advanced during a production cycle ; the average profit, however, is calculated according to invested capital. Is this equal to advanced capital ? The distinction is an important one, since if one understands invested capital to mean advanced capital plus the total capital invested in the purchase and improvement of the land, then the differential relation between value and price cannot be verified empirically. This makes it imperative to examine the analysis of these two items.

Marx's examination of the question is both clear and imprecise. It is evident that the average profit is calculated on the basis of the total capital invested, both fixed and circulating, even if only a tiny proportion of fixed capital is used up in a given cycle of production. As a result, invested capital equals advanced capital only if production requires no fixed capital at all. Otherwise the first is necessarily larger than the second (1968, p. 950). This definition is consistent with that of the average profit, which leads to the redistribution of social surplus value according to the proportion of total capital held by each capitalist on the basis of the law of competition, which equalizes the rate of profit.

Equation (6) must therefore be modified as follows :

$$\frac{C_{1\cdot}}{K_{1\cdot}} * \frac{Pl_{1\cdot}}{C_{1\cdot}} > pr'_{\cdot\cdot} \tag{20}$$

Hence

$$\frac{C_{1\cdot}}{K_{1\cdot}} * \frac{pr'_{1\cdot}}{pr'_{\cdot\cdot}} > 1 \tag{21}$$

$$\text{Hence } \frac{C_{1\cdot}}{K_{1\cdot}} * \frac{(pl'_{1\cdot})\,(t_{\cdot\cdot})\,(q_{\cdot\cdot}+1)}{(pl'_{\cdot\cdot})\,(t_{1\cdot})\,(q_{1\cdot}+1)} \qquad (22)$$

It now becomes even more important to clarify whether or not invested capital includes the market price of the land and the capital incorporated in it. The stakes are high, since if one or other of these categories of capital are included in fixed capital, one has introduced a factor of variation that can make all the "difference" to a quantitative analysis of rent.

For Marx the price of land is nothing other than capitalized rent, and as such it cannot enter into the determination of the price of commodity production. On the other hand, it plays a role as a production cost for those exploiting the land (1967, pp. 647-648). There is a paradox here, one that Marx does nothing to elucidate. While on one level he rejects totally the idea that the price of land can enter into costs or prices, on an accounting level he admits that this price is included as an individual production cost (1967, p. 808ff). But though he recognizes this contradiction, he does not propose a consistent analysis of it, simply imputing it to the capitalist mode of production.

Marx bases his thesis on two axiomatic premises : on the one hand, once the land has been acquired, the person working it must invest if production is to occur. Now this productive investment is totally separate from the price of the land. On the other hand, the capital cannot exist twice, once as "land" in the hands of the buyer and once as "money" in the hands of the seller.

> [The price of land] forms neither a part of the fixed, nor of the circulating, capital employed here ; it merely secures for the buyer a claim to receive annual rent, but has absolutely nothing to do with the production of rent itself (1967, p. 808).
>
> The buyer now no longer has capital, but in its stead a piece of land. The circumstances that the rent produced by a real investment of capital in this land is calculated by the new landowner as interest on capital which he has not invested in the land, but given away to acquire the land, does not in the least alter the economic nature of the land factor. . . (1967, p. 809).

A few pages later, however, Marx comes back on this proposition, but without making it more explicit, unfortunately :

> The conflict between the price of land as an element in the producers' cost-price and no element in the price of production . . . is but one of the forms manifesting the general contradiction between private landownership and a rational agriculture, the normal social utilisation of the soil (1967, p. 812).

The argument is unacceptable. If the price of land enters as a component of the particular cost of production, then it should be considered a part of advanced capital. As a consequence, each "amortized" part of this price will necessarily be a part of the price of production since invested capital includes advanced capital by definition. If we accept this last proposition from Marx then we are forced to reject the theory of absolute rent, hence the necessity to demarcate from this second thesis if we are to avoid a circular, tautological, argument. The fact that each farmer includes the amortization of the price of land when drawing up his balance sheet in no way implies that this amortization in fact enters into the cost of production, otherwise those who inherit land could sell their products at below-market prices. Do they ?

The second part of the question concerns capital expenditure made to permit the utilization of otherwise unusable land or to improve inferior land. Here Marx talks about capital being "incorporated" into the land ; he also qualifies it as "fixed" (1967, pp. 764-776). Here again, the attributes of this type of capital are ambiguous. If it is fixed capital it will necessarily be a part of the calculation of the average profit, and with it the price of production, and if it is put to work and used, even partially, during production, it will enter into the value of commodities. Well, apparently this is not the case :

> The so-called permanent improvements. . . nearly all amount to giving a particular piece of land in a certain limited locality such properties as are naturally possessed by some other piece of land elsewhere, sometimes quite near by . . . However, land yields rent after capital is invested not

> because capital is invested, but because the invested capital makes this land more productive than it formerly was. . . . This rent too, which may be resolved into interest, becomes pure differential rent as soon as the invested capital is amortised. Otherwise, one and the same capital would have to exist twice as capital (1967, pp. 745-746).

Marx's analysis tends to define capital incorporated in the soil as fixed capital but not as invested capital entering into the cost of production. The capitalization is necessary to increase productivity, in the case of differential rent II, or to allow the land to be used for production, in the case of absolute rent, but it is insufficient in itself for production to occur. However, since it is an expense, possibly requiring financing, the capital involved must be amortized. It cannot be amortized out of rent, hence it cannot occur at all unless the difference between the price of production and the market price is sufficiently large. It also follows that capital incorporated in the soil does not affect the organic composition.

For Marx's theory of rent to function, neither the price of land nor incorporated capital can be defined as invested capital, even if in one case it is clearly fixed capital. These two types of capitalization a landowner may carry out are absolutely independent of the nature of the economic activity the land may be used for, and neither one enters into the calculation of value or price of production. On the other hand, from the landowner's perspective, the decision to keep or acquire property, rather than investing equal capital in another sphere, must satisfy the criterion of profitability, the land in this case being more "profitable".

Given these restrictions—that neither the price of land nor capital expenditure incorporated into the soil enter into the value or price of production—Marx's definition of absolute rent is coherent and, therefore, admissible. Making use of it, however, remains a somewhat delicate operation because of the complexity inherent in its relative character. Rent is based on the disparity between the value of commodities and their general price of production, the elements of which are difficult to grasp. Marx's explanation of the chronic existence of this disparity between price of production and value is also consistent. The continued existence of this disparity seems to depend on the maintenance of the difference between the organic compositions of capital in agriculture and capital in general ; this function is assured by the right to property. By limiting the free circulation of capital, this right prevents any increase in the organic composition and, therefore, any equalization. But the organic composition of capital is not the only variable affecting the existence of rent, far from it. Lastly, value must not be seen as an absolute limit. The market price may be higher than the value if the product is under the control of a monopoly. This surplus rent is thus a monopoly rent. From Marx's point of view this would appear to be linked to the product rather than to land ownership. Here again we see a point both clear and obscure, but that is another story. . . .

Differential rent

Differential rent is based on disparities between individual production costs. Given the same total production, each producer advancing a relatively smaller amount of capital than that advanced by other producers realizes a surplus profit. Similarly, given the same individual production cost, any producer producing a greater quantity also realizes a surplus product. In either case, this surplus profit may become rent if appropriated by the landowner. This is differential rent.

Normally such disparities are understood to originate in two different sets of conditions, resulting in two types of differential rent : differential rent I, which results from conditions external to the process of production but linked to the qualities of the site (considered "natural" as a result) ; and differential rent II, which results from conditions internal to production because linked to technical productivity. Differential rent thus refers to two kinds of *a priori* conditions having nothing in common except that they are both result in surplus profits.

Consider the following formulation of the problem of differential rent in general. The unit of exploitation (j) of the sector of production (i) (agriculture), the value and the price of production present themselves as follows :*

$$V_{ij}=C_{ij}+Pl_{ij} \qquad (23)$$

* The comparisons made here presuppose the choice of a common unit of measurement, such as an acre.

$$P_{ij}=C_{ij}+K_{ij}pr'.. \tag{24}$$

where i=agricultural production sector
j=unit of production
C=advanced capital
Pl=extracted surplus value
V=value of commodities
P=price of production
$pr'..$=rate of profit
K=invested capital

If for the purposes of demonstration we assume that absolute rent does not exist, then the rate of profit in the sector (i) is equal to the general rate of profit, hence :

$$pr'i.=pr'.. \tag{25}$$

If one proposes the hypothesis that differential rent exists, this implies that value is greater than price, hence that extracted surplus value is greater than profit. Hence the following :

$$Pl_{ij}>K_{ij}\,(pr'..) \tag{26}$$

$$\text{or } Pl_{ij}>K_{ij}\,(pr'i.) \tag{27}$$

$$\text{hence } Pl_{ij}>K_{ij}\left(\frac{Pl_{i.}}{K_{i.}}\right) \tag{28}$$

$$\text{or that } \frac{Pl_{ij}}{K_{ij}}>\frac{Pl_{i.}}{K_{i.}} \tag{29}$$

As a result, the conditions for the existence of differential rent are present whenever equation (29) can be verified, in other words, each time that the individual rate of profit is greater than the agricultural rate of profit.

A particular rate may be higher for two reasons : either because the individual capital required for production is lower, or because the individual rate of surplus value extracted is higher (in such proportions that the individual rate of profit to remains above the overall agricultural rate of profit). From the examination of the nine possible combinations of variables involved in comparing the two rates of profit, as in the table below,

Surplus value	Capital $K_{i.}>K_{ij}$	$K_{i.}=K_{ij}$	$K_{i}<K_{ij}$
$Pl_{ij}>Pl_{i.}$	case 1	case 4	case 7
$Pl_{ij}=Pl_{i.}$	case 2	case 5	case 8
$Pl_{ij}<Pl_{i.}$	case 3	case 6	case 9

one can draw the following conclusions :

1° in cases 5, 6, 8 and 9, differential rent cannot exist ; 2° cases 1, 2 and 4 satisfy the conditions for the existence of differential rent, necessarily type I because $K_{ij} <= K_{i.}$; 3° in case 3 the existence of differential rent I remains contingent on a supplementary condition. The same applies to case 7, although it concerns differential rent II.

In cases 1, 2 and 4, the right to property doesn't interfere with the process of capitalist production by setting up a block to the circulation of capital. Rather it acts like a monopoly, authorized to collect relatively greater surplus value than that collected by other producers. This is the case whatever the apparent reason, whether lower production costs, greater natural soil productivity, particularities of the site, and so on. Whatever the mechanism behind it, the effect is the same and can be attributed solely to the site. Differential rent I, which can be called locational rent, is thus a type of "monopoly" because it is based on the unique properties of a particular site. It is in no way related to absolute rent.

As for differential rent II, it poses a problem that is virtually unintelligible on the level of theory. On the one hand it has been established that agricultural production permits the extraction of an absolute rent because the right of private property in land limits the circulation of capital, thus minimizing the investment of constant capital. But, inversing this logic, differential rent II presupposes precisely a level of investment superior to that made by other producers and along with it higher productivity. Thus it falls under a capitalist logic "freed" of the constraints posed by landed property. Yet this is not clearly the case. As well, depending on whether the surplus investment implied by differential rent II is made in equipment or in the improvement of the soil, it will or will not influence the individual cost of production. In effect, always according to Marx, in the first case the amortization of the surplus investment will have direct repercussions on the individual price of production, while in the second case it will be amortized out of rent. Now this cannot be absolute rent, it can only be differential rent I. If it was absolute rent one would have to ask why all farmers wouldn't invest in better equipment, since such equipment would bring in surplus profit The logic of property as a barrier to investment would collapse and the theory of absolute rent would be "absolutely" inadmissible.

If, on the other hand, the investment in question went solely to improve the land, differential rent I would be a prerequisite. Otherwise the farmer would be heading straight for bankruptcy. As a result the problem of differential rent II necessarily comes under the dynamic of differential rent I, which is based on the logic of monopoly.

Thus when all is said and done, only two types of rent exist : absolute rent and monopoly rent. Each in their own way expresses a contradiction between the logic of landed property and the logic of capital, given the place of these two categories in Marxist theory.

THE WAY OF THE WORLD

The examination we have begun requires a deeper analysis of the similarities and differences between absolute and monopoly rent. At this point it is primordial to establish the effects of these two factors on total surplus value, the point of contention of the relations of production. Our discussion has not resolved the question of a possible contradiction between the theory of value and the theory of rent. In fact, the definition of rent developed by Marx through an analysis of agricultural production does not take on its full theoretical role until he reinserts it in a more general context, which he does in Part VII of Volume III of *Capital* (1967, p. 84ff). In this section Mark analyzes the three forms of income, profit, rent and wages, and their supposed sources, capital, land and labour. His objective is clear : to show that profit and rent are simply surplus value and that, as a result, the only true source of income is labour. *Marx thus completes his analysis where he began it, with the axiom that labour is the only source of value.*

To prove his argument he resorts to proof through absurdity. Examining the contrary hypothesis, he takes it to absurdity. The reasoning is simple. If the factors of production—capital, land and labour—are all defined as sources of value, then each will give to commodities a fraction of their value. Since income signifies this value in return, it is possible to determine the value of commodities. In other words, tautology is inevitable and the question of value remains insoluble.

However, if one retains the hypothesis that labour is the only source of value, then social products only have value as commodities according to the mass of living labour incorporated within them and insofar as labour itself is defined as a commodity having an exchange value. This exchange value of labour Marx defines as a variable dependent on the relation between the amount of labour required to reproduce labour power and the amount of surplus labour furnished by this same labour power. To a theory of the absolute value of labour—which can only be proved from outside the domain of political economy if it too is not to become a tautology—Marx counterposes a theory of the relative value of labour, which is internally consistent. Thus throughout *Capital* the relation between necessary and surplus labour is conceived as the parametric function defining all other variables.

Marx's explanatory schema is more than a postulate, it is an axiom, for all intents and purposes unprovable, that must be accepted as self-evident. Departing from this axiom of surplus value in the slightest means removing all logic from *Capital's* analysis. In the entire conceptual framework forged by Marx this is perhaps the only element that could give rise to dogmatism. But it is no small element. In any case, theoretically or not, can we depart from this axiom ? Outside of God or the Absurb, we have no alternative. Is this dogmatic dimension alone sufficient to justify all those actions, both bloody and stupid, claiming to stem from a Marxist analysis ? Can the social universe deciphered by Marx not be reduced to a simple Manicheism opposing good and evil ?

So, for Marx, land rent can only be surplus value, indirect extorted labour :

> Its normal form presupposes wages corresponding to the value of labour power. Even monopoly rent. . . must always indirectly be a part of the surplus-value. If it is not part of the price excess above the price of production of the commodity itself, of which it is a constituent part (as in differential rent), or an excess portion of the surplus-value of the commodity itself, of which it is a constituent part, above that portion of *its own surplus-value* measured by the average

> profit (*as in absolute rent*), it is at least part of the surplus-value of other commodities, i.e., of commodities which are exchanged for this commodity having a monopoly price. The sum of the average profit plus ground-rent can never be greater than the magnitude of which they are components and which exists before this division (1967, pp. 832-833, our emphasis).

The statement is perfectly clear, as are his explanations. The three types of rent, differential, absolute and monopoly, do not proceed from the same rationality and, as a result do not have the same effects on social surplus value and its division, even if their ultimate cause, property, is the same. If the conclusions drawn up to now from the analysis presented in these pages are acceptable—that is, that there exist two types of rent, absolute and monopoly—we still must examine their varying effects on social relations.

Land rent has dual origins : either it comes from surplus value extracted in a given sector of production, as in agriculture, or it comes from social surplus value, that is, surplus value produced by all sectors of production. This statement conforms to Marx's propositions and could not be more consistent with the fundamental definitions of the diverse variables that go into the elaboration of his theory. Now the effects of these two types of rent are antagonistic as far as their impact on the general rate of profit is concerned, hence in the final analysis on the "value" of commodities produced. The formula $V_1. > P_1.$, resulting from the disparity between the organic compositions of agricultural and general social capital, necessarily implies that the rate of profit in agriculture is higher than in production in general, $pr'_1. > pr'..$—this is the case of absolute rent. Monopoly rent implies that $V_1 < P_1.$, hence that the sectorial rate of profit is lower than the general rate, since monopoly allows one to sell at a price higher than value, extorting a part of social surplus value that would otherwise fall under profits. Since those elements involved in calculating a sectorial rate of profit are also involved in the calculation of the general rate, one has to admit that the payment of "absolute" rent therefore increases this general rate while the payment of "monopoly" rent has the opposite effect. *This shows*, not that rent takes part in giving value to commodities, but *that the social relation underlying the existence of rent exercises a real if indirect control over the social value of labour.*

Let us digress. According to Marx the social labour furnished by a society can be divided into two types, necessary labour—labour that produces the goods "necessary" to reproduce the labour power expended—and surplus labour—unpaid labour provided by this same labour power above and beyond necessary labour. The relation between these two types of labour expresses the level of exploitation of labour power, measured in terms of time. This labour power is "put to work", that is, applied to production, in a single, continuous, recursive time period. The limit of each period is determined by the time spent on the reproduction of the labour power expended.

However, the rate of exploitation may be measured not only in terms of time, but also—and above all—according to a scale of value defined on the basis of the particular "value" that society places on labour. This is exactly what Marx wants to show, since he considers that commodities have exchange value only because they incorporate living labour, the only source of value. This attribute of labour is due to the fact that in societies dominated by the capitalist mode of production, living labour is treated as a commodity, having its own exchange value. But "logically", shouldn't this value equal its general cost of (re)production, as the following formula would indicate :

(VT.=CT. . (1+pr. .)

This would be to recognize that the social value of labour (VT) is equal to the social capital (CT) employed in (re)producing it—in the wages paid—plus the average profit on this capital. (Remembering that this capital only has value because it is itself the product of earlier living labour. Otherwise one would be forced to consider that capital has a value in itself.) Thus expressed the definition is tautological, and absurd as well. *What meaning can a measure of the value of labour have if value is itself defined according to labour* ? It is equally absurd to posit an absolute value, whether for labour, capital or land.

The rate of exploitation relates necessary and surplus labour, and this definition underlines the measure of the rate of surplus value, since surplus value and variable capital are the variables which express surplus labour and necessary labour in terms of value rather than time. Here we must recall that the existence of surplus labour is not the result of a natural law and therefore inevitable and indiscutable. Surplus labour results from a balance of power in society whereby one class "convinces" another, by force or by persuasion, to work more than is necessary and for nothing, the product of this extra labour not being equitably redistributed among individuals, groups and classes.

If the problem is posed in these terms, the implication is that for a given labour power, the less labour time and capital required to reconstitute it, the less is its value. If two units of labour power of unequal value are applied to production for the same length of time, the unit of lesser value will produce a larger amount of surplus value and, therefore, be subject to a greater rate of exploitation. As well, given that this surplus value will not be equally distributed, those individuals benefitting from this inequality will have every interest in optimizing in their favour the relation between surplus value and wages.

Notwithstanding the various techniques that exist for maximizing the rate of surplus value, a reduction in the price of labour will also involve minimizing the price of those commodities taking up a significant proportion of wages, including, among others, food and housing. Now both of these commodities are subject to the payment of rent. This implies that the payment of rent, whether absolute or monopoly, necessarily increases variable capital, thus reducing extractable surplus value. But the consequences of the payment of a rent are not identical depending upon the type involved, monopoly or absolute. One can see that the effects of variations in the rates of surplus value and profit, one upon the other, are visible in the relation between constant and variable capital. The payment of any rent whatsoever increases variable capital and thus tends to lower the value of the parameter $(c/v)+1$. However, since the existence of absolute rent implies the super-exploitation of (agricultural) labour, which tends to increase the average rate of profit, one may assume that it has little effect on the general rate of surplus value. But the payment of monopoly rent can, on the contrary, only tend to lower the rate of profit and, consequently, the rate of surplus value. This proposition implies that *the political relations underlying each type of rent are perhaps not of the same order, given what each one represents.*

Given the logic of capitalism, therefore, monopoly rent is

an "inadmissible", parasitic practice, while absolute rent acquires such a dimension only in certain situations, thus making it "tolerable". What is more, under certain circumstances, such a form of rent may even represent a disguished method of countering the tendency of the rate of profit to fall. Hence one can understand the maintenance of relations underlying this characteristic of agricultural production. On the other hand, the fact that the payment of monopoly rent continues to exist and consolidate itself, even intensifying along with the development of the principal contradiction between the socialization of labour and the concentration of ownership of the means of production, clearly implies *the existence of a contradiction within the bourgeois class itself.* This is an important point as far as urban questions are concerned, since urban rent is necessarily a monopoly rent. But it is also important from other points of view. The distinction between the production of means of production and the production of consumption goods is no doubt more than a simple analytical classification. It would perhaps be worthwhile to return to the concept of financial capital, an idea which paints too homogenous a picture of the "interest of capital". Our digression remains open . . . .

Scientific theory or dogma ?

This recapitulation of Marx's analysis shows that his treatment of the problem of rent, no matter how heuristic it may be, contains elements that remain open to interpretation. Marx has not overcome the latent paradox between the theory of value and the theory of rent, and the universality of absolute rent is extremely questionable. Demarginalizing the theory of rent in fact implies adopting a totally relativistic theory of the value of labour. But such a theory is not possible unless the political "quality" of social relations has just as much weight as their economic "quality", if not more. As a result, the determining role of economic factors on social structures, "in the final analysis", is impossible since such an assumption necessarily relegates any theory of rent to absurdity and anachronism. Moreover, this axiom—a legacy of 19th century positivism—reduces Marxism to a more subtle variation of functionalism, susceptible to being used as a disguised "bourgeois" ideology.

This general criticism does not invalidate Marx's theoretical contribution, far from it ; his analysis flows from a remarkable conceptual framework. Firstly one must recognize the general coherence of his definition of absolute rent. It presupposes a process of production dominated by the valorization of land itself under the sway of property rights. This rent therefore emerges out of the difference between the cost of production and the value of the commodity produced, which acts as the relative limit on it. This form of rent implies superexploitation of labour power and under-capitalization. The second form of rent—monopoly rent—does not necessarily presuppose a particular process of production. It is based solely on the right to private property of land and, consequently, the ownership of the natural or social "riches" inherent in it. This type of rent is thus based on the balance of power between landowners and "others", and the state of this relation is the only limit on this type of rent.

But we must recognize that while monopoly rent results solely from the exercise of the right to private ownership of a piece of land, it nonetheless presupposes the occurrence of production "somewhere else", that requires such and such a resource "here" that is a part of land "there". Monopoly rent thus presupposes the existence of a relation of production which produces a surplus value, in this case appropriated by a "distant" landowner. Hence it is a political relation that forces a bourgeois "here" to give a portion of his surplus value to a landowner "there". Now this political relation, while clearly affecting the surplus-value producing relation of production, is not a consequence of it. On the contrary, it may be its starting point. From this reasoning can we deduce that monopoly rent is a form of absolute rent ? No, because in the case of monopoly rent nothing allows us to believe that the organic composition of capital corresponds to that needed for the existence of absolute rent. We are definitely faced with two distinct types of rent. And, possibly, monopoly rent may be the more general form.

Differential rents do not in fact constitute analytical categories properly speaking. Differential rent I is just an expression of monopoly rent, while differential rent II is based on marginal logic. The "natural" advantages of a piece of land should not induce naturalistic reasoning ; these advantages have no economic value except in relation to a socially defined market and no political value except in relation to social relations defining the politico-legal force of the right to property.

On another level, one can see from Marx's analysis that the question of rent is a great source of confusion. Thus the notion of landed capital is an illusion ; the right of property is exercised either over landed property or over capital. Landed property is not a "form" of capital. Ignoring this distinction forces one to account for the same capital under two headings, which is illogical. Similarly, the capital incorporated in the soil through land improvements intended to increase its profitability does not constitute invested capital. This capital outlay can only be amortized through rent and does not imply the payment of interest. Lastly, the price of land, whatever the degree of improvement that has been made, is always equivalent only to capitalized rent, which is determinable only according to the profitability of the landed property in question.

As far as the question of urban land rent is concerned, Marx's contributions are of importance because they clearly define our field of investigation. They provide key concepts for interpreting a part of the logic of urbanization—urban rent, apparently beyond understanding. Certainly Marx peremptorily dismissed this question ; only absolute rent interested him, especially since he didn't push his analysis to the limit. A lack of time ? Perhaps. The fact remains, the question of rent, fundamentally political in its foundations, contradicts the now planetary obsession of economist determinism because it relativizes the theory of value.

RENT : AN URBAN REALITY

A distinction is generally made between rent on a conceptual level—absolute rent, differential rents and monopoly rent—and on a factual level—agricultural rent and urban rent. The distinction is important because of the passage it presupposes from the factual to the conceptual levels, from the fact to the object, the object to the concept, and vice versa.

The preceding analysis made a clear distinction between two objects : absolute rent and monopoly rent. It also showed that differential rent I (DRI), or situational rent, is monopoly, not absolute rent, and that differential rent II does not exist in agriculture. The analysis also led to a different understanding of land rent than that of Marx. On the most general level, land rent represents no more and no less than the transfer of a fraction of society's surplus value to the owners of land. This occurs on the basis of juridico-political relations that follow from the existence of property rights, not on the basis of the relations of production. Thus land rent is above all a monopoly rent, with absolute rent being simply a particular, specific form of rent. Absolute rent, in fact, does not come from social surplus value in general. It comes from agricultural surplus value because of the contradictory but limited effect of property rights on the circulation of capital in this particular sphere of production.

As well, when Marx demonstrated the possible existence of absolute rent, he only partially dealt with the latent contradiction between rent and value. In doing so, he concealed monopoly rent behind absolute rent, creating an illusion that diverts criticism to this very day. This is why it remains difficult to grasp rent in an urban context. The fact does not correspond to the object. Intentionally or not, Marx distorted the passage from concept to fact by declaring, explicitly or implicitly, that absolute rent and urban rent are equivalents. Such an equation can be refuted.

Agricultural rent is made up of absolute rent and monopoly rent (DRI), but urban rent conceals no absolute rent, and is solely a monopoly rent. This hypothesis is an admissible one, insofar as one avoids considering urban and agricultural rents as equivalents, clarifies the object of the monopoly in question, and delimits the nature of the reality in question—urban rent.

A LITERAL SETTLING OF ACCOUNTS

Repeated attempts to understand urban rent have been crippled by the false necessity of establishing an analogy between agricultural and urban rent. Did not Marx affirm that the two phenomena were one and the same. But if this analogy is accepted, it is inevitable that construction be considered a productive activity analogous to agricultural production (Alquier, 1975 ; Lojkine, 1975 ; Krifa, 1979 ; Lipietz, 1973 ; Fisette, 1978). Now if we look at the facts, the analogy is a weak one : agriculture has a yearly cycle, construction does not ; agriculture does not produce durable goods, construction does ; agricultural products are consumption goods, buildings are capital goods. In any case, construction occurs within the agricultural sector itself, since farm buildings are not products of nature. It does not take a lot of research to conclude that, as an activity, construction produces durable goods usable in any form of value-creating activity, be it agricultural, urban or extractive. It is astonishing that the impasse created by the analogy between agricultural and urban rents has not been remarked upon earlier.

In any case, an analogy wasn't what was needed, since scientifically speaking an analogy has no explicative significance. Rather the task was to identify those elements in urban rent that are homologous to elements in agricultural rent. If agriculture is understood as a set of practices contributing to the valorization of a piece of land, then only the process of urbanization, rather than construction, can be considered a comparable set of practices, also contributing to the valorization of space. But a methodological problem arises in defining such a homology between agriculture and urbanization. Is such a homology to be established on the level of forms or functions ? Now the theorization of forms is decreed to be unscientific, while that of functions goes nowhere ; your money or your life ? (Richot, 1977, 1979).

One way of dealing with this dilemma is to re-establish the relationship between form and function. Such an analysis would attempt to identify the various structural components of the form in question and relate them to the various functions either attributed to or recognized as being a part of the phenomenon being examined. From this perspective, the form/function relation would have meaning, based both on knowledge and interpretation. However, such a relation could not be considered either as an absolute or as pure contingency. It would be necessary to define it as the result of a given historical "logic", and therefore variable in time and space, with such variations being explicable. Since the existence of variations presupposes the action of forces, relating form and function implies the existence of a middle term : the social forces that are necessary for change to occur.

If agriculture and urbanization are conceived as "forms" of valorization of space, and if one postulates that their formal/functional structure follows from a "historical logic" based on the dynamic relationship between social forces, then one must admit the possible existence of several forms of agriculture and several forms of urbanization. One must also admit that these forms, or what is left of them, are determined by history. If in turn history is seen as the product of a "class struggle", these forms therefore result from past and present struggles. Of course, such a conception is potentially incompatible with any approach that declares production to be the determining factor, since the functionality of such production remains indissociable from its formal constitution, the nature of which is unknown. Whatever the case, we know that the *a priori* adoption of a productivist axiom compels any analysis to prove the existence of essential needs. The reduction of forces to needs thus turns the class struggle into a "natural phenomenon", denying the power of societies to influence history.

Lastly, it is important to point out that the search for such a homology between agriculture and urbanization would be an arduous, even impossible, task. What is more, starting from the hypothesis that such a homology exists would automatically prejudice the analysis, since the only practical approach would be to look only for those formal/structural components that might be homologous, on the basis of one's own definition of the process of valorization of a piece of land or space. Such an approach would raise as many or more problems that it resolved. Thus the definition of urban rent is likely to remain unsatisfactory for some time, just so long as the analysis, entrapped by the agricultural model, is caught between an approach by analogy (pointless) and an approach by homology (unachievable). *Perhaps the search for a solution first requires a demystification of agricultural rent as a model*?

The agricultural valorization of land involves a process of production similar and comparable to any other. Such a process brings together labour power and means of production which together produce a product that may be sold and thus bring in a profit. Once submitted to capitalist relations of production, this process involves the superexploitation of labour power, itself treated as a commodity like any other, which allows the capitalist to extract surplus value that is then accumulated as capital.

There is a strong temptation to regard agriculture as a unique production process since, after all, wheat grows "naturally". But do not all human productive activities, whatever their object, take advantage of "natural" factors? As well, all activities are inevitably "localized", that is, they occupy space in the same way that they occupy historical time. This localization is not the fruit of hazard. Ordinarily the choice of a site is justified according to a certain rationality that takes into account both natural factors like fertility, slope, and so on, and social, economic, political, cultural and other factors. On this basis, agricultural production is hardly different from the production of alumina !

Usually analyses of location forget the inherent limitations posed by the exercise of property rights over land. Certainly this is a major omission, but the question of property rights is hardly specific to agriculture. Whatever the activity, any use of space must pay for the attention of property rights. While Marx showed that in agriculture land ownership was a brake on the circulation of capital, one must ask whether this an "accidental", phenomenon or a generalized effect of property.

As far as this is concerned, one must remember that private property of land does not limit the capitalist development of natural resources, including energy. At any rate, this would appear to be the case, since these sectors have a high organic composition of capital. This type of valorization does involve the payment of a rent (Lipietz, 1973 ; Walker, 1975), although evidently not an absolute rent. So what is the basis of this rent ? Monopoly ownership of the land containing the resource or monopoly ownership of the means of production ?

In reality, agricultural production presents no notable peculiarities compared to other types of production. In general, all types of production make use of natural products and all take place in a given space, which must somehow be paid for. Only in agriculture, it would seem, do property rights come into contradiction with the flow of capital. This peculiarity is so unusual that one is justified in questioning the very existence of agricultural absolute rent. It is useful to recall here that a number of Marxist analyses have gone to the extreme of concluding that agricultural rent does not exist (Bergeron and Bouvette, 1977). In fact it is not so much the existence of agricultural rent that must be questioned, but rather that of absolute rent, which as a theoretical object is a bit too accommodating of contingencies imposed by the theory of value. Perhaps Ricardo wasn't so wrong after all.

Even elementary caution would thus counsel abandoning

agricultural rent as a model for urban rent. The fact of agricultural rent has been too compromised by the theoretical interference and manipulation it has been subjected to. The theoretical object has been made to measure, an illusion that takes the place of the "fact" that it represents, this fact being the urban "place".

IN CASE OF FIRE, LET BURN

Posing a monopoly of space as the condition for monopoly rent poses a rather delicate problem (Topalov, 1974a), and specialists, Marx included, have tried to get around it. The problem is as follows : the monopoly is an imperfect one, since scarcity of land is only relative, dependent on the voluntary retention of land by the landowners. This retention was and is possible only because it predates the establishment of capitalist relations of production. Landed property has managed to keep capital out. Thus capital must pay a tribute to property, which in return collaborates with capital to extract additional surplus labour. A preliminary remark is necessary here. The ideas of collaboration (Walker, 1975) and tribute (Lipietz, 1973) both imply recognition of the autonomy and power of juridico-political relations vis-a-vis relations of production. This in turn puts into question the final determining nature of production. Nonetheless, these two contributions in no way deal with the problem of monopoly, and their explanation leaves much to be desired.

Whether the payment of rent overdetermines or not the general rate of profit, either up or down, such rent is still a parasitic practice from the capitalists' point of view, one which implies their incapacity to fully control the redistribution of surplus value that they themselves have extracted. The most obvious reaction, following the logic of capitalist accumulation, would have the capitalists either abolish landed property or appropriate its benefits. Thus it is impossible to conceive of land rent as a one-sided relation, redistributing social surplus value (Rey, 1973) and implying a fundamental antagonism between landed property and capital. But it is equally unacceptable to consider rent a relic of the Middle Ages, a medieval pit swallowing up forever a portion of surplus value, a historical anachronism destined to disappear. The latter thesis runs as follows : the bourgeoisie tends to monopolize land because it cannot attack property for ideological reasons ; thus the historical antagonism between capital and landed property tends to disappear, while a real monopoly over land develops.

A number of historical facts cast doubt on the correctness of this idea. In Quebec, for example, the development of the mode of land tenure under the French and English regimes proceeded from a monopoly situation to one of dispersion among a proliferation of landowners (Bergeron and Bouvette, 1977). This evolution is so evident that one may even postulate that the Canadian merchant bourgeoisie was transformed into a capitalist bourgeoisie thanks to the collection of rent, which formed a sort of primitive accumulation. This proposition converges with another which sees the formation of ethnic petty bourgeoisies as based on their acquisition of property (Lavigne, 1979). So one must accept that at certain stages in its history the capitalist bourgeoisie has definitely attacked landed property, while at other times it has relinquished this fight. In ane case, the strategy of this class cannot be considered unequivocal, at least insofar as the monopolization of space is concerned.

Similarly, it is difficult to accept the idea that the bourgeoisie has not attacked the right to property in land for ideological reasons. In reality, landed property has been socialized whenever this has proved necessary, usually under the pretext of the public good. Such an observation is banal (Topalov, 1974c). Are we not forced to recognize that private land has been subject to socialization whenever it might have given rise to a monopoly over a resource ? One might, for example, reinterpret Quebec legislation on the exploitation of Crown lands, on mining claims, forestry concessions, reserves and so on, considering it as intended to establish partial socialization of the right to property, or rent, in order to prevent the monopolization of a resource and thus control access to this type of wealth (Decarie *et al.*, 1977 ; Gaudreau, 1978, 1979). The question of the historical relation between the capitalization of social production and the nature of the perennial right to landed property not only remains unanswered, it also adds ambiguity to the question of the monopolization of space.

As for the conception that defines rent as an archaic structure of redistribution of surplus value, it in no way clarifies the question (Rey, 1973). Certainly, one cannot deny that land ownership implies a redistribution of surplus value parallel to that made by the equalization of the rate of profit, but the institutionalization of this practice within a given social structure is inconceivable according to political economy if this field is defined according to the contradiction between labour and capital, or between the socialization of production and the monopolization of the means of production. This conception of political economy is too narrow; it makes the establishment of a coherent theory of rent impossible. The most rudimentary examination of urban landed property, for example, shows that this redistribution of surplus value is a part of a process of accumulation whose importance and magnitude may be difficult to evaluate but which nonetheless seems extremely large (Aubin, 1977). Given this fact, one cannot conceive of rent as a historical anachronism destined to disappear.

Any attempt to get around the problem of the monopolization of landed property goes nowhere. The collection of a monopoly rent can be considered neither as the unequivocal result of the monopolization of land, already in existence or in the process of forming, because the facts show this is not the case, nor as some misleading anachronism, since this would be an admission of theoretical impotence. In case of fire, let burn. . .and start all over again. The problem must be examined in a different light, based on the hypothesis that the payment of this monopoly rent is based on the articulation of relations of production and juridico-political relations, the latter being the foundation of the monopoly in question. Examination of certain facts underlying the urban reality will support this proposition.

An urban agglomeration is made up of a multitude of elements that can be categorized in the most trivial ways : here people, there things, and so on. Among things, urban planners tend to draw a sharp distinction between two categories : buildings and infrastructure. Infrastructure includes all those things that provide support for buildings : streets, sidewalks, sewers, water mains, electric and telephone lines, etc. This mass of urban capital goods form a framework in space that is both closed and open. Such service infrastructures may be extended without limit, since they are unfinished networks. At the same time, however, their expansion is limited by an administrative, juridical, political and economic delimitation of territory. From these two observations we can draw the following rule : the location of buildings (and developments without buildings) is dependent on the network of services, the extension and location of which is, in turn, dependent on the delimitation of territory served or to be served. Hence the question : on what and/or who does this territorial delimitation depend ?

In Quebec, as is probably the case in most countries, the state exercises clear sovereignty over the whole of its territory (within the framework of Confederation) either directly, indirectly, or both, by means of the municipalities to which it has legally delegated a part of its authority. In particular, municipalities are given control over the planning and development of their territory via the issuing of permits and their responsibility to establish, develop and manage a large proportion of public services. Today, for example, the construction and maintenance of streets, sewers, and water mains are exclusively under municipal control. The establishment and operation of other service infrastructures such as electricity or access to communications are under the control of private or public corporations which exercise legal monopolies under the "enlightened" supervision of the various levels of government. Thus the delimitation of territory served is determined by the state. It is a product of the relation between political and economic forces ; it defines an area that is subject to the exercise of real monopoly power.

Buildings are another category of capital goods, with characteristics that differ greatly from those of infrastructures. A building is a finished construction, situated on a fixed parcel of land whose unique limits are subject to a precise, legal definition. Whatever the juridico-administrative unit—the lot, the unit of evaluation, etc.—used to refer to lots, improved or not, each and every one of these units are subject to property rights, whether public or private. The territory has no empty spaces as far as land ownership is concerned. Of course, not all lots are built up or even landscaped, and land ownership is always divided among a multitude of owners. So in the usual sense of the term—one owner—there is no monopoly.

However, looked at overall, land ownership is well and truly "monopolized", since to get a piece of land one necessarily must purchase it from someone else. If the effects of monopoly are limited by the possibility of negotiating with several owners, they are strengthened by the fact that each lot has a unique location, not only in geo-physical terms, but also, and above all, in regard to the geo-political framework established by the city's infrastructure. Each lot is unique, and each lot is the property of a legal "individual".

It would thus appear that the existence of an effective monopoly is not a prerequisite for the existence of urban monopoly rent. On the other hand, the exercise of property rights over the whole of a municipal territory, as amended by the service infrastructure, poses a necessary condition for such rent.

Thus monopoly rent has its fundamental basis in the non-producible character of a "good", space, that is completely appropriated both in law and in fact. In order for landowners or capitalists having title to land to profit from this monopoly, the right to private property of land must have both a legal and political basis, and the private appropriation of a good so evidently social, space, must be backed up ideologically. In fact, the social practice in question is not based on some "natural" human attitude : many societies, including Amerindian society, consider acceptable only the appropriation of the use of land, not of the land itself. Private property of land certainly has foundations in one or more pre-capitalist ideologies, but the continued existence of the practice presupposes the existence of political relations that favour landowners. The economic dimension of rent can only be the expression of the political and ideological power of one or more classes. It is even plausible to ask whether the appropriation of the means of production, in the narrow sense of the term, is not an extension of the appropriation of space. It is also permissible to ask whether or not the foundation of all political power is based necessarily on the appropriation of territory. As a corollary, one might as whether the first step in a struggle for liberation lies on the battlefield of ideology, rather than that of the means of material production.

BACKDROP, SCENERY AND ACCESSORIES

Once liberated from its doctrinal protheses, the model of agricultural rent and the problem of monopoly of ownership, rent becomes presentable as an urban reality. But we must still present an outline of a number of elements that form the milieu within which rent develops.

Construction

Construction is an activity producing capital goods. It is extremely diversified, both in the nature of the labour process employed and in terms of its product, which is difficult to categorize. Construction may constitute an object of investigation in itself : while the work on this question is only embryonic, it is also promising (Bertrand, 1978). This type of production faces two major constraints that have slowed and limited its organization on a capitalist basis : the technical durability of its products and the obligation that they be associated with landed property (Topalov, 1973, 1974b).

The technical longevity of buildings unduly slows down the reconstruction of social capital. The "product" doesn't spoil, unlike agricultural products which may be rapidly lost in consumption. It remains, almost indefinitely if additional sums of capital are expended occasionally to maintain its functional efficiency. A quick look at advertisements in Montreal newspapers at the end of the 19th and the beginning of the 20th centuries (Durivage *et al.*, 1978, 1980) shows that for a long time promoters were content to sell unimproved lots on installments, that is, retaining full property rights until payment was complete. The sale of lots with buildings only appeared gradually, becoming a general practice around 1910. For this to happen it was necessary to find a formula whereby the constructor could rapidly be paid back all his capital (plus profit of course) and the burden of amortization be transferred to the purchaser. The beginning and generalization of mortgage financing, which appeared between 1860 and 1870, permitted this (Lavigne *et al.*, 1977). Today construction involves the intervention of numerous agents, the application of various types of financing and the integration of extremely diverse practices ; a veritable Gordian knot. The analysis of the contemporary version of construction has led to a proliferation of conceptual categories—promotion capital, real estate capital, landed capital, speculative capital—and to endemic theoretical controversies (Topalov, 1973 ; Lipietz, 1974, 1981 ; Tutin, 1981 a and b).

The "functional" reason for the existence of construction is to produce new capital goods. Thus this productive activity is, at one and the same time, subsidiary to the development of the economic forces that generate an increased demand for goods and in advance of this development insofar as it must furnish the new types of goods required for this development to occur. Since construction generates a product that is necessarily linked to a piece of land, it implies an inevitable change in the property. It thus forces the periodic readjustment of (capitalized) land rent, and even its transformation from agricultural to urban rent. Given the large sums of capital invested in construction, it is tempting to associate the mass of urban rent with the model of differential rent II. This influence is inevitable, since the concentration of capital resources aims to intensify land use ; a square metre of land with a "COS" (*coefficient d'occupation du sol*) of 12 should bring in more rent than a square metre with a COS of six.

The concentration of construction capital in certain sites does not create rent. It does, however, maximize the value of a site, which by this very fact acquires a greater value. This concentration thus strengthens the factors that make the site desirable and gives the illusion that it created them (Goux, 1980). Since, as well, these concentrations of capital are applied to the construction of buildings with highly specialized functions—high-rise residential and office buildings—they favour a functional interpretation of rent and land valorization. This epiphenomenon of construction thus greatly obscures the question of urban rent as far as its most obvious practical manifestations are concerned.

Clearly construction is an integral part of the question of urban rent, and any coherent theory of rent must also explain this particular type of production.

Functional zoning

Functional zoning is a techno-juridical practice that delimits and conditions the extraction of urban rent in various ways. On the technical level, the much discussed, and discutable, logic behind this defining and apportioning of a territory's potential uses is intended to bring into harmony different activities according to various criteria. This operation results in a plan and zoning regulations which, juridically, serve as a basis for the issuing of construction permits and, politically, contribute to decisions concerning public projects.

A zoning plan subdivides a territory into zones. The size and number of zones depends on a number of factors, including the overall size of the territory. The variety of zones depends on the zoning regulations. The principles of urban planning, in particular the idea of exclusive zones, tends to define areas according to minimal functional criteria : residential here, commercial there, industrial elsewhere, and so on. The result is more than the dividing up of the territory, since each piece is predestined for such and such a use, with such and such an intensity. Since zoning can also defer the development of some areas, it can restrain the operations of the construction industry. When zoning predates development it does not start from zero, rather it is based on previous land use and respect for acquired rights. It starts from a given state of affairs which it codifies and confirms. Hence it is easy to see the effect of zoning on rent. On the one hand it strengthens the factors behind the location of pre-existing and potentially redevelopable sites. On the other hand it apportions and determines possible locations for capital that may be invested in new urbanization.

When zoning occurs after development, it has no immediate utility, and often existing areas are not zoned. Given the massive redevelopment of old neighbourhoods and suburbs, however, this "after the fact" zoning has followed recent enthusiasm for our architectural heritage, setting territorial limits on the market in existing buildings and removing some areas from the sphere of possible redevelopment. This zoning has thus split some areas into various market categories, strengthening property values in older developed areas.

Zoning is an obvious manifestation of a relation between economic and political forces that directly influences the level of urban rent. This effect is a diverse one and is hard to evaluate because of the imponderable effects of speculation.

The land market

Property ownership in an urban area, or one that may become urbanized, is spread among a sufficiently large number of owners to constitute a market. However, this market has specific features making the operation of supply and demand problematic. Apart from the fact that elasticity of supply is only relative (that is, space is not produced according to demand), and is maintained artificially in a number of ways (addition of new areas, zoning modifications, destruction, etc.), the urban land market is structured on three levels. This complicates its operation.

The first level of structuration follows directly from the nature of the commodity in question. Each piece of property is unique because of its location, and the interchangeability of landed property is limited. The second level results from the diverse characteristics of urbanization. Because of age, form and function, each element that makes up part of an urban milieu has particular characteristics. Parity between these characteristics can only be maintained within limited groupings. The result is a formal/functional division that zoning, through rationalization, tends to strengthen and solidify. Finally, a third level of structuration follows from the fact that the market in urban property is subject to four types of demand, each with its own rules, which can be integrated only on the basis of conditions that go beyond the boundaries of the political economy of urbanization. A piece of property may be in demand for the revenue it brings in (rental), for its real estate value (investment), for its development possibilities (construction) or for its utility (occupation).

Together, the various forces that structure, and thus condition and dominate, the urban land market make up a whole that is both disparate and integrated and whose complexity is, quite frankly, tiresome. Nor does anyone doubt that the development and transformation of this market modify in return the social organization of which the market is a constituent part. The particular effect of each of these forces, whether direct or indirect, cannot even be estimated without the most detailed analysis. However, as far as the political economy of urbanization is concerned, it is certain that rent is the real question at issue behind these various phenomena. Hence the importance of understanding these elements and attempting to estimate their global importance.

Construction, zoning and the land market are not the only factors affecting urbanization, but they are the main ones. All these practices, which together make up the urban scene, appear as both the context and the result of a gigantic, Dante-esque, happening. They are a manifestation of the relation between social forces. But there is more to the urban scene. Rent, because of its economic importance, is a cause as well as an effect, since the control of rent affects a parallel redistribution of surplus value, and this is a potential source of modifications in relations among social forces. Once this is understood, we must surely admit that the backdrop to urbanization is the struggle to control and redirect this redistribution of surplus value, thus confirming that the political component of the organization of territory is a means of sociol control, operating via the control and appropriation of space.

FROM FACT TO OBJECT

At this point it is necessary to formulate a practical definition of land rent. A number of propositions provide criteria here : land rent begins where the average profit ends ; land rent does not equal the rent you pay for your appartment every month. . . Also, several conditions have emerged from our analysis so far : (1) rent is based on the exercise of private property of land ;

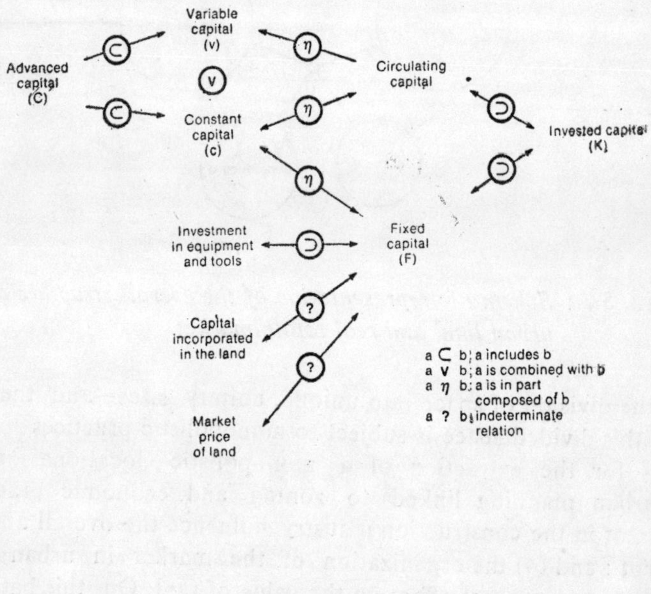

FIG. 5.1

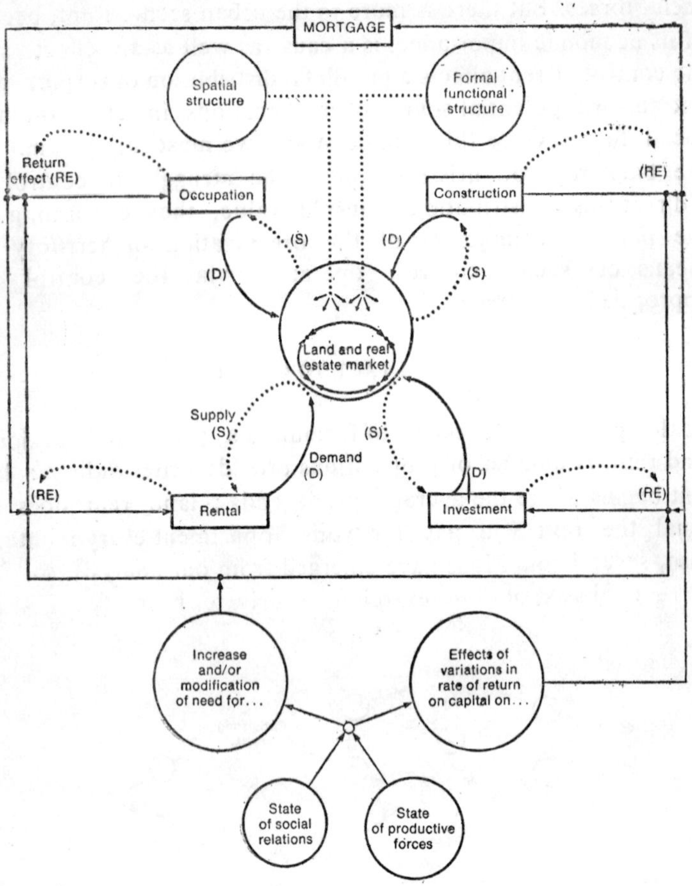

FIG. 5.2 : *Schematic representation of the overall structure of the urban land and real estate market*

(2) the division of space into unique, unitary sites—and the fact that this divided space is subject to monopolistic practices—is the basis for the extraction of a monopolistic locational rent ; (3) urban planning linked to zoning and economic practices inherent in the construction industry influence the overall amount of rent ; and (4) the organization of the market in urban land similarly has a direct effect on the value of rent. On this basis we can propose a preliminary definition : urban rent is a monopoly-

type land rent whose existence follows from two conditions—property rights and monopolistic practices—and whose mass is determined by three factors—location, utilization (type and intensity) and economic situation (demand for land).

Model of analysis

Given the unique and unitary character of any piece of landed property, given the exercise of property rights by an "individual" over any piece of landed property, given that any piece of landed property has a revenue-producing aspect (rental value), and given that any piece of landed property can be exchanged for capital (real estate value), it is possible to propose a working definition of urban rent on the level of a unit of landed property, whatever its location and utilization, on the basis of the general model establishing the relation between the value of a good and its price.

Conditional propositions :
- —urban rent exists ;
- —urban rent is monopoly rent ;
- —every piece of landed property permits the extraction of urban rent ;
- —every piece of landed property has a utilization :
- —land can be rented whatever its utilization ;
- —every service has a price of production ;
- —every price of property has a revenue-production aspect ;
- —every piece of property has a real estate aspect.

Synthesis : the urban rent brought in by a piece of landed property is equal to the difference between rental revenue and necessary operating costs, plus discounted profits on the basis of the capital value of the landed property.

A) General model

Given that : $L>P$

Where : $R=L-P$

If : $P=C+PM$

It follows that : $R=L+(C+PM)$

Where P=price of production
R=land rent
PM=average profit
L=rental revenue
C=advanced capital

B) Particular model

Normally : $PM=K^*pr$

Where K=invested capital
pr=average rate of profit

Since, on the one hand, fixed capital incorporated into the land is not invested capital and that, on the other hand, there is, strictly speaking, no production, it follows that :

$$PM=O$$

Since, however, a piece of property is exchangeable for capital and capital brings in profit according to its market value, it follows that :

$$PE=VI^*R$$

Where VI=capital value
R=discounted rate of profit
PE=discounted profits

Hence : $R=L-(C+PE)$

$R=L-(C+VI^*R)$

The general formulation thus respects our premises that land rent does not equal rental revenue, that land rent begins where profit ends and that capital incorporated in the land is not invested capital. The composition of these variables remains to be defined. If we start from the idea that house rent equals current rental income and that advanced capital covers direct operating costs, we can trace the general path taken by any real estate analysis. Certainly, a detailed definition of these items may bring up questions (for example, does one include land taxes and insurance among operating costs ?), but it cannot put into question the overall approach. On the other hand, introducing variables related to real estate value and the discounted rate of profit departs from this approach. To better understand these two components, let us examine the case of an individual summing up the situation of his property one year after acquiring it :

— first he calculates his net income (*RN*), recovering his operating costs ($L-C=RN$) ;
— then he can calculate how much his capital (*CI*) would have brought in if he had not invested in property and determine what surplus profit (or rent *R*) he has made ($RN-(CI*e)=R$) ;
— finally, considering this surplus profit has added value to his property (capitalized rent (*RC*) or landed surplus value) he can calculate the new capital value of his property ($VI=CI+RC$; $RC=R/e$) ;
— if he resells his property, he will realize the capitalized rent on top of current rent (surplus profit), and the new owner will start all over again. . . .

This situation shows that the capital value of a piece of land is simply accumulated capitalized rent, and that this depends, one, on the revenue-producing aspect of the property and, two, on the value of money capital. The problem of urban rent is thus found at the crossroads between housing (80 per cent of buildings) and the accumulation of capital (the basis of capitalist production).

To increase the model's analytical effectiveness, it is vital that other factors be added to it, in particular financing practices. Property values have the interesting quality of being buyable on margin. A purchaser need pay only a portion of the necessary capital and finance the rest with a mortgage. This time-honoured practice is now institutionalized, but it is not (yet) restricted to financial institutions. Many individuals always invest their money in this way.

Mortgage financing also underlines the illusory nature of the concept of real estate capital, which corresponds to what is only a potential reality. The capital an individual pays out to obtain a piece of landed property is divided into two parts :

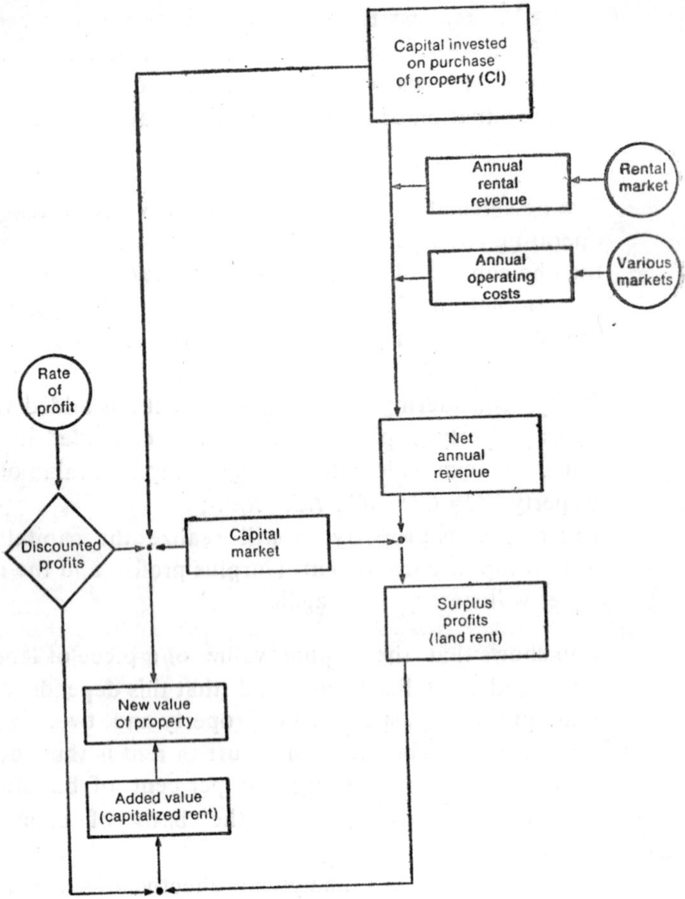

FIG. 5.3

equity, the real amount paid out, and a mortgage, i.e. a loan. Two types of rules determine a mortgage loan, those concerning financial costs (interest, which depends on the interest rate and the period determined for amortizing the loan), and those concerning the term (the arrangements for repaying the principal). The combination of these two conditions give rise to a multiplicity of possibilities that greatly complicate dealing with what are nonetheless pieces of factual information. In terms of refining

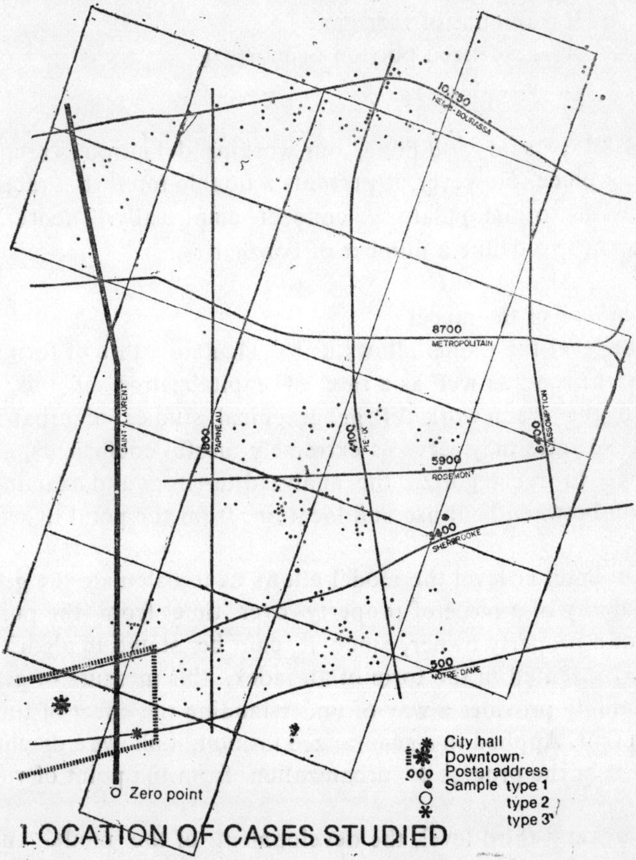

FIG. 5.4 : *Location of cases studied*

our model, only the rate of interest, the amortization period and the term constitute parametric variables. Since mortgage interest is paid out of rent, it is necessary to distinguish between gross and net rent, and since profits are calculated on capital that is actually paid out, which is less, the definition must be corrected :

$$RB = L - [C + R(E + A)]$$
$$RN = L - [C + R(E + A) + i(H - A)]$$

Where i=rate of mortgage interest
H=amount of mortgage
A=amortized portion of mortgage
E=equity

When all is said and done, our working definition is relatively commonplace. However, it presents a double interest. Practically it allows us to manipulate the concept empirically. Theoretically it allows us to define a number of corollaries.

Implications of the model

On one level the model allows us to calculate a rate of formation of current rent, as well as a rate of capitalization of this rent. Within the framework of geographical studies of urban rent, these two rates may serve as extremely useful coefficients, allowing one to recategorize the analyzed territory and examine the relation between land use and location from the point of view of rent.

On another level the model allows us to calculate the general profitability of a piece of property over time from the point of view of a property owner, since it can be stated in algorithmic form. Presented in the form of an index, this measure of general profitability provides a way of understanding the effect of time on urban rent. Applied in a generalized fashion, it allows a diachronic analysis of the process of urbanization from the point of view of rent.

On yet a third level, the development of the model enables us to examine the relation between profitability and the value of money capital as manifested in the rate of mortgage interest and the average rate of profit. Such questions are of "capital" interest to the political economy of urbanization.

The effects of time, economic situation and mortgage financing

Given a period of time of "n" years ; for each of these years a piece of property brings in a certain amount of rent and, depending on the discounted rate of profit, for each of these years the property will have a certain real estate value. However, while current rent is collected each year, the capitalized rent that is the basis of real estate value is only realized when the property is resold, that is, in our example, at the end of year "n". Thus current rent takes the form of a current asset, while capitalized rent takes the form of a fixed asset. Now normally current and fixed assets are not added together, but nothing prevents us from calculating, for purposes of comparison, an index of profitability on the basis of the average value of current rent during "n" years and the value of capitalized rent at the end of the "n" th year. Therefore, without mortgage financing :

$$Gn = \frac{1}{nCl_0}\left[\left(\sum_{i=1}^{n} R_i\right) + \frac{Rn}{en}\right]$$

(Profitability index)

with mortgage financing :

$$G'_n = \frac{1}{nCA_n}\left[\sum_{i=1}^{h} RN_i + \frac{RN_n}{en}\right)$$

where $CA_n = E \div \sum_{i=1}^{n} Ai$

If we postulate as constant the annual current rent and the discounted rate of profit, it follows that :

$G_n < G(_{n-1})$

Similarly, if we postulate that $i=e$, as $CA_n <= Cl_0$, it follows that :

$G_n <= G'_n$ (equality occurs when the mortgages is repaid, everything else being equal)

Lastly, if $e_n > e_n - 1$, it follows that :

$G_n < G_n - 1$

It becomes apparent that :

1° time represents a structural factor implying a tendency for the rate of profitability to drop, the elimination or reversal of which implies a constant increase in rent. This can only result from a constant increase in rental income and/or minimizing of operating costs ;

2° the general method of mortgage financing increases the profitability of a piece of property but strengthens the structural tendency for it to drop ;

3° the situation of the economy, which determines the value of the parametric variable "e" (discounted rate of profit), has an inversely proportional effect on the overall value of rent.

The effects of land rent on urbanization as understood in the light of the formal variations examined here would appear to be of the utmost importance. The generalization of easily accessible mortgage financing, in particular, not only multiplies the investment capacity of landowners, but also gives real estate capital a semblance of mobility. The result is a division of rent between owner and lender of mortgage funding. Since financing increases the relative profitability of a piece of property, however, the property owner loses nothing by transfering a portion of his rental income to the lender, on the contrary. However, since this practice accentuates the tendency for rent to fall over time, it inevitably entails a constant pressure to raise current rental revenue and lower operating costs. This means decreasing building maintenance and increased deterioration. Only the rate of profit can establish a potentially stabilizing bridge between urbanization and capitalization, by reducing the value of capitalized rent relative to that of capital and thus, according to the economic situation, contributing to minimizing the demand for property.

FROM OBJECT TO FACT

The working definition of a concept acquires its full significance when it is applied to reality. To judge the efficacy of our model, we tested it within the context of a subsidized research project.

Objectives

The model was applied to real data in order to evaluate :

1) its sensitivity to various factors ;
2) its capacity to distinguish between their effects ;
3) its reliability.

Measures taken

As mentioned earlier, the model makes use of simple, even commonplace, mathematical logic. It links a series of variables and conditions, which, together, give a quantitative understanding of urban rent from three, interdependent perspectives, in the form of two coefficients and one index : a coefficient of formation of current rent ; a coefficient of capitalization of rent ; and a general index of profitability. In practice it became clear that it is also useful to integrate a definition of gross revenue in order to facilitate the calculation of real estate value. As well, it was necessary to calculate the general index solely on the basis of current year figures, since figures for previous years were for all intents and purposes unobtainable.

Our working definition departs from usual practice in the fact that it makes use of a parametric variable which, without being discontinuous, poses a number of problems of evaluation that can give rise to arbitrary and discretionary choices. Unlike common practice, which proceeds from a schema based on "amortization", "capitalization", "depreciation" or "actualization", the model makes use of an uncommon notion, "discounted profits". This option was chosen in order to satisfy both the theoretical requirement posed by the idea that "rent begins where average profit ends" and the practice according to which a piece of property can always be exchanged for capital, whose return can always be calculated, depending on the types of possible investment. While the choice of an adequate value for the variable is difficult, it is no more complex than choosing a rate of capitalization or actualization. What is more, this coefficient establishes a direct link between urban rent and the economy in general, the question of rent being subordinated to the economy, since the "discounted rate of profit" ultimately depends on the value of capital at a given time and place.

Similarly, the actual measurement of capitalized rent does not correspond exactly to that proposed earlier. Nonetheless, the final result remains the same. The measurement quantifies the value of a piece of property in which land and building are taken as a whole according to the gross return the property brings in. This approach is necessary because the initial value of capital put into construction loses its significance with time. This capitalized rent, recoverable only if the property is sold or refinanced, should more or less correspond to the price of the property on the real estate market, notwithstanding any particular conditions that might give rise to "speculative" rent related to potential use of the land. If this way of measuring rent can be verified empirically, it will be a useful instrumental addition to the field.

The synthetic index of profitability establishes a sort of balance sheet of the profitability of a property from the owner's point of view. Therefore it takes into account both current rent and the capitalized rent that the owner has collected or intends to collect. As mentioned, our definition of this index perhaps comes close to accounting heresy, amalgamating current and fixed assets, but nonetheless it clearly expresses the real money income the exploitation of a property brings to its owner. The index is particularly sensitive to time and to the situation of the economy as a whole.

The measures made were as follows, on the basis of annual operation without mortgage financing :

— The return, $RD=L-C$

Where L=real rental income

C=operating expenses requiring an outlay of capital

— Current urban rent, $RU=L-C-PE=CI*e$

Where PE=discounted profits

CI=invested capital

e=otherwise discounted profits

— Capitalized rent, $RC=\frac{RU}{e}$, such that real estate value $VI=CI+RC$.

— *Or*, total capitalized rent equals real estate value such that :

$$VI=RC=\frac{RD}{e}$$

— Coefficient of formation of urban rent,

$$ru=\frac{RU}{CI}$$

— Coefficient of capitalization

$$rc=\frac{RC}{CI}$$

— General index of profitability,

$$IG=\frac{RU}{nCI}\left(1-\frac{1}{e}\right)=\frac{1}{n}\,ru\left(1+\frac{1}{e}\right)$$

Variables used

The first set of variables, which can be called factual, characterize the property concerned. They include current gross income (L), annual operating costs constituting advanced capital (C), and the capital equivalent of the property at the moment it was acquired (CI). This last given is invariable unless the property has been mortgaged. In this case it is equivalent to the equity paid out (E) plus the mortgage (H). But, according to the terms of the loan, the amount of the mortgage will diminish over time to equal the non-amortized principal (P), while the equity will increase each year by the amortized principal (A). Hence :

$$CI=\left[E+\left(\sum_{i=P}^{n}A_i\right)\right]+\left[H-\left(\sum_{i=1}^{n}A_i\right)\right]$$

where $CA_n=E+\sum_{i=1}^{n}A_i$

and $P_n=H-\sum_{i=1}^{n}A_i$

To sum up, then, two types of factual variables describe a piece of property, those concerning how it is operated and those concerning its financing.

The second set of variables, which can be called parametric, bring in external factors : the discounted rate of profit (e) and the rate of mortgage interest (i). Their values depend on the economic situation as a whole and, in theory, this should be the same no matter what property or property owner is being considered. In practice that is not the case. Mortgage rates can be negotiated and discounted profits aren't necessarily the same for everyone.

A last set includes conditional variables, that is, those over which there is no control. Our schema only makes explicit use of one, time (n), but implicitly includes at least two others, location (l) and utilization (u), In fact, location is the number one factor in the collection of urban rent, and the specific utilization of a piece of property depends on the infrastructures present, the zoning, the real or potential COS, and so on.

Treatment

The operational treatment was defined according to two different approaches involving two kinds of data :

1) To evaluate the model's efficacity, it was applied to an organized body of factual information. The purpose was to examine the effects of various factors and, therefore, the model's ability to isolate them ;
2) To estimate the structural and/or contingent effects of the parametric variables (time "n", rate of profit "e", and mortgage financing), the model was applied to a particular real case. By modifying the values of variables whose fluctuations are minimal, the intent was to show the pertinence of using these variables.

Data

The source of all data was the *Multiple Listing System* (MLS) of the Chambre d' Immeubles de Montreal. The data concerned properties sold in 1979, and the MLS listings provided all the necessary information concerning rental revenue, operating costs, financial costs, and asking price, not to mention physical description, type of building, location, use, size and so on. Information concerning mortgage financing was correlated with data from another source, Teela Survey Market Ltd. abstracts. In case of disagreement, a third, definitive source was used, the registration office of the judicial district.

The idea was to amass sufficient information to carry out a pilot project that could test the applicability of the model. The information was collected* by choosing from the MLS listings 270 pieces of property that satisfied both the criterion of

* The work was carried out as part of a FCAC research project. An interim report was published in December, 1979.

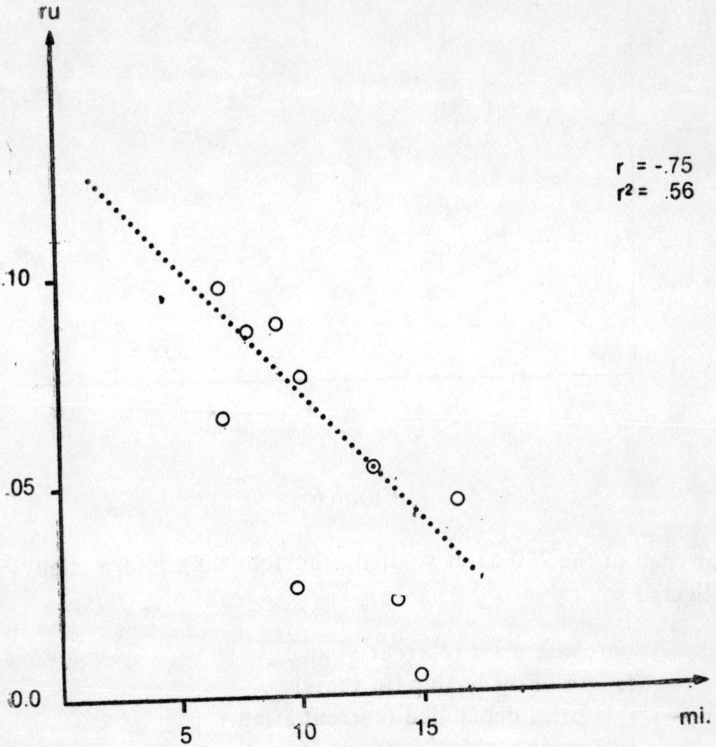

FIG. 5.5

location and that of size as indicated on the following table and map.

Size of study (number of dwellings)[1]

Location[2]	2—3	4—5	6—11	
SOUTH	30	30	30	90
CENTRE	30	30	30	90
NORTH	30	30	30	90
TOTAL	90	90	90	270

Source : 1. Categories estimated by the City of Montreal for taxation purposes.
2. MLS categories.

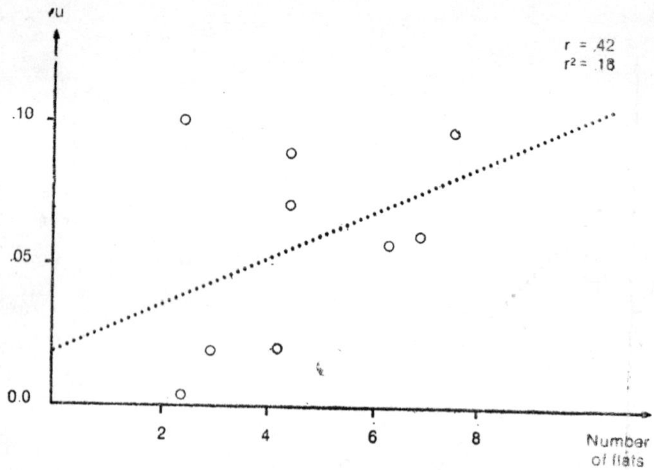

FIG. 5.6

For each of the 270 cases studied, the following information was collected :

- purchase price (current $Can.)
- length of ownership (in years)
- sale price demanded (current $Can.)
- sale price realized (current $Can.)
- number of dwelling units
- address
- estimated distance from a zero point (in miles)*
- annual income (current $Can.)
- annual operating costs (current $Can.)
- initial mortgage (current $Can.)

and if applicable :

- amount of equity
- rate of interest
- amortization period and term of mortgage (in appendix).

* The zero point chosen was that used by Montreal municipal addresses, the corner of St. Laurent and des Commissaries streets.

Since each of the nine categories presented interior variation lower than that between categories, the 270 cases were reduced to nine, each typical of their categories in terms of certain variables. This reduction, required for practical purposes, cannot influence the results given the objectives of the study. The choice of typical examples of data concerning mortgage financing was more difficult for several reasons, including an insufficient number of cases, a great variation in conditions, accumulation of two or even three mortgages, refinancing without an equity payment, and so on. Also, it was necessary to determine a profile of financing by category and then apply it to 1979 data. The following tables give the information retained.

TABLE 5.1 : **The average profile of the nine types of landed property representative of the 270 cases without mortgage financing**

Category Area	2—3 dwellings	4—5 dwellings	6—11 dwellings
South	1) 621	1,049	1,624
	2) 3,973 (2.5)	6,522 (4.5)	9,634 (7.6)
	3) 14,987 (14.2)	27,317 (9.8)	37,539 (8.9)
	4) 24,833 (5.8)	31,500 (6.2)	NA (7.6)
Centre	1) 1,037	1,450	2,171
	2) 4,331 (2.5)	7,642 (4.4)	11,574 (6.9)
	3) 22,067 (1.2)	31,824 (11.7)	49,968 (7.5)
	4) 37,700 (10.1)	50,214 (10.6)	84,100 (11.7)
North	1) 1,303	1,992	2,178
	2) 5,271 (2.3)	8,771 (4.2)	11,984 (6.7)
	3) 30,965 (8.1)	45,810 (7.9)	53,495 (5.8)
	4) 48,062 (14.9)	65,687 (14.6)	92,417 (15.2)

1) Expenditure ($).
2) Income ($) and average number of appartments ( ).
3) Purchase price ($) and length of possession in years ( ).
4) Real sale price ($) and distance in miles ( ).

As for the particular case used in the second half of the treatment, the data used was also taken from the MLS as indicated in Table 5.3.

Results

The following two tables show the values obtained from the

TABLE 5.2 : **The conditions of mortgage financing for each of the nine types**

Category Area		2—3 dwellings	4—5 dwellings	6—11 dwellings
South	1)	11,880 (10)	20,971 (19)	32,484 (22)
	2)	3,106	6,343	5,055
	3)	10.9	10.35	11.31
	4)	12.2 (0)	18,97 (9)	18.75 (10)
Centre	1)	17,393 (16)	22,592 (18)	35,838 (19)
	2)	4,674	9,232	14,130
	3)	11.2	10.69	10.86
	4)	21.4 (9)	21.6 (10)	23.07 (16)
North	1)	24,253 (18)	37,038 (23)	37,504 (21)
	2)	6,712	8,772	15,991
	3)	10.27	10.90	10.60
	4)	21.25 (13)	25.95 (18)	21.97 (16)

1) Amount of mortgage and number of cases with at least one mortgage ( ).
2) Equity.
3) Rate of interest in %.
4) Period of amortization and length of mortgage in 1979 ( ).

TABLE 5.3 : **Data concerning a income-producing building situated in Montreal and chosen at random for the study**

A) Permanent features	B) 1979 information	
Utilization : residential	Operating costs** :	$ 57,799
Age of building : 10 years	Current income :	$147,000
Number of dwellings : 60	Purchase price* :	$550,000
Surface area of building : 9,112 sq. ft. at ground level	Asking price ;	$670,000
Number of floors : 5	Mortgage :	$450,000
Surface area of land : 9,112 sq. ft.	Interest rate ;	10.25%
Occupation coefficient : 5	Amortization :	23 years

Source : *Multiple Listing Service* (MLS). Chambre d' immeubles de Montreal.

* This data is an estimate or derived from other data.

**Taxes and insurance : $35,462 ; maintenance : $4,000.

various calculations made concerning the nine test-cases, with and without mortgage financing. For the purposes of these calculations, the value "e" was set at 0.125, which corresponds to a rate of profit on capital of 12.5 per cent. Mortgage financing was treated as a new mortgage, that is, without amortization of capital and at the highest interest rates.

TABLE 5.4 : **Results of calculations without mortgage**

Category Area	2—3 dwellings	4—5 dwellings	6—11 dwellings
South	1) .10	.08	.09
	2) .79	.60	.71
	3) .06	.07	.09
	4) +8% (3)	+39% (6)	? (0)
Centre	1) .02	.07	.06
	2) .19	.56	.51
	3) .02	.05	.08
	4) —30% (10)	—1% (7)	—9% (5)
North	1) .003	.02	.06
	2) .03	.18	.47
	3) .003	.03	.09
	4) —34% (4)	—17% (5)	—15% (6)

1) Coefficient of formation of current rent "*ru*".
2) Coefficient of formation of capitalized rent "*rc*".
3) General index of profitability *G*.
4) Relative effectiveness of model at predicting market value *v* in percentage ; in parentheses, number of sales.

As for the particular case, it was submitted to four simulations :

1) value of the general index of profitability for n=1, 2, 3, 4, 5, 10, 15, and 20, all other factors being equal, without mortgage financing, with e=.125.
2) value of the general index of profitability for n=1, 2, 3, 4, 5, 10, 15, and 20, all other factors being equal, but with mortgage financing, with e=.125.
3) value of the general index of profitability for i=.05, .08, .10, .13, .18, .20, and .25, all other factors being equal, with n=1 and for e=.125.

4) value of the general index of profitability for e=.05, .08, .10, .13, .18, .20, and .25, all other factors being equal, with n=1 and for i=.1025.

TABLE 5.5 : **Results of calculations with mortgage**

Category Area	2—3 dwellings	4—5 dwellings	6—11 dwellings
South	1) .54 2) 4.30 3) .34	.40 3.17 .37	.73 5.86 .74
Centre	1) .16 2) 1.30 3) .12	.28 2.27 .22	.27 2.12 .32
North	1) .10 2) .76 3) .11	.19 1.50 .21	.24 1.92 .37

1) Coefficient of formation of current rent "*ru*",
2) Coefficient of formation of capitalized rent "*rc*".
3) General index of profitability.

Tables 5.6 and 5.7 show the results of these calculations.

TABLE 5.6 : **Effect of time alone and combined effect of time and mortgage financing on the general index of profitability**

Time n for e=.12 and i=.1025

General index of profitability	1	2	3	4	5	10	15	20
G with mortgage	.99	.49	.33	.25	.20	.10	.07	.05
G' without mortgage	6.01	1.77	1.13	.81	.62	.24	.11	.05

Analysis

Location and intensity of occupation

As the graphs here indicate, the model shows that location has a greater effect on the formation of current rent than does intensity of use, given roughly equivalent amounts (from one to three times).

It would therefore appear that, statistically, location explains a little more than 50 per cent of the variation observed in the

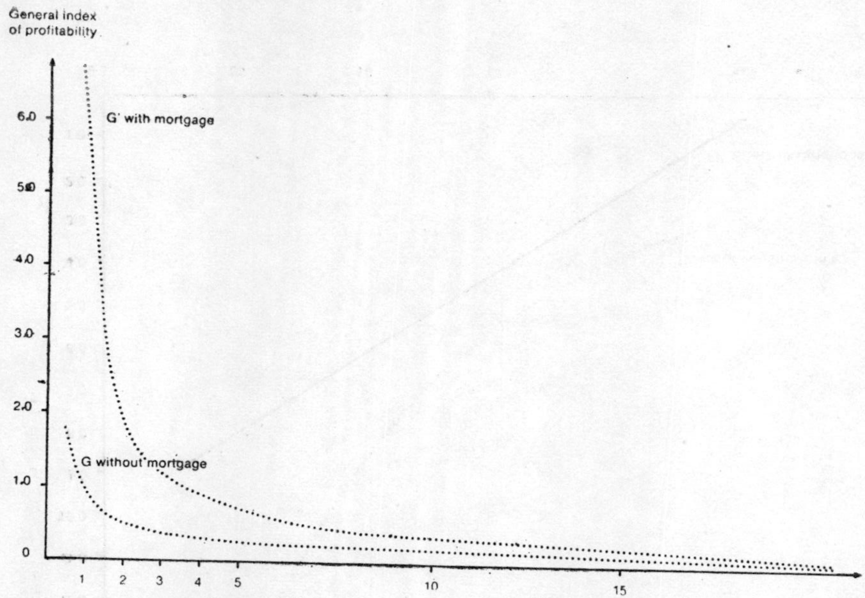

FIG. 5.7 : *Effect of time, with and without mortgage financing on the general index of profitability*

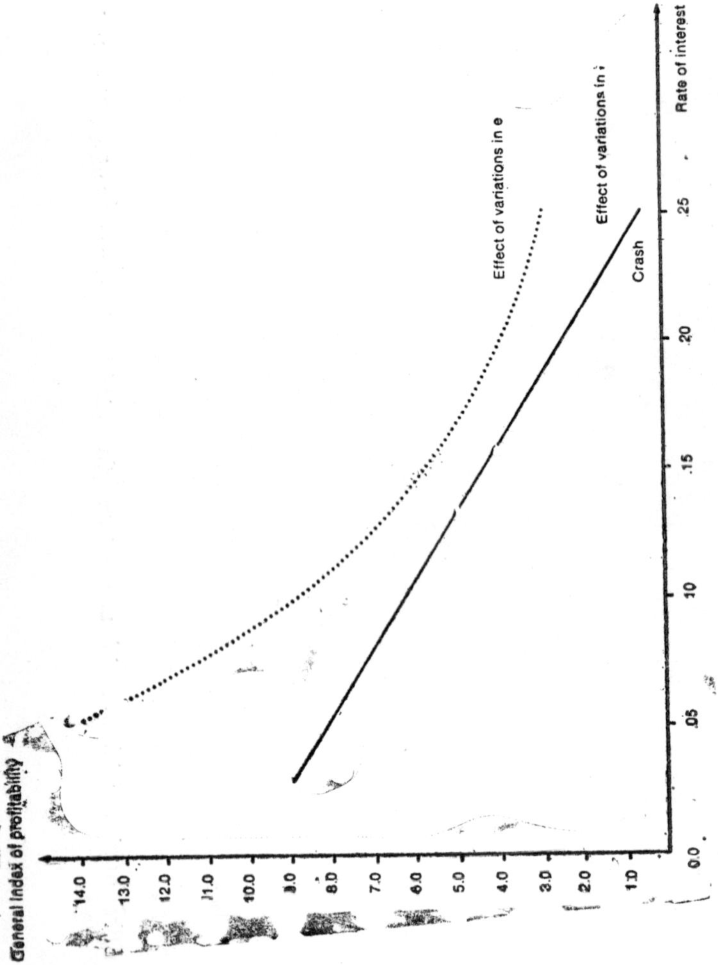

FIG. 5.8 : *Effect of the situation of economy on the general index of profitability*

TABLE 5.7 : **Effect of the discounted rate of profit and effect of mortgage interest rate on the general index of profitability**

For $n=1$

General index of profitability	0.5	0.8	.10	.18	.20	.25
	Value of discounted rate of profit e, for $i=.1025$					
G'	14.07	9.05	7.37	4.39	4.02	3.35
	Value of rate of mortgage interest i, for $e=.125$					
G'	8.01	6.85	6.08	3.00	2.23	.30

formation of both current and capitalized rent, while intensity of occupation explains a little less than 20 per cent. Thus these results correlate with previous conclusions.

Mortgage financing

When mortgage financing is taken into account, its importance is immediately evident. It increases the coefficients dramatically, as the following table shows. The magnitude of its effects make it, more than any other factor, a key aspect of the question of urban rent.

Multiplier effect of mortgage financing

Area \ Dwellings		2—3	4—6	6—11
South	1)	5.40	5.00	8.11
	2)	5.44	5.28	8.25
	3)	5.67	5.29	8.22
Centre	1)	8.00	4.00	4.50
	2)	6.84	4.05	4.16
	3)	6.00	4.40	4.00
North	1)	33.33	9.50	4.00
	2)	25.33	8.33	4.09
	3)	36.67	7.00	4.11

1) On the coefficient of formation of urban rent.
2) On the coefficient of formation of capitalized rent.
3) On the general index of profitability.

Parametric variables n, e and i
As the next graph shows, over time there is a tendency for rent to fall, and this tendency can be considered structural. While this effect is small in itself, mortgage financing increases it. Since mortgage financing is becoming a general practice, it too can be considered a structural factor.

Parameters "*e*" and "*i*" bring to the model the effects of the general economic situation on the formation of rent. In current economic circumstances, variations in these parameters are minimal. This is fortunate, since, as the following graph shows, they can have enormous effects. It can be seen that an increase in interest rates to the 25 per cent level or higher would necessarily entail a drop in the level of rent and with it the collapse of the real estate market. Since variations in the two parameters go together, their effects reinforce each other, so probably the critical level is below 25 per cent, in other words, around the levels the economy went through in 1982.

Interpretation

The model's effectiveness
Overall, the model would appear effective enough to trace the effects of the main factors influencing the formation of rent. The general index should prove a practical tool for any general study aimed at consolidating our understanding of the political economy of urbanization. The coefficients themselves should aid in geographical analyses of the urban reality. On the level of the particular unit, the model does not appear to be reliable, since the variations in its predictions of market value are too great.

Rent, urbanization and the economy
While the restricted size of our study limits the significance of any overall conclusions that can be drawn from it, a number of points should be made :

— urban rent implies a convergence of interests between landowners and financiers the moment a piece of property is mortgaged. The landowner hands over a significant proportion of current rent to the financier, who in return is responsible for the greater part of the capital investment. Thus the owner benefits from increased profitability while the financier has a stable, longterm and troublefree investment. This situation probably expresses a change in political relations.

— The generalization of mortgage financing that has occurred since the end of the 19th century has probably had three major effects on urbanization and the economy in general, via rent. By freeing landowners from the obligation to provide the total capital necessary to acquire a piece of property, mortgage financing kept a significant amount of private capital in circulation, thus multiplying investment possibilities. But, since mortgage financing also accentuates the structural tendency for rent to fall, it is very probable that it is behind a constant, dizzying rise in housing rents as well as an increased frequency of changes in ownership. Now these two results must in turn influence general economic development. Increased housing rents must necessarily have an effect on productivity, via wages, and changes in ownership drain off an increasing proportion of society's surplus value, since they involve the actualization of capitalized rent. It would be extremely interesting to attempt to evaluate what proportion of inflation is due to mortgage financing, via urban rent.

— While the determination of the discounted rate of profit and mortgage interest rates is not solely dependent on the good will of financial agents, they clearly play a role in the process. This implies, therefore, that they control in part fluctuations in the two variables that have the most effect on rent formation. Three things follow from this. The financial agents are both judge and beneficiary in the question of urban rent. As a result they are constantly faced with a dilemma. Via the phenomenon of urban rent, the whole of the urban phenomena has come under the sway of banking capital, the main source of mortgage financing.

These observations dovetail with the predictions of American analysts. The main levers of control over urban questions are, thanks to rent, out of the reach of municipal authorities, coming under economic influences of international proportions.

Rent and money

In the first part of this study, we attempted to evaluate the amount of capital involved in the redevelopment of Montreal. At this point, we propose the following approach in order to evaluate the sums involved in the phenomenon of rent. If we estimate the value of housing in Montreal alone, according to the assessment rolls, at about $6 billion ($Can), and if we apply the model, using parameters derived from our case studies to provide missing data, we see that during 1983, housing property incurred costs on the order of $200 million and brought in rental income of approximately $1.5 billion. This implies, therefore, the redistribution of some $750 million to the landlords in the form of discounted profits and $660 million in the form of urban rent, notwithstanding the form of mortgage financing. With the same logic, realizable capitalized rent would also be on the order of $6 billion. This is a large sum compared to the meagre $1.2 billion to be spent by the city in 1983. While these estimates may be imprecise, the incredible dimensions of the sums in question demand that the subject be studied systematically.

CONCLUSION

At the end of this investigation, one has the impression that while everything has not been said, neither has anything been left out. A look back reveals the contradiction inherent in a study that has been carried through but which remains incomplete. So many problems, imprecisions, and weaknesses remain that our patiently constructed edifice appears rather fragile. Everything should be begun again ; each analysis should be redone. Like a city, it remains ever unfinished.

The goal pursued throughout this reflection has been to examine the"profit and loss" of several years work on the question of rent. The aim has not been to convince anyone or prove anything, just to retrace the road taken. This wandering has obviously rekindled interest, and taken on the allure of a crusade. Why has a question as crucial as rent never raised interest equivalent to its impotance ? Why are obscure research assistants the only ones fascinated by it ? Certainly the more prestigious in the world of knowledge touch on the question, but they refuse to take it on completely. A Byzantine ignorance reigns supreme, masquerading as knowledge.

The city we have been building for a hundred years now is the incarnation of our values, ideals and beliefs. In its contemporary form it clearly shows, or so it would seem, the place that science, technology and reason occupy in our culture. But behind these obvious, and official, manifestations, the city incarnates the power and omniscience of money, that cultureless form, equivalent to everything and nothing. Ultimately, urban rent operates on this level of significance. On the scale of the enormous transactions involved, men are but bits of information, or less, since money is the only object of such transactions. When one thinks about it like the skyscrapers, all the speeches are meant to plug up the hole that rent has dug for money. Perhaps we are straying close to forbidden territory . . . .

Note : The information concerning the estimate of Montreal's housing stocks comes from the Service de l 'evaluation fonciere de la Communaute urbaine de Montreal (CUM). More precisely, in 1983 :

— the total value of building stocks in the CUM was approximately \$40 billion (\$Can) ;
— the total valve of building stocks in Montreal was approximately \$22 billion (\$Can) ;
— the value of residential housing stocks alone in Montreal was \$6,673,700,000.00 (\$Can).

REFERENCES

Alberts, W. (1944), *Rapport preliminaire au plan directeur*, Montreal, Service d'urbanisme.

Alberts, W. (1962), 'Business cycles, residential cycles, and the mortgage market', in *Journal of Political Economy*, LXX.

Alonso, W. (1960), 'A theory of urban land market', in *Papers and Proceedings of the Regional Science Association*, VI, pp. 149-157.

Alonso, W. (1964), *Location and Land Use*, Cambridge, Harvard University Press.

Alquier, F. (1971), 'Contribution a l'etude de la rente fonciere sur les terrains urbains', in *Espaces et societes*, 2, pp. 75-87.

Aubin, H. (1977), *Les vrais proprietaires de Montreal*, L'Etincelle, Montreal.

Barker, G. *et al.* (1973), 'The developers : an introduction by the authors', in *Canadian Dimension*, IX-2,

Baudrillard, J. (1972), *Pour une critique de l'economie politique du signe*, Gallimard, Paris.

Bergeron, L. et Bouvette, A. (1977), 'Pertinence de la question de la rente dans la construction d'une problematique de l'histoire de l'urbanisation', in *Notes de travail*, Montreal, Centre de recherches et d'innovation urbaines (C.R.I.U.), Universite de Montreal.

Berry, B.J.L. et Garrison, W.L. (1958), 'The functionnal bases of the central place hierarchy' in *Economic Geography*, Vol. 34-2, pp. 145-154.

Berry, B.J.L. (1964), 'Cities as system within systemal cities', in *Papers and proceedings of regional science association*, Vol. 13, pp. 151-155.

Berry, B.J.L. (1965), 'Internal structure of the city', in *Law and Contemprary Problems*, XXX Winter, p. 115.

Bertrand, J.P. (1978), Chronologie de mise en marche de materiaux et produits de la construction aux XIXe et XXe siecles, Rapp. recherche, C.R.I.U., Universite de Montreal.

Blumenfeld, H. (1955), 'The Economic base of the Metropolis', in *Journal of American Institute of Planners*, Vol. 21.

Bogue, D.J. (1949), *The structure of the Metropolitan Community*, Ann Arbor, University of Michigan Press.

Burgess, E.W. et Bogue, D.J. (1964), 'Research in urban society : a long view' in Burgess E.W. and Bogue, D.J. (ed.), Contributions to *Urban Sociology*, Chicago, The University of Chicago Press.

Burgess, E.W. (1925), 'The growth of the city : an introduction to research project' in Park R.E. et Burgess, E.W. (eds.), *The City*, Chicago, University of Chicago (1967).

Castells, M. (1968), 'Y a-t-il une sociologie urbaine ?' in *Sociologie du travail*, n° 1, pp. 72-90.

Castells, M. (1969), 'Theorie et ideologie en sociologie urbaine', in *Sociologie et Societes*, 1-2, pp. 171-190.

Castells, M. (1972), *La question urbaine*, Maspero (1977), Paris.

Chapin (Jr.) F.S. et Kaiser, Ed. J. (1979), *Urban Land Use Planning*, Urbana III, University of Illinois Press (3ieme edition, lere publication 1957).

Chapin (Jr.) F.S. *et al.* (1962), *Urban growth dynamics in a regional cluster of cities*, Wiley, New York.

Chobart De Lauwe, P. (1963), *Des hommes et des villes*, Payot, Paris.

Claval, P. (1973), *Principes de geographie sociale*, M. Th. Genin, Paris.

Claval, P. (1980), *Elements de geographie humaine*, Librairie technique, Paris.

Decarie, J. *et al.* (1977), *Le concept de reserves ecologiques : origine, signification et portee*, Montreal, Centre de recherches et d'innovation urbaines (C.R.I.U.), Universite de Montreal.

Downs, A. (1975), 'Real estate trends and their implications for property management' in *Journal of Property Management*, Sep.-Oct.

Downs, A. (1975), 'The real estate out look through mid-1976' in *Real Estate Review*, V-2.

Downs, A. (1976), 'Investing in thausing rehabilitation can be successful', in *Real Estate Review*, VI-2.

Durivage, L. *et al.* (1978), 'Histoire du quartier Rosemont, 1900-1920', in

Notes de travail, Montreal, Centre de recherches et d'innovation urbaines (C.R.I.U.), Universite de Montreal.

Durivage, L. *et al.* (1980), *Les origines de Rosemont*, Montreal, Comite de logement de Rosemont.

Fisette, J. et Quirion, D. (1978), *La rente fonciere urbaine*, Centre de recherches et d'innovation urbaines (C.R.I.U.), Universite de Montreal.

Foggin, P. et Polese, M. (1975), *La geographie sociale de Montreal en 1971*, Presses de l'Universite du Quebec, Montreal.

Gaudreau, G. (1978), 'Les politiques forestieres et de concession de force hydraulique, Quebec 1877-1910', in *Notes de travail*, Centre de recherches et d'innovation urbaines (C.R.I.U.), Universite de Montreal.

Gaudreau, G. (1979), 'Le rapport agriculture-foret au Quebec : note historiographique', dans *Notes de travail*, Centre de recherches et d'innovation urbaines (C.R.I.U.), Universite de Montreal.

Goux, J.F. (1980), *Fondements et generalisation de la loi de densite de C. Clark*, Universite de St-Etienne.

Guttentag, J.M. (1961), 'Short cycles in residential construction 1946-1959', in *American Economical Review*, LI.

Harnecker, M. (1974), *Les concepts elementaires du materialisme historique*, Contradictions, Bruxelles.

Harris, B. (1966), 'The uses of theory in the simulation or urban phenomena', in *Journal of American Institute of Planners*, XXXI-5, November.

Harris, B. (1968), 'Quantitative models of urban development : their role in metropolitan policy-making', in *Issues in Urban Economics*, Resource for the future, H. Perloff et L. Wings (ed.), Washington D.C.

Harvey, D. (1976), 'L'economic politique de l'urbanisation aux Etats-Unis', dans *Espaces et Societes*, pp. 17-18, 5-42.

Hauser, Pl. M. (1958), 'On impact of urbanism on social organization, human nature and the political order', in *Confluence*, VII Spring 58, pp. 57-69.

Heller, Agnes (1978), *La theorie des besoins chez Marx*, Union generale d'edition, Coll. 10-18, Paris.

Hill, M.D. (1965), 'A growth allocation model for the Boston region', in *Journal of American Institute of Planners*, XXXI-2, May, pp. 111-120.

Hoyt, H. (1939), *The structure and growth of residential neighborhoods in American Cities*, Federal Housing Administration, Washington D.C.

Jensen, H. (1967), 'Real estates quest for capital', in *Urban Land*, June.

Jensen, H. (1971), 'The changing world of real estate finance', in *Urban Land*, June.

Krifa, H. (1979), 'Le debat C. Topalov—A. Lipietz', *Revue d'economie regionale et urbaine*, n° 2, pp. 213-225.

Lavigne, G. *et al.* (1876), 'Development urbain et patrimoine architectural', in *Notes de travail*, Montreal, Centre de recherches et d'innovation urbaines (C.R.I.U.), Universite de Montreal.

Lavigne, G. (1979), *La formation d'un quartier ethnique : les Portuguais a Montreal* (these Ph.D.), Universite de Montreal.

Legare, J, (1965), 'La population juive de Montreal est-elle victime d'une segregation qu'elle se serait elle-meme imposee ?', in *Recherches socio-*

graphiques, IV-3, pp. 311-325.

Lipietz, A. (1974), *Le tribut foncier urbain*, Maspero, Paris.

Lipietz, A. (1981), 'Un procede de rhetorique', in *Etudes foncieres*.

Lojkine, J. (1971), 'Y a-t-il une rente fonciere urbaine ?' in *Espace et societe*, 2, pp. 89-94.

Long, C.D. (1940), *Building Cycles and the Theory of Investment*, Princeton University Press.

Lowry, I.S. (1965), 'A short course in model design', in *Journal of American Institute of Planners*, XXI-2, May.

Malinowski, Bronislaw, *A Scientific Theory of Culture*, University of North Carolina Press, Chapel Hill, 1944.

Malinowski, B., cf. *Encyclopaedia Universalis* (1968), France SA, rubrique, bibl. et correlats.

Marx, Karl, *Capital* (in three volumes), International Publishers, New York, 1967.

Marx, and Engels, *Selected Correspondence*, Foreign Languages Publishing House, Moscow.

McMahan, J. (1976), 'The post war development boom : real estate rides high', in *Real Estate Review*, VI-2.

McMahan, J. (1976), 'America urbanizes : the twentieth century transition', in *Real Estate Review*, VI-1.

McMahan, J. (1976), 'Land for all : an history of U.S. real estate to 1900', in *Real Estate Review*, V-4.

Murphy, R.E. (1966), *The American City : an urban geography*, McGraw Hill, New York.

Park, R.E. (1936), 'Human Ecology', in Theodorson G.A. (ed.), *Studies in human sociology*, Harper and Row, 1961, New York.

Park, R.E. et Burgess, E.W. (ed.) (1924), *Introduction to the social sciences*, Greenwood, New York.

Park, R.E. (1925), 'The city : suggestions for the investigation of human behavior in the urban environment', in Park R.E. and Burgess E.W. (eds.), *The City*, University of Chicago Press (1967).

Park, R.E. (1926), 'The urban community as a special pattern and a moral order', in Burgess E.W. (ed.), *The Urban Community*, University of Chicago Press (1971).

Park, R.E. (1929), 'The city as a social laboratory', in Smith, T.V. and White, L.D. (eds.), *Chicago an experimental in social science research*, Greenwood (1968), New York.

Pearson, K. (1971), 'Big business discovers real estate' in *Michigan Business Review*, March.

Pelletier, P. (1980), *Les migrations intra-urbaines et l'emergence des banlieues centrifuges de la ville de Quebec : essai de morphologie urbaine*, these de maitrise, Geographie, Universite Laval, Quebec.

Rex ,J.A. (1968), 'The sociology of a zone of transition', in Phohl, R. (ed.), *Readings in urban sociology*, Pergamon, London.

Rey, P.P. (1973), 'Sur l'articulation des modes de production', *Les alliances de classes*, Maspero, Paris.

Ricardo, D. (1973), *The Principles of Political Economy and Taxation*, Dent and Sons (1977), London.

Ritchot, G. (1977), 'Le seminaire epistemologique', in *Notes et documents de recherche*, n° 8, Department de geographie, Universite Laval, Quebec.

Ritchot, G. *et al.* (1977) *Rapport d'etuce sur le patrimoine immobilier*, Montreal, Centre de recherches et d'innovation urbaines (C.R.I.U.), Universite de Montreal.

Ritchot, G. (1979), *Plan triennal de developpement*, Geographie, Universite Laval, Quebec.

Rosenburgh, G. (1958), 'Changing structural factors in Canada's cyclical sensitivity 1902-1954', in *Journal of Political aud Economic Sciences*, Vol. XXIV, n° 1.

Samuelson, P.A., Scott, A. (1966), *Economics, an Introductory Analysis*, Canadian Edition, McGraw-Hill, Toronto.

Schnore, L.F. (1965), 'On spatial structure of cities in the two Americas' in Hauser, P.M. and Schnore L.F. (eds.), *A study of urbanization*, John Wiley, New York.

Shevky, E. et Williams, M. (1949), *The social area of Los Angeles : analysis and typology*, Berkeley and Los Angeles, University of California Press.

Shevky, E. et Bell, W. (1955), *Social area analysis : theory monstrative application and computational procedures*, Standford Calif., Standford University Press.

Smith, A. (1974), *The Wealth of Nations*, Books I-III, A. Skinner ed., Harmondsworth, Penguin Books (1977).

Sorre, M, (1952), 'L'habitat', in *Les fondements de la geographie humaine*, Tome III, Armand Colin, Paris.

Starr, R. (1975), *Housing and the money market*, Basic Books, New York.

Topalov, C. (1973), *Capital et propriete fonciere*, Introduction a l'etude des politiques foncieres urbaines, Centre de sociologie urbaine, Paris.

Topalov, C. (1974), *Expropriation et preemption publique en France, 1950-1973*, Documents pour l'etude comparative des politiques foncieres urbaines, CSU, Paris.

Topalov. C. (1974), *Les promoteurs immobiliers*, Mouton, Paris.

Topalov, C. (1974), 'La politique fonciere est-elle monopoliste ?', in 'Pour un urbanisme . . . . ', in *La nouvelle critique*, n° special 78 bis, pp. 38-48.

Tutin, C. (1981), 'Du nouveau sur la rente urbaine ?', in *Etudes foncieres*, n° 12.

Tutin, C. (1981), 'La charge de la preuve', in *Etudes foncieres*, n° 13.

Walker, R.A. (1974), 'Urban ground rent : building a new conceptual frame work', in *Antipode*, VI-1, pp. 51-58.

Walker, R.A. (1975), 'Contentious issues in marxian value and rent theory ; a second and longer look', in *Antipode*, VII-1, pp. 31-53.

Wirth, L. (1938), 'Urbanism as a way of life', in *American Journal of Sociology*, XLIV, 1, pp. 1-24.

Wirth, L. (1945), 'Human ecology', in Theodorson G.A. (ed.), *Studies in human ecology*, Harper (1961), New York.

Wirth, L. (1964), 'The ghetto', in Reiss jr., A.J. et Wirth, L. (ed.), *On cities and social life*, University of Chicago Press.

SIX

GEORGE M. JOHNSTON

SURVEY AND CRITIQUE OF EMPIRICAL STUDIES OF INTER-URBAN LAND VALUES

INTRODUCTION

THE determination of urban land values has been studied in a variety of forms : (1) the effects of changes on a particular location over time ; (2) comparison of different sites within a city at the same time ; (3) comparisons of different locations within a city over time ; and (4) inter-urban comparisons of aggregate variables.

Much of the theory used to analyze intra-urban land values is based on von Thünen's model of agricultural land rent. The basic idea is that location rent is determined by transportation cost savings and the concentric zone model of urban land use. Moreover,

> Modern economists have inserted the tools of micro-economic theory into this framework and adapted it to an urban setting. In the modern versions, Thünen's town becomes the Central Business District (CBD) of a city ; his crops become such urban uses of land as finance, retailing, housing. The object is still to show how competition determines the price of space which is shown to be a declining function of distance from the center. An optimal pattern of land use is determined that is still a sequence of rings, one to each urban use (Goldstein and Moses, 1973, p. 475).

The work of Wingo (1961), Alonzo (1964) and Muth (1971) among others is rooted in the von Thünen model. Their empirical results are weak. The problem with this approach is the changing nature of cities and assumptions which ignore the complexities of the land market.

Wendt and Goldner (1966), Romanos (1976) and Ottensmann (1975, 1977) raise similar critiques of the von Thünen model based upon the increasing complexity of spatial pulls which have replaced distance from the CBD as the transportation determinant in residential land values. The character of this diversity is discussed by Andrews (1971) who, within the sub-discipline of urban land economics, raises the diverse factors influencing the determinants of residential preferences and the factors developers must consider in location decisions. Those factors include the location of schools, business districts, recreational amenities, etc.

The recent studies which have attempted to explain inter-urban differences in land values by the use of multiple regression techniques have explored Federal Housing Administration (FHA) data on residential site prices across Standard Metropolitan Statistical Areas (SMSA).[1] Other studies looked at per capita land values or residential site prices across states.[2] Several other complementary studies examined related factors.[3] Land value appreciation, one of the approaches used in this research was first developed and empirically tested by Schmid (1968). This article will consist of both a survey of the analysis behind each aforementioned approach and the econometric methodologies used.

With one exception, previous research efforts have attempted to explain residential site values by SMSAs or states by use of cross-sectional analysis. Witte (1975), however, developed a pooled regression using time series as well as cross-section data. The independent variables used in these studies have varied. These studies will be reviewed and they key empirical issues will be summarized.

DEPENDENT VARIABLES

Geographic definitions

There are three approaches, based upon the source of the data, for geographically defining the land value variable as well as most of the associated independent variables. First is the research based on State variation done by Keiper, et al. (1961) and Gottlieb (1965). Keiper, et al.'s data was from the U.S. Census of Government. Gottlieb used FHA State data. Second, and most common is the U.S. Bureau of the Census definition of a SMSA used by Maisel (1963), Mittleback and Cottingham (1964), Muth (1971), Witte (1975) and Ottensmann (1977). These articles used the FHA SMSA market price data as the dependent variable. Observations varied from year to year based upon sample size criteria in data collection. Ottensmann also used data provided in Schmid (1968) from the National Association of Home Builders (NAHB). This data was an aggregation of local home builder associations by metropolitan areas. The exact geographic definitions of the local home builder associations are not known, but probably correspond closely to SMSAs. Schmid's econometric analysis also used the Bureau of the Census definition of Urbanized Area in conjunction with the NAHB data. Each of these geographic definitions imply different analysis and implications.

The State based studies of Keiper, et al. and Gottlieb used an estimate of the land component of taxable real property on a per capita basis and FHA average price of residential sites in states, respectively. Keiper, et al.'s results show a significant relationship between the dependent variable and income, population density and agricultural output variables. Gottlieb was somewhat successful with two income variables and a growth (employment) variable. He, however, found agriculture values insignificant. Keiper, et al.'s research was directed at explaining the geographic distribution of land values. Gottlieb argued that his approach would "yield some valuable insights into functioning of our urban land markets" (1963, p. 4). However, while use of State data, both for the dependent and independent variables, can be useful for analysis of some questions, such as the implications of demographic shifts or State policies affecting land use, the degree of insight into the functioning of urban land markets is limited.

Goldstein and Moses in their "Survey of Urban Economics" noted that "researchers exhibit an understandable tendency to avoid defining the relevant unit of study for their models because of the difficulties of obtaining adequate data" (1973, p. 172).

Conceptually, the land conversion market is that area around a metropolitan area where land is in transition from non-residential use, generally agriculture, to residential or other urban uses. It is defined by those individuals and groups whose function is to convert land to urban uses: developers, landowners, land speculators and public institutions through regulations and policies.

There is a wealth of literature, primarily by demographers and sociologists, which deals with the conceptual and operational problems of defining rural, urban, suburban, rural-urban fringe and sprawl [Kurtz and Eicker (1958), Gibbs (1961), Fuguitt (1962), Lieberson (1969), Sinclair and Manderscheid (1974) and Macura (1975)]. Sinclair and Manderscheid (1974) and Macura (1975) applied different, commonly used, definitions of rural and urban, respectively, and discovered a large variation in the population which would fall into each category depending upon the definition applied. Of course, the land conversion market is in transition. What is fringe today is most often city or suburbs in the near future. So while the concepts of fringe and land conversion markets don't necessarily overlap, the problems associated with each are similar.

Research in the area of land conversion has one of the common difficulties in working in the transition area: "Frequently, the theoretical and the empirical categories have been at variance since the former tends to focus on general social characteristics, whereas the latter usually emphasized physical, geographical, demographic or political attributes" (Kurtz and Eicker, 1958, p. 32).

The conceptual definition of fringe which seems appropriate for this research focuses on land characteristics.

> Land use in the fringe is of a unique nature which distinguishes the area from all other residence categories. This unique characteristic is the existence of mixed rural and urban land use—much of the area is still in farmland and residence of non-farm dwellers are interspersed among the farms. This mixture of land use exhibits on consistent pattern of farm and non-farm residences ; if a consistent pattern of residences exists, i.e., if there are solid groups of residential homes without interspersion of non-farm dwellings, this

> area is not considered fringe area (Kurtz and Eicker, 1958, p. 35).

It is difficult, however, to find data based on this kind of definition.

The land conversion market can take on various forms. It can be a narrow fringe or a broad belt. Also, "long ribbons of what is essentially urban development, both as regards the form of buildings and the functions performed in them, extend far out into the rural areas along the main highways" (Shryock, Siegel and Associates, 1971, p. 162). Another example is marked leap-froging to the extent that some discontinuities occur in residential patterns. Harvey and Clark (1965) defined three spatial patterns commonly associated with urban sprawl : (1) low density continuous development ; (2) ribbon development ; and (3) leapfrog development. These can be considered descriptive categories in a static sense. They may all be occurring in any particular metropolitan area, but will change over time.

The definition of the unit chosen to express some relationship, i.e., population density, will influence the results of the research. One could have population dispersed throughout the area or concentrated at a particular point in the area and get the same average density depending upon the grid chosen.

Research into land use patterns must address empirical problems of defining the density of urban development. Gross and net density are both of interest. Gross density, as used here, is the ratio of the metropolitan area to the total population. This approach has some potential in picking up leapfrog and ribbon development by including all land uses, though the variation in land used for non-residential development will exacerbate problems in analysis. Net density, the ratio of land for residential uses to people, might be able to pick up low density continuous development, though here again, the distribution of residential mixes from one metropolitan area to another will vary. The grid or grain chosen for analysis has direct impact upon the analysis. For example, one would have to have a grid capable of showing ribbon development in order to examine hypotheses associated with ribbon development. Other grids would be needed for other characteristics of concern.

While it can be aruged that low density continuous development and ribbon development might explain higher land values, land values for sites transacted over a large grid will, in the case of leapfrog development, include the expensive close-in land transactions and the less expensive, more distant transactions. Therefore, the data might inadvertently indicate that appreciation is lower with leapfrog development.

One way of capturing some of the variation in settlement patterns is to know the gross amount of vacant land in a metropolitan area. Northam (1971) and Niedercorn and Hearle (1968) surveyed the land uses, particularly vacant land, for various American cities. Both reports point to the proportion of vacant land being greater for lower population size cities. While the numbers generated provide insight on the past development patterns, and could indicate if presently vacant land is filled in later, it seems unlikely that either study rigorously defined the geographic area to which the questions were directed. Therefore, significant variations based on newness and size of the cities could exist.

Previous research has also found a statistically significant and positive relationship between site price and gross population density. More intensive use could indicate greater competition for land, hence, greater appreciation. On the other hand, higher appreciation or site price will decrease the quantity demanded and raise density. This suggests a simultaneous relationship. Income and preferences also enter into this interaction.

Idle or vacant land on the fringe remains difficult to measure, but remains a concern in land value analysis as Clawson noted :

> ...land within the suburban zone not actually used for urban purposes typically is not used at all. Our best estimate is that there is about as much idle land in and around cities as there is land used for urban purposes. In the suburbs the idled land is an even larger proportion (1971, p. 318).

If this idled land is held for speculative purposes, the level of expectations and uncertainty associated with particular markets is of interest. Ottensmann's (1977) model associated expectations with per cent of change in population. Schmid (1968) and Hansen and Schwartz (1975), however, indicated the possibility of expectations exceeding actual gains.

Another aspect of operationalizing the land conversion market concept also presents a dilemma. On one hand, one can use the U.S. Bureau of Census definition of urbanized area. The basic concept is a population density index. However, according to another Census publication, "If the suburbs are viewed as a peripheral part of the physical city, and therefore entirely urban, rather than as a traditional zone between urban and rural territory, then the former (urban fringe), more restrictive definition would be the preferable one" (Shyrock, Siegel and Associates, 1975, p. 130). Other census definitions such as SMSAs are also problematical conceptually because of their basis on political units. Unfortunately, Urbanized Areas and SMSAs are the basis of most of the available U.S. data for cross-city comparisons and so serve as the basis of measurement in the econometric models. Much relevant area information is lost; e.g., areas showing potential for population growth and increasing density ratios and areas showing marked leapfroging of residential or commercial development will not be captured by these measures.

It is clear that the method selected for operationalizing the land conversion market is critical to the definition of all variables and formation of all hypotheses. It is necessary, nevertheless, to be somewhat arbitrary and pragmatic in the choices made. The geographic problem with most of the efforts at explaining residential site or raw land values is the failure to indicate the problems associated with data using any particular geographic definition.

Comparison of dependent variables

There have been four types of dependent variables used in the studies being reviewed here. They are: (1) the land component of property value; (2) the price paid for raw land by developers; (3) the price of residential sites either received by developers (NAHB) or assessed by the FHA; and (4) land value appreciation which is calculated using raw land price or site price. Table 6.1 summarizes this research.

The estimate of the land component of taxable real property assessment ratios used by Keiper, et al.'s (1961) study from the Census of Government for 1957 was highly correlated with total real property value. "The Spearman coefficient of correlation between land and property rankings in 1956 is .96" (p. 157).

TABLE 6.1 : **Summary of empirical models of previous research**

Study/Year/ Dependent Variable	R^2	Independent Variables by Variable Type and Statistical Significance when available (*t* values in parenthesis, standard error otherwise)						
		Income	Population Density	Total Population	Population Change	Agricultural Value	Other	Other
1		2	3	4	5	6	7	8
Keiper, et al. (1961)[1] Per capita land value is States (based on an estimate of the land component of taxable real property for 1956)	.75	Per Capita Personal Income by State .51	Population Density by State .79			Value of Agricultural Output by State .64		
Maisel (1963)[2] Mean Price of Building Sites in SMSA's	.46		Population Density, SMSA, 1960 .40 (4.51)		Change in Population (z) 1950-1960 by SMSA .22 (1.98)	Value of Agricultural Land in State .29 (2.67)	FHA Price of New House, SMSA .36 (4.27)	
Mittlebach and[3] Cottingham (1964) FHA Mean Price	.27	Average Income per		Total Population SMSA,			Highest Land Value on SMSA	

of Residental Site		House-hold, SMSA, 1960 .33 (1.17)	1960 .13 (.68)			2.20 (2.52)	
Gottlieb (1965)[4] FHA Mean Price of Residential Site by States, 1961	.22	Mean Annual Per Capita Income by State, 1961 .23 (signi-ficant)		Growth in Nonagri-cultural Employ-ment, 1960 —.15 (insigni-ficant ?)	Value of Agricultural Land by State 1960 .03 (insignifi-cant)	Supply of Vacant Lots .07 (insignifi-cant ?)	Degree of Favorable Assess-ment of Vacant Land .10 (insignifi-cant)
		Per cent of Popu-lation with Income Above $10,000 by State, 1961 .44 (moder-ately signi-ficant)					

TABLE 6.1 : (*Contd.*)

1	R^2	2	3	4	5	6	7	8
Schmid (1968)[5] Net Appreciation of Raw Land Prices Above Farm Values Per Site, NAHB, 1960	.41	Median Family Income ($) 1960 Urbanized Area .129 .92	Population Per Square Mile Urbanized Area, 1960 .234 .214	Total Population Urbanized Area, 1960 —.001 .00	Per cent Change in Population 1950-1960 Urbanized Area —.493 .87		Per cent Population Living in SMSA Ring That Work in City 1960 SMSA —7.029 .30	Land Area Urbanized Area, 1960 5.044 .001
		Median Family Income 1960 (8) City .013 .71		Total Population City, 1960 —.001 .04	Per cent Change in Population 1950-1960 City 16.857 .00			Per cent Change in Land Area 1950-1960 Urbanized Area —.932 .51
				Per cent Population Living in Fringe, 1960 3.369 .60				

Muth (1971)[5] Log of the Average Price of Residential Sites in SMSA's, 1966	.76	Net Family Income 1960 .328 (1.61)				Price Per Square Foot of Residential Site, 1960 .488 (8.56)	Construction Cost Index .137 (.62)
Witte (1975)[6] Natural Log of the Price Per Square Foot of Residential Sites Across SMSA's 1969	.83	Median Income of Mortgage of FHA Loans SMSA .27 (4.72)	Population Density, SMSA 1970 .18 (3.12)	Percentage Change in Population 1960-1970 SMSA .18 (1.89)	Average Value Per Acre of Agricultural Land in State .19 (3.11)	Average Site Size —.49 (8.21)	Mortgage Interest Rate —.11 (1.40)
		Unemployment Rate, SMSA, 1970 .09 (1.38)		Percentage Change in Non-White Population 1960-1970 .05 (.70)		Housing Age .03 (.31)	Average Loan to Price Ratio —.09 (1.18)

TABLE 6.1 : (*Contd.*)

1	R^2	2	3	4	5	6	7	8
Witte (1975) Pooled Regression of Natural Log of the Price Per Square Foot of Residential Sites Across SMSA's 1966-1969	.78	Median Income of Mortgages of FHA Loans SMSA .38 (11.78)	Population Density, SMSA 1970 .20 (8.72)		Percentage Change in Population 1960-1970 SMSA .13 (5.18)	Average Value Per Acre of Agricultural Land in State .27 (10.94)	Average Site Size —.49 (20.15)	Average Terms to Maturity .07 (.93) Dummy 1967 Dummy 1968 Dummy 1969
Ottensman[4] (1977) NAHB Raw Land Price, 1964	.55	Mean Family Income, 1960 SMSA .43 .45		Total Population 1960, SMSA 1.32 .24	Per cent Change in Population SMSA 1950-1960 47.71 12.81			

Source : Some of the information on other studies in this table came from Witte (1975). Other results appeared in Schmid (1968) and Ottensmann (1977). All information from Witte (1975), Table 3, were checked against the original source. Several footnotes below were also from Witte.

[1]Other statistics were not reported.

[2]"These t-values assume that the figures in parentheses below the regression results in Mittlebach and Cottingham are standard deviations of b's". Witte (1975, p. 362).

[3]"Gottlieb did not report t-statistics so it was necessary to obtain a notion of significance of various variable from his discussion of the results of his regression analyses." Witte (1975, p. 362).

[4]Schmid's results report standard errors and are thus not in parentheses.

[5]"Muth used the log of all variables in his regression analyses. Muth's coefficients are estimated using unmanipulated not standardized variables". Witte (1975, p. 362).

[6]Witte (1975, p. 357) reported a series of cross-sectional regressions for years 1966-1969. The generalized equation for 1969 is presented here. A complete definition of Witte's variables appear in Appendix A, supplied upon request.

[7]Ottensmann (1977) reports standard errors. Best results reported.

Moreover, the regression model worked better for total property values (per capita) than the land component estimate. To Keiper, et al., the most troublesome issue arose from not only the lack of consistency of assessment practice between states, but also within states, hence, offsetting effects of different land market practices.

The best data operationally for site price or appreciation are the price paid for raw land by residential developers. While this data may exist in scattered studies, only the NAHB data for 1960 and 1964 represents significant systematic gathering of such data. These data are reproduced in Schmid (1968) from NAHB sources.

Residential site prices as reported by FHA and NAHB has several internal components : (1) development cost of a site ; (2) agricultural opportunity cost (e.g., agricultural value) ; and (3) size of the site. Each of these factors imply different policy questions. They, in turn, can explain the reason for statistical significance found in such independent variables as the construction cost index (Muth, 1971), average site size (Witte, 1975) and value of agricultural land or products [Keiper, et al. (1961), Maisel (1963) and Witte (1975)].

Schmid's land value appreciation is derived from site value. The computation process is as follows : For each city the analysis begins with the price per finished lot. The farm value of the land in the lot is computed and added to the lot improvement costs, and the total is subtracted from the finished lot price, to obtain the amount of absolute appreciation. The appreciation is then expressed as a percentage of the farm value.

Ottensmann, in commenting on Schmid's appreciation variable, notes that :

> Schmid's dependent variable has per cent appreciation over farmland values. This is highly correlated with land prices themselves, since farmland prices are much smaller and vary less. However, any error in the farm land price data is magnified by this procedure, producing large variations in the appreciation variable (1977, p. 394).

This argument notes the measurement difficulty, but does not directly challenge the underlying theoretical concept.

Independent variables and regression results of previous research

The following results of econometric research sand out : (1) Income and population density were most often found significant. (2) Total population and population growth were often found significant when either income or density were found insignificant or not used. (3) Value of agricultural land or output was found significant in three out of four studies explaining State or SMSA site variation. (4) Other variables found significant in various studies related to site size, construction cost (indices) or price of complements.

Income and population seem to have an inter-relationship which has affected which variables have been found significant in those studies. Average income of one sort or another was significant in all but two studies [Maisel (1963) and Schmid (1968)]. In both of those cases, population change was found significant. Also, in only one case out of four (Witte, 1975) did population density enter the equation with income. In other words, income seems closely associated with size variables, total population or gross population density. As the population (size) of the metropolitan area is larger, then income per family should be greater. The relationship between density and income is complex. Higher income is associated with a greater ability to purchase larger lots, but the cost of living in dense areas and the costs of congestion are also associated with greater incomes. This, of course, leads back to the problem of geographical definitions and the problems of mixing different characteristics in any of the three major geographic definitions and even within the fringe area of the urbanized area. Income may also indicate a degree of market power on the part of sellers, either direct or through expectations, to change what the buyer can pay or inversely a measure of the degree of willingness of buyers to pay.

Per cent change in population is statistically significant in four studies. This also perhaps indicates some role for expectations. Value of agricultural output or land appeared significant in three studies and insignificant in one other. This demonstrates the importance of agricultural land value as an indication of opportunity cost or competing uses of land and, hence, a supply characteristic.

The other variables were residential costs, site size and price of new homes. Construction costs could affect both supply and demand. Assuming some relationship between construction costs and development costs, the supply of lots will be affected. On the other hand, construction costs associated with the price of new homes will also affect demand. Site size was found significant by Witte (1975) and indicates a relationship between per unit prices and size of the lot.

Issues of functional form in the dependent and independent variables

The issue of functional form was raised initially in a footnote by Witte : The logarithm rather than the unmanipulated value of the price per square foot was used in order to give the dependent variable a more nearly normal distribution" (1975, p. 357). On the other hand, Witte stated that, "Muth used the log of all variables in his regression analysis. Muth's coefficients are estimated using unmanipulated not standardized variables" (1975, p. 362).

The issue of functional form is related to the hypothesized relation between a dependent and independent variable. In any given situation the researcher cannot know with complete certainty the nature of the functional relationship. "Ideally, his theory tells him unambiguously which to choose ; if he fails to utilize the appropriate one in this situation, his estimates will be biased and/or inefficient. Only if complete searching of the theory does not give the researcher any direction should he proceed to use the following ad hoc procedure, which can never completely substitute for a good theory" (Rao and Miller, 1971, p. 105). Certainly in comparing the research to date there has been little theory and no clear evidence that log forms are superior to linear forms of the equation. The practice of Witte and Muth seems to have been to use non-linear functional forms to take care of concerns about heteroskedasticity without concern for the theoretical implications of these functional forms.

Comparison of studies by Witte and Ottensmann

The two most recently published studies, by Witte (1975), (1977) and Ottensmann (1977), can be contrasted to raise several issues. These two studies represent a contrast in several areas of approach to research in this area. These include : (1) number of variables considered ; (2) functional form ; (3) regression techniques tried (e.g., Ottensmann used a recursive model and attempted some simultaneous equations, while Witte had a series of cross-sectional models and a pooled regression); (4) theoretical arguments ; and (5) results. In reference to Witte's article, Ottensmann raised the following issue to be considered here.

> Other alternative explanations of the level of land values have been provided ; however, the derived demand model developed and tested by Witte (1975) is one of the best examples. She has achieved higher coefficients of determination, but only at the expense of considering a greater number of independent variables. The simple straightforward model tested here, with but three independent variables, must be considered as a valid alternative (1977, p. 389).

Ottensman's three independent variable model offers very little new including the theory justifying their use. On the other hand, Witte presents little rationale for the use of variables or for the sometimes fanciful proxies chosen. While this may have been a function of publication space, it also seems that little attention was paid to the implications of each specification. Regarding variable selection, Witte noted :

> In many cases, a number of alternative measures of the determinants of residential site prices were found and that measure which gave the best explanation as measured by the adjusted coefficient of determination was the one utilized (1975, p. 356).

The results of both studies, however, are not reassuring for the development of instrumental variables designed to influence the land conversion market. As do earlier efforts, they do point to income, population growth, size and population density as significant variables. These alert us to the need to study in more depth the applications of urban shape and structure. We have on one hand a simple model capable of multiple explanations or vague generalities and, on the other hand, a finely manipulated model with little theory beyond the concept of derived demand.

Ottensmann experimented with a log functional form and found little improvement in results. "Different functional forms were used in regressions for some of the variables. For example, a logarithmic transformation of the population variable was tested in all of the regressions. None of the tests were conclusive" (1975, p. 395). Witte used a log form of the dependent variable in an attempt to achieve a more nearly normal distribution.

The regression techniques tried by each of these studies also need comment. Ottensmann, while reporting cross-sectional results of a recursive model using OLS, also attempted a system of simultaneous equations. He reported :

> Two-stage least-squares procedures were used to estimate the parameters, with population, income and the population change variables considered as exogenous. In each case, the parameter values associated with the original three predictors of land prices were hardly changed from those obtained with the recursive model, while the parameter associated with density of development was insignificant (p. 395).

Witte used standard multiple regression techniques. Given the number of variables used by each, it seems that the techniques used were appropriate to the other model. For example, two-stage least-squares methods raise issues of a critical nature when variables are left out of the model. Witte, however, failed to take advantage of the large number of variables used for either a recursive or simultaneously determined model. There are, of course, advantages and disadvantages of each approach, but theory clearly indicates that some variables have simultaneously determined characteristics.

SUMMARY

Inter-urban land value research has concentrated on demand variables such as total population, median family income, per cent change in population, etc., to explain a varied estimate of site price and/or appreciation. Variation in the unit of analysis and problems which arise from these difficulties have been reviewed here. In both the selection of explanatory demand variables and units of analysis, the final choice is arbitrary. Because of the complexity of the urban structure, many aspects of community characteristics are interdependent with other characteristics. While each listed variable is indicative of different trends of interest, selection of the appropriate group of variables can only be made after an analysis of the specific theoretical model to be tested. Geographical units are less amenable to such decisions and the selection of which unit is used often depends on the available data. Pragmatic choices have to then be made, but the strength and weaknesses of each geographical unit should enter in conclusions drawn from such research.

FOOTNOTES

1. These include Maisel (1963), Mittlebach and Cottingham (1964), Muth (1971), Witte (1975) and Ottensmann (1977).
2. Keiper, et al. (1961) estimates per capital land values across states based on the land component of taxable real property. Gottlieb (1965) used FHA data on the average residential price of a site by state.
3. These include a study by Van Vuuren (1976) on Canadian land values using Spearman rank correlations, a cross-sectional study of housing costs and zoning regulations in New Jersey by Sternlieb and Sagalyn (1973), and a cross-sectional study by Miller (1977) of three Californian cities.

REFERENCES

Alonso, William, *Location and Land Use*, Cambridge : Harvard University Press, 1964.

Andrew, Richard B., *Urban Land Use Policy : The Central City*, New York : The Free Press, 1972.

Clawson, Marion, *Suburban Land Conversion in the United States : An Economic and Governmental Process*, Baltimore : The Johns Hopkins Press for Resources for the Future, Inc., 1971.

Fuguitt, Glenn U., 'The Rural-Urban Fringe', *Proceedings of the Forty First Conference of the American Country Life Association, Inc.*, Washington, D.C., July 1962.

Gibbs, Jack P., *Urban Research Methods*, New York : D. Van Nostrand Company, Inc., 1961.

Goldstein, Gerald S. and Leon N. Moses, 'A Survey of Urban Economics', *Journal of Economic Literature*, Vol. XI, No. 2, June 1973.

Gottlieb, Manuel, 'Influences on Value in Urban Land Markets, U.S.A., 1956-1961', *Journal of Regional Science*, 6, 1965.

Hansen, David E. and S.I. Schwartz, 'Land Owner Behavior at the Rural-Urban Fringe in Response to Preferential Property Taxation', *Land Economics*, Vol. LI, No. 4, November 1975.

Harvey, Robert O. and W.A.V. Clark, 'The Nature and Economics of Urban Sprawl', *Land Economics*, Vol. XLI, No. 1, February 1965.

Johnston, George M., '*The Impact of Local Government Policies on Land Value and Appreciation*, East Lansing, Michigan : Michigan State University, Ph.D. Dissertation, 1980.

Keiper, Joseph S., Ernest Kurnow, Clifford Clark and Harvey H. Segal, *The Theory and Measurement of Rent*, Philadelphia : Chilton Company, 1961.

Kurtz, Richard A. and Joanne B. Eicker, 'Fringe and Suburb : A Confusion of Concepts', *Social Forces*, 37 (1), October 1958.

Lieberson, Stanley, 'Measuring Population Diversity', *American Sociological Review*, 34, December 1969.

Macura, Milos, in *Urban Researh Methods* (Jack P. Gibbs, ed.), New York : D. Van Nostrand Company, 1961.

Maisel, S., *Land Costs for Single Family Housing*, Berkeley : California Housing Studies, Center for Planning and Development Research, University of California, 1963.

Miller, Kenneth, *An Intertemporal Cross-City Comparison of Single-Family Housing Prices*, Research Reports on Public Policy, No. 12, Urban Economics Program, University of California, Santa Barbara, April 1977.

Mittleback, Frank G. and Phoebe Cottingham, *Some Elements in Interregional Differences in Urban Land Values*, Los Angeles : Real Estate Research Program, UCLA, June 1964.

Muth, R.F., 'The Derived Demand for Urban Residential Land', *Urban Studies*, 8, 1971.

Niedercorn, John H. and Edward F.R. Hearlean, 'Recent Land-Use Trends in Forty-Eight Large American Cities', *Land Economics*, Vol. XL, No. 1, February 1964.

Northam, Ray M., 'Vacant Urban Land in the American City', *Land Economics*, Vol. XLVIII, No. 4, November 1971.

Ottensmann, John R., *The Changing Spatial Structure of American Cities*, Lexington, Massachusetts : Lexington Books, D.C. Heath and Company, 1975.

Ottensmann, John R., 'Urban Sprawl, Land Values and the Density of Development', *Land Economics*, Vol. 53, No. 5, November 1977.

Rao, Potluri and Roger Miller, *Applied Econometrics*, Belmont, California : Wadsworth Publishing Company, 1971.

Romanos, Michael C., *Residential Spatial Structure*, Lexington, Massachusetts : Lexington Books, D.C. Heath and Company, 1976.

Sagalyn, Lynn B. and George Sternlieb, *Zoning and Housing Costs*, Rutgers University : Center for Urban Policy Research, 1973.

Schmid, A. Allan, *Converting Land from Rural to Urban Uses*, Washington, D.C. : Resources for the Future, Inc., 1968.

Shryock, Henry S., Jacob S. Siegel and Associates, *The Methods and Materials of Demography*, Washington, D.C. : U.S. Government Printing Office, 1975.

Sinclair, Bill and Lester V. Manderscheild, *A Comparative Evaluation of Indexes of Rurality—Their Policy Implication and Distributional Impacts*, Michigan State University, Department of Agricultural Economics, CRMPA, Special Report 22, August 1974.

Van Vuuren, W., *Distribution of Gains and Losses Resulting From Planning Legislation : The Compensation-Betterment Problem*, University of Guelph Publication AE/76/8 CRD, No. 76, August 1976.

Wendt, Paul F. and Uiam W. Goldner, 'Land Values and the Dynamics of Residential Location', in *Essays on Urban Land Economics*, Los Angeles : Real Estate Research Program, U.C.L.A., 1976.

Wingo, Lowden, *Transportation and Urban Land*, Washington : Resources for the Future, 1961.

Witte, Ann Drysen, 'The Determination of Inter-Urban Residential Site Price Differences : A Derived Demand Model With Empirical Testing', *Journal of Regional Science*, Vol. 15, No. 3, 1975.

Witte, Ann Drysen, 'An Examination of Various Elasticities for Residential Sites', *Land Economics*, Vol. 53, No. 4, November 1977.

SEVEN

TONU PUU

ON THE EQUILIBRIUM DISTRIBUTION OF POPULATION AND LAND VALUE IN AN URBAN REGION

THE purpose of this paper is to construct a model for the spatial equilibrium distribution of population within some urban area. There is an equilibrium when all locations are considered as equivalent and no reasons for migration exist. To escape the complicated utility approach introduced by Wingo (1961) and Alonso (1965) we simply state that there is equivalence of location when the sum of housing and communication costs for an individual balance so that more expensive accommodation is compensated by less expensive communication and *vice versa*.

The cost of housing is supposed to be determined by land value, which is itself determined by population density.

Communication cost, on the other hand, depends on the need of communication with other locations and on the facility of movement at various points of the region. The latter is taken as dependent on congestion expressed as the ratio of traffic to capacity. For each individual the former is taken as proportionate to population at the points of destination.

Fixed transportation capacity, or road capital, is assumed to be distributed on the region by some road-building authority that minimizes the sum of the capital-maintainence costs for the fixed capital and the total costs for transportation.

To make things simple we assume the region to be one-dimensional, the closed interval $\{x \mid x^2 \leqslant 1\}$. This is the "long narrow city" introduced by Solow and Vickrey (1971).

Population, traffic and total transportation cost

We need an expression for total transportation or communication cost to start with. Supposing that we can define the cost of transfer or displacement across a unit distance by some function $f(x)$ that varies with the coordinate x of location we get the cost for transportation between the points x and y as

$$\int_x^y f(z)\, dz$$

Suppose that a number of communications proportionate to the product $p(x)\, p(y)$ of population densities at x and y is needed. This follows from the gravity or the entropy model if for simplicity the distance dependence is disregarded. The total communication cost for the region $(-1, 1)$ is

$$\int_{-1}^{1} \int_x^{1} \int_x^{y} p(x)\, p(y)\, f(z)\, dz\, dy\, dx \qquad \ldots(2)$$

If we now use the formula for integration by parts twice subsequently (2) is transformed into

$$\int_{-1}^{1} P(x)\, Q(x)\, f(x)\, dx \qquad \ldots(3)$$

where $$P(x) = \int_{-1}^{x} p(y)\, dy \qquad \ldots(4)$$

and $$Q(x) = \int_{x}^{1} p(y)\, dy \qquad \ldots(5)$$

As $P(x)$ is population to the left of x and $Q(x)$ is population to the right of x the product PQ obviously represents traffic going through x. Hence we define traffic

$$i(x) = P(x)\, Q(x) \qquad \ldots(6)$$

and can obtain total transportation cost as

$$\int_{-1}^{1} f(x)\, i(x)\, dx \qquad \ldots(7)$$

Intuitively it is reasonable that total transportation costs are obtained by multiplying the cost of displacement $f(x)$ by local traffic $i(x)$ at each point x of location and by summing, i.e., integrating, over all locations of the region.

We have seen from (4), (5) and (6) how one of the factors, namely traffic, is determined. We next turn to the question of how the other factor, transfer cost, should be determined. In a congested urban region it is reasonable to take all costs of transportation (fuel, wear of vehicle and driver's work) as proportionate to travel time. This is the starting point for our discussion.

Traffic flow, capacity and velocity

We need some hypothesis about how the velocity of the flow of traffic is related to the intensity of this flow. It is expected that increasing flow intensity reduces the speed when the capacity of the road is given, so that at a certain congestion traffic comes to a complete stand-still.

For simplicity we consider traffic along one lane without crossings and without overtaking. We want to determine the minimum space, s, between two cars that makes it possible to bring each following car safely and smoothly to a complete stop if the preceding one should come to a sudden stop through an accident.

Denote the maximum safe retardation by β. Of course it depends on the quality of the road and on the car, the weather etc., and hence varies from one point to another along the lane; but suppose that it is a universal constant. If the initial velocity of a car at time $t=0$ is v_0, then its velocity at time t is $v=v_0-\beta t$. The time needed to halt the car is thus $t=v_0/\beta$. During this time the car travels a distance of $v_0t-\beta t^2/2$. Substituting v_0/β for t we obtain $0.5\ v_0^2/\beta$ for the space needed.

This, however, is relevant only provided that the driver reacts immediately. If we allow a time-lag of ρ for the reaction the car with velocity v_0 travels the distance ρv_0 before retardation begins. Thus "safe" space between two cars is

$$s=0.5\ v^2/\beta+\rho v \qquad \ldots(8)$$

where we drop the index, as we consider a steady state of motion without acceleration or retardation. The equation relates space to velocity, or reversing causality, it relates velocity to space available, provided that the drivers drive "safely".

Now, the space available depends on the concentration of vehicles and their average length. If the concentration, i.e., the number of cars per kilometer is denoted c and the average length of one car is δ, we have the space $s=1/c-\delta$ kilometers.

Substituting this into equation (8) we get $0.5\ v^2/\beta+\rho v =(1/c-\delta)$.

Supposing that the maximum possible retardation β is infinite we get $v=(1/\rho)\ (1/c-\delta)$. Retarding $1/\delta$ as the "bumper-to-bumper" jam concentration we have arrived at an expression that exactly corresponds to the "follow-the-leader" model. See Herman (1966). Velocity is brought to a complete stop at the jam concentration.

It seems, however, that another simplification than putting β to infinity is more reasonable. Supposing that in general the concentration is far from the jammed state δ is small in relation to $1/c$ and we can ignore it. Thus $s=1/c$. We now wish to express the concentration in terms of the flow of traffic i, measured in cars per hour. As the velocity, v is measured in kilometers per hour and the concentration, c, in cars per kilometer we obviously have $i=vc$ *along one lane*. We now assume there to be l lanes at a certain spot. Hence $i=vcl$. This makes it possible to solve for $1/c=vl/i$. This is equated to s and substituted into (8). This yields the two equations $v=0$ and $v=2\beta(l/i-\rho)$. We ignore the former uninteresting case of a sequence of cars standing still bumper to bumper and adjust the units of measurement of velocity and traffic so that $\beta=1/2$ and $\rho=1$.

Hence $$v=(l/i-1) \qquad \ldots(9)$$

and the reciprocal of velocity that represents the time of transfer is

$$f=(i/l)/(1-i/l) \qquad \ldots(10)$$

Supposing transportation costs to be proportionate to time we conclude that f represents the cost of transfer or displacement over one distance unit.

Equation (10) is an important expression in the formulation of transportation or communication costs. As an idealization we let i and l that represent numbers of cars and numbers of lanes be continuous variables that measure traffic and capacity (or real road capital) respectively in the following optimization problem.

Optimal quantity and allocation of road capital

We are now prepared to answer the question : How much road capital should the authorities allocate to each point of the region ? A reasonable rule is that the sum of total transportation costs and total costs for building and maintaining road capital is minimized. It is reasonable to assume that the yearly cost for amortization and interest and maintainence of each unit of road capital is the sum of a constant building and maintaining costs A and of a location-dependent acquisition cost V.

Hence $$\int_{-1}^{1} [A+V(x)\; l\,(x)\, dx \qquad ...(11)$$

is total (periodized) cost for road capital, whereas

$$\int_{-1}^{1} \frac{[i(x)/l(x)]\; i(x)}{[1-i(x)/l(x)]}\, dx \qquad ...(12)$$

is total communication cost according to equations (7) and (10).

As we wish to minimize the sum of these cost expressions we have to differentiate the sum of the integrands partially with respect to l at each x taking i as given and to put the derivative equal to zero. This obviously yields

$$A+V=(i/l)^2/(1-i/l)^2 \qquad ...(13)$$

or $$A+V=f^2 \qquad ...(14)$$

as the first order condition. Due to convexity the second-order conditions are fulfilled, so that (13) really yields a minimum.

The condition prescribes a relation that must hold between transfer cost $f(x)$ and land acquisition cost $V(x)$ *at all points* of the region. As transfer cost f is in one-to-one correspondence with the ratio i/l according to (10) we can say that land value decides the ratio i/l of traffic to capacity, that we may call congestion, for each point of the region. By this relation an optimal amount of road capital is invested and it is optimally allocated in space in the sense that the sum of capital and communication costs are minimal. As traffic i is determined by the distribution of population p from (4), (5) and (6), the road capital distribution l is decided along with i/l.

Balance of costs of housing and communication

We now turn to the criterion of equivalence of all locations. In order that all locations shall be equivalent the sum of communication costs and accomodation costs should be constant everywhere. The latter cost for a standard accomodation should, like road capital cost, be the sum of one contant, B, and a location-dependent term that is proportionate to land value V. Denoting a necessary proportionality constant by λ, we get accomodation cost as

$$B+\lambda V(x) \qquad \text{...(15)}$$

The communication costs $C(x)$ for one individual, living at location x, are obtained as

$$C(x)=\int_{-1}^{x} p(y)\int_{y}^{x} f(z)\,dz\,dy+\int_{x}^{1} p(y)\int_{x}^{y} f(z)\,dz\,dy \qquad \text{...(16)}$$

We have to make it a sum of two integrals because they take care of trips rightwards and trips leftwards respectively. The integral $\int f(z)\,dz$ is the cost for one trip and as, due to hypothesis, $p(y)$ trips go to location y the formulation is straight-forward.

By integration by parts the formula (16) is easily transformed into

$$C(x)=\int_{-1}^{x} P(y)\,f(y)\,dy+\int_{x}^{1} Q(y)\,f(y)\,dy \qquad \text{...(17)}$$

where P and Q again, by (4) and (5), denote, population to the left and to the right of a point respectively.

If we differentiate (17) we obtain

$$C'(x)=[P(x)-Q(x)]\,f(x) \qquad \text{...(18)}$$

Differentiating once more : $C''=(P'-Q')\ f+(P-Q)f'$. But, due to (4) and (5), $P'=-Q'=p$. Substituting this along with $(P-Q)=C'/f$ from (18) we get

$$fC''=2\,pf^2+C'f' \qquad \text{...(19)}$$

For equivalence of location $C(x)+B+\lambda V(x)\equiv constant$ for some $\lambda>0$ must hold true. Differentiating once and twice respectively we get

$$C'+\lambda V'=0 \qquad \text{...(20)}$$

$$C''+\lambda V''=0 \qquad \ldots(21)$$

As, however, from (14), $V=f^2-A$ we get

$$V'=2ff' \qquad \ldots(22)$$

and

$$V''=2\,(f'^2+ff'') \qquad \ldots(23)$$

Substutiting from (20)–(21) and (22)–(23) into (19) we get the differential equation

$$-\lambda f''=p \qquad \ldots(24)$$

as the final condition for equivalence of location.

By straight-forward integration we can hence determine the transfer cost function $f(x)$ from a *given* distribution of population $p(x)$. On the other hand by (14) the distribution of land value $V(x)$ is determined along with $f(x)$. As we have seen from (10) an optimal allocation of roads determines the distribution of $i(x)/l(x)$ as well, and $i(x)$ being determined by (4), (5) and (6) from $p(x)$, the proper distribution $l(x)$ of road capital is determined. Hence *for any distribution of population* we can now determine all the other distributions of the model.

It is, however, reasonable to assume that there is an additional condition in the system. Land value should, by the mechanism of supply and demand, depend on the density of population according to some function $V=F(p)$. For completeness the amount of land used for roads should be taken in account as well, but for simplicity we abstract from this. As $V=f^2-A$ from (14) and as $p=-\lambda f''$ from (24) we get the equation

$$F(-\lambda f'')+A-f^2\equiv 0 \qquad \ldots(25)$$

Only transfer cost functions f (and corresponding population distributions $p=+\lambda f''$) that fulfil this identity are possible.

Equation (24) leads to some qualitative conclusions. As $p>0$ and $\lambda>0$ we obviously have

$$f''<0 \qquad \ldots(26)$$

everywhere, i.e., the transfer cost function is *strictly concave* everywhere. This implies that there is some center (which may be one of the boundary points) where *transfer cost* is maximal. Transfer cost and congestion decrease monotonically with the distance from this center. Along with transfer cost, we know from (14) that land value is maximal in the center and that it decreases with the distance from it. Accordingly, with equivalent locations, communication costs are minimal in the center.

There is hence a unique center with high land value and low communication costs for people living there along with a heavy load of traffic to road capacity and low speed of traffic. Observe that this is not socially inoptimal. The inoptimality of tolls has been demonstrated in Puu (1978).

We exemplify by a special case where land value is proportionate to the square of population density, i.e., $F(p)=p^2$ and $A=0$. Then the equation (25) renders the differential equations

$$\lambda f''+f=0$$

and $$\lambda f''-f=0 \qquad \ldots(27)$$

As $f''<0$ only the second one makes sense as we want $f>0$. The solution is

$$f=a\cos(x/\sqrt{\lambda}+b) \qquad \ldots(28)$$

Suppose that the solution is symmetric. Then $b=0$ and $f=a\cos(x/\sqrt{\lambda})$. As $f''<0$ must hold we have $\lambda\leqslant 4/\pi^2$. Immediately we get $p=f$ and $V=p^2$. Integrating (4) and (5) we get $P=a\sqrt{\lambda}\,[1+\sin(x/\sqrt{\lambda})]$ and $Q=a\sqrt{\lambda}[1-\sin(x/\sqrt{\lambda})]$. Hence, from (6), $i=a^2\lambda\cos^2(x\sqrt{\lambda})$. Substituting into (17) we next get $C=a^2\lambda[1+\sin^2(x/\sqrt{\lambda})]$. As $C+\lambda V=2a^2\lambda$ all locations are equivalent.

As another example we try the possibility of having $p\equiv 1$. From $V=F(p)$ we conclude that then $V\equiv$ *constant*. Then the equivalence condition implies that $C\equiv$ *constant*. But, from (18), $C'\equiv 0$ everywhere only if $f\equiv 0$, because $(P-Q)$ changes continuously at the rate $2p=2$. This is only possible with $i\equiv 0$, as we see from (10). But, as $P=1+x$ and $Q=1-x$ with unitary population, $i=(1-x^2)$. Hence we arrive at a contradiction and conclude that a constant population density is not possible in the model.

A two-dimensional model

Despite the intuitively appealing conclusions the model has an obvious unrealistic feature, as it deals with a one-dimensional region. It is most desirable to generalize to a two-dimensional region. There is a simple way of doing this, namely the one used by Solow (1972) in generalizing his one-dimensional "long narrow city" to a circular one. If all distributions on the circular region possess circular symmetry and especially if *all transportation moves radially,* so that the only possible connection between two points in the circular disk is a pair of radials that me et in the center, we can very easily make the model two-dimensional.

Most of the formulae remain unaffected by this. So, even though the capital-maintainence costs and the transportation costs are now obtained as double integrals the *minimization* of their sum still yields the *same conclusion* as before

$$A+V=f^2 \qquad \text{...(29)}$$

where still $f=(i/l)/(1-i/l)$ .. (30)

The only difference is that all distribution functions V, f, i, l etc. now depend on a pair of Cartesian co-ordinates x, y or, in view of the circular symmetry, on $r=\sqrt{(x^2+y^2)}$ if we for convenience place the origin of the co-ordinate system in the center of the disk. The equations stated must now hold at all points x, y of the region.

The same obviously holds true for the condition of equivalence of location, namely that $B+C+\lambda V=constant$ must hold at all x, y. For this to be true

$$C'+\lambda V'=0 \qquad \text{...(31)}$$

must still be fulfilled. The derivative is now taken with respect to $r=\sqrt{(x^2+y^2)}$, as C and V depend on x, y only through r due to symmetry assumptions. (B is still a constant that vanishes at differentiation).

The only part of the model that we need to reconstruct is the derivation of traffic distribution $i(r)$ and of cost distribution $C(r)$. For the simple case we can use a heuristic reasoning.

Let us begin with traffic at distance r from the center. For simplicity we take the radius as unitary and assume total population to be π. If it is distributed with equal density we hence have $p\equiv1$. Now, define

$$P(r)=2\pi\int_0^r q\,p(q)\,dq \qquad \text{...(32)}$$

and $$Q(r) = 2\pi \int_r^1 q\, p(q)\, dq \qquad \ldots(33)$$

to represent the totals of population that live in the disk $\{(x, y) \mid x^2+y^2 \leqslant r^2)\}$ and in the ring $\{(x, y) \mid r^2 \leqslant x^2+y^2 \leqslant 1\}$ respectively. Due to assumption

$$P+Q \equiv \pi \qquad \ldots(34)$$

for the whole unit disk $\{(x, y) \mid x^2+y^2 \leqslant 1\}$.

We can ask : how many transports cross the circle $x^2+y^2=r^2$?

As the demand of transportation was taken as proportionate to the product of population densities at origin and at destination of each trip we can represent the numbers of various types of trips as products and squares of P and Q. Hence P^2 represents the number of trips between points within the r-circle which (moving radially) do not cross it at all. Q^2 represents the number of trips between points in the ring outside the r-circle. They cross the circle twice, on the way inward and on the way outward. PQ represents the trips between the disk inside the r-circle and the ring outside it. Unlike the squares that account for trips in two directions the product only accounts for trips outwards *or* trips inwards. Hence, $2PQ$ is the number of trips that cross the r-circle once. This is verified by the fact that $P^2+2PQ+Q^2=(P+Q)^2=\pi^2$ as is reasonable.

The number of intersections is hence $0.P^2+1.2PQ+2.Q^2 =2Q(P+Q)=2\pi Q$. To get the density of intersection we have to divide this number by the perimeter $2\pi r$ of the r-circle. Hence

$$i=Q/r \qquad \ldots(35)$$

If, as an example, $p\equiv 1$ we get from (33) $Q=\pi(1-r^2)$ and from (35) $i=\pi(1-r^2)/r$. Compared to the one-dimensional case the concentration of traffic to the center is much more pronounced when population density is constant.

We can also easily calculate communication cost $C(r)$. We first observe that for all transportation, except to points lying on the same radial as the starting point (which can be ignored as the areal content of the set of zero), all trips have to go to the center. The cost for *each* such trip is

$$\int_0^r f(q)\,dq \qquad \ldots(36)$$

The total number of trips is π, so that for total cost (36) should be multiplied by π. From the center the trips go radially to all points of the region. The cost for that is

$$2\pi \int_0^1 r\,p(r) \int_0^r f(q)\,dq\,dr \qquad \ldots(37)$$

which by integration by parts can be put in the form

$$\int_0^1 Q(q)\,f(q)\,dq \qquad \ldots(38)$$

and so $$C(r)=\pi \int_0^r f(q)\,dq+\int_0^1 Q(q)\,f(q)\,dq \qquad \ldots(39)$$

Observe that the second term in the right hand member is a *constant* and that *only this constant depends on how population is distributed.* Hence, the derivative is

$$C'=\pi f \qquad \ldots(40)$$

which is independent of p.

As $C'=-\lambda V'$ from (31) and $V'=2ff'$ (from (29) we finally get

$$2\lambda f'+\pi=0 \qquad \ldots(41)$$

Thus we can solve the differential equation for $f(r)$ which is now independent of $p(r)$. The solution is linear. We can easily obtain the land value function $V(r)=f(r)^2-A$, once we have determined $f(r)$. Also the non-constant term of $C(r)$ is obtainable from (39) by simple integration. The interesting thing is that now everything is determined without the population distribution, or, which is the same, *any population distribution is possible.* If we specify $V=F(p)$ then this relation determines a unique population distribution (as $F'>0$). In conclusion this "two-dimensional" case is actually simpler than the one-dimensional case.

Difficulties in the two-dimensional case

The two-dimensionality is, however, only spurious. If we make two radial cuts in the disk and clasp the two sectors together to line segments we arrive at the one-dimensional case. Sectorial areas turn into line segments and this accounts for the changed formulae, but there is *nothing* in the two-dimensional case that occurs that cannot occur equally well in the one-dimensional case. Hence, this change is no real generalization and on this account Angel and Hyman (1976) criticize Solow and other authors constructing models with a central business district to and from which all transportation goes radially. It must be stressed that a real generalization to two dimensions is a very difficult task, demonstrated by the fact that Angel and Hyman do not manage to define even a correct measure of traffic for it.

The problem is that the routes that transportation takes are no longer fixed, like being confined to the line segment that the long narrow city itself was or to the radials of the circular city. The route itself is an object of choice and, given f, it could be determined by solving the variational problem of minimizing $\int f(r)\sqrt{[r^2+(dr/d\omega)^2]}d\omega$ where ω is the angular coordinate satisfying $x=r\cos\omega$ and $y=r\sin\omega$. Such problems have been solved in a multitude of works, such as Beckmann (1952), Wardrop (1969) and Angel and Hyman (1970) to mention a few.

The determination of traffic is, however, very complicated except for a few simple cases. Angel and Hyman use the heuristic approach outlined in the preceding paragraph, namely to simulate end-points for trips at random to decide the number of intersections, (0, 1 or 2) between a circle of given radius and the optimal path corresponding to the end-points. Thus they expect to arrive at a measure of traffic by counting the average intersection density for the trips.

Doing this they miss one important point. If we regard the circle (or "cordon") intersected, not as an actual circle, but as a very thin ring, then we see that the length of the segment of an intersecting route cut off by the ring *depends on the angle of incidence*, and so does the load of traffic created by this trip. The "cordon crossings" should not only be counted, but weighted. In Puu (1977) I have demonstrated that weights equal to the secants of the incidence angle are reasonable.

It was also shown that the measure obtained in this way agreed with one, implicit in Beckmann (1952), where traffic flow was treated as anelogous to an incompressible fluid. In hydrodynamics the conservation equation for the fluid relates the divergence of the flow to the distribution of sources and sinks. The sources and sinks in our case would be the trips starting and ending at various points. In Beckmann's case a single type of goods is studied as it flows from excess supply sources to excess demand sinks. The present case would be more complicated as the communication between all pairs of points corresponds to a non-denumerable infinity of vector fields, that, unlike physical fields, do not fuse into one resultant field. The reader may find something about all these matters and a few traffic distributions resulting from very simple transfer cost functions and population distributions in Puu (1979).

Equally difficult to derive are the communication cost distributions. For some simple cases the reader may find examples in Puu (1979).

Much work is, however, needed to construct a theory of population distribution equilibria for real two-dimensional cases like the one developed above for the one-dimensional case.

In a more general model one should also ask to what extent the single lane model for speed and flow of traffic is relevant as traffic in all directions is incessantly crossing at all points of the two-dimensional region.

Addendum on the case of the entropy model for interaction

In the main text we for simplicity disregarded the fact that transportation demand is sensitive to distance even in an urban area of limited size. We could quite easily bring this dependence into the picture. The demand for transportation would then no longer be $p(x)\ p(y)$ in the one-dimensional case, but rather $p(x)\ p(y)e^{-\gamma\,|\,y-x\,|}$. If we then modify the definitions (4) and (5) to

$$P(x)=\int_{-1}^{x} p(y)\ e^{-\gamma(x-y)}\ dy$$

and

$$Q(x)=\int_{x}^{1} p(y)\ e^{-\gamma(y-x)}\ dy$$

then the definition of traffic (6) and the cost expression (7) hold as before. The same is true for (17), the final expression of $C(x)$.

Also (18) is left unchanged. On the other hand (19) is changed into

$$fC''=2pf^2+C'f'-\gamma(P+Q)f^2$$

and this changes the differential equation (24) into the integro-differential equation

$$-\lambda f''=p-\gamma(P+Q)/2.$$

Observe that the expression $(P+Q)$ is no longer a constant, but for each x is a functional of p. This sum represents communication from each point with the rest of the region.

REFERENCES

Alonso W, 1966 *Location and Land Use* (Harvard University Press, Cambridge, Mass.).

Angel S, Hyman G.M., 1970 "Urban velocity fields", *Environment and Planning*, 2 : 211.

Angel S, Hyman G.M., 1976 *Urban Fields—A Geometry of Movement for Regional Science* (Pion, London).

Beckmann M.J., 1952 "A continuous model of transportation", *Econometrica*, 20 : 643.

Herman R, 1966 "Theoretical research and empirical studies in Vehicular Traffic", *Proceedings of the Australian Road Board*, 3 : 25.

Puu T, 1977 "A proposed definition of traffic flow in continuous transportation models", *Environment and Planning*, 9 : 559.

Puu T, 1978 "On traffic equilibrium, congestion tolls and the allocation of transportation capacity in a congested urban area", *Environment and Planning*, 10 : 29.

Puu T, (forthcoming) 1979 *The Allocation of Road Capital in Two-Dimensional Space—A Continuous Approach* (North-Hollan, Amsterdam).

Solow R., Vickrey W, 1971 "Land use in a long narrow city", *Journal of Economic theory*, 4 : 430.

Solow R., 1972 "Congestion, density and the use of land in transportation", *The Swedish Journal of Economics*, 74 : 161.

Wardrop J.G., 1969 "Minimum cost paths in urban areas", *Strassenban-und Strasseuverkehrstechnik*, 86 : 184.

Wingo L, 1961 *Transportation and Land Use* (Resources for the Future, Washington).

EIGHT

MALCOLM FAIRWEATHER

LAND VALUES AND LAND USE INTENSITY IN THE NORTH AMERICAN CENTRAL BUSINESS DISTRICT
An Appraisal

INTRODUCTION

LAND values in the Central Business Districts (CBD) of North American cities have long been studied by geographers for the purpose of assessing their spatial characteristics and furthermore to determine if common distributional patterns exist. In a 1903 study Hurd[1] developed the idea that in cities the economic rent of a piece of land was based upon its locational characteristics and that the most accessible points in the city would have the highest land values. Later, in the 1920's, Haig[2] discussed a threefold interrelationship between location, transport costs and land values. His concept was that the most accessible location in the CBD had the lowest transportation costs from which to serve the entire city. This land, therefore, would be at the most desirable location in the CBD and the great competitive bidding for such property would result in its value being extremely high. Such a location is often described as the Peak Value Intersection (PVI). Since increasing distance from the most accessible point or PVI will cause a concomitant increase in relative transportation costs for each piece of real estate, the value of such land would be lower. This relationship between the land values and distance from the most accessible point in the CBD has been demonstrated by Alonso[3] to be in the form of a negative exponential curve. Thus, as distance increases from the PVI, land values decline and Hartshorn has stated that the drop in these values is particularly sharp within the first few blocks from the PVI.[4] Furthermore, Carter has determined that since land values reflect demand for a scarce commodity, land use intensity or building height "...is an attempt to squeeze maximum use out of a limited resource, that is, central city land, and therefore, *a priori*, there should be a clear relationship between value and height......hence it is impossible to maintain that a height of building-land value relationship does not exist."[5]

THE PROBLEM

It would seem that the above relationship would require little further documentation. The CBD's are the most visible areas of cities, their land values are high and they do possess the majority of high rise structures, whose profiles can be seen easily. Such a land value/intensity of use relationship should be clearly evident, even to the untrained observer. This concept, however, is static and does not take into consideration past and present CBD building trends; trends that have been the result of technological change and prevailing economic conditions. Furthermore, the concept is rigid and assumes a regularity of patterning that may be difficult or even impossible maintain in this uncertain everchanging world. Thus the question must be raised as to the validity of the land value/land intensity relationship generalization cited above. Is it a model whose simplicity is appealing but yet not found in reality?

During recent years the CBD's of North America have witnessed a change in function with the decline of retailing and an increase in the number of office operations; a change that caused Garner and Yeates to state that "...most downtown areas have experienced striking structural and functional alterations since the mid 1960's."[6] It must be stated, however, that this trend started many years ago. In the 1920's, for example, about 90 per cent of the total retail sales in urban areas were from the CBD, but by the 1960's Hartshorn estimated the CBD proportion of metropolitan-wide sales to be between 10 and 20 per cent and to have dropped below 10 per cent for the 1970's.[7] This reduction in sales was paralleled by a decline in the number of retailing establishments in the CBD, dropping about 38 per cent in cities with populations of between one quarter and one million, and by about 26 per cent for cities with over a million people, during the period 1954 to 1967.[8] Since it may be assumed that the suburbanization of retailing continued at an even faster rate throughout the decade of the 1970's, it may be stated that there are proportionately fewer dollars being spent in CBD retailing and that there are fewer retailing establishments operating there today than was the case in 1967.

The decline in retailing illustrates the dynamic processes at work in the CBD. While retailing was moving out of the area, office development was growing and Manner's study of selected Standard Metropolitan Statistical Areas indicated that there was greater than a 41 per cent increase in the gross floor space given over to office functions during the period 1960-1972.[9] The proportion of these new office functions that were location in new structures is not known but it was probably significant and the boom in the construction of office buildings during this and later periods did have a noticeable impact upon the CBD skyline. It is clear that the newer structures tended to be taller than the ones that they replaced. Furthermore, such periods of construction came in spurts. The 1970's, for example, witnessed two such growth periods from 1971 to 1974, with a second period beginning in 1978 and extending into the 1980's.[10] It is obvious that with ever increasing land values the new CBD structures had to be tall in order to amortize the high cost of the land. Such is the case in Houston, Texas, where the new Texas Commerce Tower, First International Plaza and Three Allen Center are all 50 or more stories in height. Since all of these new tall structures were not able to be located on the most accessible or most expensive land in the CBD, it is apparent that the perceived relationship between building height aud land values may not be as strong as one believed, especially when analyzed on a block by block basis in the CBD. Furthermore, Johnson[11] has noted that the new office struetures tend to cluster. This concentration of newer structures must, therefore, distort the CBD profile to a greater extent today than was the case in the past, especially since offices are now the "...major central city employers (and) the major sources of property tax revenues."[12]

CASE STUDY

To test the hypothesis that functional change and the normal growth processes at work in the CBD will not produce regular land use intensity pattern in the CBD and that such intensity distributions will not necessarily conform to land value patterns, the city of Rochester, New York was studied. An urban community of nearly 300,000 people, Rochester has a well defined commercial core and statistics available on a block by block basis. For the purpope of this study, three variables were analyzed and mapped (Figs. 8.1, 8.2 and 8.3), namely land values,

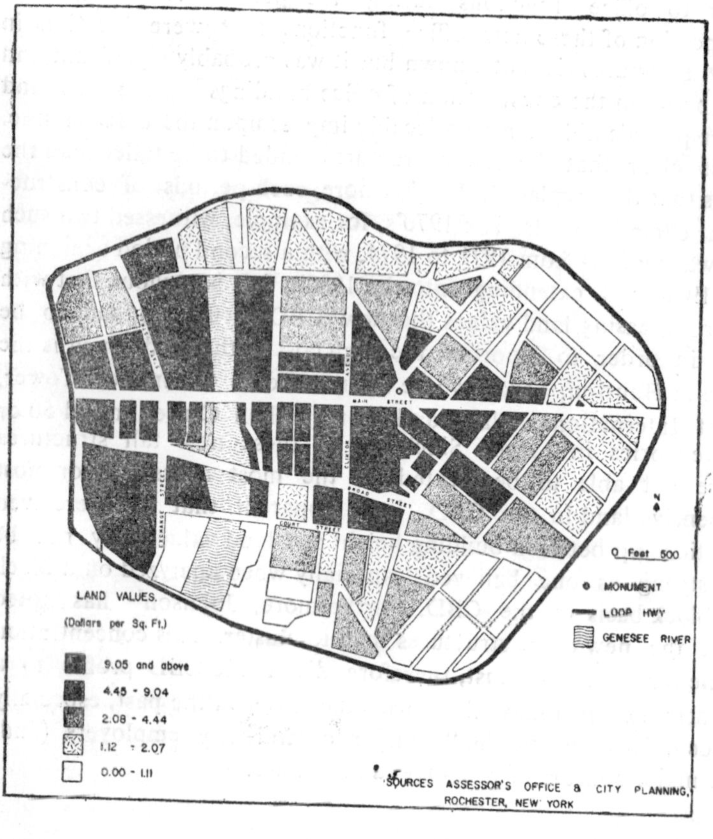

FIG. 8.1 : *Land values in central Rochester*

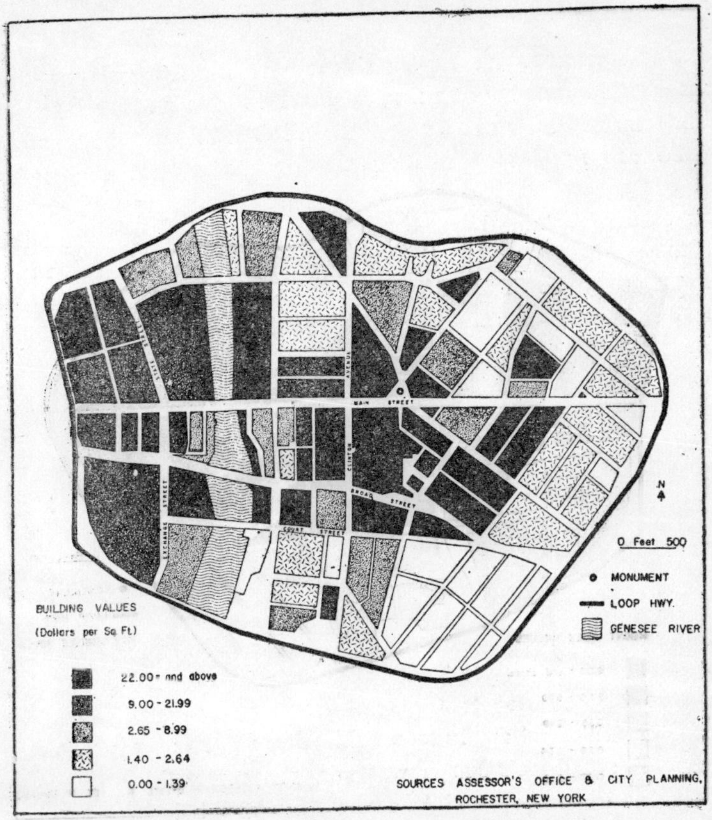

FIG. 8.2 : *Building values in central Rochester*

building values and the Murphy and Vance Central Business District Height Index (CBDHI).[13] The use of the CBDHI was necessitated by the fact that the buildings on any city block were of different heights and that the proportion of the block that each occupied varied widely. It was imperative, therefore, that a standardized measure of building height or land use intensity be utilized, hence the selection of the CBDHI.

A visual comparison of the three maps indicated that there was some level of similarity in the distributional patterns of the land values, building values and the CBDHI. Since the studies cited earlier indicated that there should be a significant level of

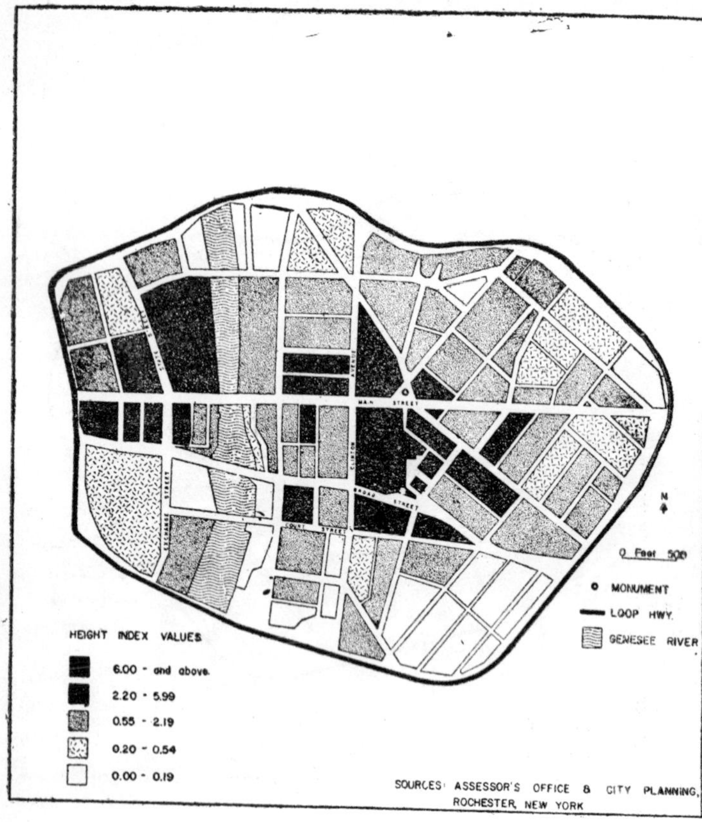

FIG. 8.3 : *Height index values in central Rochester*

spatial correspondence between these distributions, Pearson Product Moment correlations were applied to the data. The results were lower than had been expected. The relationship between high land values and high building values was set at +0.6221, indicating a spatial correspondence in about one third of the cases. A much lower level of correlation was found for the CBDHI and the land values (r=+0.2920), illustrating a positive relationship but a weak one. These relatively low correlation coefficients for Rochester indicated that broad generalizations about CBD land and building values as well as the intensity of land use may not be quite so valid when analyzed at the micro level of the CBD. Perhaps a new avenue of approach should be taken to explain the relationshp between CBD property values and the intensity of land use.

The CBD continues to occupy a location at the center of most cities. A position not modified greatly by suburban expansion at the periphery of the urban area and one maintained by the existing transportation infrastructure. While the ease of access of the CBD to the city as a whole may remain unchallenged, congestion in the inner city has increased traval times to the CBD and extensive freeway construction in suburbia has greatly facilitated movement in the outer city. These events, however, have not changed the accessibility rating of the CBD nor have they altered the level of bidding for sites in the CBD for establishments serving the whole city. As a result, land values are still highest in the CBD and may be expected to remain so into the foreseeable future. In the case of Rochester, the land value pattern conformed to the expected, with values declining with increasing distance from a central, somewhat elongated, peak. The question arose therefore, as to why the relationship between the value of the land and the intensity of the land use was so poorly correlated.

The physical characteristics of a CBD site are extremely difficult, if not impossible, to change but the structures upon them are an entirely different matter. Buildings change functions, they get old, they burn down and they outlive their usefulness. Furthermore, structures may be owned by conservative organizations like churches and trusts or they may be owned by dynamic real estate developers. As a result the land may not change in value or form but the structures built upon it will. Such change is more likely to be random, due to multifaceted extraneous forces, rather than to conform to any highly organized land use intensity model. This situation arises because there are no systematic patterns of property ownership. For example, certain groups hold on to structures long after others would have replaced them with more profitable buildings ; buildings probably taller than those being replaced and thus representing a greater intensity of land use. Furthermore, some property owners tend to wait until the time that structures fail to yield profits before rebuilding while others wait only for the time when a more profitable situation occurs before they redevelop their property. Any of these factors can occur at any time but they do not occur all of the time and they are unlikely to be distributed evenly throughout the CBD, hence the lack of a pattern to CBD buildings in terms of their land use intensity.

THE MODEL

It can be shown that even under the best possible of cases, where the land is owned by individuals whose aim is to maximize profits, there may be times when a tract of CBD land use intensity does conform to a negative exponential format, while in other locations in the CBD and at other times in the tract under review, the expected pattern does not exist. The model introduced here approximates wave theory in terms of the fluctuations in structure height and it assumes that older buildings are less profitable and replaced sooner than newer ones.

In Fig. 8.4 illustrating a section through an hypothetical CBD. In time period one (T-1) the section east of the Peak Value Intersection (PVI) approximates the standard model of declining land use intensity with increasing distance from the PVI, while to the west no such relationship exists. During time period two (T-2) the small structure on block A is replaced by a new taller building, to better maximize the utilization of the increasing land values in the CBD. This taller structure may have also changed its function. In time period three (T-3) block B is replaced and finally in time period 4 (T-4) block C (the newest and tallest structure in T-1) is replaced. A similar cycle was at work for the area to the west of the PVI but not synchronized with that to the east. Given, that in the above it was the older structure that were being replaced during each time period, even this element of regularity failed to produce an intensity distribution that approximated the land value pattern at all times. When applied to the CBD as a whole the relationship would be even less clear. Furthermore, since the above fails to take into consideration fires, bankruptcies and other disasters that affect CBD users, as well as the conservative or aggressive nature of the property owners, it may be stated that CBD land use intensity, as measured by the height of structures or the Murphy and Vance CBDHI, should not be expected to correlate highly with land values for the CBD as a whole. This was the

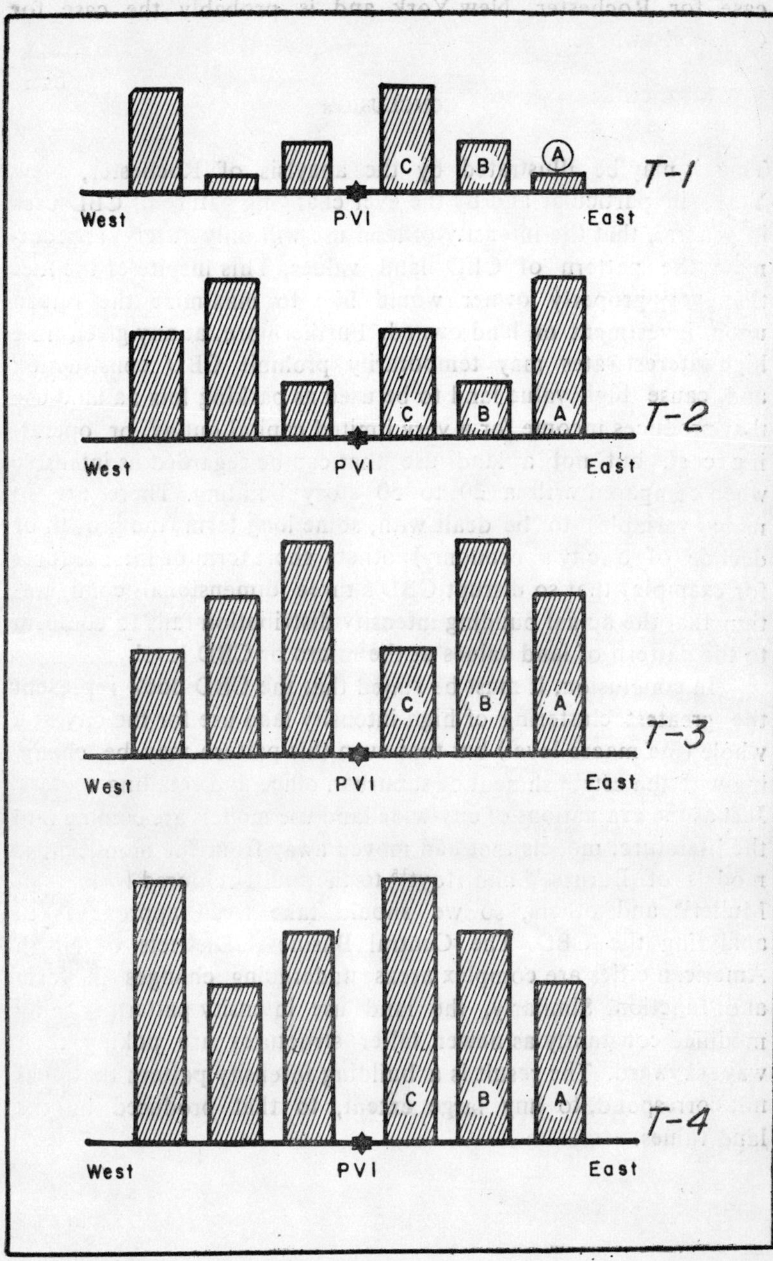
T-1
C
B
A
West
PVI
East
T-2
C
B
A
West
PVI
East
T-3
C
B
A
West
PVI
East
T-4
C
B
A
West
PVI
East

FIG. 8.4

case for Rochester, New York and is probably the case for CBD's elsewhere.

CONCLUSION

Thus it may be illustrated by the anaylsis of Rochester, New York, in particular and by the ever changing nature of CBD uses in general, that the intensity of land use will only rarely approximate the pattern of CBD land values. This inspite of the fact that every property owner would like to maximize the return upon investment on land owned. Furthermore, at any given time high interest rates may temporarily prohibit CBD construction and cause high value land to be used as parking lots ; a land use that produces income for a very limited capital outlay or operating cost, but not a land use that can be regarded as intensive when compared with a 20 to 50 story building. There are so many variables to be dealt with, some long term (the growth or decline of a city's economy) others short term or intense (fires for example) that so disrupt CBD's three dimensional configuration that the actual building intensity distribution fails to conform to the pattern of land values at the micro or CBD level.

In conclusion, it must be stated that the CBD does represent the greatest clustering of high intensity land use for the city as a whole (the macro level) but that even this pattern may be changing with the establishment of suburban office and retailing centers. Just as the evaluations of city-wide land use models are coming into the literature, models that had moved away from the monocentric models of Burgess[14] and Hoyt[15] to the multi-centered formate of Muller[16] and others, so we should take fresh approaches to analyzing the CBD. The Central Business Districts of North American cities are complex areas undergoing changes in form and function. Similarly, the land use intensity pattern is being modified constantly as newer, taller structures are poking their way skyward. The result is a building intensity pattern that does not correspond, to any large extent, to that produced by the land values.

FOOTNOTES

1. R.M. Hurd, *Principles of City Land Values*, New York; Record and Guide, 1903.
2. R.M. Haig, "Toward an Understanding of the Metropolis," *Quarterly Journal of Economics*, Vol. 40, 1926, p. 421.
3. W. Alonso, "Theory of the Urban Land Market, "*Papers and Proceedings of the Regional Science Association*, Vol. 6, 1960, pp. 149-157.
4. T.A. Hartshorn, *Interpreting the City*, John Wiley and Sons, New York, 1980, p. 214.
5. H. Carter, *The Study of Urban Geography*, John Wiley and Sons, New York, 1976, p. 207.
6. M. Yeates and B. Garner, *The North American City*, Harper and Row, 1980, p. 336.
7. T.A. Hartshorn, p. 322.
8. B.J.L. Berry and U.S. Cohen, "Decentralization of Commerce and Industry : The Restructuring of Metropolitan America," in L.H. Masotti and J.K. Hadden (eds.), *The Urbanization of the Suburbs*, Sage Publications, London, 1973, p. 443.
9. G. Manners, "The Office in Metropolis," *Economic Geography*, Vol. 50, 1974, pp. 93-110.
10. *Time*, July 20, 1980, p. 56.
11. R.J. Johnston, *The American Urban System*, St. Martins Press, New York, 1982, p. 213.
12. Ibid., p. 213.
13. For details see : R.E. Murphy and J.E. Vance, Jr., "Delimiting the CBD," *Economic Geography*, Vol. 30, 1954, pp. 189-222.
14. E.W. Burgess, "The Growth of the City : An Introduction to a Research Project" in R.E. Park (et al.) *The City*, The University of Chicago Press, Chicago, 1925.
15. H. Hoyt, "Tne Structure and Growth of Residential Neighborhoods in American Cities", U.S. Government Printing Office, Washington, D.C., 1939.
16. P.O. Muller, *Contemporary Suburban America*, Prentice Hall, Inc., Englewood Cliffs, N.J., 1981.

SECTION THREE

SEGREGATION AND HOUSING MARKET

NINE

SHARON G. LEVIN

PROPERTY TAX INCENTIVES FOR HOUSING REHABILITATION
Theory and Evidence

THE system of local property taxation in the United States is not without its critics. One area which has borne substantial criticism is the effects of the system on allocative efficiency within urban housing markets. Simply stated, it is contended that the property tax system[1] discourages the upkeep and upgrading of the existing housing stock and, as a result, contributes to the now familiar pattern of urban housing decay and abandonment. Increasing concern with this problem has led many states to pass special legislation enabling their cities to implement program providing property tax relief for rehabilitation activities. As of 1979, a survey of eighty-two cities by the Urban Institute [26] finds that twenty-eight have active, on-going programs, with another twelve cities in the process of establishing their own programs.

Unfortunately, as one author observes, "[such programs are costly in terms of property tax revenue foregone, yet no evidence exists to confirm that upgrading results from such programs [6, pp. 45-50]. This study reviews the theory and design of local government property tax incentives for housing rehabilitation with the purpose of evaluating their effectiveness.[2] With this objectivein mind, Section I reviews the economic justification for government activity in the urban housing market. Section II sets the scene for the ensuing analysis of tax incentives by presenting a simple model of the urban housing market. The design and expected effects of property tax relief measures for housing rehabilitation are examined in Section III. And finally, Section IV reviews the design, operation, and cost-effectiveness of several programs which had sufficient data for analysis.

I. Property tax relief for rehabilitation of the existing housing stock in urban areas can be justified on both economic efficiency and equity criteria. To the extent that local property taxes can be viewed as partial excises[3] levied on the value of improvements (capital added) to the housing stock, economic decision-making leads to the substitution of current operating and maintenance inputs for capital inputs and to an overall reduction in the quantity of housing services forthcoming from the existing stock.[4] Property tax relief measures, by lowering the cost of capital and as a result, lowering the supply price of housing services from the existing stock, as demonstrated below, can lead to an increase in welfare.[5] Moreover, to the extent that the deterioration of individual housing units contributes to "neighborhood" or "external" effects, local government excise tax subsidies can be used to stimulate the optimal amount of additional upgrading. In addition, in cases of urban blight, it may also be desirable to offer tax incentives for rehabilitation rather than pursuing a strategy of demolition and new construction, since rehabilitation may be less costly, involving fewer dislocations of existing businesses and residences and less need, perhaps, for major changes in the area's infrastructure. Finally, property tax relief measures can also be targeted to "needy" citizens such as the elderly or poor and can be used as an effective tool for racial desegregation in the urban housing market, by providing rehabilitation scattered site low income housing units rather than units in public housing projects, with their unintended negative spillover effects on property values. Thus there are well-established grounds for considering government property tax incentives for housing rehabilitation. As discussed above, however, the cost-effectiveness of these programs is questionable. To set the stage for evaluation, the next section depicts the operation of a "representative" urban housing market[6] so that the effects of alternative property tax relief measures can be studied.

II. It is useful, first, to define more precisely two concepts used throughout the discussion : the quantity of housing services and the price per unit of housing service. Since housing is a heterogeneous commodity, the quantity of housing services contained in each dwelling needs to be measured in a standardized way. The conventional method is to develop an "hedonic" index[7] based on all the characteristics of value that a housing unit delivers. Price per unit then refers to the price at which a "standardized unit" of housing services is bought and sold.

It is well-recognized [14, 24, 28, 32] that a large degree of variation exists in the supply and demand for houses across geographic submarkets or neighborhoods within an urban area. The housing stock is normally dispersed among neighborhoods or submarkets in such a manner that households of roughly similar house-type offering similar quantities of services per unit. The neighborhoods may either be independent political jurisdictions with their own fiscal instruments and packages of public goods and services (the fragmented local government model) or they may be part of a metropolitan-wide system of control (the centralized local government model). In addition, zoning and other land-use controls often serve to re-enforce the market segmentation. As a result, the price per unit of housing service differs according to the relative supplies and demands for the various types of houses—neighborhoods.

Equilibrium prices and quantities of housing services in the different submarkets results from the interactions of the self-seeking behavior of the market participants : households demanding housing, owners of existing units producing services, firms offering new construction services, and local governments enacting various zoning ordinances.[8] Households choose housing along with other private and public goods in order to maximize satisfaction. The quantity of housing services desired by the household depends on its real income, tastes for housing versus other goods, the price per unit of housing services, and the price of related goods and services. Households can fulfil their desired quantity demanded either with an existing unit, which may be upgraded or downgraded, as necessary, or with a new housing unit expressly built to the desired level (and design) of housing services. The least costly alternative will be chosen.[9]

The demand curve for housing services by household "*i*" in neighborhood "*j*" can be written in inverted form as

$$P_{ij}^{D} = f(Q_{ij}, Y_i, D_i, P^R, N_j) \qquad \text{...(1)}$$

where P_{ij}^{D} is household's *i* demand price per unit of housing service, Q_{ij}, in neighborhood j; Y_i is the household's real income ; D_i is a set of demographic factors, such as age of head of household and family composition, which influence the household's tastes for housing ; P^R is the price per unit of related goods, notably existing housing units in different neighborhoods and newly constructed units ; and N_j is a set of neighborhood characteristics including accessibility, natural and physical amenities, racial, social and/or wealth composition, crime rates, and quality of public schools, for example, which influence the willingness to pay for housing in j. This demand curve is normally negatively sloped ; that is, P^D_{ij} and Q_{ij}, other things being equal, are inversely related. Changes in Y_i, D_i, P^R and N_j on the other hand, increase or decrease the demand price (shift the demand curve), *ceteris paribus*.

Owners of existing housing units can produce housing services with current inputs, which are operating and maintenance variables, and capital inputs. For existing dwellings, the land input is generally considered to be fixed. Thus owners of existing dwellings can increase (decrease) the quantity of housing services offered by altering the level and relative proportions of current and capital inputs.

Given the price per unit of housing services established in the market and expectations concerning future prices and costs in the market, an owner of an existing unit will produce the quantity of housing services which maximizes expected profit. Simply speaking, expected profit is maximized when for the very last increment of housing service produced, the expected market price (extra revenue) just covers the expected extra cost. This requires that capital and current inputs be used in "optimal" proportions, where the extra output produced per last dollar spent on each input is equal. If, in any market period, however, operating at the profit-maximizing level of output means that the expected total revenue falls short of the expected variable cost, then the owner will let the housing unit run down. Furthermore, if this situation continues in the long run, then the owner will either convert the building to a more profitable use or sell it, and if neither of these alternatives proves feasible, the profit-maximizing owner will be forced to abandon the housing unit.[10]

The quantity of housing supplied from an existing dwelling

in the current market period depends upon the services provided by the unit during the previous period (or initial house design) and the short-run price elasticity of supply, by how much the housing services of the unit can and will be increased or decreased in response to a price incentive. Diminishing returns and the rate of economic depreciation, however, tend to limit the adaptability of the existing housing stock to price incentives in the short-run. Furthermore, both owner and tenant characteristics as well as owner's expectations concerning neighborhood viability also influence the short-run supply of housing services from the existing stock.[11]

The supply price for housing services from the existing stock, by owner "*k*" in neighborhood "*j*", $P_{kj}^{(SO)}$ can, on an annualized basis, be written as

$$P_{kj}^{(SO)} = g[C^0(i+d+t),\ X_{kj},\ E_{kj}] \qquad \text{...(2)}$$

where C^0 is the present value of the variable cost of producing housing services from the existing stock, $S(O)$; i is the opportunity (interest) cost of capital, d is the depreciation rate, and t is the effective property tax rate ; X_{kj} is the set of owner-tenant characteristics influencing the supply decision ; and E_{kj} is the owner's measures of neighborhood confidence. Changes in any of the parameters in (2) will shift supply and consequently influence the price and quantity of housing services offered in the different submarkets.

To simplify the analysis below, it is assumed that neighborhoods (j) are identified by similar household (i) and owner (k) characteristics, so that differences due to household and owner characteristics within neighborhoods can be safely ignored. It is also useful to assume that the new construction industry is perfectly competitive and exhibits constant-costs in the long-run. Moreover, the price per unit of new housing services, $P^{S(N)}$, acts as a ceiling on the price per unit of service found in closely related submarkets in the urban housing markets.

Finally, representative local governments impose property taxes, provide local public goods and services, and enforce various land-use controls presumably in the interest of their resident-voters. If there are a large number of local governmental units offering a wide range of choice over public service levels, and capital and households are mobile within the urban area, then one expects the system of local property taxes to function as if user charges existed.

Two results of this system of local public finance are important for the urban housing market model : (1) the supply of low-income housing will tend to be restricted,[12] and (2) local property tax subsidies for housing rehabilitation targeted to selected neighborhoods ultimately will be capitalized in property values in the preferentially treated areas.[13]

Market equilibrium is said to exist when a set of prices and quantities is established such that neither producers nor consumers want to alter their respective production and consumption plans. To reach an equilibrium allocation of households over neighborhoods in the urban housing market, two conditions must be simultaneously met : households must maximize utility given market opportunities, and owners of income producing properties must maximize profits. Thus, if there are two households bidding for the same house, the owner will rent it to the highest bidder, and if the house cannot be rented at a price sufficient to cover variable costs per unit of service, then the owner will desire to disinvest in the unit.[14]

Fig. 9.1 depicts a set of equilibrium prices and quantities for a hypothetical urban housing market segmented into three submarkets, providing low (H^1), medium (H^2), and high (H^3) quantities of housing services per unit. D^1, D^2, and D^3 denote the respective demand curves for these markets ; housing services will be cut-back if price falls below P^M ; new construction services are forthcoming at a constant long-run supply price of $P^{S(N)}$; and housing codes mandate that new housing units produce the minimum of $\overline{Q}$ housing services.

In submarket H^1 the price per unit of housing service is P^1 and the quantity of housing services consumed per unit is Q^1. P^1 lies above the long-run supply price of new construction services, $P^{S(N)}$. Residents may be willing to pay a premium for location in H^1, if neighborhood features make location there more attractive than elsewhere. Also possible, however, in this sector of the housing market, is that supply has been artificially restricted by urban renewal or by local zoning and housing codes. Otherwise, if the premium was not accounted for by nonreproduceable factors capitalized in property values, capital would tend to flow

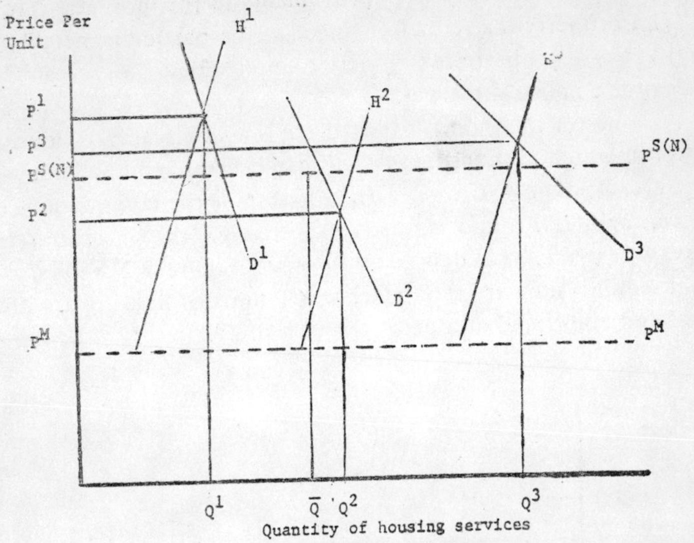

FIG. 9.1 : *Quantity of housing services*

into this sector bringing down prices. Note that new housing is not an option for families seeking housing in this submarket, since housing codes require that units contain the minimum quantity ($\bar{Q}$) of housing service.

Price P^2 and quantity of housing services per unit Q^2 are found in submarket H^2, while P^3 and Q^3 result in submarket H^3. This latter result suggests that submarket H^3 is blessed with valuable features, otherwise a close substitute, new housing, available at a lower price per unit of service, would tend to be preferred by the utility maximizing household.

III. Now it is possible to examine the relationships between property tax incentives and the quantities of housing services produced in the urban housing market. The analysis begins with a discussion of a general tax incentives such as a uniform reduction in the property tax rate for all housing in the housing market, and proceeds to determine the effects on the volume of housing rehabilitation of more narrowly defined programs. Of particular interest are the differential effects of (1) a property tax reduction for housing, in general, versus a property tax reduction applicable only to improvements to the housing stock, and (2) a property tax reduction specific to a particular neighborhood, versus a property tax reduction applicable to all neighborhoods in the housing market.

Assume for the moment that there is a single unified housing market in which all housing services can be supplied at a constant annual cost of $P^1 = C(i+t_1+d)$, where C is the cost per unit of service, and i, t_1, and d, are respectively, the interest rate, property tax rate, and depreciation rate. Figure 9.2 shows the initial equilibrium in this market Q_1 units of housing are produced and consumed at a price per unit of P^1.

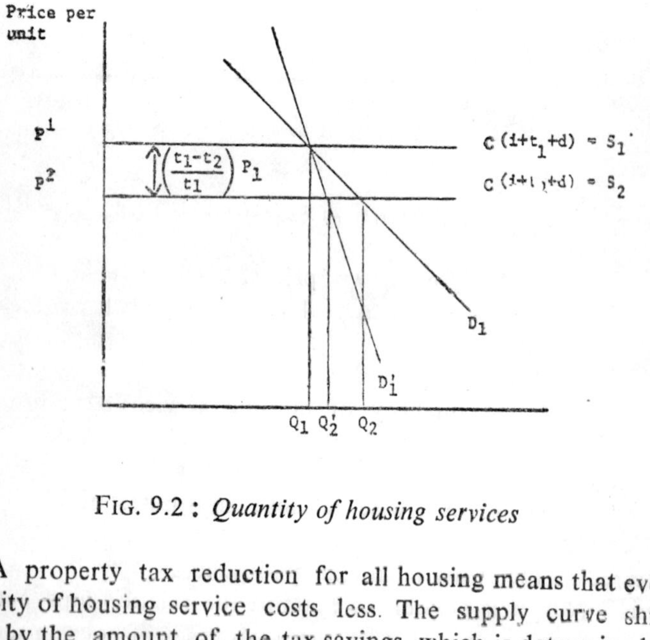

FIG. 9.2 : *Quantity of housing services*

A property tax reduction for all housing means that every quantity of housing service costs less. The supply curve shifts down by the amount of the tax savings, which is determined by the percentage reduction in cost (as determined by the program design) and the level of C, i, d, and t in the housing market. The new supply curve is S_2, where $P^2 = \left(\frac{t_1 - t_2}{t_1}\right)[C(i+t_1+d)]$, and the resulting equilibrium quantity produced is Q_2 units. In this case, the percentage increase in housing services depends solely on the price elasticity of demand. The more responsive is the quantity demanded to price changes, i.e., the more elastic is demand, other things being equal, then the larger will be the increase in services provided. If demand was less elastic, such as D_1' in Figure 9.2, then the quantity produced will increase by only $Q_2'-Q_1$ units.

Figure 9.2 shows only the partial equilibrium effect of the tax reduction in the general housing market. Effects of this tax reduction will be felt in other product markets and factor markets as consumption plans and input combinations are altered as a result of tax reduction. In general, the smaller the partial elasticities of substitution between the differentially tax inputs (housing-land and capital) and other inputs (labor), and the smaller the elasticity of substitution between housing and other goods and services consumed, the larger will be the percentage of the tax reduction passed on to consumers in the form of lower housing prices. Furthermore, if inputs supplied to the housing market are not perfectly mobile, their prices will be affected as well.[15] Consequently, the smaller will be the effect of the tax reduction on the quantity of housing services produced.

Figure 9.3 shows the partial equilibrium effect of a property tax reduction on increased production from the *existing stock* in a single "representative" neighborhood. D_1 and S_1 are the initial demand and supply curves for housing services per unit in this neighborhood. Initially, the price per unit of services is P^1 and the quantity of housing services produced is Q_1. A fall in

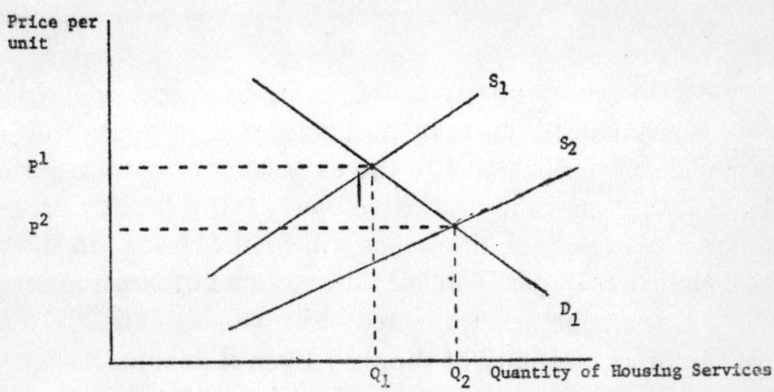

FIG. 9.3

property tax rates shifts the supply curve from S_1 to S_2, with the result that price falls to P^2 and the quantity of housing services increases to Q_2.

Now the effects of the tax reduction depend on both the price elasticities of supply and demand. Here a general property tax reduction for housing will result in a larger increase in housing production and capital demanded, the higher the supply price of housing, the more elastic the demand for housing services, and the more elastic the supply of housing services. Moreover, compared to the initial example, one expects that the price elasticity of demand in a single market would be higher than in the overall housing market because the fall in price attracts some purchases away from new (unsubsidized) housing and investments in other neighborhood housing stocks, in addition to attracting the previously expected purchases from other goods and services.

A property tax reduction granted only for improvements to the housing stock affects housing production in the same manner as a general property tax reduction, although the subsidy mechanism is slightly different. Here both owner-occupants and investors are constrained by what they can do with the savings resulting from the property tax reduction—that is, the property tax savings result only after the completion of the housing improvement activity. The savings are realized on future housing improvements, not on the cost of supplying the existing supply of housing services. Of course, some such as Curran[2] and others would argue that this distinction is immaterial, because owners decide to carry out housing improvements for non-tax reasons anyway.

To sum up, the property tax subsidy, by reducing the price of capital relative to current inputs leads to the substitution of capital for current inputs and to the expansion of output. Furthermore, the more specific the coverage of the subsidy program, other things being equal, the larger will be the price elasticity of demand and the larger will be the volume of housing services produced in the submarket affected. But what about the magnitude of the price elasticity of supply ? Even if demand is perfectly elastic, supply may be perfectly inelastic in some submarkets, and as a result, as shown in Figure 9.4, regardless of the magnitude of the property tax subsidy, no upgrading of the housing of stock

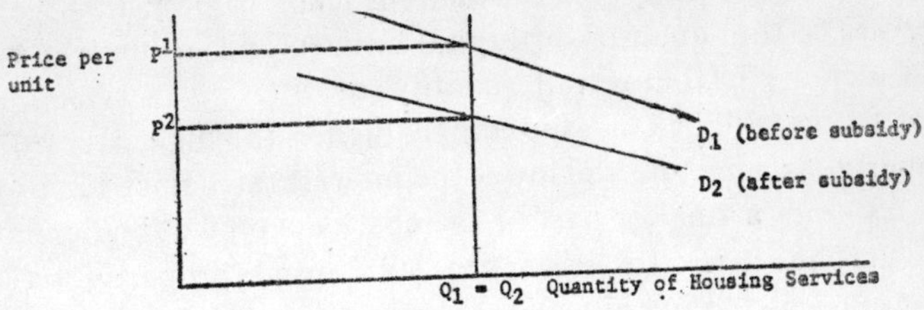

FIG. 9.4

will take place. The net price paid by the consumer falls by the amount of the tax reduction, but no increase in output is forthcoming from the existing stock.

Previous work [10], [17], [24], [25], [26], [32], [34] suggests that this result is most likely to occur under conditions of unfavourable owner expectations such as in downward transitional and blighted neighborhoods and in neighborhoods with long-term elderly owner-occupants who face higher input prices[16] and have shorter time spans over which to recoup their investments than other owners. The price elasticity of supply will also be affected by type of structure and tenant characteristics.[17]

Dougharty's work on the rental housing market[8] provides some insight into the sensitivity of capital inputs and the quantity of housing services to property tax reductions. Some of his estimates for an effective property tax rate of 2 per cent and in interest rate of 8 per cent are shown in Table 9.1.

TABLE 9.1 : **Tax sensitivity of housing investment**

Price Elasticity of Demand for Housing	Tax Elasticity of Capital Inputs	Tax Elasticity of Total Housing Services
— .7	—.14	—.07
—1.0	—.17	—.10
—1.5	—.22	—.13
— ∞	—.58	—.41

Source : Dougharty [8].

It is evident that even under the most favorable demand conditions for upgrading, a price elasticity of demand=—∞, a

10 per cent property tax reduction leads to only a 5.8 per cent increase in the quantity of capital utilized and to only a 4.1 per cent increase in the overall quantity of housing services. These percentages will be correspondingly higher, the higher the effective property tax rate, and the lower the interest rate (since the property tax becomes a smaller part of the cost of capital at higher interest rates). Thus it is clear that even substantial property tax relief "is not likely to radically alter the size or condition of the existing housing stock except in the special cases of overassessed slums and political fragmentation [8, p. 10]." If property tax relief is to be used in an effective manner to improve the urban housing stock, it should be targeted to "selective" submarkets with high effective tax rates, and expected high price elasticities of demand and supply. The next section reviews the United States' experience with local property tax relief programs for urban housing rehabilitation.

IV. The design features of sixteen of the active local property tax relief programs are summarized in Table 9.2. The basic terms of these programs are listed in the first three columns : size (column 1), length (column 2), and type (column 3).

Size refers to the amount of the improvement subject to the relief measure. All cities provide 100 per cent coverage, with the exception of Wilmington, with 150 per cent coverage. Three cities (Buffalo, Hartford, and Philadelphia) provide coverage with a sliding benefit which declines to zero over the period of tax relief granted. The length of the period for tax relief generally ranges from one year to twelve years, with the majority between one-five years. One city, Boston, provides relief for the economic life of the capital improvement.

Three types of relief measures are provided : exemptions (*E*), abatements (*A*), and rebates (*R*). An exemption grants the value of the improvement immunity from local property taxation, an abatement provides for relief from prior property tax obligations, and thus is a form of tax credit, and a rebate provides for a cash grant upon completion of approved work. Thirteen cities offer just exemptions, two cities (Buffalo and New York) offer abatements together with exemptions, and one city, Boston, offers a rebate together with an exemption.

The depth of the subsidy offered by these programs is compared by calculating the percentage reduction in the cost of capital provided by each program for a proto-typical home improvement project. The cost of capital, before tax relief, for this project is shown in Appendix A, and columns 5-7 of Table 9.2 show the effective percentages of tax relief implied by the exemptions, abatements, and rebates. These range from a modest 2.0 per cent in Seattle to a substantial 60.0 per cent in Buffalo. Thirteen out of the sixteen programs offer less than a 10 per cent reduction in the effective cost of capital, however.

The eligibility requirements for participation in the programs vary from city to city as shown in columns 8-10 of Table 9.2. Most cities limit participation by specifying types of eligible structures. Boston provides for an income limit on eligible participants as well, and three cities (Buffalo, Newark, and Yonkers) impose restrictions on the locations of the units.

Several evaluative statistics are presented in Table 9.3. The participation rates (column 3) are generally low, with thirteen out of the sixteen falling below one per cent. The authors of the Urban Institute study[26] from which these data come attribute this result to a host of factors including the newness of most of the programs and the competition from other programs offering more substantial subsides to the cost of capital.[18]

The aver ge value of the investment in rehabilitation per year of program activity is shown in column 4. These figures are estimates of the maximum amount of investment stimulated by the tax subsidies since no data exist to control for the amount of investment that would have been carried out in the absence of the incentives. These data together with the terms of the program and the effective property tax rate (column 5) are used to calculate the "real" cost of an "average" year's program activity (column 6), the present value of the stream of foregone property tax revenue (plus rebates, in the case of Boston). These costs range from a low of $ 751 per year in Pittsburgh, with a low participation rate, a low average value of work done, and a modest capital cost subsidy, to a high of over $ 7 million dollars per year in New York City, with a higher participation rate, a higher average value of work done, and a more substantial capital cost subsidy.

A cost-effectiveness index is calculated in column 7 of Table 9.3, since benefits of these programs are not measureable. The cost index shows the average value of rehabilitation expenditures[19]

TABLE 9.2 : **Program**

	Terms of Program			Year Started	Depth of Subsidy		
					Source		Total
	(1)	(2)	(3)	(4)	(5)	(6)	(7)
	Size	Length	Type[a]		E	A or R	%
Boston, MA	100%	Life	E and R	1973	24.5	15.4[b]	39.9
Buffalo, NY	Sliding	8	E and A	1976	10.3	43.7[c]	60.0
Chicago, IL	100%	4	E	1975	3.5[d]		3.5
Cranston, RI	100%	5	E	1973	6.2		6.2
Denver, CO	100%	5	E	1977	4.5		4.5
Hartford, CT	Sliding	10	E	1974	9.4		9.4
Hoboken, NJ	100%	5	E	1976	7.7[e]		7.7
Honolulu, HI	100%	7	E	1967	3.0		3.0
Newark, NJ	100%	5	E	1977	5.4[e]		5.4
New York City, NY	100%	12	E and A	1955	11.2	46.0[f]	57.2
Philadelphia, PA	Sliding	5	E	1974	2.2[e]		2.2
Pittsburgh, PA	100%	3	E	1974	2.5[e]		2.5
Providence, RI	100%	5	E	1968	9.3		9.3
Seattle, WA	100%	3	E	1975	2.0		2.0
Wilmington, DE	150%	5	E	1974	8.8		8.8
Yonkers, NY	Nego-tiated	1-3	E	1976	—		—

Source : [26, Table 2 and Table 7] with corrections.

Notes : (a) E=Exemption, R=Rebate, A=Abatement ;
(b) Based on average of 20, 40 and 50 per cent rebates, weighted by number of participants in each category ;
(c) Assumes abatement of 8 1/3 per cent of cost of rehabilitation for a period of 10 years ;
(d) $ 15,000 limit on value of property subject to exemption ;
(e) Assumes abatement of 8 1/3 per cent of rehabilitation for a period of 10.8 years.

design

Eligibility Requirements		
(8)	(9)	(10)
Structures	Persons	Areas
Owner-occ, 1-6 unit : 5-10 cm, owner-occ, lodging houses	Net taxable Income ⩽ $16,000	No limit
Multi-family ; 3 units	No limit	Designated only
No limit	No limit	No limit
Own-occ, single family more than 5 yrs. old	No limit	No limit
3 units or less at least 30 years old	No limit	No limit
Easily met restrictions	No limit	No limit
More than 20 yrs. old	No limit	No limit
Own-occ, in conjunction with other restrictions	No limit	Designated only
More than 20 yrs. old	No limit	No limit
Multi-unit including conversions and condos.	No limit	No limit
Own-occ, 1-3 units, Ass. value ⩽ $ 10,000 per unit	No limit	No limit
No limit	No limit	No limit
1-3 family units	No limit	No limit
Own-occ, single family	No limit	No limit
No limit	No limit	No limit
Multi-family > 40 units	No limit	Blighted area

TABLE 9.3 : Evaluation

	Eligible Population[a]	Average Annual of partici-pants	Partici-pation Rate %	Average Value Rehab. per year	Effective Property Tax Rate	Cost of Average Year's Program[b]	Cost Index[c]	Break-Even Level of Stimulant[d] %
	(1)	(2)	(3)	(4)	(5)	(6)	(7)	(8)
Boston,[e] MA	50,080 (S)	3,039	6.07	10,106,861	3.81	5,785,670	1.75	57.1
Buffalo, NY	70,643 (DU)	177	.25	477,692	3.72	68,277	7.00	14.3
Chicago, IL	481,576 (S)	3,295	.68	138,219	1.66	7,273	19.00	5.3
Cranston, RI	13,750 (S)	52	.38	80,990	1.91	5,864	13.81	7.2
Denver, CO	65,852 (S)	400	.61	g	1.33	—	—	—
Hartford, CT	15,687 (S)	43	.27	1,282,680	3.09	152,778	8.40	11.9
Hoboken NJ	3,976 (S)	11	.28	84,900	6.20	19,956	4.25	23.5
Honolulu, HI	66,757 (S)	68	.10	328,727	.65	10,403	31.60	3.2
Newark, NJ	29,208 (S)	27	.09	287,345	3.77	41,046	7.00	14.3
New York City,[f] NY	2,500,000 (DU)	60,593	2.42	51,499,777	1.91	7,299,325	7.12	14.0
Philadelphia, PA	266,000 (S)	31	.01	g	2.11	—	—	—

Pittsburgh, PA	124,278 (S)	15	.01	12,122	2.44	751	16.14	6.2
Seattle, WA	104,490 (S)	785	.75	695,718	.88	15,226	45.69	2.2
Wilmington, DE	22,491 (S)	30	.13	801,875	1.78	81,166	9.88	10.1
Yonkers, NY	34,855 (DU)	1,057	3.03	1,182,500	3.10	g	—	—

Source : Columns 1-5, [26].

Notes : (a) S=Structures, DU=Dwelling Units ;

(b) Present Value of foregone revenue calculated using terms of the program on the average value of rehabilitation undertaken for a year ;

(c) Average value of rehabilitation per year per dollar of foregone revenue—column 4 divided by column 6 ;

(d) Percentage of rehabilitation required to have been stimulated by the subsidy for the program to have broken even, i.e., Cost Index=1 ;

(e) Figure calculated for years 1975-1978 ;

(f) Figures calculated for years 1969-1978 ;

(g) Data not available.

per dollar of real cost, excluding administrative expenses. Column 8 presents a complementary index to the cost index. It shows the minimum percentage of the rehabilitation expenditures that has to be assumed as being stimulated by the program in order for the program to break-even.

These data are troublesome, particularly in the case of Boston which has the lowest cost-index ($ 1.75) and correspondingly requires the largest break-even level percentage of stimulated investment (57.1%). Moreover, assuming that administrative expenses run on the order of 10 per cent of the value of rehabilitation expenditures,[20] then seven of the twelve programs with cost-effectiveness data will have "total" cost-indices (including administrative expenses) less than $ 5 and break-even percentages of stimulated investment exceeding twenty per cent. Given that available survey data [26, p. 182] suggest that it is highly likely that much of the rehabilitation activity would have taken place even without property tax incentives, it is clear that the cost-effectiveness of these programs is questionable.

In conclusion, that evaluative statistics presented in Table 9.3 cast considerable doubt on the effectiveness of these property tax subsidies in stimulating investment in the existing housing stock. Clearly, local property tax incentives for housing rehabilitation alone cannot ensure that urban housing conditions will improve dramatically. But such local policy instruments, if properly designed and understood, could prove to be cost-effective tools in a multi-dimensional approach towards meeting the dual objectives of efficiency and equity : conserving as well as improving the existing housing stock and providing "decent" housing for "needy" citizens.

FOOTNOTES

* The author is Associate Professor of Economics and Public Policy at the University of Missouri-St. Louis. Initial work on this project [16] was carried out while the author was on professional leave at the Urban Institute. Financial support during this period was from a National Science Foundation Science Faculty Professional Fellowship.

1. This assumes that the property tax system works as it was designed to operate, increasing assessed valuation in a timely fashion to reflec hanges in housing stocks.

2. This effort is hampered by the paucity of data. The data used in this study were collected by the Urban Institute [26].
3. Only those local rates of property taxes which are not compensated for by public service benefits and which are in excess of corresponding charges in other communities.
4. This is demonstrated more formally in Levin [16].
5. This assumes all other conditions for economic efficiency, i.e., Pareto optimality, are met.
6. This presentation follows closely the modelling of deLeeuw and Struyk [4].
7. For a complete description of the properties of such an index see S Rosen, 'Hedonic Prices and Implicit Markets : Product Differentiation in Price Competition', *Journal of Political Economy*, 82 (Jan./Feb. 1974) : 35-55.
8. The fragmented local control model is assumed.
9. This requires qualification. Optimum housing quantities may not exactly be met because of information and moving costs and the possibility that new construction activity may be restricted by zoning ordinances.
10. For examples of the financial difficulties that landlords face leading to abandonment in declining markets, see Peterson, *et al.* [24], and Sternlieb and Burchell [34].
11. See, for example, Goetze [10], Peterson [25], and Mayer [18].
12. See, for example, the results of Hamilton [13].
13. Only current owners of homes in the preferentially treated areas will likely experience gains in property values. But these gains may be instrumental in restoring neighborhood confidence.
14. For a complete description of the equilibrium solution process, see deLeeuw and Stuyk [4].
15. For a general discussion of the general equilibrium effects of a tax change, see Peter Mieszkowski [19].
16. For example, because of their inability to utilize sweat-equity.
17. See, for example, the discussion in Muth [22] and Peterson [25].
18. These include, for example, interest rate subsidies, federal tax subsidies for housing rehabilitation which include depreciation subsidies for low income housing and historic preservation provisions, and other grant programs.
19. This is calculated assuming an average year of program activity.
20. In Boston the administrative expenses were estimated at 13 per cent for the first two years of operation.

REFERENCES

Aaron, Henry, *Shelter and Subsidies*, Washington, D.C. : Brookings Institute, 1973.

Curran, Donald J., 'The General Property Tax and Residential Rehabilitation'. In *Proceedings of the Fifty-Seventh Annual Conference on Taxation*, pp. 250-8, Pittsburgh : National Tax Association, 1964.

deLeeuw, Frank, and Ekanem, Nkanta, 'The Supply of Rental Housing', *American Economic Review*, 61, (December 1971) : 806-71.

deLeeuw, Frank, and Struyk, Raymond J., *The Web of Urban Housing : Analyzing Policy with a Market Simulation Model*, Washington, D.C. : The Urban Institute, 1976.

Denne, Robert C., 'Explicit Property Tax Policies and the Promotion of Specific Land Use and Economic Development Objectives : A Review', *Assessors Journal*, 11 (March 1976) : 13-46.

DeSalvo, Joseph, 'Effects of the Property Tax on Operating and Investment Decisions of Rental Property Owners', *National Tax Journal*, 24 (March 1971) : 45-50.

Dildine, Larry L. and Massey, Fred A., 'Dynamic Model of Private Incentives to Housing Maintenance', *Southern Economic Journal*, 40 (April 1974) : 631-39.

Dougharty, L.A., 'The Magnitude of the Effects of the Property Tax on Operating and Investment Decisions in the Rental Housing Industry' *Rand Paper*, p. 5469, Santa Monica, CA : The Rand Corporation, 1973.

Eilbott, Peter and Kempey, William M., *An Analysis of the J-51-2, 5 Tax Abatement and Exemption Program for Stimulating Housing Rehabilitation in New York City*, New York : The City University of New York, 1974.

Goetze, Rolf, *Building Neighborhood Confidence : A Humanistic Strategy for Urban Housing*, Cambridge, Massachusetts : Ballinger Publishing Company, 1976.

Grieson, Ronald E., Effects of Property Tax on Operating and Investment Decisions of Rental Property Owners : A Note', *National Tax Journal*, 26 (March 1973) : 127-28.

Grigsby, William G. and Rosenberg, Louis, *Urban Housing Policy*, New Brunswick, New Jersey : Rutgers University Center for Urban Policy Research, 1975.

Hamilton, Bruce W., 'Capitalization of Intrajurisdictional Differences in Local Tax Prices', *American Economic Review*, 66 (December 1976) : 743-53.

Heilbrun, James, *Real Estate Taxes and Urban Housing*, New York : Columbia University Press, 1966.

James, Franklin, *Back to the City : An Appraisal of Housing Reinvestment and Population Change in Urban America*, Washington, D.C. ; The Urban Institute, 1977.

Levin, Sharon G., 'Analyzing the Investment Effects of Property Tax Incentives', *Urban Institute Working Paper*, 1130-02, Washington, D.C. : The Urban Institute, 1978.

Lowry, Ira S., Rydell, Peter C. and deFerrante, David, 'Testing the Supply Response to Housing Allowances : An Experimental Design', *Rand Paper*, WN-7711-UI, Santa Monica, California : The Rand Corporation, 1971.

Mayer, Neil S., 'Rehabilitation Decisions in Rental Housing : An Empirical Analysis', *Journal of Urban Economics*, 10 (July 1981) : 76-94.

Mieszkowski, Peter, 'The Distributive Effects of Local Taxes : Some Extensions', July 1975 (Mimeographed).

Mendelsohn, Robert, 'Empirical Evidence on Home Improvements', *Journal of Urban Economics*, 4 (October 1977) : 458-68.

Moorhouse, J.C., 'Optimal Housing Maintenance Under Rent Control', *Southern Economic Journal*, 39 (July 1972) : 93-106.

Muth, Richard F., *Cities and Housing*, Chicago : University of Chicago Press, 1969.

Ozanne, Larry and Struyk, Raymond J., 'Housing from the Existing Stock : Comparative, Economic Analyses of Owner-Occupants and Landlords', *Urban Institute Paper*, 221-10, Washington, D.C. ; The Urban Institute, 1976.

Peterson, George E. ; Solomon, A.P. ; Madjid, H. ; and Apgar, W.C., *Property Taxes, Housing and the Cities*, Lexington, Massachusetts : D.C. Heath-Lexington Books, 1974.

Peterson, George E., 'Housing Prices and Tenant Characteristics', *Working Paper*, 0785-01, Washington, D.C. : The Urban Institute, 1974.

Reigeluth, George A., Reinhard, Ray M. and Kleinbaum, James, *Property Tax Relief for Housing Rehabilitation, Final Report*, Volume I, Washington, D.C. : The Urban Institute, 1979.

Rosen, Sherwin, 'Hedonic Prices and Implicit Markets : Product Differentiation in Price Competition', *Journal of Political Economy*, 82 (January/February 1974) : 35-55.

Schnare, A.B. and Struyk, R., 'Segmentation in Urban Housing Markets', *Journal of Urban Economics*, 2 (April 1976) : 146-166.

Shoup, Donald C., 'The Effect of Property Taxes on the Capital Intensity of Urban Land Development'. In *Metropolitan Financing and Growth Management Policies*, pp. 105-32. Edited by George F. Break, Madison, Wisconsin : University of Wisconsin for the Committee on Taxation, Resources and Economic Development, 1978.

Skouras, Athanassios, 'On the Analysis of the Property Tax Effects on Operating Investment Decisions of Rental Property Owners', *National Tax Journal*, 26 (March 1973) ; 173-75.

Smith, Vernon L., *Investment and Production : A Study in the Theory of the Capital Using Enterprise*, Cambridge : Harvard University Press, 1961.

Stegman, Michael, *Housing Investment in the Inner City : The Dynamics of Decline*, Cambridge : MIT Press, 1972.

Sternlieb, George, *The Tenement Landlord*, New Brunswick, New Jersey : Rutgers University Press, 1966.

Sternlieb, George, and Burchell, Robert W., *Residential Abandonment : The Tenement Landlord Revisited*. New Brunswick, New Jersey : Rutgers University Center for Urban Policy Research, 1973.

Sweeney, James L., 'Housing Unit Maintenance and the Mode of Tenure', *Journal of Economic Theory*, 8 (June 1974) : 111-38.

APPENDIX A

GROSS[a] CAPITAL COSTS OF PROTOTYPE REHABILITATION PROJECT ($ 20,000 PROJECT COST)

Source	Description	Annual Cost	Present Value[b]
A. Principal and Interest	Home Improvement Loan ; 12.5% for 5 years	5,400	21,177[c]
B. Economic Depreciation[d]	Assumes 20 year project life	238	2,027
C. Property Taxes	Assumes effective property tax rate=2% and market value of rehabilitation is $ 20,000	400	3,406
D. Income Tax Subsidy From Depreciation Allowance	Excess of 125% declining balance over true economic depreciation multiplied by the investor's marginal tax rate=50%	374	—3,184
	Gross Capital Costs		23,426

Source : [25].

Notes : (a) Includes amortization of principal amount of loan ;
(b) Assumes 10 per cent discount rate ;
(c) Computed from Real Estate Tables ;
(d) Based on estimates prepared by Rand [17].

TEN

DETLEV IPSEN

SEGREGATION, MOBILITY AND OPPORTUNITY ON THE HOUSING MARKET
An Empirical Study in Mannheim

HOUSING MARKET AND HOUSING POLICY

THE housing market has been closely connected to global and specific housing policies of the government since the end of the First World War (Haring 1974). Thus the question of the structure and function of the housing market is always at the same time the question of direction and dimension of housing policy. Recently the voices calling for a strengthening of the market in housing supply have become numerous. Officially supported demand for housing should be given up entirely ; in its place, the free market should take over housing supply, and the government should intervene only in the case of real need (Biedenkopf and Miegel, 1978).

Supporters of official housing policy demand a qualitative change in it. The government would then have to worry less about the basic supply of infrastructure policy. The subsidisation of housing and of high-quality neighbourhoods would be essential to the creation and stabilisation of a labour market which can satisfy the growing demand for highly qualified workers. This would be an important aspect of decisions by entrepreneurs concerning site and investment, and thus of the development opportunities of an area (Joachim/Gustaffson, 1970).

Both tendencies encourage the growth of a high-quality housing supply, so that the question of securing housing for groups with average and below-average income takes precedence.

The press is (once again) reporting housing shortages in the metropolitan areas (see for example the *Suddeutsche Zeitung*, October 30, 1979). In the constellation which is only briefly indicated here, the 'filtering theory' of the housing market provides a model which posits a compatibility of luxury with mass housing and also a compatibility between economic and social goals in government housing policy.

The filtering theory

The statement "until the present there has been no satisfactory economic theory of the housing market" (Forster/Steinmuller 1976, p. 118) holds true for the filtering theory as well. Even the definition of terms and the operational recommendations for the "filtering process" vary greatly from author to author. While Ratcliff understands "filtering" to mean that, because of falling market prices, a dwelling unit can be occupied by a lower-income group which thus has improved its living conditions without having had to pay more to rent or buy (Ratcliff 1949, p. 321), this idea is not to be found in fisher or Winnick. "Filtering is defined as a change over time in the position of a given dwelling unit. . . within the distribution of housing rents and prices in the community at whole" (Fisher/Winnick 1951, p. 52). This definition implies that a filtering-down process is necessarily accompanied by a rise in prices for new housing units (Grigsby 1963, p. 89f), and it thereby deprives the theory of its political explosiveness : movements in price on the housing market are no longer connected with the problem of the level of the housing supply. While it must be admitted that the filering theory of the housing market is far from being clearly formulated, let alone able to show convincing empirical evidence, it is still the most advanced attempt to clarify the behaviour of the housing market. In essence the filtering theory hypothesises that *unequal* rates of change of price and quality are typical of the development of the good "housing". Prices for housing (rents or selling prices) fall more rapidly than the housing ages, that is, falls below changing quality standards or disintegrates physically. Consequently, the price-quality relationship changes to the extent that, for lower-income groups, a better quality of housing becomes available for the same financial outlay. Every round of new tenants moving in sees the housing units taking a step down in quality and price, right down to the lowest level, at which point it drops out of the market (Grigsby 1963 ; Ohls 1975). This process is explained by the observation that the wealthy classes do not demand new housing because the old housing is threatened by disintegration, but because their demand follows dynamically the standard of living. So it is that with the change of housing on the part of the wealthy classes, good quality housing comes onto the market, *on top of* that housing already on the market, pushing the price down to that of the next lowest level by oversupply. Only then will this housing be demanded, putting into operation the filtering-down process, as it descends, from one level of quality to the next.

Insofar as this theory corresponds to reality, it has important political consequences for the housing market, as already indicated. The private housing market always supplies by new production the demand for housing only of the financially strongest consumer groups, because it is only here that the relation of costs to receipts promises attractive profits. The filtering-down process, however, improves the supply of housing with the passage of time for all consumer groups, and along with it the average level of housing quality. The theory can justify the withdrawal of the government from the area of housing supply. Accordingly, the same is true also for public housing construction ; it can concentrate on "elevated" consumer groups and thereby harness housing policy to city development plans which are economically oriented. At the same time, according to the filtering theory, a sustained average improvement in the housing supply will follow.

Criticism of the filtering theory

The filtering theory has not remained uncriticised. The basis for the criticism has been an "demand for internal plausibility", especially doubts of the reality of some assumptions which the theory presumes as preconditions. The price-depressing effect, therefore, can only operate when there is an over-supply in the market for a respective quality level. If the market is not balanced, in general or on a particular quality level, the prices will not fall (Westphal, 1978). If, because of a balanced market situation, prices fall, the price-quality relationship will change only if the owner of the housing unit undertakes appropriate maintenance and modernisation in spite of falling income. However, such measures would not correspond to economic behaviour, in connection with which we would rather expect disinvestment as a means of securing profits (Lowry, 1969). Finally, the filtering theory implies a *unified* market, high mobility on the part of many consumers and no barriers to mobility. Inquiries into the social structure of the city, however, indicate that probably the opposite is true. Thus only the extent rather than the existence of social segregation is controversial (Herlyn, 1974). The existence of segregation, the unequal distribution of social groups in a defined urban unit of area, makes it probable that barriers to mobility exist, if one does not assume that the concentration of social groups in particular quarters in entirely voluntary. Voluntary segregation in its contemporary form is all the more unlikely, as research has been able to demonstrate a very uneven quality in the outfitting of apartments in the social infrastructure (and the standard of living conditions which go along with it—Billerbeck 1975). So we can assume that social segregation and the direction of the process of mobility (in orientation and intensity) set up market conditions opposed to the filtering process, or at least to its realisation. From this it follows that the housing market falls along "segregation boundaries" into market segments, which only function as substitutes for each other in a confined sense or not at all. If the above sketch truly corresponds to reality, then the filtering theory—if indeed empirically valid at all—can only explain the movements of prices, standards of living quality and households *inside* the boundaries of the separate market segments. If one further assumes that the structure of the market segments is correlated to the structure of the housing supply, a particular market segment having a "good supply" and another a "poor supply", then the significance of the filtering theory in terms of housing and social policy is considerably reduced. The filtering-down process then takes place only within narrow boundaries, so that the transition from a problematic to a normal, and from a normal to a good housing supply will not be brought about.

PURPOSE OF THE STUDY

It is the purpose of the following study to show, using empirical evidence, that the housing market is in fact divided into market segments which offer varying and characteristic opportunities on the housing market. The following will explain the data on which this study is based (section III). Several theoretical considerations on the sociological boundaries of these market segments will then be developed. It will be shown that, theoretically, the market segments are determined on the one hand by the intensity of mobility and on the other hand by the concentration of certain social classes in particular living areas (segregation—section IV). A presentation of the results of our empirical research on the various market opportunities of different social classes on the individual market segments will follow (section V). Section VI will provide some empirical indicators of the barriers to mobility which form the basis of the creation of such segregated market segments. Some indications of the consequences of our findings for housing policy close the paper (section VII).

EMPIRICAL MATERIAL

Our analysis is based on a series of data sources in *Mannheim*. Part of the data was collected for other purposes and reanalysed by us ; part was collected specifically for our research. In particular, the following data sources were used in the study.

Building and housing unit census, 1968
Only units financed on the free market were considered here. Because no errors due to random sampling could occur in this source of data, it is especially appropriate for determining the structure of the housing supply and of prices. Several secondary analyses were carried out here.

Random sample of housing units, 1973
A total of 691 households in buildings financed on the free market were investigated. Because it could not be broken down by statistical areas, this data source could only be used for a few questions. See the description by Bachmann, Ipsen, and Solowjew (1973).

Random sample of housing units, 1975

A total of 837 units in buildings financed on the free market were investigated. The data could be broken down by statistical area. However, because of the relatively small extent of the data, the exactitude of the results must be viewed with caution. See Bachmann, Ipsen, and Solowjew (1975).

Random sample of housing units, 1977

We investigated 1,464 households in buildings financed on the free market. The data source was made available to us by the city of Mannheim and the Center for Polls, Methods, and Analysis.

Survey of tenants, 1979

A total of 2,072 households were investigated—grouped clustered into 379 apartment houses ; see Ipsen et al. (1979b).

Limiting the field of observation to one city brings both advantages and disadvantages. An advantage is the possibility of relatively intensive and longterm observation (1968-1979) and the combination of several representative studies. On the other hand, the results can be said to hold strictly true only for Mannheim. A replication of the research in Kassel, now in process, will probably demonstrate that the form and nature of market behaviour are not related to any specific location, but rather to the character of the location (situation in an agglomeration vs. periphery, growth vs. shrinkage of the area of settlement, occupational structure and type of demand). In this sense, one can assume that results similar to those reported here will show up in all industrial cities in densely settled areas, but that variations will be found in metropolises and in large cities in isolated situations or in cities where the tertiary sector of the economic structure is dominant.

THEORETICAL DETERMINATION OF HOUSING MARKET SEGMENTS

The argument up to now has come to the conclusion that two social processes—segregation and mobility—decisively influence the process of economic distribution. This was the result of the criticism presented above of some implications of the filtering theory (unified nature of the market and free mobility of the households). Furthermore, certain characteristics of the variation in rents point to the possible effects of these factors ; namely, the relation between the quality of the outfitting of flats and their rents is not a linear one (see Table 10.1).

TABLE 10.1 : **The relationship between quality of the outfitting and rents in Mannheim (German marks/square meter—in parentheses, the number of cases)**

Housing quality	Construction year	All construction years
Poor	4.85 (147)	2.77 (6361)
Simple	2.30 (312)	2.10 (12373)
Middle	3.78 (1654)	2.53 (25393)
Good	4.29 (6181)	3.79 (15242)

1 Poor : without toilet facilities.
Simple : with toilet facilities but without central heating and without a bath.
Middle : with toilet facilities and with either bath *or* central heating.
Good : with toilet facilities, bath, and central heating.
Source : Census of Buildings and Flats, Mannheim, 1968 ; author's calculations, only residential construction financed on the open market.

The average rents for flats of all ages indicate that poor quality flats bring the second-highest rents. We can assume that a division of the market sets in leading to a particular price structure in the segment of the market having housing of poor quality. Such an isolation of one market segment cannot itself depend on economic factors, since every customer left to his free choice would prefer a better outfitted, more economical flat. Thus we are justified in suspecting a segregation effect here.

Similar observations have been documented for a considerable time in connection with "ghetto research" in the United States. Old and rundown housing inhabited mainly by black Americans, with inadequate plumbing facilities and an unsatisfactory living environment, often goes for higher rents than housing of better quality, primarily inhabited by whites (Walzer and Singer, 1974). "The poor pay more," etc. This situation can be explained by a confined access to the market for certain (black) segments of the population. Economic, social and cultural differences lead to sharply defined borders between individual ethnic groups, so that the flow of information, goods and migration is not free (Haugen and Heins, 1969). Thus, because of barriers like these, an excess of demand arises and prices in certain segments of the market rise. For the Federal Republic, it is questionable whether ethnic discrimination, such as against foreign workers, offers an adequate explanation for the segregation effect. As Table 10.1 shows, the U-shape of the relation between the quality and the price of flats in buildings of recent construction is particularly marked. But this is just the place where foreign families would be rather weakly represented.

It is only a small step from observing the separation of individual markets to the idea that the housing market consists of different market segments, identificable by analysis. Thus N. Walzer and D. Singer (1974) distinguish among three sections of the market. "The first section, the slum, is an area in which undesirable minority groups have traditionally resided . . . . The second market segment, the transitional market . . . . The third market segment is characterized by housing of above average quality and a high level of community services" (Walzer and Singer, 1974, p. 226f.). Even if this distinction is unsatisfactory because it is only slightly systematic (the dimensions of resident status, mobility and living quality are applied without any intermediate factors determining the sections), nevertheless the essential thing is that the division of the market into market segments is made explicitly. Market segments—no matter how they are concretely determined—are relatively closed structures of supply and demand. Substitutability of demand and/or supply between the individual market segments is relatively slight. Market segments are only relatively closed, since we cannot assume that no interaction at all takes place between the separate market segments.

Social segregation is a necessary and sufficient condition for the establishment of market segments. This is, however, not to say that segregation necessarily leads to high rents for lower income groups. Thus Zelder, for example, shows for the United States that a reduction in the number of poor households during the 'sixties led to a relative reduction in rents (allowing for inflation) during this period, since the demand for living quarters in these areas was reduced (Zelder, 1972). In view of *high* rents in the market segment in which chiefly poor elements of the population live, segregation is simply a necessary but not a sufficient condition. This constellation of the determining factors means that a rise in wages for the lower income groups can lead to rent relief even for those groups not benefiting from a rise in income. On the other hand, a decrease in segregation can lead to rent relief and thus has a redistributive effect, even when the distribution of income remains unchanged. Accordingly we find a negative correlation between the index of segregation and expenditures for rent (Walzer and Singer, 1974). In reverse manner, a worsening of the income situation of lower-income households leads to an additional burden on the family budget through rising rents when segregation remains the same ; or, alternatively, the negative effect of a loss of income is reinforced when segregation is simultaneously intensified (which is likely).

Mobility and rent level

Before we undertake an approach to determination of the market segments, we should report on a second observation related to the economic effects of spatial mobility. A study carried out in 1975 of a big city rental market showed that the length of residence had a distinct influence on the rent level (Ipsen 1976). The difference between a brief stay (up to two years) and a long stay (sixteen years and longer) amounted to between 30 per cent and 140 per cent depending on the quality category in which the apartment was located (see Table 10.2). In my opinion these results can be explained by the nature of transactions on the rental market. The determination of prices by supply and demand is distinct from the use value of the good being exchanged. Or, expressed in a different way, insofar as market conditions determine the price, this price-creating effect is independent of the use value of the good. On the other hand, we can assume that the motivation of the customer in the purchase, and in many cases also that of the seller, is the use value of the good. Thus, the more anonymous the transaction is, the more the price will be determined by the market value, because then the motivation of customer and seller will not be determining the price. According to this interpretation, the different mobility or length of residence conditions the truly price-determining factor, which is the anonymity of the personal side of the transaction. A landlord will not be able to raise the rent of a longtime tenant, or will not do so to the extent that market conditions would allow, because the use value of the flat cannot be considered in isolation from the personal aspect of the transaction. The use value of the flat will, however, sink absolutely or relatively over the course of time. With short residences, however, anonymous conditions can prevail, allowing market forces to become decisive. This interpretation becomes more plausible because the effect of the length of residence on the rent in poorly outfitted flats with a slight use value is particularly high.

TABLE 10.2 : **Price per square meter for various qualities according to length of residence**

Quality	Length of residence up to 2 years	up to 6 years	up to 15 years	16 years and over
Good	4.85 DM	4.64 DM	4.11 DM	3.40 DM
Middle	3.84 DM	3.33 DM	3.30 DM	2.83 DM
Simple	3.66 DM	3.43 DM	2.41 DM	2.45 DM
Poor	6.48 DM	4.74 DM	2.50 DM	1.99 DM

Source : A study of the housing market in 1975, documented in Bachmann, Ipsen and Solojew, 1975.

The sociological identification of the market segments by segregation and mobility

We now have two arguments with a certain empirical plausibility at our disposal for theoretically identifying the market segments. According to the first, it is likely that segregation, defined as the spatial concentration of certain social groups, leads to "special" interactions between supply and demand. The dominance of a particular social class in a neighborhood will thus have a price-determining effect if and as long as barriers to mobility stabilise or reinforce this social-spatial structure. So in this case, segregation effects the price of housing through a quantitative determination of the transaction. According to the second argument, the intensity of mobility affects the level of rents through a qualitative determination of the transaction. In housing areas where mobility prevails, anonymous transactions are rule ; but in areas of where the population is immobile, personal ones dominate. If we combine the two arguments, we arrive at a quantitatively and qualitatively defined structure of market segments, determined by social factors. Such a picture assumes a dichotomising of mobility variables and a trichotomising of the social structure. A combination of the two variables of social class and mobility yields six possible market segments, according to the selected scheme of classification (see Schema 1) :

SCHEMA 1 : **Sociological identification of market segments**

	Mobility (frequency of moving) in a given neighborhood high	low
Upper class	M 1	M 2
Middle class	M 3	M 4
Lower class	M 5	M 6

An essential weakness of this market typology is the arbitrary categorising of the variables, which a larger or smaller number of market types respectively is produced. At the moment I see only one way to resolve this problem : conducting empirical studies of the housing market in large cities so as to gather material which would make plausible a limitation on the possible market types. This limitation would be workable and with time would become systematically justified. The goal of our thoughts up to now has not been to posit a market typology "per se", but rather to formulate hypotheses about characteristic socio-structurally conditioned opportunities on the housing market. Opportunity on the market has less to do with whether one obtains a flat on the housing market at all, but rather with what quality housing is obtainable for what price. The opportunity a family has on the housing market is thus defined by the prevailing relationship between quality and price. Residents in a market segment have a given opportunity on the market when identical living situations are available on different market segments but at different prices. Since we assume that certain classes dominate individual market segments, this thesis posits at the both market-segment-specific opportunities and class-specific opportunities in obtaining housing. Thus an opportunity on the market formulated in this class-specific way means not (*only*) different availability of housing on the basis of different incomes, but (*in addition*) a relation between quality and price varying from class to class and disadvantaging the lower classes.

Market segments and market opportunities : Four hypotheses

In order to structure this train of thought more clearly (and not claiming that all the theses were first formulated theoretically and only subsequently tested, as the textbooks prescribe), we posit four hypotheses:

(1) Market segments in which intensity of migration is above average are marked by relatively high rents for various quality levels. This relationship is in turn the result of a high frequency of anonymous transactions.

(2) Market segments in which the lower classes dominate are marked by relatively high rents for the respective quality levels. This relationship is in turn the result of firmly effective barriers to mobility (segregation) among these groups. In addition, there is a tendency to scarcity of simply furnished and older flats owing to demolition, clean-up operations, and only minimal new construction in this category.

Neither of these hypotheses would diminish the number of market types as shown in Figure 10.1. Instead, they posit only particularly poor market opportunities for the mobile lower class and particularly advantageous ones for the stable upper class. The third hypothesis supposes a relation between belonging to a particular class and frequency of moving.

(3) The upper and lower classes tend more toward intra-regional migration than do the middle classes.

Some arguments for the plausibility of this thesis may be advanced. The upper classes are more highly mobile because their resources available for moving are relatively generous. For this reason, they can realise a change in their housing preferences more frequently. At the same time, the upward mobility of the upper classes is more marked than that of other classes, and it thus creates horizontal mobility as a consequence of vertical mobility. On the other hand, the lower classes are forced to

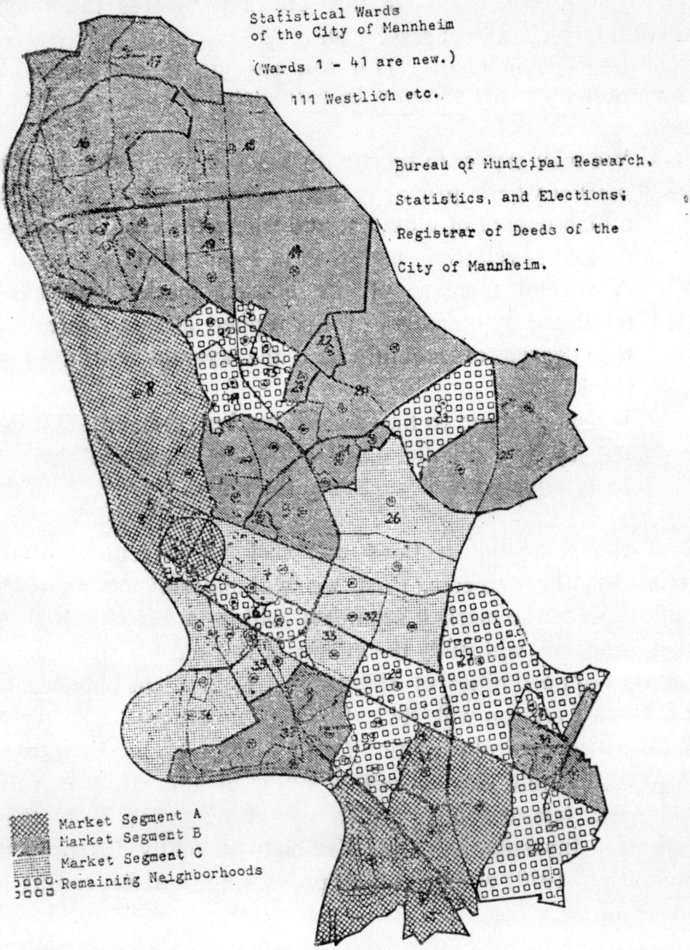

FIG. 10.1 : *Spatial identification of the market segments*

change their living quarters more frequently. They are displaced as a consequence of city development activities (clean-up operations) and because of their more limited resources. They are able to improve their living situations only in small and never fully satisfactory steps, and so they frequently undertake little adjustments "upward" and "downward". None of these arguments holds true for the middle classes, who thus are neither under strong pressure to move, nor do they possess the means for a voluntary change of residence.

On the basis of theses (1) to (3), specific theses about the three market segments can now be formulated :

(4) We may expect to meet with a segment of the housing market where primarily the lower classes live, which has a high degree of mobility, and where the cost of accomodations is relatively high (M5 in Figure 10.1).
A second segment of the housing market is primarily inhabited by members of the upper classes. Here also the degree of mobility and the average rents are high (M 1).
We may expect to find a third market segment dominated by the middle classes. The degree of mobility will be relatively low here, as are the rents.

Both of the following sections will seek to present empirical material for these theses. First we will undertake an empirical identification of the market segments within a big-city housing market, and we will study the effects of this market structure on the market opportunities of the respective resident populations. The following section will look for and investigate barriers to mobility as the central condition for the degree of social segregation. We have not carried out a study of the conditions for greater and less mobility, which would be called for by these hypotheses. Investigations by Kreibich currently in progress (Jessen et al., 1979) will be able to provide up to date results in the near future.

EMPIRICAL STUDY OF SEGMENTS OF THE HOUSING MARKET

In theory, the segmentation of the market is determined by the intensity of mobility and the concentration of certain social strata (segregation). Our hypotheses dealt with three segments of the market :

— a mobile lower-class market (market segment A).
— an immobile middle-class market (market segment B).
— a mobile upper-class market (market segment C).

Each of these three market segments is characterised by a certain level of quality and certain rents. Furthermore, in each market segment, the size, quality and price are related in a specific fashion to each other ; that is, one finds a relation between quality and price specific to a certain area, which can be favourable (good quality for a reasonable price) or unfavourable. Table 10.2 summarises these hypotheses, which will be tested below. The highly changeable market for the lower classes is marked by a lower quality level, relatively high prices and an unfavourable relation between quality and price. According to this hypothesis, the opportunities on the housing market will be relatively unfavourable for the lower classes in market segment A. On the other hand, the middle classes will have good opportunities in market segment B. The opportunities for the upper classes in market segment C are ambivalent, according to our theses ; while the supply of quality housing is naturally good, the relation between quality and price will be rather unfavourable. The fact that the prevailing unfavourable quality-price relationship affects the dominant income groups there is an important aspect of all this.

TABLE 10.2 : **Hypotheses about the connection between market segments and market opportunities**

Degree of Mobility	Characteristics of Residexts Lower Class	 Middle Class	 Upper Clas
Mobile	*Market Segment A* Quality : poor Price : high Q-P relation : unfavourable		*Market Segment C* Quality : poor Price : high Q-P relation : unfavourable
Immobile		*Market Segment B* Quality : middle Price : low Q-P relation : favourable	

In testing these theses with empirical data, the theoretical interest remains in the foreground. So we are reconciled to the fact that perhaps we will not be able to divide up the entire city of Mannheim exhaustively among the three market segments ; instead, the "residual" areas will have to be omitted from the study. The investigation proceeds on the aggregate level of statistical districts, to which socio-economic homogeneity cannot be attributed. All variable empirical characteristics and relationships yet to be discussed are accordingly dominant traits only within a single market segment ; other characteristics are present but are not taken into account. While this lack of focus is a result of aggregations on a relatively high level, it does not run counter to the heuristic goals of this study. Market segments are theoretical abstractions and become politically significant when they are reinforced by the empirical dominance of certain traits.

Territorial identification of the market segments

The point of departure for identifying the territorial borders of the market segments is an investigation of the migration pattern. An observation of the currents of migration between 1966 and 1973 made three spatially distinct processes distinguishable. Together with prior knowledge of the "quality" of the residential areas, the territorial identification of the market segments—in the sense of an operational hypothesis—came about in this way. Schematically, the outline of the migratory process resembles a fishpond, with an intake, a drain and a calm central area. Only the part of the city to which a lower-class market can be attributed had a positive balance in migration. The dynamics of movement were very strong. If we figure immigration as a percentage of the resident population in 1965, we arrive at the result that, statistically, the entire population was replaced in ten years. Sharply lower was the intensity of migration in the second section of the city, which we have characterised as a stable middle-class market. The emigration balance was negative ; however, it was clearly less in both absolute and relative terms as was the case in the third area, which was designated as a mobile upper class market. Table 10.3 provides the data of the migratory movement ; the map (Figure 10.1) shows the position of the three market segments and of the remaining areas within the city limits.

Social structure of the market segments

For explaining the social structure, legal rather than social categories are most useful to us. The 1970 census distinguished

TABLE 10.3 : **Population change and migratory movements in the three market segments from 1966 to 1973**

Market segment	Population change	Change[1] in %	In migration	%	Out migration	%	Balance, in and out of the city	%	Balance, within the city	%
Type A :	—6,433	—7.2	72,706	81.8	68,234	76.8	+4,472	+5.0	—10,762	—12.1
Type B :	—8,466	—6.8	53,407	43.0	57,765	46.5	—4,358	—3.5	— 3,871	— 3.1
Type C :	—6,161	—8.8	38,816	55.3	45,149	64.3	—6,333	—9.0	962	1.4
Market segments overall :	—21,060	—7.4	164,929	58.2	171,148	60.4	—6,219	—2.2	—13,761	— 4.8
Mannheim overall :	—3,006	—0.9	196,152	59.6	199,801	60.7	—3,649	—1.1		

1 Basis of the respective percentage changes is the population status at the end of 1965.
Four city wards, comprising about 18% of the residential population in 1973, could not be clearly assigned in this breakdown of the mobility situation. One case posed a statistical problem, where a single city ward included two apparently different neighborhoods. In a second case, extensive street construction had led to a drastic reduction of population (i.e., houses were being torn down). The third case was that of a bedroom suburb from the 'sixties with a large proportion of public housing. The omission of the fourth ward in question has yet to be accounted for. On the whole, the results of the division into the three market segments is, in my opinion, not unsatisfactory, as long as the hypotheses concerning the market segments can be confirmed. In the case that such a confirmation was not possible, or was only partially possible, a complicated situation would arise, since it would involve a falsification both of the spatial identification of the market segments and also of the analytically postulated connections between them.
Source : Annual Statistical Reports of the city of Mannheim ; my own calculations.

occupational categories (worker, employee, self-employed) and nationality. Considering the variations in on-the-job status and nationality, we suppose a clear relation to exist to a hierarchy of income categories and the lifestyle opportunities deriving from it. Aspects of prestige and influence on the job and in public life point in the same direction. The tentative nature of these hypotheses becomes clear when the untrained sales girl is classified as an "employee" while the skilled craftsman is a "worker", to say nothing of the heterogeneity in the group of "self-employed". Table 10.4 shows the breakdown according to occupational category and nationality for the respective market segments. According to these criteria, market segment C is clearly distinguishable ; the proportion of self-employed and employees is above average here. Thus we can speak, albeit with caution, of a market segment for the upper class. The situation is more difficult with market segments A and B, where the hypothesis supposes a distinction between lower and middle class. Only the larger proportion of foreigners can be interpreted as an indication in this direction. Supporting these data, a study we conducted in 1975 indicated that the proportion of unskilled labourers in market segment A was 7% higher than in market segment B.

TABLE 10.4 : **Market segments and social structure in 1970 (according to census)**

Market segment	Absolute residential population	Self-employed %	Employees %	Workers %	Foreign nationals %
Segment A	84,973	6.0	38.7	53.3	14.2
Segment B	119,900	5.6	41.9	50.3	7.7
Segment C	66,364	10.5	62.0	24.7	5.1
Over all average :		6.6	45.5	45,6	8.9
Total :	332,163				

The same conclusions were indicated by a poll of tenants carried out in 1979. It indicated a difference in net family income per wage earner in the market segments (in market segment A, DM 1363.00 ; B=DM 1450.00 ; C=DM 1569.00).

The present outlook for characterising the market segments by their social structure looks something like the following. Market segment A is dominated by the lower working class. The probability (which, however, has not been tested) is that the self-employed are primarily small shopowners and artisans and that the employees to a great extent belong to the group without high qualifications. Market segment B is likewise a workers' quarter. The proportion of employees is, however, greater ; and the level of qualification is probably higher on the whole. Finally, market segment C is dominated by the middle class, at any rate. To this extent, we can speak of two rental markets for workers and one for the middle class. In workers' areas, a difference between a lower and an upper working class is indicated. Compared to the hypothesis as originally formulated, a shift of the social level "downwards" can be seen, a result which is plausible in view of Mannheim's character as a "working-man's town.

The supply of housing

In describing the housing market in the market segments, we used the plumbing in the flats and their size as indicators. Table 10.5 shows the development of the housing market in the three market segments between 1968 and 1979. Although the different sizes of the random samples for 1975, 1977 and 1979 must be taken into account in evaluating the figures, and although a certain distortion in representativeness should be noted with the cluster sample of 1979 ; nevertheless, the frequency of the observations makes possible a statement about consistency and change in the *structure* of supply in the market segments. Both consistency and change are clearly seen when one considers the supply of good flats in the market segments between 1968 and 1979. Clear differences emerge at all times between the market segment of the lower and upper class on one hand and the middle-class market on the other ; that is, we find a greater share of well-outfitted flats in market segment C. The differences between the market segments decrease slightly with time but remain considerable. The market segment of the working class in 1979 had not even reached the level of the middle-class market of

TABLE 10.5 : **Outfitting of available flats broken down by market segments in the year 1968, 1975, 1977, 1979 (in %)**

Outfitting	Market Segment A				Market Segment B				Market Segment C			
	1968	1975	1977	1979	1968	1975	1977	1979	1968	1975	1977	1979
Poor	15.0	14.1	5.7	4.1	9.5	5.7	5.0	—	4.8	2.2	1.3	0.2
Simple	25.7	20.0	22.5	6.0	4.4	20.8	19.2	4.8	6.2	5.8	2.6	2.8
Middle	37.5	36.8	37.1	51.6	[illegible]9.7	44.3	41.7	46.6	39.8	40.9	27.0	33.1
Good	21.8	29.1	34.7	38.3	16.2	29.2	34.0	48.6	49.2	51.1	69.0	63.9
N	19,386	220	458	585	21,609	269	614	457	14,599	225	381	532

Poor=without bath, toilet facilities, or central heating.
Simple=with toilet facilities, but without bath or central heating.
Middle=with toilet facilities and with either bath or central heating.
Good=with toilet facilities, bath and central heating.
Source : Census of Buildings and Flats, Mannheim, 1968 ; author's calculations.

1968. A levelling-out of the demand structure between the market segments is not found at the upper, but rather at the lower end of the housing market. The share of badly or sparely equipped flats decreases rapidly in both workers' housing markets by 1979. However, the well-equipped flats, which could be counted as a normative standard, do not increase ; instead the flats of average quality do. In concrete terms, this means that the essential change in both of these housing markets in ten years consisted only of the installation of toilets and baths.

Often it is objected that a description of the flat outfitting confining itself to the presence of a bath, toilet and central heating is not differentiated enough, and that both the actual quality of life and the rent demanded are essentially determined by many other features. For our purposes, we examined eleven further features of the layout in the different market segments, from kitchen equipment to carpets to the balcony and the yard. Only in the provision of balcony and a yard were significant differences found ; 51% of the households in market segment A had neither garden nor balcony, in comparison to 34% in market segment B and 20% respectively in market segment C. Except for this single case, one can assume a random distribution of additional features of the flats.

If we summarise the description of the housing market in its three segments, we see particular differences in quality between the market segments of the lower and upper working class on the one hand and that of the middle class on the other (even if we wanted to neglect entirely the differences between the two markets for workers).

Rents

With our study of rents, the analysis arrives at the dependent variable. A claim has been made that segregation, forcibly limiting mobility on the housing market, particularly for the lower classes, influences rents in a market segment-specific way by conditioning the interaction of supply and demand. Second, it has been claimed that the degree of mobility, working through the mode of interaction (anonymous vs. personal) is important for the rent level. In testing these theses, the determining factors are not seen in isolation, but rather appear in combination in determining the price. We should still indicate at the outset the extent to which segregation and mobility can be expected to influence rents. Our concept leads us to see the rent as determined by a number of elements working in combination. The basis of the rent is made up of the ground rent plus construction costs. In addition to these come financing expenses, which vary in turn depending on how much financing comes from outside sources and on interest levels. Ups and downs on the market come into play only after these cost factors have been taken into account ; they effect only a certain proportion of the rent in turn. Only within this restricted sphere can segregation and mobility exert an influence on housing prices.

Table 10.6 shows rents in the market segments for the years from 1968 to 1979. The data show for each year in the study a

TABLE 10.6 : **Average rent per square meter, broken down by market segment (in German marks)**

Market segment	Year of the sample			
	1968	1975	1977	1979
A	DM2.39	3.77	3.81	4.29
B	2.09	3.48	3.58	4.11
C	2.76	3.96	4.19	4.62
Mannheim overall ;	2.34	3.72	3.85	4.34

Source : Census of Buildings and Flats, Mannheim, 1968 ; author's calculations.

higher rent level in the market segment of the lower working class (A) than in that of the upper working class (B). In all years, the rents in the middle-class market (C) are the highest. These figures say nothing about the structure of supply in the individual market segments. While indeed the higher rents on the C-market, as we know, can be caused by a higher average quality, this was not the case with the difference between the A- and B-markets, since the lower quality was found, if at all, in the A-market. The development of the rents shows an increase of 85% in the period from 1968 to 1979 for the rental market as a whole. The increases were the least in the middle-class market (67%) and highest in the market for the upper working class. The heterogeneous nature of the development in rents caused a convergence between the market segments, at least in average rents. Thus the difference between the B-market and the A-market amounted to 14% in 1969, while in 1979 it was only 4%. Also the differential between the B-market and the C-market decreased during this period from 32% to 12%. We shall have more to say later about this development.

First of all, however, the data presented in Table 10.6 are not related to the thesis that was to be tested, since the quality of the apartments was not taken into account. Hence we are not dealing with quality-price relations, but rather only with price relations. Since a complete picture of the housing market for the year 1968 is available, it is possible to carry out an investigation of housing quality with great precision for this time In Table 10.7, the outfitting as well as the year of construction are taken as indices of the quality of flats. The table therefore provides the rents for comparable flats in the respective market segments.

TABLE 10.7 : **Rents (in German marks) by market segment, taking into account outfitting and year of construction—for the year 1968**

Quality		pre-1918	1918-1948	1949-1960	1961-1968
	A	1.77	1.89	2.86	3.58
Poor	B	1.65	1.75	2.20	4.08
	C	1.76	2.20	3.73	3.48
	A	1.70	1.73	2.11	2.57
Simple	B	1.65	1.71	2.06	2.02
	C	1.71	1.85	2.23	4.08
	A	2.03	1.82	2.47	3.67
Middle	B	1.88	1.86	2.36	2.92
	C	2.07	2.02	2.50	3.33
	A	2.52	2.65	3.37	4.22
Good	B	2.42	2.31	2.36	3.38
	C	2.68	2.54	2.50	3.90

Source : Census of Buildings and Flats, 1968 ; author's calculations.

In fifteen out of sixteen cases, the quality-price relation is worse on the market for the lower working class than for the upper (B) ; in six out of sixteen cases, the quality-price relation in this market segment is less favorable than on the middle-class market. It becomes clear precisely in this situation that particular qualities in the living environment cannot account for these differences in rents. The residential areas in market segment A consist to a great extent of closely spaced, multistory construction with only sparse open areas. The nuisances of street and industrial noise, odours and air pollution are greater than average. We can also varify statistically that flats in a residential area with dense construction and the nuisance of streets and industrial noise have a higher price per square meter than flats in quiet residential areas with green space.

Likewise in fifteen out of sixteen cases, the relation between quality and price is worse on the middle-class market than on the market for the upper the working class. Even if we are rather inclined at first sight to attribute the higher price level to the quality of the environment, this is still not plausible in the case of the market for the upper working class, for it is exactly here (even if it is not universally so) that we find a high quality living environment. Often there is a low-profile construction, with garden apartment developments ; in other cases there are authentic downtown advantages. So we can assume that these results do not reflect any differences in residential quality, but rather unequal market opportunities, conditioned by social differences and conveyed through economic factors.

A further objection against such an interpretation could be made, namely that the relatively high price per square meter with no better quality on the lower working class market could be caused by the smaller average size of the flats there. Smaller flats are more expensive than larger ones because the investment costs per square meter of living space are relatively greater. But we should consider that such an argument would be valid only after toilet facilities had been installed. Such was certainly not the case in the quality categories "poor" and "simple", and was only partially true for apartments of middling quality (in the cases where the landlord had installed any bath at all).

The data recorded here confirm the existence of a segmented rental market, even when we include the data from the random sample of housing in 1979 (=1179). Flats of average quality were 6% more expensive on the mobile rental market for workers ; well-outfitted flats brought 9% more in this market segment. Thus segregation and mobility influence movements on the market in a class-specific way. Depending on the period in time and the type of flat, this influence amounts to over 30% (for well-outfitted postwar flats in 1968), or perhaps "only" 6%. Even if it is clear that the market for the upper class as well as the lower working class is relatively poor, this market discrimination doubtless hits the lower class harder—not only from the monetary point of view, but also considering the environmental factors prevailing in market segment A: industrial and traffic noise, troublesome odours and the lack of green space are found here together with relatively high rents.

BARRIERS TO MOBILITY—ON THE TRAIL OF EMPIRICAL INDICATORS

Segregated market segments arise through barriers to mobility, which direct and confine mobility on the housing market. Market segments can thus change (that is, be converted totally or partially into other market segments) when old barriers to mobility are simultaneously overcome or new ones are erected. Segregation is not a statistical artifact, but is at every point the result of a system of distribution (of flats and housing-seekers) whose dynamics produce our social organisation of space. The distribution is conditioned by the economics of land utilisation and of infrastructure development on the part of the suppliers and the class structure on the part of the tenants. In this sense barriers are not the cause but rather only mechanisms of the distribution system.

Preferences in mobility have the same character as barriers to mobility, but sociopolitically they are less significant. Segregation is seen to be a one-sided constraint. Some people can't go where they want, while others don't go where they could. These are decisively different situations, especially in the context of market opportunities that interest us here.

In this section, the search for empirical indicators of the existence of mobility barriers is presented. The search for such indicators serves the purpose of reinforcing with intermediate mechanisms our claim that mobility, segregation, market segment structures and opportunities on the housing market are interrelated. In this way the functional operation of the housing market ought to become clearer.

We distinguish three conditions acting as constraints on the housing market : informal brokerage on the rental market, a resigned decision not to change flats, and the anticipation of barriers in the search for a flat. Here we always keep the focus on differences among the three market segments. In general, one can assume that the market segment for the lower working class is hardly able to seal itself off from the outside (that is, it is open for people moving in). On the other hand, it is quite tightly sealed from the inside (outmigration is difficult). For this market segment, the barriers thrown up by other market segments are hindrances, but it has also thrown up hindrances of its own. The situation in the market segments of the upper working class and the middle class looks different ; here strong barriers will shield against migration "from below".

Informal brokerage is an indicator of a barrier to mobility insofar as it guarantees a preservation of the status quo. This is particularly true when locating a flat is carried on by friends and relatives, since one can assume a high degree of class homogeneity here.

TABLE 10.8 : **Locating flats through friends and relatives, by market segments (in % ; N=2072)**

Market Segment		
A	B	C
40.7	51.0	36.7

Source : Tenant survey, 1979.

In the market segment of the upper working class (B), locating a flat through friends and relatives was particularly common. The barrier in this case consisted of a sharply marked form of social self-recruiting. If we take other forms of informal flat-locating into account—such as through the previous tenant or through other tenants in the same building—then new leases in 63.5% of all flats in the B-market were concluded in this way. The chances of having a fair choice are thus unevenly distributed.

Seen in a passive sense, a decision not to change one's lodgings can indicate a barrier. We regard a failure to change flats as indicating a barrier only in cases where the desire to move existed but no action took place because the tenant assumed that his purpose in moving—improving his living conditions—could not be attained. Such cases of a resigned failure to move are considered as signs of barriers. In order to gather information on this, the question was asked why a person did *not* intend to change his flat. Table 10.9 presents the answers.

TABLE 10.9 : **Market segments and reasons for not moving, in per cent (in parentheses—number of responses)**

Market segment	Flat OK	Moving expensive/ difficult	Search for a flat too hard	New flat no better	Avg. % (total responses)
A	61.8 (34)	12.7 (7)	3.6 (2)	21.8 (12)	29.3 (55)
B	75.8 (47)	1.6 (1)	12.9 (8)	9.7 (6)	33.0 (62)
C	83.1 (59)	7.0 (5)	2.8 (2)	7.0 (5)	37.8 (71)
Totals	74.6 (140)	6.9 (13)	6.4 (12)	12.2 (23)	100.0 (188)

Source : Tenant survey, 1979.

Obviously a large segment of the people polled responded that they were not moving because they were pleased with their flats. In a different connection, we tried to show that this response could not be taken literally until we had checked out what chance the respondent had of actually changing his residence. In the above case, 34.9% of those not wanting to move because their flats were allegedly "well equipped" had no central heating, and some didn't even have bathing facilities ! This gives at least some idea of the degree of resigned making-do in this response.

We take as indirect indicators of resignation the response that the move would be too expensive or difficult. Direct indicators were responses that the search for a flat would be too difficult or that one couldn't find a better one in any case. If we combine the direct and indirect indicators of a resigned decision not to change flats, we arrive at 38% of the responses in market segment A and 16.8% in market segment C. In these percentages, rationalisations with the response "flat OK" were not included. Even if the small number of cases studied do not make a definitive conclusion possible resignation seems nevertheless to be an important indicator of barriers to mobility. It is theoretically plausible that people anticipate barriers, and so they confine their search for a flat to certain sections of the city where they are most likely to meet with success.

This in turn has consequences for the geographical direction of actual migration processes. At the beginning of this section the claim was made that market segment of the lower working class is "sealed from within" (i.e., it is hard to get out), while the other two market segments are "sealed from without". If this is the case, then it must be apparent in the direction of the intra-city migration. According to this hypothesis, migrations originating in the market segment of the lower working class (A) would be confined to a greater extent to this market segment. In 307 households we asked for the address of the flat preceding the current one so that we could discover the direction of migration in a change of flat. Table 10 shows the results.

TABLE 10.10 : **Situation of previous and current flat in % (N in parentheses)**

Current flat in market segment	Previous flat in market segment			Residual
	A	B	C	
A	72.9 (51)	11.4 (8)	12.8 (9)	2.8 (2)
B	17.9 (15)	71.5 (60)	5.8 (5)	4.8 (4)
C	33.3 (26)	21.9 (17)	42.3 (33)	2.6 (2)

Source : Tenant survey, 1979.

These data show for all market segments a concentration of migration in the inner area of each segment. Accordingly, the correlation between the current and earlier residence is relatively high (Cramer's V=0.55). Furthermore, it is evident that the degree of confinement—in the sense of circular migration within a single market segment—in the market for the lower and middle working class is practically the same, while in the middle-class market it is conspicuously smaller. Our hypothesis would, however, have led us to expect differences between market segments A and B. So although barriers in form of circular migration are clearly present, some questions remain unanswered even here.

This section has provided three examples of indicators of the existence of barriers to mobility. Barriers to mobility are essential mechanisms by which the economic unit of the market segment constitutes itself in terms of social space. Even if the pilot study presented here makes the existence of barriers to mobility appear likely, it is nevertheless clear that extensive theoretical and empirical work in this area remains to be done.

SOME SUGGESTIONS ON THE CONSEQUENCES FOR HOUSING POLICY

The findings of a sociological analysis of the housing market presented here should be regarded as tentative both in their geographical representativeness and in the refinement of their theoretical and empirical argumentation. Nevertheless, their potential significance for housing policy seems to be considerable. As was stated at the outset, the government has increasingly withdrawn from mass construction of housing projects, and support for private home construction has been increased. The justification for such a policy has been drawn from the "filtering theory", which claims that a housing policy for the middle classes is also, at each level, beneficial to the lower income groups and that the investment of private capital—stimulated by government subsidies—increases the efficiency of government programs. One of the essential requirements for the functioning in the filtering effect is free movement of those seeking housing and the nonexistence or minimal significance of social segregation. Our investigations have provided indications that mobility and segregation have contributed to the growth of market segments which cannot be substituted for one another or which can only be substituted to a limited degree. Thus it is likely that filtering effects, insofar as they can be empirically documented at all, break off at the socio-political relevant boundaries of the market segments. The inadequate housing of the lower 50% of income-earners is not essentially improved by benefiting the upper 50%. On the contrary, structural disadvantaging of the lower classes is increased when the supply of apartments is reduced by construction projects (building transportation systems, expanding the city centre, urban renewal) or when the demand is increased by programs in labour policy such as importing foreign workers. Thus if we want to supply the lower classes with housing, then programs are necessary which concentrate directly on those groups.

Furthermore, the small size of the market segments prevents our expecting much success from drastic measures in housing policy. In this context we should reflect on how the administration of housing policy can be shifted to a greater extent to the communal level and then further to the level of individual neighbourhoods, if we take as the chief purpose of housing policy meeting the needs of the lower and middle classes.

SECTION FOUR

INTRA URBAN LOCATION OF ECONOMIC ACTIVITIES

ELEVEN

B. MERENNE-SCHOUMAKER

ANALYSIS OF THE MOBILITY OF ECONOMIC ACTIVITIES IN URBAN AREAS

SINCE 1950 there has been a marked change in the localisation of many economic activities. Although the process is especially typical of industrial enterprise, tertiary activities such as the retail trade or services to industry have also been affected and even activities which, we call "heavy tertiary" (wholesale trade, garages, forwarders, etc.) which, due to their surface area and transport requirements are in many ways similar to manufacturing industry.

In spite of the numerous articles written about this problem, exhaustive analyses are relatively rare and often limited to the most striking aspects, such as the creation of big industrial estates or activities, the opening of new shopping centres or the development of large office areas. On the other hand nothing, or hardly anything, is known about changes in localisation in the heart of an urban centre or in a suburban district and often little is known about the changes of occupations in the pre-existent urban network.

The aim of this article is to show the interest of studies about the mobility of business organisations and to present some types of research that could be done in this field of investigation.

THE CONCEPT OF MOBILITY

By mobility we mean any change in the *civil status* of the businesses with results in a change in *the localisation of these businesses*. Any extension on the spot as well as any internal changes in the business (e.g. modification of the activity, growth or decline, legal or financial change) are not taken into consideration.

Four kinds of situations are therefore valid :

— creations or openings,
— cessations or closures,
— extensions on a site different from the original one,
— transfers.

However, as the table clearly shows, the same situation can be classified differently depending on the point of view concerned. Thus, if a spatial point of view is adopted—as is often the case in geographic studies—the opening of a new business by a firm from outside the region is considered as a creation, whereas, as far as the firm is concerned, it is an extension of its activity and, from an industrial point of view, it is either a creation (if the field of activity is new) or an extension (if the new business is working in the same field of activity as the parent company). Likewise, the cessation of a business due to the transfer of its activities outside the region represents a closure for the region whereas it is a change in localisation for the firm.

It would therefore seem to be of the utmost importance that in studies on the mobility of activities, the researcher clearly defines his *point of view of analysis* in order to be able to make further comparisons. Personally we tend to prefer the spatial point of view but we are aware that the resulting classification is extremely dependent on the area studied, e.g. in urban areas : the city centre, the agglomeration or the urban region.

Furthermore, attention should be drawn to the misunderstanding produced by certain individual concepts such as "spreading out" or "decentralisation" which are used in French studies. By "decentralisation" French authors generally mean the total or partial transfer or extension of a company out of the limits of the Ile de France region (on this subject see T. Saint-Julien, 1973) whereas if the new division remains in the region the operation is called "spreading out".

TABLE 11.1 : **Classification of the kind of operation of localisation according to the spatial point of view, the industrial point of view and the firm's point of view**

Kind of operation of localisation	Spatial point of view	Industrial point of view	Firm's point of view
1. Opening of a new business by individuals or a new company	creation	creation	creation
2. Opening of a new business by a company from outside the region but already working in the same field of activity	creation	extension	extension
3. Ditto but a new field of activity for the company	creation	creation	extension
4. Opening of a new business by a company already in the region and already working in the same field of activity	extension	extension	extension
5. Ditto but a new field of activity for the company	extenison	creation	extension
6. Cessation of the activity of a business—voluntarily or due to bankruptcy	closure	closure	closure
7. Cessation of part or all of the activity due to its transfer elsewhere in the region	dislocalisation	dislocalisation	dislocalisation
8. Ditto but complete transfer out of the region	closure	dislocalisation	dislocalisation
9. Ditto but partial transfer out of the region	dislocalisation	dislocalisation	dislocalisation
10. Opening of a business originally transferred from a place outside the region	creation	dislocalisation	dislocalisation

MEASUREMENT OF MOBILITY

This measurement necessarily involves the existence of a card index of the companies and businesses. Such a *card index* would include, for a given period, any changes in localisation that have affected production or services units.

With official statistics and particularly the data transmitted after census, it is not possible to keep a check on the civil status of the businesses. In addition, this information does not permit studies on the significant spatial sub-groups : city centre, old suburbs, harbour areas, etc. Indeed, if only 2 or 3 sets of statistics are available it is only possible to analyse the balance of the evolution, often on a local or regional scale. In addition, comparisons are made difficult by the changes which often affect the spatial divisions (e.g. changes in the limits of the agglomerations) or the activity code numbers of the businesses.

On the other hand, with a precise card index of all the business in the study area at two different dates it is possible to analyse the mobility components precisely.

From this point of view the study done by P.E. Lloyd and C.M. Mason (1978) of the city and conurbation of Manchester is a very good example. As is shown in Fig. 11.1 components of industrial change have been taken into account ; the exits, the in situ changes and the entries. Under exits the authors have separated closures and transfers whereas under entries the creations are separated from the dislocalisations. The figure clearly shows that the balance of the evolution is, in fact, only the difference between all the growth and reduction operations of both businesses and employment.

The existence of exact data about the number of businesses, the staff employed or all other quantitative variables which show the size of the businesses (e.g. surface occupied or sum of investments) also make it possible to calculate certain *rates*.

Let us suppose that for a given period $t0$-$t1$ we have the following information about the number of businesses :

- x or the number of businesses in $t0$
- y or the number of businesses in $t1$
- a or the number of businesses which did not change their localisation during the period $t0-t1$

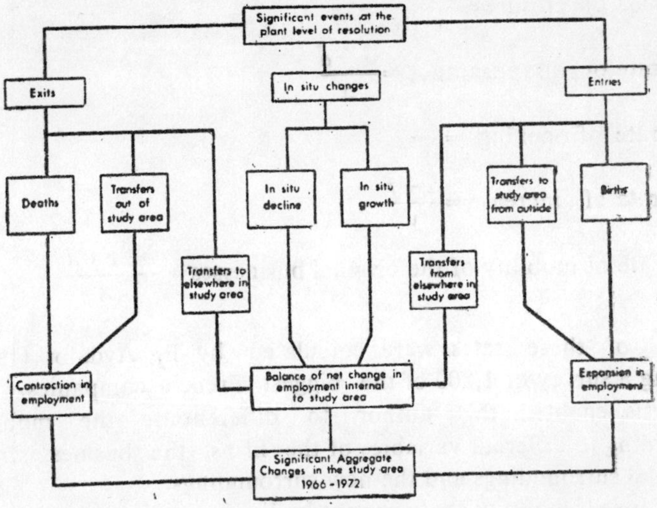

FIG. 11.1 : *Components of industrial change*

Source : P.E. Lloyd and C.M. Mason, Manufacturing industry in the inner city : a case study of Greater Manchester, in Transactions, *Institute of British Geographers*. Vol. 3, n. 1, 1978, p. 79.

b or the number of businesses which ceased their activity entirely

c or the number of businesses which were transferred within the study area

d or the number of businesses which were transferred out of the study area

e or the number of new businesses created during the period $t0—t1$

f or the number of businesses which were the result of a transfer from outside the study area

The following can therefore be calculated :

increase in number of businesses $=e+f$
decrease in number of businesses $=b+d$
balance of evolution $=y—x$

$$\text{rate of closure} = \frac{b}{x}$$

$$\text{rate of disappearance} = \frac{b+d}{x}$$

$$\text{rate of openings} = \frac{e}{y}$$

$$\text{rate of increase} = \frac{c+f}{y}$$

$$\text{rate of mobility of the original businesses} = \frac{b+c+d}{x}$$

Some of these rates were calculated by P. Aydalot (1978) during a survey of 1,800 of the biggest French companies. The analysis enabled this author to differentiate the mobility according to different variables of the firms, the businesses, the original surroundings and the new surroundings.

Indeed, mobility study cannot be limited to simple calculations on the number of businesses. It is advisable to integrate *various characteristics of the firms and businesses* involved, e.g.

— the branch of activity (e.g. manufacture of clothing, wholesale),
— the function of the business (e.g. factory, laboratory, sales office, etc.)
— the size of the business (number of people employed, ground surface),
— the localisation of the registered office,
— the size of the firm to which the business belongs (translated for example by the number of businesses which belong to the firm),
— the date of implantation.

The calculation of the rates defined above by category of business proves very interesting as it makes it possible to pick out the commonest features of the most or the least mobile units according to the mobility situations (creation, transfer, closure, etc.) (see P. Aydalot, 1980, pages 9-25, in particular).

SPATIAL TRENDS IN MOBILITY

In addition to measuring mobility, it is also necessary to study the movement itself by analysing the *characteristics of the areas* affected by the movement as well as the *directions* and *distances covered* in the case of extensions and transfers.

In order to achieve this, maps have to be made. As in research on changes in industrial localisations in the area of Liege (B. Merenne-Schoumaker, 1980, planche 34) the following can be mapped :

— the businesses according to the type of localisation operation which produced them ; cessation (proper or due to a transfer), creation, extension ;
— for transfers and extension, the point of departure and the point of arrival of the business as well as the journey effected by joining these two points by a segment of a straight line.

It is also advisable to study the main features of the areas involved in the different changes principally by distinguishing those where the closures and/or transfers have taken place and those where there have been creations, extensions and transferred units (also see under head—Spatial Results of Mobility).

In urban areas it is especially interesting to separate intra-urban migrations from inter-urban ones as the firms responsible for these migrations generally differ and the processes originate in different causes.

In Western Europe, on the whole, the businesses in urban regions very often move a limited distance (5, 10, 20 kilometres depending on the size of the regions concerned) due to the management's desire to keep its customers, labour and human and economic relations. Furthermore, they generally move in a specific radius of the conglomerations, e.g. businesses in the north of the city will settle in the northern outskirts of the agglomeration (B. Merenne-Schoumaker, 1974, pages 49-50). Moreover, there is a big intra-urban movement which is strongly influenced by the land and property market. This diagram proves correct in both the case of a big city like Paris (see J. Palierne, 1964, pages 85-111 and A. Delobez, 1981, p. 77

in particular) and the case of an average city like Liege (see our research in the bibliography at the end of the article).

CAUSES OF MOBILITY

Although it is often difficult to know the true causes of the closure of a business exactly, it is, on the other hand, possible to find out the factors of localisation of both new units and dislocalisations.

As regards the latter, we believe like A. Fischer (1973, pages 96-97) that the *expulsion factors* (from the original localisation) must be distinguished from *attraction factors* (of the new site). Indeed, all the surveys we have done in industrial enterprise (B. Merenne-Schoumaker, 1978) in heavy tertiary (B. Merenne-Schoumaker, 1981a and 1981b) and in retail trade (B. Merenne-Schoumaker, 1979) show that most transfers are due, in the first place and above all, to difficulties encountered in the original localisation. In the case of industry and heavy tertiary activities the main causes of dislocalisation are : the decrepitude and unsuitability of the buildings, traffic and parking conditions, difficulties of proximity and pressure of land prices accentuated by town planning operations. In the case of retail trade the main factors of explusion are : end of a lease, unsuitability of the premises, their price or the bad situation of the shop.

The requirements concerning the new site are therefore only taken into account at a second stage, when looking for a new localisation. The factors of attraction are principally : the surface area and the cost of the ground and/or buildings, the situation of the site, the policy of the authorities, the environment of the new site, etc.

The analysis of the causes of mobility therefore involves precise surveys with the firms in order to analyse the decision-making process. The quality of the work is very dependent on the investigator and the means of investigation (see B. Merenne-Schoumaker, 1982a, pages 106-107).

It should, however, be noted that in spite of a growing rationalisation of choices, precise studies of localisation are still rare, particularly in the case of directors of small businesses and when businesses are created. It is therefore advisable to be very careful in this kind of analysis and to accept answers that are fragmentary but true rather than answers that are complete but incorrect.

SPATIAL RESULTS OF MOBILITY

In addition to research on the mobility of businesses it is also very interesting to study the areas affected by the changes, particularly, as already mentioned, the areas under development and those abandoned.

In actual fact the dislocalisation of many activities creates various problems. Generally the situation of most European cities is the following.

In the city centre premises are rarely abandoned but, helped by land speculation, there is a clear whittling down of functions and the "noble" activities (decision, research, offices of industrial firms, luxury trade) are often the only ones which can pay the price asked for. Certain economic fields are therefore ejected from the city as well as a certain type of population except from the dilapidated areas where the "marginals" are becoming more and more concentrated.

In the outskirts of the agglomerations the chief problem is the anarchic growth of urbanization and the recession of farmland. The city is diluting hence the difficulties for both the rural world (seriously threatened by the progression of the urban front) as well as for the city (faced with the problems of providing services and organising public transport).

It is, however, in the *close suburbs* and especially in the old industrial suburbs that the most acute problems exist due to the multiplication of wasteland and to the difficult conversion of activities (B. Merenne-Schoumaker, 1982b).

Thus one can see the interest of precise analysis of the changes in the activities of the various urban sub-spaces—these analyses being essential for any development or renovation operation. The research done by J.P. Bondue (1982, pages 356-402) on the evolution of acquisitions liberated by wholesale activities in the conurbation of Lille is a very good example from this point of view.

CONCLUSION

The mobility of businesses, major process of the evolution of cities and of the changes in urban spatial structures, appears to us to be one of the principal subjects to be explored when analysing cities.

That is why we have tried, in this article aimed at methodology, to demonstrate different ways of research that are possible as well as various methods that can be used effectively.

Doubtlessly the concept of mobility is often ambiguous. In addition the analysis requires lengthy and sometimes tedious research but the results of this research are very rich and indisputably likely to renew traditional studies of urban functions and areas.

REFERENCES

Aydalot, P. (1978).—La mobilite des activites et de l'emploi. Resultats d'une enquete nationale menee aupres des grandes entreprises, in Revue d'Economie regionale et urbaine, n° 3, pp. 299-328.

Aydalot, P. (1980).—L'entreprise dans l'espace urbain, Collection Economic publique de l'Amenagement et des Tradsports, n° 8, Economica, Paris.

Bondue, J.P. (1982).—La mobilite spatiale du commerce de gros et des entrepots dans la conurbation lilloise (1964-1980), These de 3e cycle, Universite de Lille 1, 420 p.+24 p. d'annexes.

Delobez, A. et Collaborateurs (1981).—Les mutations recentes du stade commerce de gros en Ile-de-France, Laboratoire Analyse de l'Espace, Action concertee Urbanisme commercial, Paris, 226 p.+108 p. d'annexes.

Fischer, A. (1973).—Pour une etude de la mobilite geographique des activites industrielles en France, in Annales de Geographie, n° 449, pp. 93-101.

Lloyd, P.E. et Mason C.M. (1978).—Manufacturing industry in the inner city : a case study of Greater Manchester, in Transactions, Institute of British Geographers, Vol. 3, n° 1, pp. 66-90.

Merenne, Schoumaker B. (1974).—Elements entrant concretement en compte pour le choix d'une localisation, in Localisation des entreprises et development regional, Premier Congres des Economistes belges de Langue Francaise, Rapports preparatories, Charleroi, pp. 33-55.

Merenne, Schoumaker B. (1978).—L'analyse des localisations industrielles : des schemas classiques aux etudes de comportement, in Bull. de la Societe belge d'Etudes geographiques, t. 47, pp. 39-60.

Merenne, Schoumaker B. (1979).—Motivations des localisations commerciales au centre-ville. Le cas des nouveaux commerces de l'hyper-centre liegeois, in Revue de la Societe d'Etudes et d'Expansion, n° 281, pp. 541-550.

Merenne, Schoumaker B. (1980).—Les industries, in Liege prepare son avenir, E. Wahle, Liege, pp. 119-127.

Merenne, Schoumaker B. (1981a).—Analyse de la localisation des garages et des societes de transport dans la region liegeoise, in Wallonie 81, n° 3-4, pp. 269-290.

Merenne, Schoumaker B. (1981b).—Le commerce de gros a Liege. Permanence et renouveau des localisations, in Bull. de la Societe geographique de Liege, n° 16-17, pp. 49-64.

Merenne, Schoumaker B. (1982a).—Perceptions spatiales et localisations, in Percevoir l'espace. Vers une geographie de l'espace vecu, Actes de la Table ronde 1981, Universite de Geneve, Department de Geographie, Geneve, pp. 103-116.

Merenne, Schoumaker B. (1982b).— L'amenagement des friches industrielles, dans Notes de Recherches de la Societe geographique de Liege, n° 2, pp. 29-40.

Palierne, J.L. (1964).—Mouvement des establissements industriels dans la region parisienne, Cahiers de l'I.A.U.R,P. (Institut d'Amenagement et d'Urbanisme de la Region parisienne), Vol. 1.

Saint, Julien T. (1973).—Signification geographique des implantations industrielles decentralisees en province, in Annales de Geographie'n° 453, pp. 557-575.

TWELVE

FABIO LANDO

FUNCTIONAL AREAS IN THE TOWN
The Example of Venice, Italy

VENICE is a city which is not only at the service of its residents but pursues a number of different functions : it is a tourist and cultural centre of international value, plays a directorial role towards a large part of the region, is the integral part as "historic centre" of a large lagoon conurbation, and finally, is the Venetians' city.[1] And these functions intermingling, occupy various areas, and render inextricable the various roles of the economic urban space. Moreover, the number of retail activities and the services offered is not only notable in respect to the limited space in Venice, but seems to be almost uniformly distributed along the various streets.

Then the fact that it is almost exclusively a city for pedestrians, in which not only are the "economic distances" limited and therefore well-definable within the urban space, but also its being well-limited by the lagoon makes it particularly attractive for analyses of this kind. So to verify the existence of this economic zone and then attempt to designate the relevant area two principal component analyses were made and one potential was calculated.[2]

THE TWO PRINCIPAL COMPONENTS ANALYSES

In the first analysis of the principal components the variables consist of the percentage of each economic activity[3] in every Census section.[4]

In this way the characteristics of a series of 139 "tertiary structures" are made evident, each of which is considered of equivalent importance, whatever the service being offered. In one respect the analysis did not produce the hoped for results : a good 15 components were obtained with eigenvalues above the unit, capable of explaining just 68% of the total variance (see Table 12.1). A result that if no use from the geographical point of view does say a lot about the extreme complexity of the localization of the offer and thus the impossibility of identifying with this analysis the economic areas that are—if not specialized—at least homogeneous.

Given these results the analysis was repeated keeping the values relative to the services intact, without translating them into percentages to try and make the *mass effect* evident. The breaking down of the data into percentages could be understood as a kind of prenormalization : it underlines the likeness in the composition of the services offered in the sections (mix) at the expense of the similarity of the distribution (mass) of the various services. So the analysis, before beginning the calculation of the correlation matrix carried out an effective normalization. And in this way, without this "premanipulation", that is, admitting in the analysis the data with its mass, one can obtain from the analysis itself a type of *mass effect* that can be read in the factor scores, in as much as it results from the product between the loading factor and the normalized value of given data. If the data has a distribution of "abnormal" average and standard deviation—high factor scores are obtained.

Now 8 components succeed in explaining 70% of the total variance (see Table 12.2). Even though halved, the number of the components remains high while the variation explained remains the same : another confirmation of the complexity of the tertiary-commercial structure of insular Venice.

Fortunately the first component, with almost 20% of the variance, clearly demonstrates the fact that there is a *commercial centrality*. It is known that the graded positions of a nucleus of shops depends not only on the type of goods offered but also on the quantity of the items offered, and in fact shops offering different goods, but with similar scope, tend to be grouped together in the same place. The possibility of stocking up on many goods during the course of shopping has an extremely

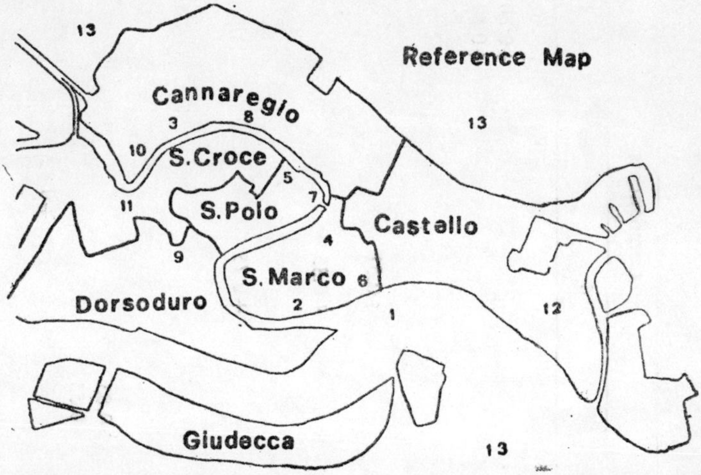

FIG. 12.1 : *Reference map : Principal places cited*

1. St. Mark's Basin
2. Calle Larga XXIII Marzo
3. Lista di Spagna
4. Mercerie
5. Pescheria (Fish market)
6. St. Mark's square
7. Rialto
8. S. Leonardo
9. S. Margherita
10. Railway terminal
11. Road terminal
12. Via Garibaldi
13. The Lagoon

positive effect on the potential buyer : it could be likened to a discount, or better to a reduction of the "economic distance" that the consumer evaluates in "time and cost". In this way the quantity, the type and the quality of the goods offered, in a very restricted territorial environment, is important for the significance of a "commercial centrality".

As far as we are concerned it is a question of shops that offer both clothes and their accessories and unusual products for the house : all goods, that for the consumer correspond to purchases not made very frequently and related to the necessity of systematically having to compare prices and quality.

The factor scores demonstrate a large central area corresponding to the "Mercerie" : that part of the district of St. Mark's comprising the area between the Rialto and St. Mark's Square in

TABLE 12.1 : Analysis with percentage values (Varimax Rotated Component Matrix)

Variables	Components							
	1	2	3	4	5	6	7	8
1. Grocer		−0.40						
2. Butcher								+0.80
3. Grenegr								+0.80
4. Fish								
5. Clothing			+0.66					
6. Fashion				+0.44				
7. Shoes			+0.36			+0.51		
8. Showroom								
9. Electric			+0.52			+0.35		
10. China	+0.81							
11. Arts				+0.59				
12. Hardware						+0.75		
13. Perfumery			+0.62					
14. Tobacco								
15. Books								
16. Jewel	+0.72							
17. Florist					+0.85			
18. Toyshop					+0.55			
19. Pharmac							+0.82	
20. Photo								
21. Hairdre								
22. Restaur								

23. Bar								
24. Pizza	+0.30							
25. Pl. Entret.	+0.75							
26. Lar. Hot				+0.59				
27. Med. Hot								
28. Smal. Hot							+0.76	
29. Tour. Ag				+0.77				
30. Esta. Ag						+0.81		
31. Ship. Ag								
32. Law. Off		+0.80						
33. Architect		+0.32						
34. Account		+0.76						
35. Bank								
Eigenvalues	2.15	1.88	1.87	1.87	1.85	1.84	1.64	1.62
Variance exp.	6.15	5.38	5.35	5.34	5.29	5.27	4.68	4.62

TABLE 12.1 : (*Contd.*)

Variable			Components			
9	10	11	12	13	14	15
						+0.49
			+0.88			
				+0.37		
				−0.75		
					−0.75	
				+0.60		
	+0.81					
	+0.57	+0.42				
						+0.84
			+0.60			

Components						
Variable						
9	10	11	12	13	14	15
		−0.68				
+0.84					+0.53	
					+0.76	
1.42	1.39	1.35	1.34	1.26	1.25	1.25
4.04	3.97	3.86	3.83	3.60	3.56	3.56

TABLE 12.2 : Analysis with total values (Component loadings) (Varimax Rotated Component Matrix)

Variables	Components								
	1.	2.	3.	4.	5.	6.	7.	8.	
1. Grocer			+0.64						0.64
2. Butcher			+0.91						0.85
3. Greengr			+0.86						0.84
4. Fish			+0.80						0.81
5. Clothing	+0.86								0.89
6. Fashion	+0.57								0.65
7. Shoes	+0.58						+0.40		0.72
8. Showroom						+0.74			0.69
9. Electric	+0.82								0.78
10. China	+0.78								0.70
11. Arts	+0.75	+0.50							0.85
12. Hardware					+0.61				0.45
13. Perfumery	+0.50						+0.47		0.72
14. Tobacco	+0.42							+0.56	0.64
15. Books	+0.58								0.56
16. Jewel	+0.75								0.82
17. Florist						+0.70			0.58
18. Toyshop						+0.46	+0.42		0.62
19. Pharmac					+0.60				0.51
20. Photo	+0.81								0.82
21. Hairdre					+0.66				0.55
22. Restaur		+0.42			+0.42				0.72

23. Bar	+0.55							+0.42	0.81
24. Pizza					+0.66				0.63
25. Pl. Entert		+0.61							0.46
26. Lar. Hot		+0.83							0.77
27. Med. Hot		+0.79							0.72
28. Smal. Hot		+0.69			+0.46				0.80
29. Tour. Ag	+0.45	+0.67							0.68
30. Esta. Ag				+0.70					0.62
31. Ship. Ag								+0.68	0.60
32. Law. Off				+0.84					0.85
33. Architec				+0.66					0.63
34. Account				+0.72					0.72
35. Bank	+0.51	+0.46							0.75
Eigenvalues	6.70	4.07	3.20	2.94	2.88	1.68	1.53	1.42	
Variance expl.	19 14	11.63	9.15	8.41	8.23	4.81	4.38	4.07	

which more than a third of the shops offering "non-banal" goods are crowded along the streets of the said "Mercerie" (see Table 12.3 and Fig. 12.2). From this compact central nucleus ramifications seem to branch out that, following the main routes reach the two secondary nuclei of S. Leonardo and S. Margherita, arriving then at the two terminals for road and rail.

The second component—accounting for 11.63% of the total variance—indicates a "tourist centrality", showing up the areas where the hotels are concentrated (see Table 12.4 and Fig. 12.3), the tourist agencies, the fine art shops and the restaurants. In fact, the scores immediately emphasize the important hotel nucleus located around St. Mark's Square and overlooking St. Mark's Basin. Here we find the most famous and important hotels and restaurants in the city : Danieli, Gritti, Regina, Harry's Bar—enjoying a position and a view among the most prestigious and renowned in Venice.

The second and far less important nucleus regards the Lista di Spagna, a distinctly inferior hotel centre adjacent to the railway terminal.

The third component regards the *daily supplies* of the urban population : groceries, meat, fish, fruit and vegetables. In Venice, these are services that are found concentrated (see Table 12.5 and Fig. 12.4) in only two Census sections : the Rialto, where the wholesale market is situated and the most important retail fruit, vegetable and meat market in the city, and the fish market (Pescheria) where the majority of fishmongers are concentrated.

Every morning the hotels and the Venetian housekeepers make their daily purchases. And this is by now a long standing tradition, and typical of many Veneto cities : almost at the geometric centre of the city, very near to the town square the most important city food market is to be found—perhaps the only one that could be termed as such ; regularly frequented by housekeepers from both the city and outskirts. The map then shows the other two much less important nuclei of San Leonardo and Via Garibaldi.

The fourth component regards the professions (see Table 12.6). It shows the zone in which there is the maximum concentration of law, architectual, and accountancy offices and so demonstrates the marked *tertiary function* of Venice. It picks

TABLE 12.3 : **First component : Census section with factor scores higher than +1.0 and the original values of the relative variables having a saturation higher than 0.7**

Census Section	Scores	Clothing T	Clothing %	Electrical T	Electrical %	Fine Arts T	Fine Arts %	Jewellers T	Jewellers %	Photo T	Photo %	China Shop T	China Shop %
96	5.634	23	6.4	6	5.1	33	13.9	6	6.3	6	8.8	9	15.3
97	6.523	26	7.2	8	6.8	64	26.9	8	8.4	8	10.8	3	5.1
98	2.464	16	4.4	4	3.9	12	5.0	4	4.2	2	4.2	5	8.5
108	1.615	15	4.2	3	2.5	3	1.3	4	4.2	4	5.4	1	1.7
109	4.299	18	5.0	9	7.6	10	4.2	6	6.3	5	5.8	5	8.5
110	2.299	22	6.1	6	5.1	2	0.8	3	3.2	1	1.4	2	3.4
1	1.971	15	4.2	1	0.8	13	5.5	15	15.8	1	1.4	1	1.7
Total Nucleus		135	36.5	37	31.4	137	57.6	46	48.4	27	36.5	26	44.1
38	1.674	12	3.3	6	5.1	2	0.8	5	5.3	—	—	2	3.4
Total Venice		370	100.0	118	100.0	238	100.0	95	100.0	74	100.0	59	100.0

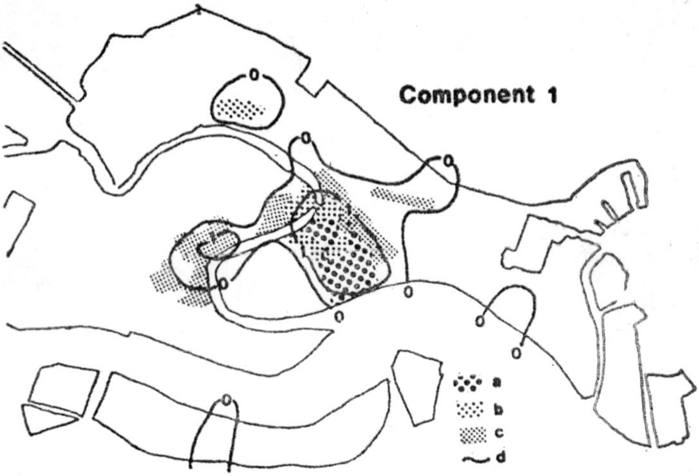

FIG. 12.2 : *Commercial centrality*

(a) Score values higher than +3.0 ;
(b) Score values rancing from +1.0 to +3.0 ;
(c) Score values rancing from +0.4 to +1.0 ;
(d) Isopotential.

out Venice's City, the core of which—the Stock Exchange, the Chamber of Commerce and the local branch of some large national banks—is clearly shown up in Cens. sect. 102 of Calle Larga XXIII Marzo that features the highest scores.

The remaining four components, although presenting own eigenvalues well above the unit seem to be clearly residual and the resulting outlines are not very convincing.

THE ANALYSIS WITH THE POTENTIAL

To see how and to what extent these economic areas relate to the inhabitants of Venice a correlation has been measured between the areas and the total population, the residential density and the social structure, i.e. social-economic status (Lando, 1978).

The correlations obtained are extremely low, but despite that it is possible to pick out some significant indications (see Table 12.7). The population, both in number and in density,

TABLE 12.4 : **Second component : Census section with factor scores higher than +1.0 and the original values of the relative variables having a saturation higher than 0.7**

Census Section	Scores	Pl. entert		Large Hot.		Medium Hot.		Small Hot.		Tourist Ag.	
		T	%	T	%	T	%	T	%	T	%
86	3.839	—	—	1	7.7	2	7.7	12	8.8	2	8.3
97	4.054	1	5.9	1	7.7	3	11.5	4	2.9	5	20.8
100	4.33	1	5.9	2	15.4	1	3.8	3	2.2	6	25.0
102	5.551	2	11.8	3	27.1	3	11.5	5	3.7	1	4.2
Total Nucleus		4	23.6	7	53.9	9	34.5	24	17.6	14	58.3
30	2.020	1	5.9	—	—	2	7.7	7	5.2	—	—
31	5.354	1	5.9	2	15.4	3	11.5	13	9.6	2	8.3
Total Nucleus		2	11.8	2	15.4	5	19.2	20	14.8	2	8.3
Total Venice		17	100.0	13	100.0	26	100.0	136	100.0	24	100.0

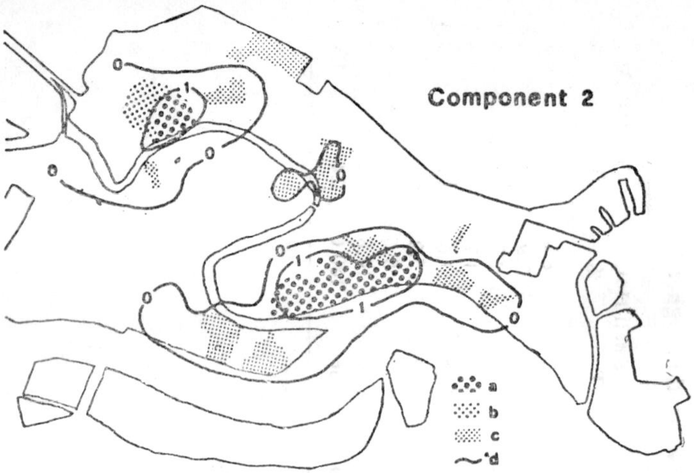

FIG. 12.3 : *Tourist centrality*

(a) Score values higher than +3.0
(b) Score values rancing from +1.0 to +3.0
(c) Score values rancing from +0.4 to 1.0
(d) Isopotential

is correlated negatively to the first, second and fourth components : in an ambient characterized by a limited and costly available space, the distribution of the population—in as much as it is a consumer of space—clearly runs counter to the distribution of shops, hotels and professional offices, which are also large consumers of space. The social-economic status, that seems to be orthogonal to the first three components, is correlated positively to the fourth—that regards the distribution of the professions : the positive co-relation is obvious between the high status zone (understood as those parts of the city in which a prevalence of directors, professionals, or office workers reside who have a high level of education, live in large houses, with little crowding, and are well-equipped with comforts) and the localization of the professional studios.

In accord with these analyses we can distinguish—and therefore outline—precise and distinct *social economic areas*.

To depict these areas that go over the limits placed by the

TABLE 12.5 : **Third component : Census section with factor scores higher than +1.0 and the original values of the relative variables having a saturation higher than 0.7**

Census Section	Scores	Grocer's		Butcher's		Greegrocer		Fish	
		T	%	T	%	T	%	T	%
1	5.369	15	3.0	8	5.2	50	22.8	—	—
2	8.955	11	2.2	13	8.5	34	15.5	25	50.0
Total Nucleus		26	5.2	21	13.7	84	38.3	25	50.0
35	1.983	6	1.2	4	2.6	9	4.1	2	4.0
37	1.121	4	0.8	4	2.6	8	3.7	2	4.0
Total Nucleus		10	2.0	8	5.2	17	7.8	4	8.0
37	1.137	6	1.2	2	1.3	10	4.6	3	6.0
Total Venice		500	100.0	153	100.0	219	100.0	50	100.0

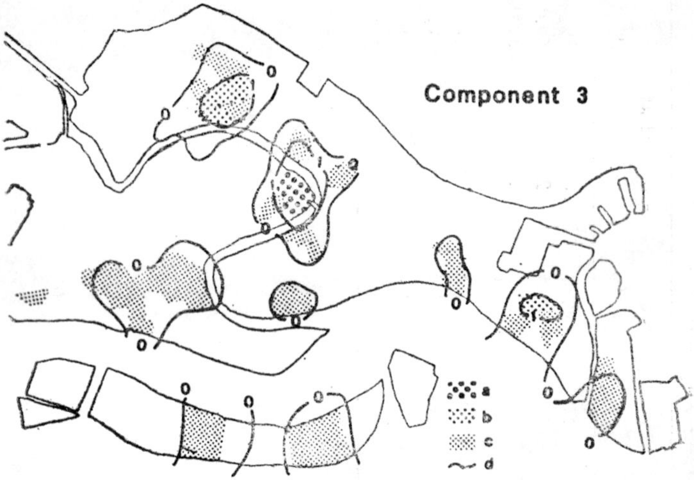

FIG. 12.4 : *Daily supplies*

(a) Score values higher than +3.0
(b) Score values rancing from +1.0 to 3.0
(c) Score values rancing from +0.4 to 1.0
(d) Isopotential

confines of the Census sections, the potential :

$$Vi=\sum \frac{f(M)}{f(d)}$$

has been used that we can consider as a synthetic indication of the distribution of the phenomenon, in that it as signs a value to every place– estimated by the "nearness" of that place to a distributed phenomenon.

From time to time, the factor scores of the four components and the scores of the status have been applied to the numerator $f(M)$. The most important square of the Cens. sect. was that considered for peak load.

Obviously the most important problem has been the choice of distance function, i.e. the spatial friction connectable to the considered phenomenon. As is known, the choice of such functions has been and is the object of notable controversy.

It can however be affirmed that : indicating with R^+ the aggregate of the non negative real numbers, it is possible to define

TABLE 12.6 : **Fourth component : Census section with factor scores higher than +1.0 and the original values of the relative variables having a saturation higher than 0.7**

Census Section	Scores	Estate Agency T	Estate Agency %	Law Offices T	Law Offices %	Architect. Studio T	Architect. Studio %	Accountant's T	Accountant's %
87	1.314	1	8.3	2	1.4	2	2.6	—	—
90	1.021	—	—	4	2.7	3	3.9	—	—
99	3.098	+	+	8	5.5	4	5.2	7	9.5
101	3.303	1	8.3	16	11.0	1	1.3	3	4.1
102	4.889	2	16.7	10	6.9	3	3.9	7	9.5
103	1.228	—	—	9	6.2	—	—	1	1.4
104	3.100	1	8.3	8	5.5	2	2.6	7	9.5
107	4.196	—	—	16	11.0	7	9.1	6	8.1
108	4.230	2	16.7	13	8.9	1	1.3	5	6.8
109	2.060	—	—	14	9.6	2	2.6	3	4.1
110	3.550	1	8.3	10	6.9	5	6.5	3	3.1
Total Nucleus		8	66.4	110	75.6	30	39.0	42	57.1
Total Venice		12	100.0	146	100.0	77	100.0	74	100.0

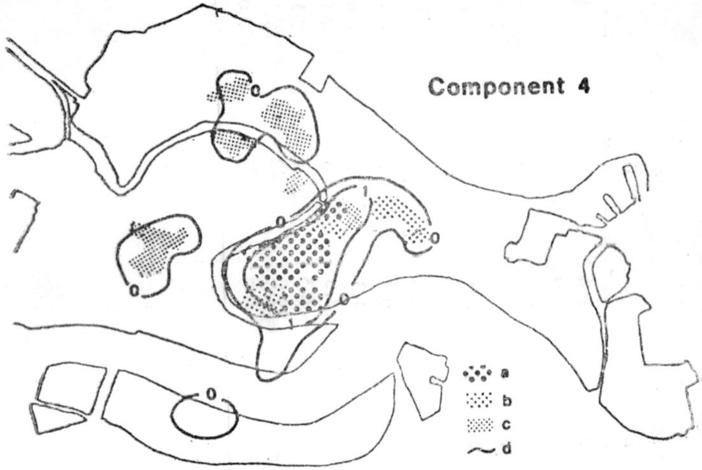

FIG. 12.5 : *Tertiary function*

(a) Score values higher than +3.0
(b) Score values rancing from +1.0 to 3.0
(c) Score values rancing from +0.4 to 1.0
(d) Isopotential

TABLE 12.7 : **Correlation**

	Population	Density	Status
Component I	—0.236	—0.042	+0.148
Component II	—0.240	—0.309	+0.112
Component III	+0.054	+0.028	—0.087
Component IV	—0.215	—0.103	+0.390

as a function of spatial friction any function $f(d)$ of $R^+ \to R$, such as to satisfy the following property :

a) continual and monotonic decrease
b) $\lim_{d \to +\infty} f(d)=0$
c) $0 \leqslant f(d) \leqslant 1$, for every $d \in R^+$
d) there exist two values d_1 and d_2 $(0<d_1<d_2)$ such that in the interval $(0, d_1)$ the decrease of the $f(d)$ is very slow

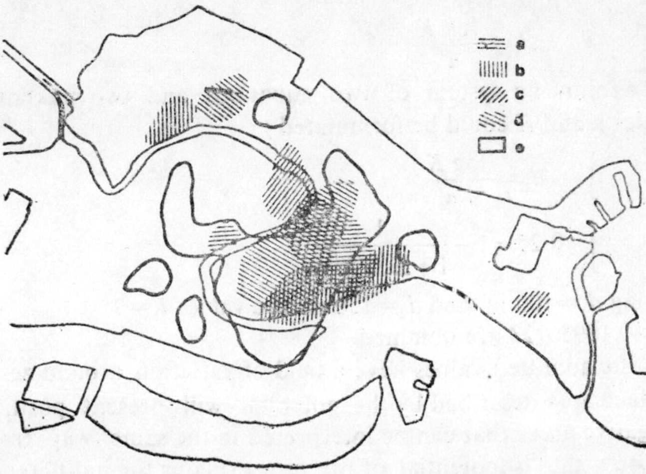

FIG. 12.6 : *Economic areas*

(a) Commercial centrality
(b) Tourist centrality
(c) Daily supplies
(d) Tertiary function
(e) High status areas

if not completely zero, while in the interval (d_1, d_2) the decrease is quite rapid (Canestrelli, 1978).

There are many functions that can satisfy all four properties (Ingram, 1971 ; Hutchinson, 1975) but here the logistical function is utilized or rather its reciprocal :

$$1-\frac{1}{1+Ke^{(-\alpha d)}}$$

with α and K positive parameters to be determined.

Lacking the data necessary to calibrate the function, the two parameters α and K were calculated keeping in mind some hypotheses that could be formulated concerning the point where d_1 is found—in which the function could be worth 0,5 and the point d_2 where it could be worth 0.25.[5] Observing that :

$$f(0)=\frac{K}{K+1}$$

$$(d_1)=0,5$$

when, $$d_1=\frac{\log K}{\alpha}$$

The following system of two equations and two unknown quantities α and K could be formulated :

$$\begin{cases} d_1=\dfrac{\log K}{\alpha} \\ 0.25=1-\dfrac{1}{1+K_e^{(-\alpha d_2)}} \end{cases}$$

Supposing $d_1=100$ m. and $d_2=150$ m. the values $K=9$ and $\alpha=0.10986123$ are obtained.

As the admitted values have a field of variation around zero[6] the surface area described by the potential will present positive and negative areas that can be interpreted in the same way from the score : the isopotential of the zero explains the indifference to the phenomena while the positive values, in agreement with our analysis, will indicate the concentration of the centrality or of the high status.

In agreement with the initial assumptions regarding the choice of variables the scores of the four components present few positive values, but very high and relative to adjacent sections, countering many—however, extremely low—negative values. Analogous results are obtained with the potential : very high positive values concentrated in small areas and predominantly low in negative values.

In our case the area enclosed by the isopotential (+ 1) is that which could be considered the most significant for our purposes : it marks the area of maximum concentration both of the centrality, defined by the four components, and of the high status.

CONCLUSIONS

Excluding the *daily services*—third component regarding the food shops—the values higher by one to all the other components dwell principally on the St. Mark's area. Even in the orthogonal way in which their structural characteristics are expressed, these components—with their higher scores—indicate adjacent areas with some points overlapping. So the Northern part of the

St. Mark's zone which is less densely inhabited and is placed almost in the geometric centre of Venice, encloses the maximum concentration of the three central areas, whose importance could qualify them as the Venetian centre, the influence of which extends well beyond the lagoon. This description of the town centre tallies well with what the various schemes or theories, from Burgess to the gradient of density, express about the composition of the City of any town with demographic dimensions analogous or superior to those of Venice. Here instead, it is the high status area, that takes in and incorporates the town centre, which does not seem to conform with what is defined for the other cities—at least those of Anglo-Saxon culture, which are those that have been studied the most. Present-day Venice recalls the Chicago of Burgess : but here the invasion and the succession, whose evolution can be traced, has the middle and high classes as protagonists—not the poor immigrants. As is demonstrated in other analyses here it is the rich who desire the centre ; they invade it and substitute the less rich by buying, restoring and restructuring the houses. The earning mechanism here has an eminent role in establishing an equivalent between the cost of the site, social class, quality of the district, and the presence of prestigious activity. But to fully understand this intermingling Venice cannot be considered as an isolated city enclosed in its lagoon : we must remember its integration in the "Venetian conurbation" of which it represents the residential, tertiary, commercial, tourist centre.

FOOTNOTES

1. With regard the special characteristics of Venice—its history, its residential, tourist, industrial and commercial functions, see : F.C. Lane 1973 ; P. Costa, B. Dolcetta and G. Toniolo 1971 ; V. Piasentin, P. Costa and D. Foot 1978 ; G. Zanetto 1981.
2. Principal Component Analysis is a data transformation technique. Often used in geography and in particular in urban geography (J. Goddard A. Kitby 1976 ; S. Daultrey 1976). The potential model has appeared frequently in the human geography literature as an index of the intensity of possible interaction between social or economic groups at different locations (D.C. Rich, 1980).
3. The data relative to the retail activity comes from a "census" which

I effected in the first days of July 1978 ; the various shops wer, classified according to what appeared to be their dominant activity after a careful look in the window. For the service activities reference was made to the 1978 telephone directory. For the analyses were used the following variables : 1-Grocer's ; 2-Butcher's ; 3-Greengrocer's ; 4-Fishmonger's ; 5-Clothing and Haberdasher's ; 6-Shoe Shop ; 7-Fashion and furs ; 8-Furniture Showroom ; 9-Electrical goods shop ; 10-China Shop ; 11-Fine arts shop ; 12-Hardware store ; 13-Perfumery ; 14-Stationer's and Tobacconist's ; 15-Bookshop ; 16-Jeweller's ; 17-Florist's ; 18-Toyshop ; 19-Pharmacist's ; 20-Photographer's ; 21-Hairdresser's ; 22-Restaurant ; 23-Bar ; 24-Pizza Parlour ; 25-Places of Entertainment ; 26-Large Hotel (with more than 150 beds) ; 27-Medium sized Hotels (with from 76 to 149 beds) ; 28-Small Hotels (with less than 76 beds) ; 29-Tourist Agency ; 30-Estate Agency ; 31-Shipping Agency ; 32-Law Offices ; 33-Architectural Studio ; 34-Accountant's ; 35-Bank.

4. The Census Section represents the smallest territorial unit of importance that was assigned to each census taker. For Venice there are 149. The average surface area, not including water surfaces and those relative to the bridges, is of 2.80 hectares, and on average each one is composed of about 650 inhabitants.
5. The point at which the function is rated at 0.50 has been set at 100 metres while at 150 metres it is rated at 0.25. To obtain these figures reference was made to the surface area of the census section, for each of which the radius of equivalent surfaces was calculated, that on average is about 100 metres, while the maximum radius (excluding the sections that include the road and rail terminals) is of about 290 metres. In this way it is arranged that every phenomenon manifesting itself in the centre of the average Census section would feel, at the borders after 100 metres, an influence equal to 50 per cent of its intensity and that this influence would practically tend to annul itself only beyond the 300m. These 300m. constitute the radius equivalent to the Census section with the greatest surface area.
6. The field of variation of the four components being examined is respectively : of (—1.72 ; +6.52) for the first ; of (—1.12 ; +5.55) for the second ; of (1.02 ; +8.95) for the third ; of (—2.40 ; +4.89) for the fourth and of (—2.77 ; +2.28) for the status scores.

REFERENCES

Canestrelli, E., *L'accessibilita al sistema urbano italiano : methodologia e primi risultati*, Venezia, G.R.E.P.R.U., paper no. 20 (1978).

Costa, P., B. Dolcetta and G. Toniolo, *The new scale of the city*, Architectural Review, 149 (1971), pp. 310-312.

Daultrey, S., *Principal Component Analysis*, Norwhich, Geo Abstracts, Catmog n. 8, 1976.

Goddard, J., A. Kirby, *An introduction to factor analysis*, Norwich, Geo

Abstracts, Carmog n. 7, 1976.

Hutchinson, B.G., *Principles of urban transport systems planning*, New York, McGraw Hill, 1974.

Ingram, D.R., *The concept of accessibility : a search for an operational form*, Regional Studies, 5 (1971), pp. 101-107.

Lane, F.C., *Venice. A maritime republic*, Johns Hopkins University Press, 1973.

Lando, F., *La struttura socio-economica veneziana : un tentativo di analisi*, La Rivista Veneta, 28/29 (1978), pp. 125-140.

Rich, D.C., *Potential models in human geography*, Norwich, Geo Abstracts, CATMOG, n. 26, 1980.

Piasentin, U., P. Costa and D. Foot, *The Venice problem : an approach by urban modelling*, Regional Studies, 12 (1978), pp. 579-602.

Zanetto, G., *A definition of Venice in a metropolitan context*, R.J. Bennet (ed.), European Progress in Spatial Analysis, London, Pion, 1981, pp. 297-300.

THIRTEEN

CLIFFORD M. GUY

CLASSIFICATIONS OF URBAN RETAIL FACILITIES

INTRODUCTION

THIS paper examines a topic of considerable importance to geographers and planners alike—the classification of retail facilities in urban areas. The view is taken that, while it is relatively easy to devise detailed descriptive classifications of shops, a generally agreed parsimonious list of retail types selected on some consistent and rational basis does not currently exist, at least in the U.K. or North America. Those classifications used in planning practice tend to be inconsistent and illogical, or at best, vague and incapable of precise application.

In order both to demonstrate this proposition, and to seek improvement, it is necessary to review relevant existing practice in three areas of research which have normally been pursued independently, although a number of conceptual links will become apparent. These areas are, firstly, market research, which (among other things) seeks to explain the shopping behaviour of consumers, paying particular attention to the ways in which behaviour appears to be affected either by economic, social and psychological characteristics of consumers themselves, or by characteristics of retail commodities and of the methods used in selling them. (For a summary see Guy, 1980, ch. 5.) The second area is the concern of the conventional urban geographer, who tends to be concerned most with physical attributes (size, location and characteristics) of shopping centres (e.g. Warnes and

Daniels, 1980 ; Dawson, 1980 ; Davies, 1976). Thirdly, some spatial analysts have examined the spatial distribution of shops of various types in cities, partly with a view to explaining some aspects of the locational behaviour of retailers (e.g. Rogers, 1974 ; Sibley, 1972).

The discussion of the first two areas of research mentioned above needs no justification. Spatial analytical work on locational patterns of retail facilities has however tended to be neglected in most conventional urban geographic reviews. This is unfortunate, because not only does this work offer some insights into the locational behaviour of retailers and consumers, but it also allows the possibility of more precise definition of types of retail facility than has emerged from the work of either market researchers or conventional urban geographers.

One further introductory point should be made. The geographic work to be reviewed below has concentrated mainly upon shops (retail *outlets*) and their locational patterns. In contrast, much of the market research has been into retail goods and services (or *commodities*). This paper deals with both outlets and commodities, since they are intimately related : the classification proposed in the final section is actually of retail commodities, but could be adapted to form a classification of retail outlets. Hence the neutral title (retail *facilities*) used in this paper.

The paper proceeds as follows. In Section 2 summaries are made of ways in which retail commodities and outlets have been classified by market researchers, economists and geographers. The locational implications of these various classifications are discussed. In Section 3 the work of spatial analysts on patterns of retail location is briefly discussed, with particular attention paid to suppositions about locational decision-making on the part of retailers. In Section 4 some results of research into retail location in the Reading area, carried out by the author from 1974 onwards, are summarised and some measures of spatial distribution of various retail commodities are discussed. These measures are related to aspects of classifications of retail commodities discussed in Section 2. Finally, some broad conclusions about problems in retail research are drawn.

CLASSIFICATIONS OF RETAIL COMMODITIES AND OUTLETS

It may be assumed that individual types of retail commodity (defined as consumer goods or services normally made available to the public without prior appointment, in premises devoted mainly to their sale) can be distinguished relatively unambiguously. The problem is to classify these commodities into distinctive groups : this is necessary not only for research purposes but often also for the clarification of policies in marketing or property development, or town planning. A logical basis for classification would be that each group or commodities implies a particular set of decision-making rules on the part of retailers and/or consumers. These 'rules' might also imply certain patterns in space of location and consumption respectively.

Behavioural classifications

A well known classification of retail goods was first devised by Copeland (1924), and as revised by the American Marketing Association (1948) is as follows :

> Convenience Goods : Consumers' goods which the consumer usually purchases frequently, immediately, and with a minimum of effort.
>
> Shopping Goods : Consumers' goods which the consumer, in the process of selection and purchase, characteristically compares on such bases as suitability, quality, price and style.
>
> Speciality Goods : Consumers' goods on which a significant group of buyers is habitually willing to make a special purchasing effort.

This classification is made on the basis of assumed behaviour of consumers, related to physical or financial characteristics of the goods themselves. Since consumers vary a great deal in their attitudes to many aspects of shopping (Guy, 1980, Chapter 5 ; Bowlby, 1979 ; Williams, 1979), any commodity might fall into any category ; but experience and common sense suggests which category is on the whole most appropriate.

The A.M.A. classification carries implications for spatial patterns of shops selling the three types of commodity, which have been stated by several authors, including R. Nelson (1958) and Rogers (1974, p. 72). Shops selling convenience goods tend to locate close to the consumer, and gain little or no benefit from proximity to one another. Thus they are likely to be widely dispersed over residential areas. Shops selling shopping goods are likely to cluster together to aid the consumers' search process. Shops selling speciality goods may locate virtually anywhere in an urban area, as they tend to generate single-purpose trips whose outcomes are important relative to the effort involved.

Product classifications

Classifications by characteristics of commodities themselves are often used (e.g. foods/non-foods ; durable goods ; household goods). Classifications of 'retail establishments' (in Britain) and of 'business types' (in U.S.A.) are similar, grouping shops according to the principal types of goods that they sell.

P. Nelson (1970) has attempted to relate product classification to consumer behaviour. He classified goods as :

(i) Experience Goods : the consumer determines the utility of these goods through purchasing them and testing them at home, e.g. canned foods, paint, TV and radio.

(ii) Search Goods : the consumer can assess their utility visually in the shop, e.g. clothing, floor covering.

Nelson suggests that stores that sell search goods will tend to cluster more than those selling experience goods. The former appear to be similar in nature to comparison goods, but the latter can also include some goods classified normally as comparison, as well as some convenience and speciality goods.

'Order' classifications

One of the necessary assumptions for Christaller's (1966) formulation of central place theory is that retail commodities can be ranked according to characteristics of consumer demand for them. Beavon (1977, Chapter 3) suggests that the 'marketing principle' hierarchy (k=3) is most easily deduced if commodities are ranked in order of range (the distance beyond which consumers are not prepared to travel in order to obtain the commodity). 'High order' commodities are, according to this theory, available only in 'high order' centres : those centres which are relatively large and well spaced apart. 'Low order' commodities, having much smaller ranges, are available in 'low order' centres (small and frequent), as well as in the high order centres. An alternative formulation of central place theory (Berry and Garrison, 1958) ranks commodities in order of threshold (number of consumers needed for profitable operation of one retail or service establishment providing the commodity concerned).

Several authors (e.g. Garner, 1966) have suggested a correspondence between high order commodities and comparison goods, and between low order commodities and convenience goods. These links are not inevitable, however, because central place theory does not assume any wish on the part of consumers to compare outlets for any type of commodity, but only to minimise distance travelled. Also, the position of speciality goods becomes unclear. Although these are likely to be high order commodities, we have already deduced that they may be sold at any location and not just in the high order centres. Perhaps because of these problems, little attempt has been made to generalise any empirical findings concerning perceived 'orders' of either commodity types or retail outlet types (e.g. Berry, 1963 ; Stafford, 1963 ; Golledge et al., 1966).

Critical comments

The overall situation regarding classificatory systems for retail outlets and commodities seems very unsatisfactory. The most consistent system would appear to be that of the American Marketing Association ; however it is probably too vague to be of practical value in any detailed exercise. 'Product' systems are clearer in detailed applications, but carry little or no implications for spatial patterns of commodities or outlets, because they do not immediately suggest any patterns of behaviour. The situation is confused further when inconsistent systems of classification are used, such as the convenience/durable classification commonly applied both to goods and shops in the U.K.

A further criticism of the behavioural and order classifications is that they are based upon assumptions about consumer shopping behaviour which are either untested or have been found to be untenable, such as the 'nearest centre' hypothesis of central place theory (Hubbard, 1978). It is unclear to what extent shoppers distinguish between commodities or outlets according to their product or locational characteristics, and how much variation exists between shoppers. Suppositions about retailers' motives for locational choice are also, on the whole, untested.

SPATIAL ANALYSIS OF RETAIL LOCATION PATTERNS

Several geographers have analysed retail location point patterns, usually those formed within urban areas by shops of one 'type'. (For a general review of point pattern analysis, see Getis and Boots, 1978.) In so doing the assumption has to be made that all shops within any one type are similar enough to be influenced in their location by some common process or set of processes. This assumption usually appears to be implicit, and variations in size of shops, characteristics of ownership, quality of goods, exact nature of goods, etc., are often ignored.

Spatial affinities

Spatial affinities are said to exist where shops (either of the same or of two specified types) tend to be sited physically next to one another significantly more often than would be expected under a random point process. Under this severe definition of clustering the only affinities commonly observed have been between various sub-types of clothing store (Getis and Getis, 1968; Davies, 1972).

It is not clear what process is assumed to occur here. It is reasonable to suggest that comparison goods retailers will want to locate so as to facilitate comparison, but this does not require that retailers offering similar goods actually locate next to one another. In any case, the opportunity to do so will be restricted by imperfections in the property market.

Distance measures

Davies (1972) computed standard distance measures for several types of retail and service establishment within the central area of Coventry. He found that shoe shops possessed the smallest standard distance (25.56), and building services the largest (60.69); the mean distance for all shops was 44.10. Davies infers that low values indicate a "tendency towards clustering", and high values a "tendency towards dispersal". These conclusions seem to be derived from internal comparisons and not from any comparison with the standard distance that might arise from a random point process.

Davies (1972 ; 1976, pp. 128-135) suggests that these results provide support for Garner's (1966) hypotheses concerning the bid-price curves (Alonso, 1964) of various types of retail firm : those placing a high emphasis on comparison will be prepared to bid high prices for the most central sites in the city, thus tending to cluster around their centre of gravity. Other firms prepared to accept non-central locations will show a more dispersed pattern. These firms are likely to offer convenience or speciality goods rather than comparison goods.

Nearest neighbour analysis

This technique has some advantage over those outlined above in that a characteristic of the observed point pattern (its mean nearest neighbour distance) can be compared with that which would arise due to a random spatial point process. A nearest-neighbour statistic below 1.0 suggests that some form of clustering has occurred : tests of significance can be used in this respect (Clark and Evans, 1954 ; Haggett et al., 1977, Chapter 13 ; Getis and Boots, 1978, Chapter 2).

Rogers (1974, p. 97) found that for each of four types of store (grocery, food, non-food, apparel) the nearest neighbour statistic in Ljubliana (Yugoslavia) was below 1.0. This matches conclusions drawn from his quadrat analysis. Rogers also (p. 10) warns against the possibility of misleading results from this form of analysis, which cannot distinguish between a pattern of isolated clumps and a perfectly clustered pattern.

Quadrat analysis

Another method of assessing the probability that some form of clustering has influenced a spatial point pattern is to take counts of the occurrence of points in equal size quadrats. The numbers of quadrats with 0, 1, 2, etc. occurrences can then be compared with those numbers that would have arisen under some specified spatial point process. Under a random spatial point process, a Poisson distribution is likely to occur, in which the mean and variance are equal (Rogers, 1974, p. 4).

Rogers (1974) has carried out the most complete analysis to date of spatial patterns of retail location, dealing mainly with data of the location of four broad types of store in Ljubliana. Various measures demonstrate clustering in all instances, although much more strongly in the case of apparel and non-foods than for food or grocery stores, as predicted above. He compared frequency distributions derived from observed point patterns with those derived from several probability distribution functions, and found that in all cases the results of a X^2 test indicated that a negative binomial distribution provided a satisfactory fit. Since this distribution can be generated in several different ways (Boswell and Patil, 1970) it is impossible to make conclusive statements about processes which have led to the observed point pattern. Rogers states (p. 96) that two types of process might be involved. First, retailers "carrying the same class of shopping goods merchandise do indeed appear to be attracted to one another." Second, all types of retailer are also "attracted to purchasing power". This means that the apparent spatial clustering of convenience goods outlets may be due to the clustered distribution of the residential population themselves, rather than to any desire for clustering on the part of retailers. Rogers shows that the population of Ljubliana is itself clustered, providing a close fit to the negative binomial distribution among others.

Temporal spatial analysis

The probability distribution functions used in quadrat analysis are intended to replicate the effects of specified dynamic processes. It is relevant therefore to investigate actual changes in spatial point patterns over time, since this may provide greater insight. Getis (1964) investigated the spatial pattern of grocery stores in Lansing, Michigan, at 10-year intervals over the period 1900-1960. This pattern appeared to be 'random' in 1900, 'clustered' over 1910-1950, and 'random' again in 1960. The early lack of clustering was ascribed to a lack of spatial organisation at an early stage in the city's development, while the recent trend towards a less clustered pattern was said to be connected with a greater use of the car for grocery shopping. This latter argument is not wholly convincing : a possible alternative argument might be that land costs are lower outside existing business centres, thus encouraging retailers to open new stores in locations between these centres.

Sibley (1972) investigated temporal changes in spatial patterns of greengrocers, chemists and jewellers in Leicester and Northampton over the period 1880-1969. He considers that "we may expect to find patterns approaching the optimum only in the long run, as marginal operations are liquidated and as retailers adapt to, or are adopted by, the urban system." Patterns were described at 10-year intervals, using order-neighbour randomness ratios (Dacey, 1962) and the variance-mean ratios from quadrat analysis. The results of these analyses were not entirely consistent, but suggest in general that the pattern of greengrocers has been essentially random throughout, although with some local clustering. That of chemists was clustered initially, but has tended to become more random over time ; that of jewellers has become increasingly more clustered.

The behaviour of jewellers thus suggests a dynamic clustering process, not surprisingly as jewellery is usually considered to be a 'shopping' good. Sibley believes that the contrast in behaviour between greengrocers and chemists reveals differences in the locational strategy of independent and multiple retail firms. The former do not generally seek to maximise profits, and are likely to be content with the location originally made available (Guy, 1980, Chapter 4). Thus the initial set of locations, essentially 'chance events' (Sibley, 1972, p. 156), possess stability over time. However, the multiple retailer is more aware of the advantages to be gained by locational adjustment : in the case of the chemist, advantage is gained through establishing local monopolies, which process will normally lead to greater regularity in the spatial point pattern.

Comments on the use of spatial analysis

A number of themes emerge from this work. There has been increasing concern with the inference of process from the observed spatial point pattern. This has been hindered, not only by problems of choosing quadrat sizes, parameters for distribution functions, and measures of significance, but also by the ability of certain distribution functions (such as the negative binomial) to replicate the effects of several dissimilar processes.

Two ways have been suggested in which processes of retail locational pattern formation can better be explained. The first is in the direct historical study (e.g. Sibley, 1972). This still however seems to require rather imaginative inferences, in the lack of direct knowledge of retailers' decision-making processes.

A second way lies in the linking of retail point patterns to patterns of population distribution, as suggested by Rogers in the development of bivariate distributions (1974, Chapter 8). Dacey (1966 ; 1972) has formulated models of retail location in urban areas in which the location of centres of retail clusters is determined by some function such as the circular normal distribution, which approximately replicates the distribution of population density in several major cities. The number of shops in each cluster is then generated by a random variable.

This indicates that in the analysis of retail point patterns, it is important to establish the degree to which an observed pattern is 'regular', 'random', or 'clustered' with respect to the pattern of residential population. This rather imprecise statement implies a number of methods, including that of Getis (1963), who transformed geographic space into 'income space' for the purpose of examining the market areas of grocery stores. Given this transformation, the point pattern of these stores tended to be more regular than random. Other possible methods are discussed in the following section.

Finally, there seems to be confusion over the properties of retail commodities (goods and services) and retail establishments (shops). It has been noted above that, as in Section 2, commodities have been defined with respect to typical decision-making strategies on the part of consumers. The optimal behaviour of retailers has been assumed to be that which allows consumers most easily to adopt the appropriate strategy for those commodities offered by the retailer. This reasoning seems only justifiable if the retailers is offering a bundle of commodities clearly associated with a particular strategy. Where this is not the case (as with the umbrella categories of 'food' and 'non-food' used by Rogers, for example), then it is by no means clear why the disparate types of retailer included should locate according to one spatial point process, rather than several.

RETAIL LOCATION PATTERNS IN THE READING AREA

In this section it is shown that information on retail point patterns can in fact be used to classify retail facilities. The results given here also represent a preliminary attempt to remedy two deficiencies of previous spatial analyses of retail location, identified at the conclusion to the previous section. These are the lack of disaggregation of point patterns, and the problem of establishing associations with observed spatial distributions of residential population.

The survey data

Members of a student class recorded the goods and services available at every retail and service establishment in the Greater Reading area. The type of good or service was entered from a pre-coded list based upon that used in current Family Expenditure Survey reports (Department of Employment, 1974). Because of limited time it was not possible to survey the size of each establishment, or its 'quality' of goods or services. Further details are given in Guy (1976 ; 1977a).

Subsequently, the location of each establishment was digitised (to 10-metre intervals). This means that for any of the 146 classes of goods and services, a full list of locations is available for point pattern analysis. It should be noted that since any shop may sell several goods or services, the following discussion relates to commodities, not outlets.

Spatial point patterns for retail commodities

Figures 13.1 to 13.4 depict the point patterns for 4 commodities, chosen to represent regularity, marked clustering, clumping, and patterns difficult to summarise, respectively.

Some statistics describing the spatial point patterns of outlets for all types of retail good and service in the Reading area are shown in Appendix I. First, the table shows the frequency of occurrence of each type. The most obtainable good was 'soft drinks and sweets', with 370 occurrences (i.e. in 18.8% of all retail and service outlets surveyed ; and one point of sale for every 515 residents of the survey area). This is followed in rank order by several items normally sold in supermarkets, food shops or tobacconists.

Two simple indices of spatial dispersion are also given in Appendix I : the nearest neighbour index and variance-mean ratio, for each commodity. These findings are not to be discussed

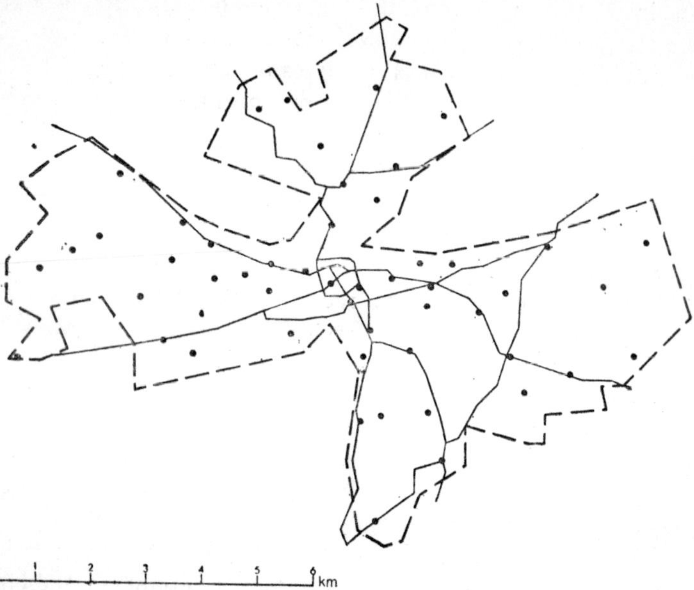

FIG. 13.1 : *A regular pattern : Sub-post Offices in Greater Reading*

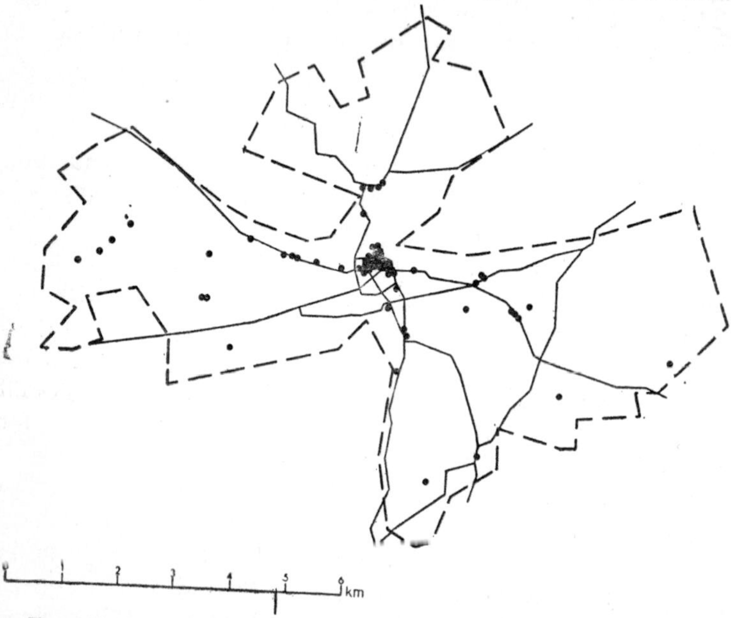

FIG. 13.2 : *A highly clustered pattern : Women's outer clothing sales in Greater Reading*

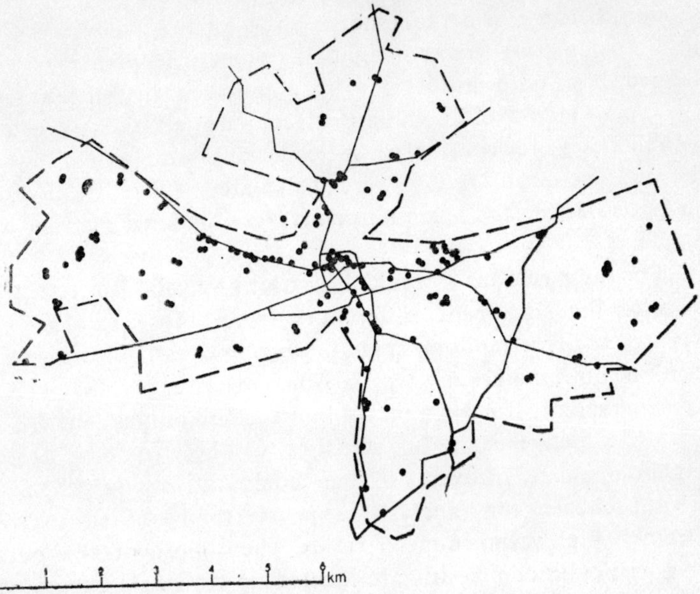

FIG. 13.3 : *A clumped pattern : Fresh meat sales in Greater Reading*

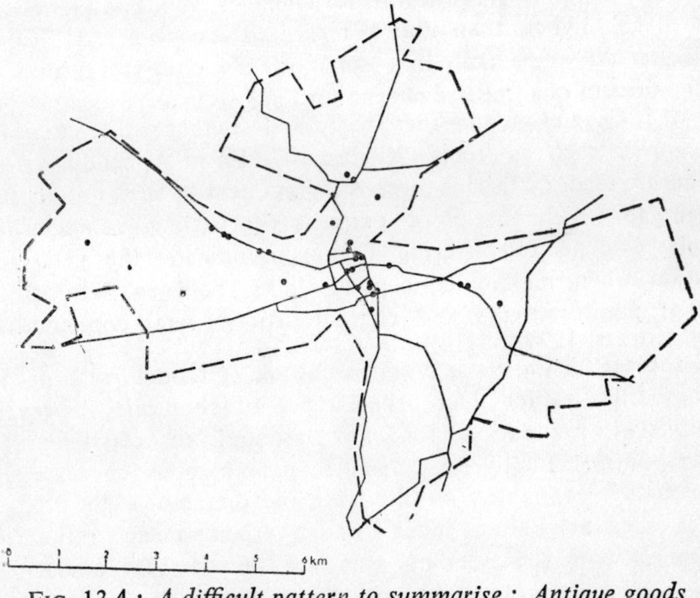

FIG. 13.4 : *A difficult pattern to summarise : Antique goods sales in Greater Reading*

in detail, because of certain shortcomings in the analysis carried out. In calculating nearest-neighbour indices, the points were not mapped first onto a torus, as recommended by Haggett et al. (1977, p. 441) to avoid boundary effects ; also all points for each commodity were considered instead of a sample (*ibid*, p. 440). The variance-mean ratios were calculated for only one size of quadrat (1 km^2), and again all points were included instead of a sample.

For these reasons it would be strictly invalid to test these statistics for significant differences from those values to be expected under a random spatial point process. However, the values of both indices shown in Appendix I suggest that clustering is prevalent : for example, only 10 commodities out of the 137 for which meaningful statistics can be given have nearest-neighbour indices of over 1.0. The comparatively large size of quadrat chosen for analysis appears to have led to some extremely high variance-mean ratios, when most of the outlets for a particular commodity are located in the single quadrat that includes most of the town centre shops (e.g. 'men's outer clothing', ratio of 43.94). Ratios for chemists' goods and jewellery are much higher than those measured by Sibley (1972) in Leicester ; it seems likely that some of the contrast is due to differences in quadrat size chosen for analysis.

It is clear even from these basic analyses that within umbrella categories such as 'food' (Codes 101-119 in Appendix I) or 'apparel' (Codes 401-416) there is a great deal of variation in the extent to which the point patterns for various commodities display evidence of clustering. This again indicates the need for caution when making conceptual links between features of spatial point patterns and characteristics of retail commodities (e.g. Rogers, 1974, p. 116).

Indices such as those described above, although relating to commodities rather than broad types of shop are, however, insufficient foundation for any attempt to classify such commodities. Firstly, no single unambiguous measure of dispersion is available : to illustrate the difficulties, the values of nearest-neighbour index and variance-mean ratio for commodities in the Reading area are only weakly associated ($r^2=0.157$). Secondly, since nearly all commodities appear to possess clustered point patterns, there is no obvious means to distinguish types of commodity according to some feature of their spatial dispersion.

Residential point patterns

The conclusion was drawn in Section 3 that measures of dispersal of retail point patterns might usefully be related to characteristics of the distribution of population in the area concerned. Rogers (1974, Chapter 8) tackled this through bivariate distribution functions, but his attempts to fit such functions to the observed distribution of population and shops taken together in Ljubliana were not very successful. In any case, the process of calibrating such functions appears to be complex and it is not clear whether the moment estimators used by Rogers are actually efficient enough to be useful. Instead, some much more simple methods of relating observed retail point patterns to variations in population density are to be suggested. The results of one of these methods are then discussed in relation to typologies of retail commodities.

The first step in these methods is to depict the distribution of residential population as a spatial point pattern. If a random sample of population is chosen, the home locations of those chosen can form a spatial point pattern. Thus, distance-based measures of dispersion, such as nearest-neighbour statistics, can be used. These can then be compared with similar measures for the spatial point patterns for various retail commodities. This will suggest whether clustering of outlets for the commodities is more or less pronounced than for the population as a whole.

A further step would be to examine directly the spatial association between the point patterns of shops and homes. A simple set of methods of examining 'segregation' in a two-species population have been developed by ecologists (summarised in Pielou, 1969, pp. 159-171 ; Getis and Boots, 1978, pp. 34-35). For example, when the two patterns are both realisations of a Poisson process, then the value of a 'coefficient of segregation' (S) is close to zero ; if they are spatially associated, S approaches-1.

Accessibility analysis

A test of the method above against the Reading data has not yet been carried out. However, some results of another method of analysis can be described. This does not seek to relate the extent of clustering of outlets to the distribution of residential population, but examines contrasts between commodities in their degree of accessibility for the residential population. This leads to the tentative proposal of a new classificatory system for retail commodities.

Points were chosen to represent the distribution of residential population in the Reading area, as follows : a regular sample of 1 in 200 registered electors was made, starting at elector no. 100 in every polling district, and their home addresses were digitised. This gave a total of 657 points in the Reading area (Figures 13.5 & 13.6). This procedure creates an unbiased sample, but one which probably has somewhat different properties from a random spatial sample. The main purpose of taking a regular sample was to achieve full areal coverage of the Reading area in order to examine the effects upon accessibility of shop closures in the area (Guy, 1977b).

The intention was to measure from each of these points the

FIG. 13.5 : *Location of sampled residential addresses in Greater Reading*

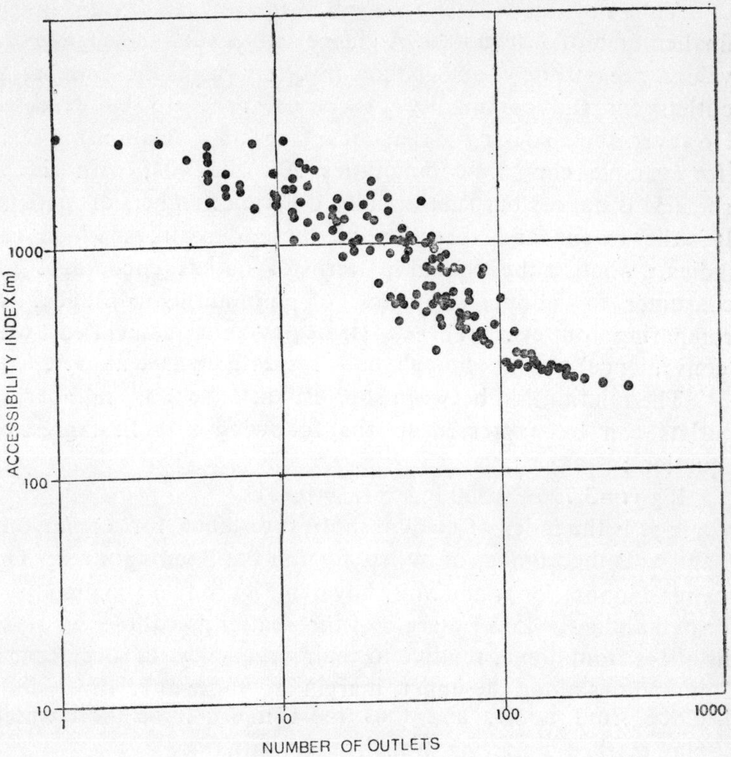

FIG. 13.6 : *Scatter diagram of accessibility and frequency of outlets by function*

distance to the nearest outlet at which commodity *i* was available (i=1,. . . , 146). From these data some 'average' would be obtained, to represent accessibility to that commodity in the Reading area. Preliminary analysis showed that a reduction in the number of sample homes to 219 (i.e. every 600th elector) still gave a frequency distribution of home-nearest outlet distances closely similar to that derived from analysis for all 657 points, and so the smaller sample of 219 homes was used in order to save computer processing time. Further analysis showed that this frequency distribution tended to be strongly skewed, so the measure of 'average' shortest distance chosen was the median of the 219 values measured.

Values of this index, expressed in metres, are given in the final column of Appendix I. A glance at this column suggests that values are strongly associated inversely with the number of outlets for the commodity concerned, as is to be expected. However, some striking departures from this relationship exist (for example, compare commodities 301 and 404, with similar shortest distances but substantially different numbers of outlets). It is the extent and direction of these departures which can indicate whether the spatial pattern of outlets encourages the consumer to adopt strategies of minimising distance, or comparing outlets. These strategies are associated with 'convenience' and 'shopping' goods respectively (see above).

The relationship between shortest distance and number of outlets can be expressed in the following best fit regression equation :

$$\log y_i = 3.796 - 0.580 \log x_i \quad (r^2 = 0.831)$$

where y_i is the index of median shortest distance for commodity i, and x_i is the number of outlets for i in the Reading area. The scatter diagram for y_i and x_i is shown in Figure 13.6 : commodities located along the lower margin of the scatter are those at short distances from home, relative to their frequency of occurrence. Commodities along the upper margin are those at relatively long distance from home, and thus most likely to be those which display marked clustering in their point patterns.

A classification of retail commodities

These features can now be related to strategies likely to be used by consumers. Those commodities which are relatively widely dispersed through residential areas, or which are in any case usually available within a short distance of home, encourage the consumer to make frequent short trips, and can be termed 'accessibility' commodities. A tentative method of definition is to include in this category all those commodities which are (i) relatively easily available (at least 20 occurrences in the Reading area), and are either (ii) commonly available within a short distance of home (within 600m. of home for at least 90 % of the sampled residential locations), or (iii) relatively widely dispersed (have median shortest distances of at least one standard residual below the value expected from the best fit regression given above).

When defined in this manner, 'accessibility commodities' include many goods commonly accepted as 'convenience', such as several types of food, and newspapers, tobacco products, cleaning materials, etc. Other commodities often classed as 'durable' such as chemists' goods, toys and stationery, and services such as hairdressers, launderettes and betting shops, are also included. These are listed in Appendix II to this paper.

The consumer strategy of comparing outlets for a commodity is assisted where the outlets are strongly clustered. The category 'comparison commodities' in Appendix II includes those which are (i) relatively easily available (at least 20 occurrences in the Reading area), *and* (ii) relatively clustered (have median shortest distances at least one standard residual above the expected value). These definitions are thus comparable with those adopted for "accessibility commodities'. The commodities defined in this manner for the Reading area include several clothing, furniture and electrical goods generally regarded as 'shopping goods', and three service uses.

This leaves several 'intermediate commodities' which do not display marked degrees of dispersal or clustering in their spatial patterns in the Reading area, and are not very widely available. Most of these are well represented in the town centre of Reading and in the larger suburban centres. These include commodities sometimes regarded as 'convenience' (hardware items) or 'shopping' (e.g. footwear).

For completeness the 'scarce commodities' (those with 20 occurrences or less) are also listed in Appendix II. These may to some extent correspond with 'speciality goods' and show considerable variation in locational pattern.

CONCLUSIONS

The work described above should be regarded as an initial attempt at improving methods of interpretation of retail locational patterns. The improvements lie first, in examining patterns for commodities at individual level instead of for broad and possibly ill-defined groups; and second, in establishing measures of dispersion which are related to the distribution of population, and thus to those aspects of consumer behaviour which in turn affect the commonly accepted typology of retail commodities. Finally, a classification of retail commodities has been made which is similar to previous attempts but defined on a more precise basis.

Some basic research questions need further investigation: for example, the ways in which commodities are typically grouped in retail outlets, the extent to which retailers are aware of possible advantages of dispersal or clustering, and the ways in which consumers respond to different spatial patterns in their shopping behaviour. In this area of research it seems almost impossible to avoid either making unsupported assumptions about aspects of human behaviour, or indulging in circular arguments. Clearly many spatial aspects of consumer behaviour are affected by spatial aspects of retailer behaviour, and *vice versa*. The nature and extent of these inter-relationships appears to vary not only according to observed characteristics of retailers, consumers, and the commodities themselves, but also according to the temporal and spatial scales adopted for analysis. It is hoped that this paper has at least indicated the magnitude of the research problems involved, and the limited degree of success of investigations to date.

REFERENCES

Alonso, W., 1964, *Location and Land Use*, Cambridge, Mass.

American Marketing Association, 1948, Report of the Definitions Committee, *Journal of Marketing*, 13, pp. 202-217.

Beavon, K., 1977, *Central Place Theory, a reinterpretation*, London.

Berry, B.J.L., 1963, Commercial structure and commercial blight, *University of Chicago, Department of Geography Research Paper*, 85.

Berry, B.J.L. and Garrison, W.L., 1958, Recent development of central place theory, *Papers and Proceedings, Regional Science Association*, 4, pp. 107-120.

Boswell, M.T. and Patil, G.P., 1970, Chance mechanisms generating the negative binomial distribution, in Patil, G.P. (ed.) *Random counts in scientific work*, Pennsylvania State University, vol 1, pp. 3-22.

Bowlby, S.R., 1979, Accessibility, mobility and shopping provision, in Goodall, B. and Kirby, A. (eds), *Resources and Planning*, Oxford.

Christaller, W., 1966, *Central places in southern Germany*, Englewood Cliffs, N.J.

Clark, P.J. and Evans, F.C., 1954, Distance to nearest neighbour as a measure of spatial relationships in populations, *Ecology*, 35, pp. 445-453.

Copeland, M.T., 1924, *Principles of merchandising*, Chicago.

Dacey, M.F., 1962, Analysis of central place and point patterns by a nearest neighbour method, *Land Studies in Geography, Ser. B.*, 24, pp. 55-75.

Dacey, M.F., 1966, A model for the areal pattern of retail and service establishments within an urban area, *Department of Geography, Northwestern University, Research Report No. 30*, Evanston, III.

Dacey, M.F., 1972, An explanation for the observed dispersion of retail establishments in urban areas, *Environment and Planning*, 4, pp. 323-330.

Davies, R.L., 1972, The retail pattern of the central area in Coventry, in Institute of British Geographers, Urban Study Group, *The Retail Structure of Cities*, pp. 1-32.

Dawson, J.A. (ed.), 1980, *Retail Geography*, London.

Department of Employment, 1974, *Family Expenditure Survey : Report for 1973*, London.

Garner, B.J., 1966, The internal structure of retail nucleations, *Northwestern University, Studies in Geography, No. 12*, Evanston, III.

Getis, A., 1963, The determination of the location of retail activities with the use of a map transformation, *Economic Geography*, 39, pp. 1-22.

Getis, A., 1964, Temporal land-use pattern analysis with the use of nearest neighbour and quadrat methods, *Annals of the Association of American Geographers*, 54, pp. 391-399.

Getis, A. and Boots, B., 1978, *Models of Spatial Processes*, Cambridge.

Getis, A. and Getis, J., 1968, Retail store spatial affinities, *Urban Studies*, 5, pp. 317-332.

Golledge, R.G., Rushton, G. and Clark, W.A.V., 1966, Some spatial characteristics of Iowa's dispersed farm population and their implications for the grouping of central place functions, *Economic Geography*, 42, pp. 261-272.

Guy, C.M., 1976, The location of shops in the Reading area, *University of Reading, Geographical Paper No. 46*.

Guy, C.M., 1977a, *Local shops in a changing retail environment*, Unpublished Ph.D. thesis, University of Reading.

Guy, C.M., 1977b, A method of examining and evaluating the impact of major retail developments upon existing shops and their users, *Environment and Planning A*, 9, pp. 491-504.

Guy, C.M., 1980, *Retail location and retail planning in Britain*, Farnborough.

Haggett, P., Cliff, A.D. and Frey, A., 1977, *Locational methods*, London.

Hubbard, R., 1978, A review of selected factors conditioning consumer travel behaviour, *Journal of Consumer Research*, 5, pp. 1-21.

Nelson, P., 1970, Information and consumer behavior, *Journal of Political Economy*, 78, pp. 311-329.

Nelson, R.L., 1958, *The selection of retail location*, New York.

Pielou, E.C., 1969, *An introduction to mathematical ecology*, New York.

Rogers, A., 1974, *Statistical analysis of spatial dispersion*, London.

Sibley, D., 1972, Strategy and tactics in the selection of shop locations, *Area*, 4, pp. 151-157.

Stafford, H.A., 1963, The functional bases of small towns, *Economic*

Geography, **39**, pp. 165-175.

Warnes, A.M. and Daniels, P.W., 1980, Urban retail distributions : an appraisal of the empirical foundations of retail geography, *Geoforum*, **11**, pp. 133-146.

Williams, N.J., 1979, The definition of shopper types as an aid in the analysis of spatial consumer behaviour, *Tijdschrift voor Economische en Sociale Geografie*, 70, pp. 157-163.

SPATIAL STATISTICS FOR RETAIL GOODS AND SERVICES IN THE READING AREA

Code	Description	Number of outlets Number	Rank	Nearest-neighbour statistics	Variance/ mean of distri-bution	Shortest home-to-outlet distance
1	2	3	4	5	6	7
	1. *Food*					
101	Bread, cakes, pies (cold), etc.	198	5	0.621	5.25	252
102	Meat, sausages, etc.	186	8	0.519	4.72	261
103	Poultry, bacon, eggs	192	6	0.579	4.73	269
104	Fish (fresh)	20	101	1.207	2.32	881
105	Milk (liquid)	131	17	0.808	2.99	276
106	Butter, margarine, cheese, fats	154	13	0.800	4.33	270
107	Fruit (fresh)	161	12	0.664	4.47	269
108	Vegetables (fresh)	147	14	0.726	4.32	280
109	Canned fruit and vegetables	210	4	0.591	4.67	246
110	Groceries in bulk, for freezers	20	101	0.721	2.82	1,072
111	Other packaged, frozen, or canned groceries	237	3	0.569	6.93	240
112	Imported cooked meats, cheeses, etc.	69	37	0.908	3.18	414
113	Soft drinks and sweets	370	1	0.388	11.53	220
114	Ice cream, lollies, etc.	191	7	0.678	4.91	261
115	Fish, hot pies, etc. and chips to take away	53	53	0.847	1.92	453
116	Indian, Chinese, etc. food to take away	22	97	0.695	2.13	919
117	Sandwiches to take away	32	85	0.705	8.08	895
118	Cafe or snack bar (counter service)	54	51	0.699	11.20	773

APPENDIX I (*Contd.*)

1	2	3	4	5	6	7
119	Restaurant (waiter service)	39	72	0.468	13.70	1,012
	2. *Drink and Tobacco*					
201	Beer, cider, etc.	85	26	0.888	3.51	361
202	Wines, spirits	85	26	0.858	3.80	364
203	Cigarettes	280	2	0.520	8.63	232
204	Pipe tobacco, snuff, cigars	167	10	0.674	7.54	283
	3. *Personal Goods*					
301	Medicines (dispensary)	34	81	1.029	1.53	539
302	Medicines, pills, etc. (open sale)	128	18	0.613	3.99	313
303	Surgical goods	54	51	0.955	3.35	440
304	Cosmetics, perfume, etc.	81	29	0.714	5.50	388
305	Other toilet requisites (e.g. soap, toothpaste)	170	9	0.647	5.97	280
306	Sunglasses	42	70	0.788	5.30	582
307	Handbags	39	72	0.546	18.52	906
308	Jewellery	49	61	0.331	27.54	1,035
309	Smokers' goods (e.g. pipes)	21	99	0.443	9.46	1,426
	4. *Clothing and Footwear*					
401	Men's outer clothing	83	28	0.413	43.94	731
402	Men's underclothing and hosiery	55	49	0.470	25.78	857
403	Men's and women's sportswear	20	101	0.217	6.32	1,237
404	Women's outer clothing	100	24	0.492	35.35	550
405	Women's underclothing and hosiery	114	21	0.557	17.18	396
406	Boys' clothing	62	43	0.658	16.51	596
407	Girls' clothing	65	40	0.806	12.14	488

408	Infants' clothing	55	49	0.766	8.76	544
409	Knitting wool	36	78	0.930	4.93	563
410	Gloves, scarves, handkerchiefs, ties	66	38	0.493	33.00	741
411	Haberdashery (e.g. sewing cotton, ribbons)	46	68	0.912	4.48	491
412	Dressmaking material	22	97	0.810	4.95	992
413	Men's footwear	63	42	0.331	32.83	753
414	Women's footwear	57	45	0.501	26.14	725
415	Children's footwear	56	47	0.660	16.87	563
416	Second-hand clothing, footwear	10	125	0.346	2.21	2,012
	5. *Household Goods*					
501	Cleaning materials, soap powder, etc.	141	15	0.701	4.01	294
502	Tissues, kitchen paper, toilet paper	137	16	0.680	4.20	311
503	Cutlery, cooking utensils, other kitchen goods	74	32	0.812	12.09	471
504	China, pottery and glassware	73	33	0.594	12.83	589
505	Paint, paint brushes	66	38	0.766	4.27	447
506	Wallpaper	49	61	0.672	3.42	539
507	Ironmongery (e.g. nails, hammers, drills)	70	36	0.741	4.28	466
508	Timber and hardboard (retail sales)	28	89	0.847	1.61	666
509	Electrical accessories (e.g. plugs, flex, batteries)	93	25	0.610	9.93	435
510	Gardening tools and equipment	72	34	0.736	4.67	455
511	Seeds and plants	65	40	0.810	3.22	420
512	Flowers and indoor plants	56	47	0.647	3.94	532
513	Animals and pets	6	134	0.696	0.89	1,789
514	Petfood and equipment	80	30	0.764	3.49	380

APPENDIX I : (*Contd.*)

1	2	3	4	5	6	7
	6. *Durable Goods and Furnishings*					
601	New furniture-upholstered or finished (beds, suites, etc.)	45	69	0.513	23.93	1,503
602	New furniture—plain wood or unfinished	38	75	0.649	13.86	1,033
603	Office furniture	5	138	0.216	3.31	2,721
604	Second-hand furniture	14	112	0.581	1.88	1,245
605	Antique furniture	19	103	0.199	3.38	1,568
606	Carpets	50	58	0.727	12.26	804
607	Floor coverings (e.g. lino, tiles)	38	75	0.407	5.34	854
608	Household textiles (e.g. curtain material, chair covers)	33	83	0.799	13.23	911
609	Soft furnishings (e.g. pillows, cushions)	38	75	0.670	15.23	1,057
610	Towels, bed linen. blankets	32	85	0.391	23.71	1,586
611	New televisions, radios, record players, etc.	57	45	0.464	14.28	878
612	Second-hand televisions, etc.	10	125	0.564	1.61	1,557
613	TV rentals	29	88	0.531	7.56	1,057
614	Hi-Fi equipment, tape recorders	47	66	0.373	14.07	990
615	Radio spare parts	23	96	0.652	2.48	1,030
616	Records, tapes	59	44	0.607	10.73	529
617	Musical instruments	8	129	0.079	7.85	2,741
618	New gas appliances	8	129	0.893	1.10	1,472
619	New electrical appliances (large) (eg. cookers, washing machines)	37	77	0.417	7.87	1,052
620	New electrical appliances (small) (eg. electric kettles)	51	55	0.468	13.57	932
621	Second-hand gas or electric appliances	5	138	0.644	2.91	1,968
622	Solid fuel appliances	5	138	1.089	0.91	1,565
623	Other heating appliances (e.g. paraffin stoves)	12	118	0.375	2.27	1,378

7.	*Other Goods*					
701	Leather and travel goods, umbrellas	50	58	0.419	32.90	996
702	Sports goods	18	106	0.687	7.44	1,313
703	Fishing tackle	12	118	0.873	1.94	1,021
704	Antique goods and bric-a-brac	34	81	0.488	5.48	1,015
705	New watches and clocks	49	61	0.467	18.20	990
706	New fancy goods and small gifts (e.g. souvenirs, mirrors, thermometers)	72	34	0.609	14.47	553
707	Second-hand fancy goods, clocks, etc.	18	106	0.396	2.10	1,395
708	New books (hard-cover), maps, etc.	52	54	0.719	8.67	567
709	Second-hand books	10	125	0.525	2.01	1,621
710	Newspapers	109	22	1.063	3.18	278
711	Magazines and periodicals	107	23	1.048	3.32	280
712	Toys, indoor games	164	11	0.677	11.42	278
713	Writing paper, pens, pencils etc.	116	20	0.882	5.09	327
714	Office stationery	47	66	0.678	5.56	636
715	Greetings cards	118	19	0.964	5.16	277
716	Paintings (new), reproductions, posters, art materials	32	85	0.420	22.33	1,389
717	Stamp and coin collecting equipment	6	134	0.926	2.89	2,062
718	Typewriters, distating machines	14	112	0.373	8.59	2,163
719	Adding machines, calculators	11	121	0.059	10.79	2,802
720	Cameras, photographic goods	26	93	0.428	5.59	932
721	Binoculars, telescopes, microscopes	10	125	0.568	2.21	1,594
722	Home brewing, wine-making equipment	10	125	0.544	4.01	1,515
723a	Cars and vans	(12	118	0.418	2.61	1,930)
724	Car spares and accessories	49	61	0.682	5.18	641
725a	Mopeds and motorcycles	(7	131	0.930	1.73	1,802)

APPENDIX I : (*Contd.*)

1	2	3	4	5	6	7
726	Cycles and accessories	19	103	0.614	4.96	1,251
727a	Caravans and accessories	(3	143	0.161	1.61	2,840)
728a	Boats and accessories	(5	138	0.477	2.11	2,321)
729	Camping equipment	6	134	0.978	1.55	1,670
730	Prams and nursery goods	12	118	0.389	4.77	1,747
731	Paperback books	50	58	0.907	5.50	530
732	Other goods	27	91	(0.473	7.75	1,278)
	8. *Services*					
801	Men's hairdressing	41	71	1.051	3.69	526
802	Women's hairdressing	79	31	1.036	5.38	388
803	Women's beauty treatment	7	131	0.496	2.01	1,757
804	Hearing-aid service	2	145	0.294	0.96	2,806
805	Optician	13	114	0.555	4.14	1,543
806	Sauna or massage	5	134	0.667	2.11	2,051
807	Post office (main)	1	146	—	0.96	2,994
808	Sub-Post Office	51	55	1.589	0.59	332
809	Shoe repairs	15	109	0.703	1.52	1,064
810	Watch and clock repairs	18	106	0.408	4.88	1,155
811	Furniture repairs, upholstering	4	142	0.474	0.92	2,355
812	Radio, etc. repairs	11	121	0.649	1.70	1,722
813	Launderette	35	80	1.171	1.03	458
814	Laundry (collection)	8	129	0.619	1.35	1,413
815	Dry cleaning	32	85	0.913	1.65	567
816	Bank	48	64	0.338	5.93	764

817	Estate agent	47	66	0.365	15.94	1,140
818	Travel agent	14	112	0.561	8.59	1,765
819	Insurance, loans, etc.	25	95	0.555	12.93	1,480
820a	Motoring school, car hire, taxi service	(15	109	0.291	3.65	2,016)
821	Employment bureau	13	114	0.236	10.91	2,219
822	Armed Forces requirement	3	143	0.139	2.94	2,809
823	Funeral services	5	138	0.296	2.11	2,471
824	Betting shop, turf accountant	36	78	1.076	2.10	540
825	Studio photography	12	118	0.533	2.27	1,350
826	Building, plumbing, heating supplies	26	93	0.369	3.59	1,301
827a	Wholesale supplies	(16	108	0.897	3.07	1,312)
828	Building society	27	91	0.090	16.27	1,630
829b	Other services	27	91	(0.299	14.71	1,842)
901	Vacant shop premises	120				

a Coverage of these functions is likely to be particularly incomplete, therefore all data should be used carefully.

b Miscellaneous category : spatial statistics have little meaning here.

APPENDIX—II

RETAIL AND SERVICE FUNCTIONS CLASSED BY ACCESSIBILITY

Code	Description	Accessibility	
		Absolute	Relative
	I. ACCESSIBILITY FUNCTIONS		
101	Bread etc.	**	
102	Meat etc.	**	
103	Poultry, bacon, eggs	**	
105	Milk	**	++
106	Butter etc.	**	+
107	Fruit	**	+
108	Vegetables	**	+
109	Canned fruit and vegetables	**	
111	Packaged etc. groceries	**	
113	Soft drinks, sweets	**	
114	Ice cream	**	
115	Fish etc. and chips		++
201	Beer, cider	*	+
202	Wines, spirits	*	+
203	Cigarettes	**	
204	Tobacco, cigars	**	
301	Medicines (dispensary)		++
302	Medicines (open sales)	*	+
303	Surgical goods		++
305	Toilet requisites	**	
409	Knitting wool		++
411	Haberdashery		++
501	Cleaning materials	*	+
502	Tissues etc.	*	+
508	Timber and hardboard		++
514	Pet food	*	+
710	Newspapers	**	++
711	Magazines	**	++
712	Toys etc.	**	+
713	Stationery	*	+
715	Greeting cards	**	++
801	Men's hairdressing		++
802	Women's hairdressing	*	+
808	Sub-post office	*	++++

813	Launderette	+++
815	Dry cleaning	++
824	Betting shop	++
	II. INTERMEDIATE FUNCTIONS	
104	Fish (fresh)	+
110	Groceries in bulk, for freezers	
112	Imported meats etc.	+
116	Indian, Chinese food to take away	
117	Sandwiches, to take away	
118	Cafe, snack bar	—
304	Cosmetics, perfume	+
306	Sunglasses	+
307	Handbags	—
309	Smokers' goods	—
403	Sports wear	
404	Women's outer clothing	—
405	Women's underclothing, hosiery	
406	Boy's clothing	
407	Girls's clothing	
408	Infants' clothing	
412	Dressmaking material	
413	Men's footwear	—
414	Women's footwear	—
415	Children's footwear	
503	Kitchen goods	
504	China, pottery, glassware	
505	Paint etc.	+
506	Wallpaper	+
507	Ironmongery	
509	Electrical accessories	
510	Gardening equipment	
511	Seeds, plants etc.	+
512	Flowers, indoor plants	
606	Carpets	—
607	Floor coverings	
608	Household textiles	
613	TV rental	—
615	Radio spare parts	
616	Records, tapes	
704	Antique goods	—
706	Fancy goods, gifts	
708	Books (new)	
714	Office stationery	
720	Cameras etc.	
724	Car spares and accessories	
731	Paperback books	
816	Bank	

APPENDIX II : (*Contd.*)

Code	Description	Accessibility	
		Absolute	Relative
	III. COMPARISON FUNCTIONS		
119	Restaurant		– –
308	Jewellery		– – –
401	Men's outer clothing		– –
402	Men's underclothing		– –
410	Gloves etc.		– –
601	Furniture (upholstered)		– – –
602	Furniture (unfinished)		– –
609	Soft furnishings		– –
610	Towels, blankets etc.		– – – –
611	Television, radio		– –
614	Hi-fi equipment		– –
619	Electric appliances (large)		– –
620	Electric appliances (small)		– –
701	Leather and travel goods		– –
705	Watches, clocks		– –
716	Posters, art materials, etc.		– – –
817	Estate agent		– – –
819	Insurance, loans		– –
826	Building supplies		– –
828	Building society		– – –
	IV. SCARCE FUNCTIONS		
416	Second-hand clothing, footwear		–
513	Animals, pets		+
603	Office furniture		
604	Second-hand furniture		
605	Antique furniture		– –
612	Second-hand televisions etc.		
617	Musical instruments		– –
618	New gas appliances		+
621	Second-hand gas or electric appliances		+
622	Solid fuel appliances		+++
623	Other heating appliances		
702	Sports goods		
703	Fishing tackle		++
707	Second-hand fancy goods		–
709	Second-hand books		
717	Stamp and coin collecting		
718	Typewriters and dictating machines		– – –
719	Adding machines and calculators		– – – –
721	Binoculars etc.		

722	Home brewing and wine-making	
726	Cycles and accessories	
729	Camping equipment	+
730	Prams and nursery goods	—
803	Women's beauty treatment	
804	Hearing-aid service	++
805	Optician	
806	Sauna, massage	+
807	Post office (main)	(+++++)
809	Shoe repairs	+
810	Watch and clock repairs	
811	Furniture repairs	+
812	Radio etc. repairs	
814	Laundry (collection)	+
818	Travel agent	—
821	Employment bureau	——
822	Armed forces recruitment	+
823	Funeral services	
825	Studio photography	

Notes : 1. Functions with incomplete coverage, or of a miscellaneous nature, are excluded (these are listed in Appendix IV).

2. ** indicates that the function is accessible within 600 metres of at least 90 per cent of the sampled homes in the study area ;* indicates similar access within 800 m.

3. + and — signs indicate the size and direction of standard residuals from the best-fit regression equation between the median value of shortest home-to-outlet distances for the function, and the number of occurrences of that function (see text). Negative residuals indicate better accessibility than predicted, so signs are reversed :

$\text{s.r.} \leqslant -2.5$	+++++
$-2.5 < \text{s.r.} \leqslant -2.0$	++++
$-2.0 < \text{s.r.} \leqslant -1.5$	+++
$-1.5 < \text{s.r.} \leqslant -1.0$	++
$-1.0 < \text{s.r.} \leqslant -0.5$	+
$-0.5 < \text{s.r.} < 0.5$	
$0.5 \leqslant \text{s.r.} < 1.0$	—
$1.0 \leqslant \text{s.r.} < 1.5$	— —
$1.5 \leqslant \text{s.r.} < 2.0$	— — —
$2.0 \leqslant \text{s.r.} < 2.5$	— — — —
$2.5 \leqslant \text{s.r.}$	— — — — —

FOURTEEN

S. BANERJEE AND S.R. JOSHI

SPATIAL STRUCTURE OF RETAILING ACTIVITIES IN PUNE CITY

INTRODUCTION

SPATIAL arrangement of commercial activities in an urban area is far more important than the limited amount of space they cover. This is largely because their distribution on space reflects the aggregate demand conditions (i.e. population status) of a city (Goodall, 1972). Their concentrated and deconcentrated patterns are related to the intra-urban mobility and the social status of the people. The number and the size of the retail units, on the other hand, depict the economic characteristics of the population. The overall distribution and nature of commercial activities have been found to closely follow the distribution of population in many metropolitan cities (Racine, 1973). Therefore commercial activities in an urban area have varied locations. Location of highest accessibility and centrality in the city core is found side by side with arterial locations. Sometimes random distributions throughout the city with low threshold market is also a phenomenon (Boyce, 1974). All these patterns and sub-patterns are primarily the outcome of interaction between demand and supply sectors because population happens to be one of the direct forces that changes commercial structure in a city (Simmons, 1964). This calls for a study on the dynamism of intra-urban commercial pattern focussing the growth, maturity and decline of commercial areas together with the population change.

The present study attempts to analyse the changes that took place in the spatial structure of commercial activities* in a period of twenty years, 1961-1981. Special care has been taken to bring out the relationship between population termed as 'demand sector' and commercial units termed as 'supply sector'.

Review of spatial structure of commerce in Pune

Agglomeration of non-residential activities in the town centre ultimately leads to congestion. Hence, shift of shopping activity from the town centre to the adjoining areas, especially when the town is old, is a common feature. Space in town centre is always scarce and restricted. In town-centres of old cities, however, the street network is older and hence narrow and constricting. In some cases it forces the concentration of shopping activity at the adjacent areas as in 20th century Oxford on Rouen (Garnier and Delobez, 1977). Thus, the road network of the urban core besides conferring an enormous privilege of accessibility also causes a serious handicap. This aspect of an old town-centre with mixed activity (i.e. commercial and residential) is found to be present in the core area of Pune city. Laxmi Road, the major retail-trade area of the city, is not exclusively commercial. Quite a considerable portion is occupied by residential activity. Moreover, though the area enjoys a fairly high degree of accessibility, this locational advantage has been largely diminished by the constricted road network of the area.

Within the core area also the commercial pattern has undergone considerable change. When Poona was a small village, the market was situated in the 'Kasba' area later to be shifted to the Shaniwar ward outside the royal residence during Maratha rule. During the later part of the Peshwa period the main shopping activity shifted to Raviwer ward in a north-south alignment. During the British period east-west area became more important. Since then only, Laxmi Road became an important retailing area (Deshpande, 1978).

In 1822 Budhwar, Raviwar and Shukrawar together accounted for more than 50% of the total commercial establish-

*For the present analysis only retailing and wholesaling have been considered as commercial activities.

ments. These wards were experiencing high density of population, median location and better accessibility. From 1822 to 1940 Poona developed as an administrative and educational centre. With further population growth and physical extension of the city and extreme congestion in the core area, commercial activities started getting decentralised. From 1940-50 influx of refugees helped maintain the above trend and population increased by 85%. Introduction of city-bus service as means of mass transportation carried this process farther.

Besides the commercial core, the arterial pattern of commercial activity came into being. Major roads cutting across the well-developed residential areas in Sadashiv Peth, Deccan Gymkhana and the newer areas in the periphery are good examples. Arterial shopping areas in Tilak Road, Karve Road, Fergusson Road are characterized by mixed functions or neighbourhood functions e.g., grocery, bakery, food-stores etc. that serve the local residential areas.

Apart from the above pattern, commercial activity has recently developed in the high-class residential districts which have grown in the redevelopment process after the 1961 floods. Mukund-nagar colony in Gultekadi, Sahakarnagar, Padmavati, Mitramondal colony in Parvati, Deepnagar and Gokhalenagar colonies in Shivajinagar are apt examples.

Mention should also be made of retail clusters with low threshold convenience goods shops. These are located in low-class residential areas and in slums along Sholapur Road, Nagar Road, extension of Karve Road to Kothrud, Yeravada, Parvati, Dapodi, Bopodi etc. (Fig. 14.1)

Pattern of concentration

In 1961, six peths located at the heart of Pune city with a central location were having the highest concentration of retail units.* The areas were Nana, Bhawani, Shukrawar, Budhwar, Raviwar and Sadashiv housing more than half of the total retail units of the city (56.17%) within a very small area. Apart from this major concentration, Ganesh, Kasaba, Saniwar and Narayan Peths which are also located very near to the core area had 14%

***Kirkee and Pune cantonment areas have been excluded from the present analysis due to non-availability of data.**

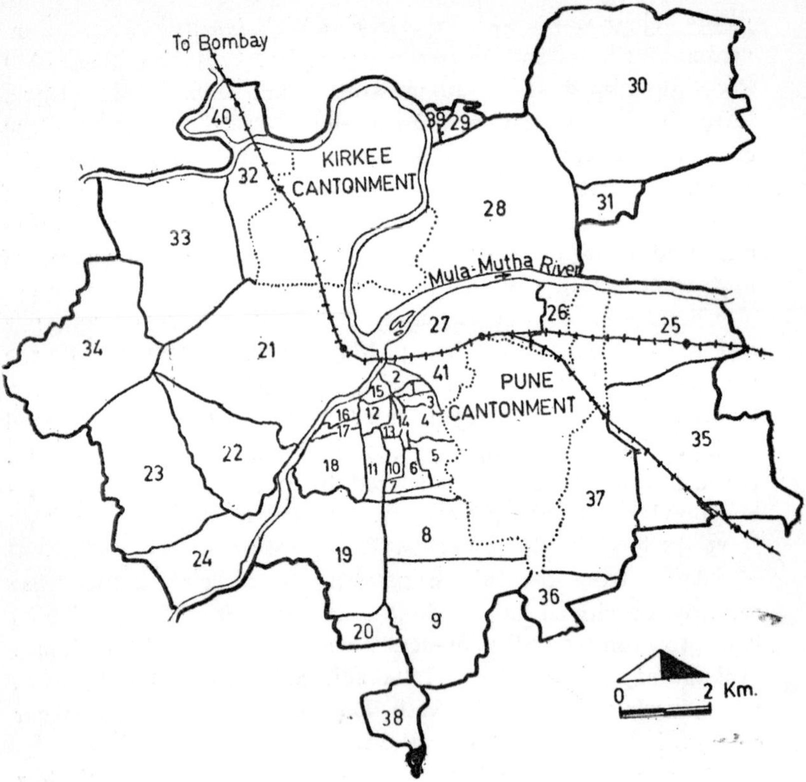

FIG. 14.1 : *Pune city* : *Administrative divisions*

1. Somwar
2. Mangalwar
3. Rasta
4. Nana
5. Bhavani
6. Gatj
7. Ghorpade
8. Gultekadi
9. Bibvewadi
10. Guruwar
11. Shukrawar
12. Budhwar
13. Raviwar
14. Ganesh
15. Shaniwar
16. Kasaba
17. Narayan
18. Sadashiv
19. Parvati
20. Dhankavadi
21. Shivajinagar
22. Erandvana
23. Kothrud
24. Hingane
25. Randhawa
26. Ghorpadi
27. Bund Garden
28. Yeravada
29. Dhanori
30. Lohagaon
31. Wadgaonsheri
32. Bopodi
33. Aundh
34. Pashan
35. Hadapsar
36. Kondhawa
37. Wanawari
38. Katraj
39. Kalas
40. Dapodi
41. Pune Suburban

of the total retail units. Thus 70% of the total retail units in 1961 were concentrated within a very small area in the centre of Pune city (Fig. 14.2).

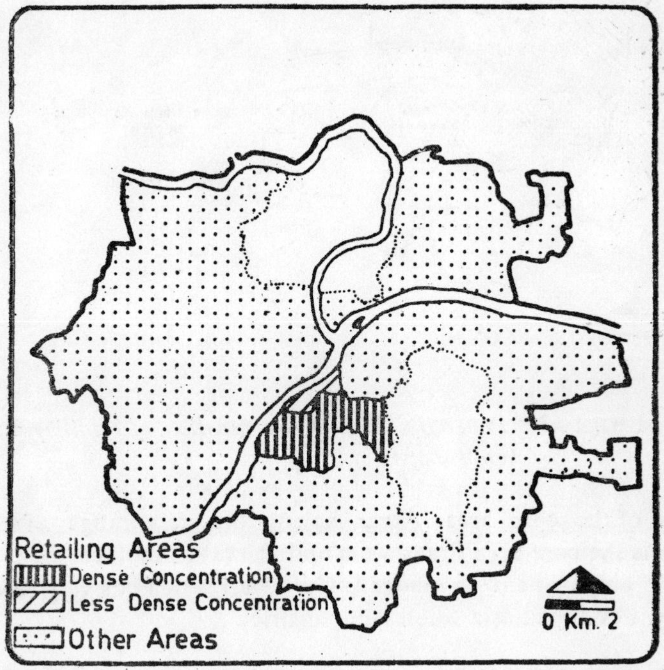

FIG. 14.2 : *Concentration of retailing units, Pune city, 1961*

After twenty years in 1981 the pattern of distribution of shops in Pune showed some changes. Bhawani, Nana, Budhwar, Raviwar, Sadashiv and Shukrawar still are the major concentration areas housing 58% of the total retail units of Pune. Besides the core area, three new residential areas e.g. Shivajinagar, Erandwana and Parvati also show a high concentration of shops with 17% of the total. Together the core and the newer areas comprise 75% of the total retailing units of the city (Fig. 14.3).

When the map of concentration areas of shops is compared with the map of shop-size, the trend becomes clearer (Fig. 14.4). Areas having the biggest size of shops with largest employment is Shivajinagar, a high-class residential area, located to the north-

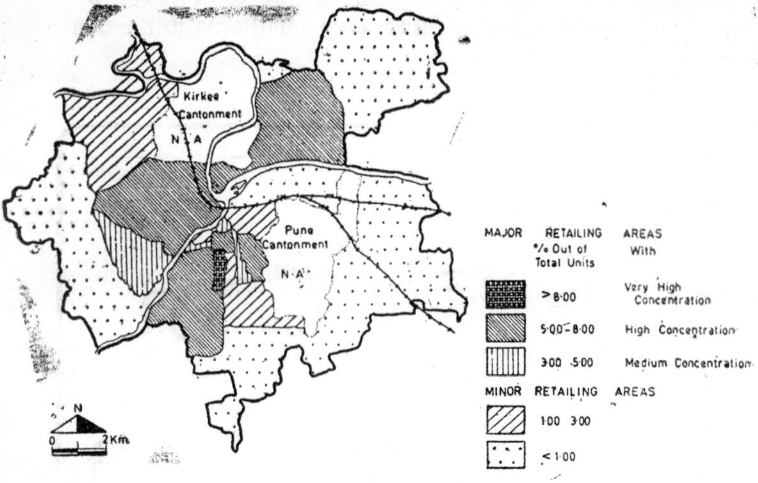

FIG. 14.3 : *Pune city 1981 : Concentration of retailing units (only shops)*

west of the core area. Areas having the next range of shop-size is the core area Erandwana and Parvati. Another area with high employment in shops is Gultekadi which has very recently been developed as a wholesaling district.

Relationship between demand and supply sectors

Correlation co-efficient between population density (considered as the demand sector) and number of commercial units (considered as supply sector) for 1961 and 1981 has been calculated. R values for both the years were .72 and .75 respectively indicating a positive but medium degree of relationship between the two variables. Regression analysis has been then carried out of the same data to bring out the inter-action pattern between the two sectors in each peth [Fig. 14.5(a), and 14.5(b)].

Definite groups of peths can be traced from the regression diagram. For 1961 groups of peths have been identified according to homogeneity in the relationship between population and shops in the following manner :

(1) Peths with less than 20,000 people and shops less

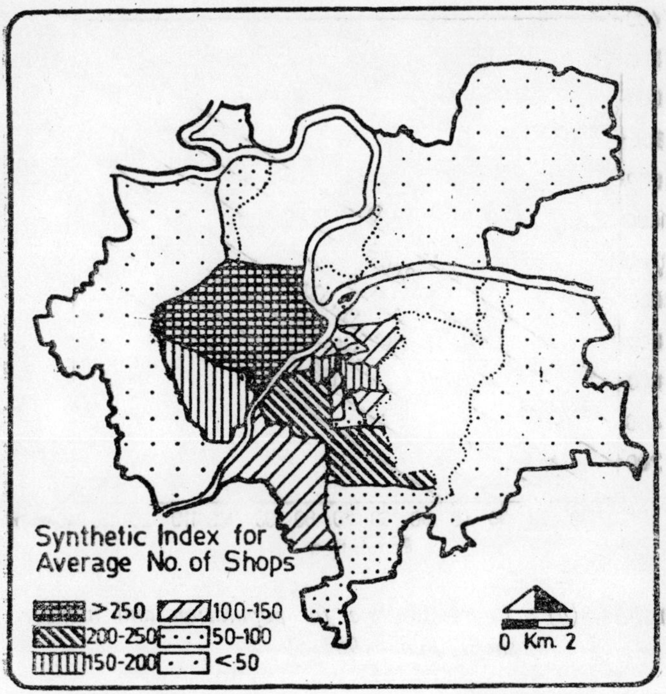

FIG. 14.4 : *Size of retailing units, Pune city, 1981*

than 100

(2) Peths with population of 15,000--30,000 and shops ranging from 100—400

(3) Peths with population of 30,000—50,000 and shops ranging from 400--800

Peths belonging to the last category were having retailing as a major activity. But these areas were also simultaneously experiencing residential activity as evidenced from the large number of population. However, Budhwar peth stood out as a separate type as a major commercial area with a population of only 29,067 but with 1,310 shops.

In 1981 the number and range of groups were not the same, change in population size and number of shops were the major

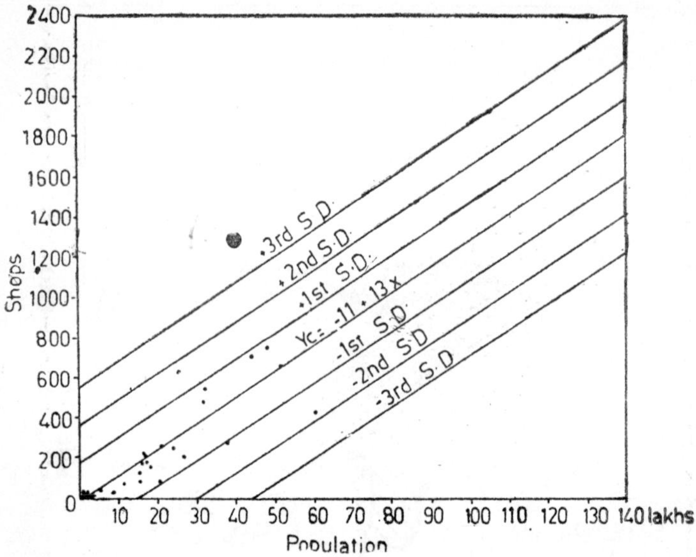

FIG. 14.5(*a*) : *Regression line for population and number of shops, Pune, 1961*

reasons behind it. The groups of 1981 have been arranged as follows :

(1) Peths with less than 15,000 people and shops less than 100
(2) Peths with less than 50,000 people and shops between 100—400
(3) Peths with less than 50,000 people but shops ranging from 400—800
(4) Peths with less than 50,000 people but shops ranging from 800—1,600
(5) Peths with less than 50,000 people but shops more than 1,600
(6) Peths with more than 50,000 people and shops also more than 1,600

Considering the overall size of population and shops it can be concluded that peths belonging to Group 5 are the major

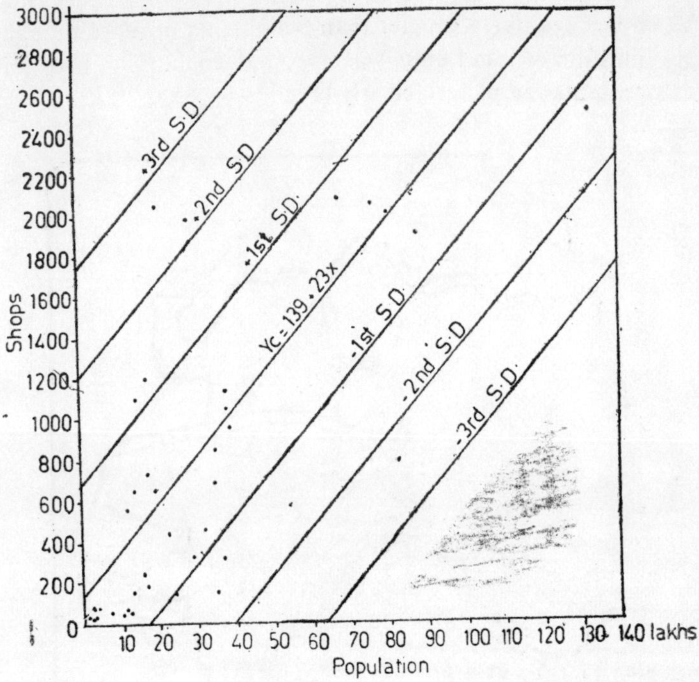

FIG. 14.5(*b*) : *Regression line for population and number of shops, Pune, 1981*

commercial areas while peths belonging to group 6 are commercial areas with mixed residential activity.

Analysis of residuals

In 1961 Ganj, Nana, Shukrawar, Budhwar and Raviwar Peths were all showing positive deviation values. Non-residential activities in these areas can be said to have a slight dominance over the residential ones. But Sadashiv was showing a negative value indicating that in 1961 population was comparatively larger (48,181) than the number of retail units though the area was having very high concentration of retail units. Budhwar and Raviwar peths yield the highest positive values forming the retail core of CBD in Pune in 1961 with population of 29,067 and 25,291 respectively. Naravan situated south of Sadashiv, at the edge of the core, however, was giving positive results because the population was relatively smaller than the number of shops though the concentration of retail units was not that high. The map of residuals presents the picture clearly (Fig. 14.6).

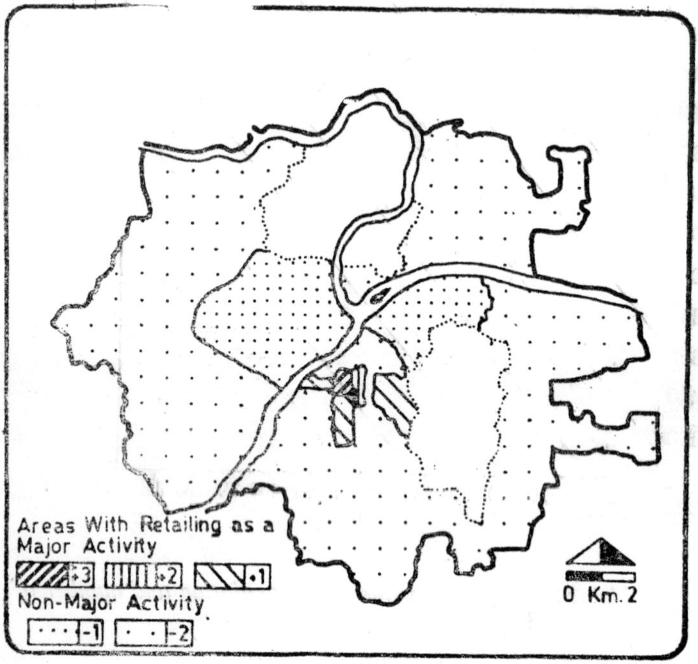

FIG. 14.6 : *Residual map showing relationship between population and retailing units, Pune city, 1961*

In 1981 the relationship between the two sectors changed. By then the process of decentralization due to population shift has started. Nana and Bhawani again give +1 deviation values. Shukrawar, however, giving very high +3 values, can claim to be included in the CBD core together with Budhwar and Raviwar. In all these 3 peths population has decreased from 1961 to 1981 establishing their major activity as non-residential. Ganesh, Kasaba, Shaniwar, Somwar and Ghorpadi which were giving negative residuals in 1961 give positive residuals in 1981. The change might be a result of the extension of the main business area into these adjoining peths. Population has increased to a very small extent in all these peths from 1961—1981. Sadashiv gives a + value of residuals with a large population. Position of Parvati and Shivajinagar shows that growing competition for land from non-residential users in those areas have already started. The map of concentration shows that in 1981 these 2 areas were experiencing concentration of retailing activities. However, the primary activity here is residential as evidenced from population figures. Erandwana is showing positive values in 1981 indicating decentralization of retailing activity in the peripheral areas along arterial routes. The area is higher and middle class residential area with a number of large departmental stores (Fig. 14.7).

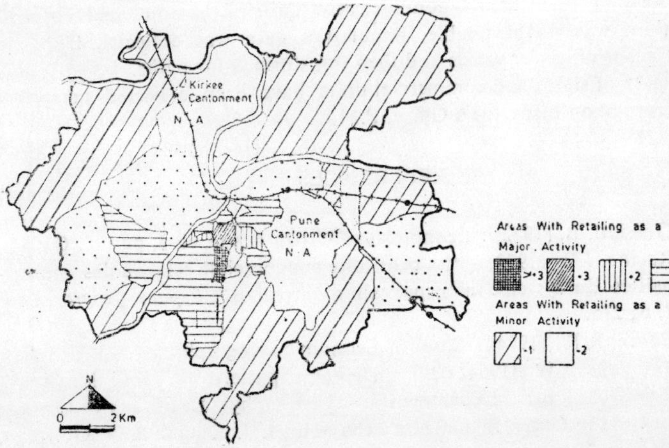

FIG. 14.7 : *Pune city 1981 : Residential map showing the relationship between population and retailing units shps)*

CONCLUSION

The above analysis reveals the trend of retailing activity in Pune over a time period of 20 years from 1961 to 1981. For Pune there 20 years are very important because the spurt of industrial activities which rapidly transformed the nature and face of the city started only during the early 60's. The spatial pattern of retailing corroborates this fact, the centralized retail activities in the hard core of the city in 1961 experienced decentralization to a large extent during '61—'81. As population of the city grew enormaly retailing had to serve its growing demand and consequently there was spill-over of the hard retailing core in the adjoining areas. Further, many newer residential areas of high, middle and low income groups, evolved all over the city. This led to multi-nucleation or poly-nucleation of retailing activities, its degree and quality depending on the socio-economic status of the residential areas.

FOOTNOTES

1. As data for peths, the administrative units of the municipal corporation, was not available, population data was collected from the Census office for wards and then transformed for peths.
2. Data of shops and commercial units have been collected personally from Shop Inspector's Office, P.M.C.

REFERENCES

1. Goodall, B. (1972) : Economics of Urban Areas, ch 5, pg 138, Oxford.
2. Racine, J.B. (1973) : "La centralite commerciale relative des municipalites du systeme metropolitain montrealais", *Espace geographique*, 2, pg 275.
3. Boyce, R.R. (1974) : Bases of Economic Geography, pg 293, U.S.A.
4. Simmons, J.W. (1964) : "The changing pattern of retail location", Research Paper, Department of Geography, University of Chicago as cited in Cities, Space and Behaviour, L.J. King & R.G. Golledge, ch 6, p. 195.
5. Garnier, J.B. and Delobez, A. (1979) : Geography of Marketing, Part II, ch 4, pg 18, Paris.
6. Deshpande, C.D. (1978) : Pune—a metropolis in transition, in 'Million Cities of India' ed. by R.P. Misra, New Delhi.

SECTION FIVE

URBAN TRANSPORTATION

FIFTEEN

C. JOHN LANGLEY, JR.

HIGHWAYS AND PROPERTY VALUES
The Washington Beltway Revisited

THIS study is a continuation of an investigation of the impacts of the Washington Capital Beltway (I-495) on residential property values in the adjacent community of North Springfield, Virginia. A 17-year (1962-1978) time series of property values represents the longest continuous longitudinal data base used in any analysis of highway impacts on residential communities. The results show conclusively that properties near the highway increase in value at a rate less than those more distant. It was found that properties in proximity to I-495 sell for approximately $3,000-$3,500 less than the others.

Today's society has placed an extremely high priority on the development of transportation systems that will facilitate the movement of both goods and people in a swift and reliable fashion and with the greatest convenience, comfort, and privacy. Although conflicts of interest are inevitable on the design and modification of alternative systems transportation planners attempt to select those projects that will provide the greatest net benefit to society. As a result, there are a number of tools and techniques available for facilitating the integration of social impacts into the transportation planning process.[1] Although efforts to gain a more meaningful understanding of the benefits and costs of transportation improvements have considered a number of modal scenarios, a predominant share of attention has been directed toward the case of highways.

Specific benefits and costs that are likely to be associated with the construction or improvement of a limited-access highway are noted below. Benefits have been divided into two classes—those for which highway users are the principal beneficiaries and those that represent a gain accruing primarily to nonusers; alternatively, because a dichotomy of costs by user status would represent a more narrow, less-meaningful perspective, costs have been considered as being either direct or indirect:

1. Benefits: (a) for the user—accessibility (speed and reliability), fuel cost savings, maintenance cost savings (vehicular), safety, comfort and convenience, and aesthetics of travel; and (b) for the nonuser—reduced congestion in general area, economic efficiency, property value changes, economic development, and income and employment; and

2. Costs: (a) direct—right-of-way acquisition, construction, improvement, maintenance, operation, and relocation; and (b) indirect—loss of tax base, provision of additional community services, degradation of community qualities, property value changes, environmental degradation, and loss of income and employment.

In order to achieve a greater understanding of the extent to which the net of highway benefits and costs is reflected in the values of nearby residential properties, I conducted and reported the results of a time-series analysis of residential property values along a portion of Interstate 495 (the Washington beltway).[2] The research methodology included an analysis of sale-resale data during the period 1962 through 1972 exhibited by 1676 residential properties. A principal finding of that study was that those properties in North Springfield, Virginia, located in proximity to I-495, exhibited a tendency (particularly during the last 3 years of the time series) to increase in value at a rate significantly less than that for properties more distant from the highway. The study results suggested that highway-related environmental externalities were responsible for a lowering of values of nearby properties compared with those of properties more distant from the highway. Aside from the specific findings of the study, the effort was notable in that it represented the first attempt to analyze the impacts of a highway on residential property values through the construction of a time series of property value index numbers.

The study reported in this paper is a revision and update of the findings of the earlier study, based on the addition of several more years of data to the already-existing time series. As a result, 17 years of data (1962 through 1978) were made available for analysis. This study incorporates a longer time series of residential property sales data than has been used previously in any investigation of the effects of highways on property values. Following a brief review of the recent literature and a profile of the highway-community interface that exists in North Springfield, a summary of the methodological approach and the results achieved is presented.

RECENT LITERATURE

An examination of the published literature indicates that a continuing high level of importance is attached to achieving a greater understanding of the determinants of relative house and land prices. In addition, recent research efforts have placed added emphasis on how neighborhood amenities are valued by people and how such values are translated into prices of land and/or improvements.

Although it preceded publication of the earlier Washington beltway study, a number of empirical efforts into the determinants of relative house prices were surveyed.[3] Emphasis was placed on the inclusion of studies that served to isolate and quantify a variety of attributes associated with housing, particularly those that were related to environmental quality in both a physical and a social context. Each of the studies selected for discussion was limited somewhat in that its respective methodological approach incorporated the use of regression analysis (and factor analysis in some cases) as applied to cross-section data. None of those surveyed were based on time series of data.

A recent study analyzed the impact of railway externalities on residential prices.[4] Another research effort[5] measured the extent to which variations in levels of local property taxes and public expenditures affect residential property values. Alternatively, the technique of using a time series of property value data was employed in a study on the effects of airports on land values.[6] The procedure followed was to measure changes in mean selling prices for various study areas at differing distances from the airport.

Contemporary interest has shifted somewhat from attempting to explain variation in house or land prices, to estimating the implicit valuation of the specific locational features or amenities that have a major impact on the selling prices of properties.[7-10] The major research questions raised collectively focus attention on topics such as the relative usefulness of land only versus the selling prices of land plus improvements; the extent to which hedonic prices (assumed to be equilibrium prices paid by informed, willing buyers) are representative of the more theoretically acceptable willingness-to-pay prices;[11] and the development and refinement of models and techniques for estimating price gradients for a number of amenities simultaneously. Finally, a cross section of residential property values was used to determine a set of implicit marginal prices for air quality.[12] In combination with income and other variables, the prices are incorporated into a two-equation demand-and-supply model.[13] Results are expressed in terms of both price and income elasticity of demand.

STUDY AREA DESCRIPTION

The predominantly residential community of North Springfield is located in Fairfax County, Virginia, along the southwest portion of the Washington beltway. The study site is bisected by the highway, and residential structures are limited to single-family dwellings, of which there are nearly 1,700. As computed from Fairfax County courthouse records, property sales prices averaged $22,456 in 1962, $33,440 in 1970, and $65,182 for the first quarter to 1978. Numbers of property turnovers per year were typically between 125 and 200. Additional descriptive information regarding the study site may be found in Langley.[2]

As indicated in Fig. 15.1, a variety of highway-related changes has taken place in the time period of interest, with the most notable occurring in recent years. The first is that data from the Common-wealth of Virginia[14] indicate that average daily traffic (ADT) volumes have risen from 8,845 vehicles/day in 1961-1962 to 113,790/day in 1978. Second, a widening of the relevant section of I-495 from two lanes in each direction to four lanes, begun in 1974, was completed in 1977. Third, noise barriers were constructed beginning in 1974 in a continuous pattern on both the

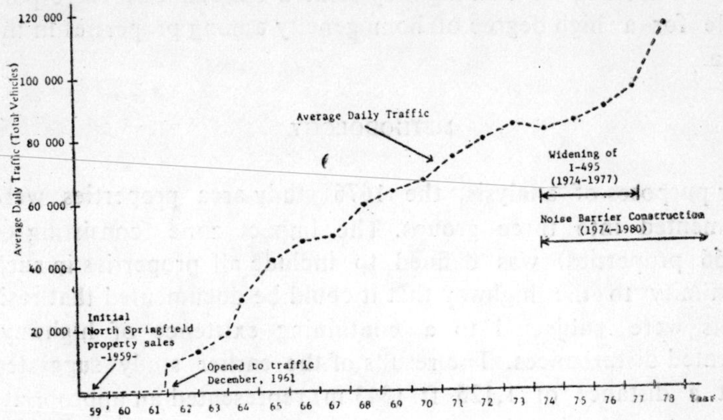

FIG. 15.1 : *Traffic profile of I-495, North Springfield, Virginia : 1959-1978*

north and south sides of the highway right-of-way, and minor alterations to the existing walls were being made as recently as 1980. Technically, the barrier type is metal wall on earth berm, and the height of the barrier above the road is 7.6 m. Federal Highway Administration (FHWA) tests have concluded that noise levels in proximity to the highway have been reduced by approximately 15 dB (A), thereby reducing loudness at least by half.[15] In addition to measuring the effectiveness of various types of noise barriers, the study evaluated the accuracy of the FHWA Highway Traffic-Noise-Prediction Model. It is interesting to note that the same section of the Washington beltway investigated in the study reported in this paper was also included among the sites selected by FHWA for noise barrier analysis. As a result of personal visits to the study site before, during, and after such construction, it was evident to me not only that noise levels had been lowered as a result, but also that the highway itself was much less obtrusive, and generally less noticeable.

In an overall sense, therefore, North Springfield continues to be the type of community that lends itself appropriately to a study of highway impacts on residential property values. While an inherent stability in the area under study is certainly an attribute from the perspective of research methodology, the general absence of non-highway-related externalities is responsible for a high degree of homogeneity among properties in the area.

METHODOLOGY

For purposes of analysis, the 1676 study-area properties were segmented into three groups. The impact zone (consisting of 1,056 properties) was defined to include all properties in such proximity to the highway that it could be documented that residents were subjected to a continuing existence of highway-oriented disturbances. The results of the earlier study suggested that a distance of 1,125 ft (343 m) represented an appropriate delimiter, and this measure was used once again in this study. Second, the subset of impact zone properties that were located immediately adjacent to the highway were classified as abutting properties (99 in number). Finally, those properties beyond the boundary of the impact zone were referred to as being located in the nonimpact zone (610 in number).

The research plan included these two major objectives: (a) to construct for each distance-related category a time series of property value index numbers that could be used to describe the behavior of aggregate property values over time and (b) to compare statistically the yearly index numbers among the various property classifications to determine whether any significant differences exist. To the extent that discrepancies are noted, it is accurate to claim that highway-related environmental externalities are the primary contributing factors.

In order to accurately interpret the study results, it is necessary to recognize an important distinction that must be drawn between rate of price appreciation and total or gross impact on property values. The former places no restriction on the actual years to be included in a highway impact study, while the latter would certainly require the measurement of effects on values beginning before construction or even anticipation of the highway. The approach taken in this study emphasizes the rate of price appreciation.

The methodology for price index construction used in this study incorporates only sale-resale pairs of property transaction values, and employs regression analysis to estimate the index numbers.[2,16] Courthouse records from Fairfax County indicated that a total of 1,322 valid pairs of study area property transactions were recorded for the years 1962 through 1978. Prior to the regression analysis, all property sales values were deflated by using the implicit price deflators for gross national product.[17] Although the time series of interest began in the year 1962 (the first full year in which the highway was opened to traffic), the base year for applying the price deflators was selected to be 1959 (the year in which the first property sales were recorded for the study area).

Finally, it is important to understand that the general approach of this study is valid, even when one considers some of the recent findings regarding the appropriateness of methodologies for studying the impact of location dependent amenities on property values. For example, one study suggests that regression studies cannot be used for predictive purposes except to the extent that the city is small, and there is mobility among cities.[18] This means that property values at a particular location depend only on amenities (and other relevant variables) at that location.[19] Aside from the fact that the approach of this study is not regression-oriented in the same sense as referred to by those authors, the nature of size and mobility characteristics has no direct bearing on an interpretation of the results. This is because the study findings are expressed in terms of differences in rates of price appreciation among the various North Springfield property groups, and no attempt is made to derive an implicit, generalizable valuation for the existing externalities.

FINDINGS

Table 15.1 summarizes a variety of residential property sales data for North Springfield during the years 1962 through 1978. All valid property transfers are included and, in addition to being presented for all properties, yearly information is subdivided by property category. Two principal observations are notable: (a) the mean selling price of abutting properties tended to be lower on a year-to-year basis than for the other property types in the study area and (b) yearly increases in the mean selling prices of impact zone properties approximated those of the nonimpact zone. The former is explained largely by the fact that abutting

TABLE 15.1 : North Springfield, Virginia, property sales data : 1962-1978

Year	All Properties[a]			Abutting[b]			Impact[c]			Nonimpact[d]		
	N	$\bar{x}$($)	Deflated[e] $\bar{x}$($)	N	$\bar{x}$($)	Deflated $\bar{x}$($)	N	$\bar{x}$($)	Deflated $\bar{x}$($)	N	$\bar{x}$($)	Deflated $\bar{x}$($)
1962	226	22,456	21,489	10	20,719	19,827	87	22,584	21,611	139	22,375	21,411
1963	238	22,774	21,485	21	22,857	21,563	94	32,432	22,106	144	22,345	21,080
1964	214	23,222	21,562	16	24,544	22,789	84	24,396	22,552	130	22,464	20,858
1965	162	24,224	22,002	11	24,733	22,464	69	24,914	22,629	93	23,712	21.537
1966	162	25,319	22,268	13	24,557	21,598	62	25,534	22,457	100	25,186	22,151
1967	147	26,189	22,384	11	25,441	21,744	52	26,460	22,615	95	26,041	22,257
1968	143	28,730	23,491	6	31,633	25,865	58	29,625	24,223	85	28,120	22,993
1969	129	31,257	24,343	5	28,683	22,339	51	31,324	24,396	78	31,213	24,309
1970	127	33,340	24,715	8	30,521	22,558	42	33,329	24,633	85	33,495	24,756
1971	161	35,517	24,977	16	34,985	24,603	57	36,247	25,490	104	35,117	24,695
1972	157	39,290	26.529	9	40,272	27,192	56	39,808	26,808	101	39,003	26,336
1973	133	46,897	29,928	12	47,216	30,131	44	47,919	30,580	89	46,393	29,606
1974	135	52,009	30,273	6	49,658	28,905	43	51,245	29,828	92	52,366	30,481
1975	121	56,449	29,978	9	55,416	29,430	45	56,688	30,105	76	56,307	29,903
1976	112	58,905	29,735	5	57,667	29,110	35	58,075	29,312	77	59,282	29,925
1977	159	62,817	29,956	9	57,800	27,562	52	62,541	29,824	107	62,952	30,020
1978	33	65,182	29,914	1	65,000	29,830	13	67,446	30,954	20	53,711	29,239
Total	2559			168			944			1615		

[a]Within 1676 ft.
[b]Within 99 ft.
[c]Within 620 ft.
[d]Within 1056 ft.
[e]Mean sales values were deflated to base year=1959 by using the implicit price deflator for gross national product.[17]

properties were priced lower than other properties during the early years of the time series, and the discrepancy has continued throughout the period under consideration. The latter observation could be construed to imply that the existence of highway-associated externalities is not reflected in property values since the averages remain approximately the same throughout the 17 years. As will be indicated subsequently, such a conclusion is not only premature but inaccurate.

The results of residential property price index construction are exhibited in Table 15.2 by distance category. In addition to the yearly index numbers, the logarithms and standard errors of the logarithms of the index number are shown, as well as the total number of initial plus final sales in each year. The three time series of index numbers are depicted in Figure 15.2. Major observations of interest include the following: (a) the time series of index numbers for abutting properties consistently shows less-than-comparable figures for impact and nonimpact zone properties (aside from the slight aberration of data in the year 1974), (b) with the exception of one year early in the time series, index numbers for impact zone properties are less in magnitude than those for nonimpact zone properties, and (c) the apparent divergences among index numbers of various property types are the greatest in years subsequent to 1973. It is evident, therefore, that properties nearer the highway exhibit a very definite tendency to increase in value at a rate less than those more distant from the highway.

One-tailed student-t tests were used to test for statistical significance among the various index number differences noted above. Table 15.3 notes those pairs of index numbers for which the differences were found to be significantly different at the 10 per cent level, or better. While 12 of the 17 years in the time series are represented in Table 15.3, a preponderance of attention is focused obviously on the years from 1970 to 1978. These findings lend conclusive support to the contention that highway-related environmental externalities from I-495 are responsible for an adverse impact on nearby residential property values in North Springfield. It is quite likely, however, that the widening construction from 1974 through 1977 was responsible for a portion of the differences in recent years that are apparent in Table 15.3.

An added feature of Table 15.3 is that the significantly different

TABLE 15.2 : **Real estate price indexes, North Springfield, Virginia : 1962-1978**

Aburting Properties[a]					Properties in Impact Zone[b] (within 1125 ft from highway)					Properties in Non-impact Zone[c] (>1125 ft from highway)				
Year	Index	Log of Index	S_e Log	N	Year	Index	Log of Index	S_e Log	N	Year	Index	Log of Index	S_e Log	N
1962	1.000	0.000,00	0.000,00	8	1962	1.000	0.000,00	0.000,00	62	1962	1.000	0.000,00	0.000,00	96
1963	0.987	—0.005,83	0.015,78	12	1963	1.011	0.004,81	0.006,32	68	1963	1.024	0.010,42	0.005,31	107
1964	0.990	—0.004,33	0.014,19	18	1964	1 031	0.013,10	0.006,14	70	1964	1.033	0.014,14	0.005,03	108
1965	1.030	0.012,66	0.015,52	10	1965	1.084	0.035,08	0.005,48	78	1965	1.071	0.029,71	0.005,49	83
1966	1,037	0.015,82	0.015,75	13	1966	1.088	0.036,51	0.000,23	71	1966	1.097	0.040,10	0.004,97	107
1967	1.082	0.034,08	0.013,90	15	1967	1.096	0.039,93	0.006,38	57	1967	1.101	0.041,87	0.005,08	118
1968	1.122	0.049,83	0.017,49	8	1968	1.124	0.050,59	0.006,40	66	1968	1.132	0.053,90	0.005,16	112
1969	1.122	0.050,06	0 018,77	6	1969	1.167	0.067,19	0.006,37	65	1969	1.185	0.073,76	0.005,19	107
1970	1.142	0.057,82	0.017,09	9	1970	1.207	0.081,56	0.006,70	56	1970	1.222	0.087,20	0.005,25	113
1971	1.197	0.077,93	0.014,09	24	1971	1.213	0.083,71	0.006,13	74	1971	1.245	0.095,33	0.050,09	123
1972	1.233	0.090,99	0.016,13	11	1972	1.268	0.103,09	0.006,49	67	1972	1.307	0.116,44	0.005,03	131
1973	1.427	0.154,66	0.014,21	13	1973	1.471	0.167,65	0.006,98	47	1973	1.504	0.177,20	0.005,27	114
1974	1.444	0.159.67	0.019,20	6	1974	1.422	0.152,86	0.007,05	46	1974	1.472	0.167,90	0.005,42	98
1975	1.378	0.139,32	0.015,13	12	1975	1.434	0.156,60	0.006,90	51	1975	1.507	0.178,21	0.005,82	79
1976	1,392	0.143,79	0.020,03	5	1976	1.411	0.149,58	0.007,80	31	1976	1.491	0.173.47	0.006,07	69
1977	1.333	0.124,88	0.018,88	6	1977	1.419	0.152,06	0.007,34	44	1977	1.487	0.172,33	0.005,43	96
1978[d]					1978	1.403	0.146,92	0.011,06	13	1978	1.466	0.166.13	0.010,08	17

[a] R^2=0 8278.
[b] R^2=0.7824.
[c] R^2=0.8085.
[d] Insufficient sales of abutting properties.

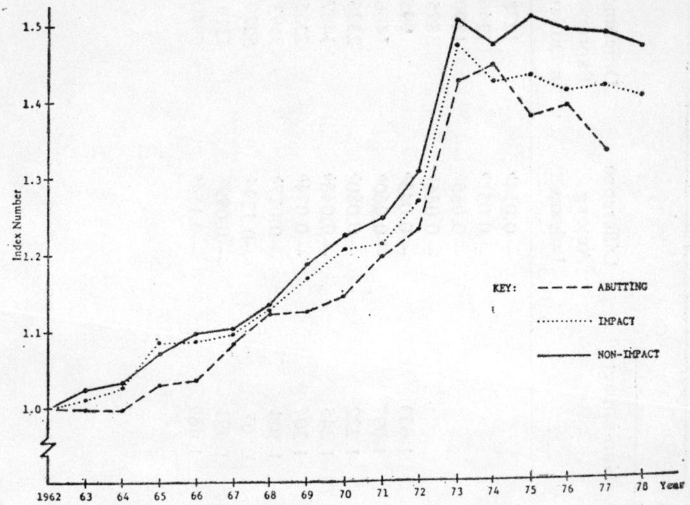

FIG. 15.2 : *Property value price indexes : 1962-1978*

index numbers are transformed into dollar differences that have been inflated to reflect real dollar values in the respective years. These are shown in column 7 of Table 15.3. Although the value differences are greatest for abutting versus nonimpact zone properties, the recent differences between impact and nonimpact area properties are more representative of the impact on nearby properties in general. With reference to the dollar differences shown in the bottom portion of column 7 of Table 15.3, therefore, it can be stated that properties in proximity to the highway (within 1,125 ft) sell for approximately $3,000-$3,500 less than equivalent properties located farther from the highway.

EVALUATION

This study proves conclusively that highway-originated environmental externalities are the major cause of an inverse relationship between yearly increases in North Springfield property resale values and proximity to I-495. Aside from simply revising and updating the results of the earlier study, the current effort found significant differences among distance-related property value index

TABLE 15.3 : **Significant differences among index numbers and conversion to value differences in dollars**

Year	Price Deflator	Index Numbers			Difference Among Indexes	Difference Expressed in Dollars[a]
		Abutters	Impact	Non-impact		
1965	1.101	1.030	1.084		—0.054[b]	1278
1966	1.137	1.037	1.088		—0.051[b]	1246
1970	1.353	1.142	1.207		—0.065[b]	1890
1977	2.097	1.333	1.419		—0.086[b]	3875
1964	1.077	0.990		1.033	—0.043[b]	995
1966	1.137	1.037		1.097	—0.060[b]	1466
1970	1.353	1.142		1.222	—0.080[b]	2326
1971	1.422	1.197		1.245	—0.048[b]	1467
1972	1.481	1.233		1.307	—0.074[b]	2355
1973	1.567	1.427		1.504	—0.077[b]	2593
1975	1.883	1.378		1.507	—0.129[d]	5220
1976	1.981	1.392		1.491	—0.099[b]	4214
1977	2.097	1.333		1.487	—0.154[c]	6940

1971	1.422	1.213	1.245	—0.032[b]	978
1972	1.481	1.268	1.307	—0.039[b]	1241
1974	1.718	1.422	1.472	—0.050[b]	1846
1975	1.883	1.434	1.507	—0.073[d]	2954
1976	1.981	1.411	1.491	—0.080[c]	3406
1977	2.097	1.419	1.487	—0.068[c]	3064
1978	2.179	1.403	1.466	—0.063[b]	2950

[a]Dollar differences have been inflated to reflect real value in each respective year. Computation : $ 22,456 × price deflator × difference among indexes.

[b]Indicates significance at 10 per cent level.

[c]Indicates significance at 2.5 per cent level.

[d]Indicates significance at 1 per cent level.

numbers in 12 of the 17 years under study. Although significant differences were found in each of the latest nine years in the time series under study, it is likely that the highway widening construction from 1974 through 1977 had some impact on the magnitude of such differences in those particular years. In general, therefore, the overall results justify a much stronger statement concerning highway impacts on property values than did the findings of the 1962-1972 analysis. An additional contribution of this study is that the length of the time series (17 years) was unprecedented in previous highway impact investigations.

Although the study findings are valid in a statistical sense, caution should be exercised regading their overall generalizability. It would be misleading to attempt to apply the results of this study directly to the situations of other highway-community interfaces. It would be very useful, however, to employ the methodology and procedures of this study for the purpose of gaining insight into the net economic impact of highways on property values in other areas.

It was interesting to note that noise barriers had been constructed along the right-of-way boundaries of the Washington beltway in North Springfield and that reductions of up to 15 dB (A) in noise levels were estimated. As a result, the loudness of traffic noise has been reduced by at least onehalf. Unfortunately, such improvements occurred so recently that any possible impact on property sales values could not have been detected. Perhaps a future study may investigate this. While it is well documented that highway-originated disturbances can have adverse impacts on the values of nearby residential properties, it will be interesting to see if such a trend reverses, given that the level of disturbance has been reduced significantly.

Finally, it is appropriate to mention that the findings of this study are quite consistent with generally accepted theories of capital asset pricing. That is, each yearly deflated housing price actually represents the present value of a stream of anticipated housing services and locational amenities. If such anticipations were to have remained constant over time, no changes in deflated housing prices could have been expected. Property sales prices in North Springfield did change throughout the period under observations, however. This phenomenon can be attributed to two general factors : (a) changes in the level or degree of an externality and (b) changes in consumer attitudes (preference or tastes) toward an externality. Traffic volumes on I-495 (level of externality) have increased quite dramatically and, without any doubt, people have become much more cognizant and concerned about environmental issues, including traffic-generated noise and air pollutants, since the environmental movement began approximately with Earth Day in 1969. Also, the construction that took place in order to widen the highway and the erection of noise barriers must be regarded as having been annoying sources of environmental externalities. These had an adverse impact on those residents in proximity to the highway.

ACKNOWLEDGEMENT

This study was supported in part by a grant from the Faculty Research Fellowship program of the University of Tennessee's College of Business Administration.

REFERENCES

1. M. Stein, Social-Impact Assessment Techniques and Their Application to Transportation Decisions. Traffic Quarterly, Vol. 31, April 1977, pp. 297-316.
2. C.J. Langley, Jr., Time Series Effects of a Limited Access Highway on Residential Property Values. TRB, Transportation Research Record 583, 1976, pp. 36-44.
3. M.J. Ball, Recent Empirical Work on the Determinants of Relative House Prices. Urban Studies, Vol. 10, June 1973, pp. 213-233.
4. L.C.L. Poon, Railway Externalities and Residential Property Prices. Land Economics, Vol. 54, May 1978, pp. 218-227.
5. G.R. Allen, An Investigation of the Combined Effects of Property Taxes and Local Public Spending on Property Values : The Case of Virginia. James Wilson Department of Economics, University of Virginia, Charlottesville, Ph.D. dissertation, 1978.
6. R.W. Crowley, The Effects of an Airport on Land Values. Journal of Transport Economics and Policy, Vol. 7, May 1973, pp. 144-152.
7. F.C. Emerson, Valuation of Residential Amenities : An Econometric Approach. Appraisal Journal, April 1972, pp. 268-278.
8. B.A. Smith, Measuring the Value of Urban Amenities. Journal of Urban Economics, Vol. 5, July 1978, pp. 370-387.
9. P.W. Abelson, Property Prices and the Value of Amenities. Journal of Environmental Economics and Management, Vol. 6, March 1979,

pp. 11-28.

10. D.B. Diamond, Jr., The Relationship between Amenities and Urban Land Prices. Land Economics, Vol. 56, Feb. 1980, pp. 21-32.
11. A.A. Walters, Noise and Prices. Oxford Univ. Press, London, England, 1975, pp. 33-35.
12. J.P. Nelson, Residential Choice, Hedonic Prices, and the Demand for Urban Air Quality. Journal of Urban Economics, Vol. 5, July 1978, pp. 357-369.
13. S. Rosen, Hedonic Prices and Implicit Markets : Product Differentiation in Pure Competition. Journal of Political Economy, Vol. 82, Jan. 1974, pp. 34-55.
14. Average Daily Traffic Volumes on Interstate, Arterial, and Primary Routes. Traffic and Safety Division, Department of Highways, Commonwealth of Virginia, Richmond, Volumes for 1962-1978.
15. R.E. Armstrong, Effectiveness of Noise Barriers Along the Capital Beltway (I-495) in Northern Virginia. Presented at 59th Annual Meeting of the Transportation Research Board, Washington, DC, 1980 (mimeo).
16. M.J. Bailey, R.F. Muth, and H.O. Nourse, A Regression Method for Real Estate Price Index Construction. Journal of the American Statistical Association, Vol. 58, Dec. 1963, pp. 933-942.
17. Economic Report of the President Transmitted to the Congress, January 1979, Together with the Annual Report of the Council of Economic Advisors. U.S. Government Printing Office, 1979, p. 186.
18. A.M. Polinsky and S, Shavell, The Air Pollution and Property Value Debate. Review of Economics and Statistics, Vol. 57, Feb. 1975, pp. 100-104.
19. A.M. Polinsky and S. Shavell, Amenities and Property Values in a Model of an Urban Area. Journal of Public Economics, Vol. 5, 1976, pp. 119-129.

SIXTEEN

MASATOSHI A. ABE

THE PROBLEM OF PEAK LOAD PRICING

INTRODUCTION

THIS paper discusses the peak-load pricing problem in the framework of urban transportation. Professor William S. Vickery wrote [13, p. 452], "In no major area are pricing practices so irrational, so out of date, and so conducive to waste in urban transportation. Two aspects are particularly deficient : the absence of adequate peak-off differential and the gross underpricing of some modes relative to others."

As it is well known, traffic congestion results from not using a proper price mechanism. A relatively low price charged during peak periods invites an excess number of road users during peak-periods. This would imply inefficient allocation of road users, for traffic congestion results from too many users during peak periods and fewer users during off-peak periods.

If we can persuade the peak-period users to switch to the off-peak-period users, we may be able to solve the problem of traffic congestion. This is where the price mechanism comes in. (Of course, we are here ignoring the fact that people have to use roads during peak periods to get to work. However, we can persuade some peak-period users to abandon their automobiles for mass transit.) A relatively lower price charged during peak periods and a relatively lower price charged during the off-peak periods would accomplish the transfer of some of the peak-period users to the off-peak-period users.

The proper use of the price mechanism will thus theoretically solve the problem of traffic congestion, but it will create another formidable problem—the problem of inequity. A higher price charged to the peak-period users reduces traffic congestion only by denying the poor their right to use the roads during peak periods. If this policy is pushed too far, we can conceive of a situation where the peak period road use is limited only to the rich and mass transit to only the poor.

We face, therefore, a problem of choice between various combinations of efficiency and equity. What we should aim at, in this regard, is to set price so as to maximize welfare and to achieve allocative efficiency.

We believe, therefore, that the pricing of public facilities such as transportation should be used as a possible means to direct a smooth flow of traffic and to enhance social welfare by income redistribution.

In what follows, therefore, we use a rather general social welfare function, i.e., a linear function of individual utility functions with weights. With this formulation we explicitly take into consideration the fact that society does not value equally a dollar received by its members.

Our problem is then to accomplish Pareto-optimality by setting up proper price levels and by redistributing income. This framework is a follow-up of three papers by Mohring,[5] Marchand[6] and Sherman.[9] We will show that given today's pricing practice of urban transportation service a strict adherence to marginal cost pricing does not yield Pareto-optimality. Rather a systematic deviation from m:rginal cost is required for attainment of maximum social welfare.

THEORETICAL FRAMEWORK

In this economy there are n consumers ($i=1, 2, \ldots n$) and each derives satisfaction from t_1^i peak period auto travel, t_2^i off-peak period auto travel, and from consuming units of composite commodity x^i. Each consumer possesses a utility function of the form

$$(1) \qquad u^i = u^i\,(t_1^i, t_2^i, x^i)$$

Utility functions are quasi-concave, continuous, and twice differentiable.

Average input quantity required to provide a unit of t_i is represented by composite variables (including fuel, tires, vehicles, etc.)[1] g, i.e.

(2) $g_1 = g_1 (t_1)$

and $g_2 = g_2 (t_2)$

g_1 is a convex twice continuously differentiable function of total traffic t_1, and will take a form presented in Figure 16.1.

Figure 16.2 shows the form of g_2, where no traffic congestion exists. Under congested conditions an additional vehicle journey

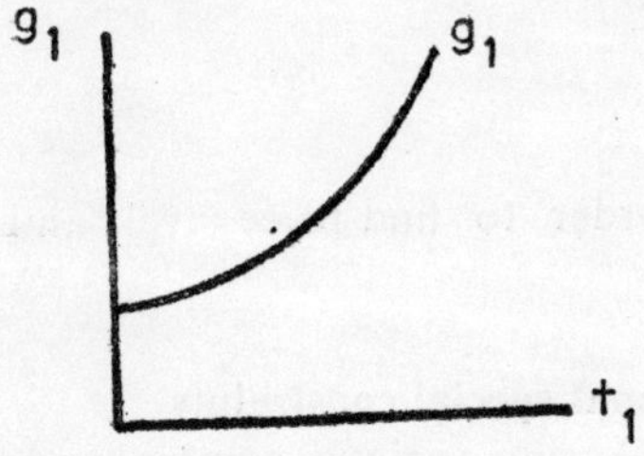

FIG. 16.1

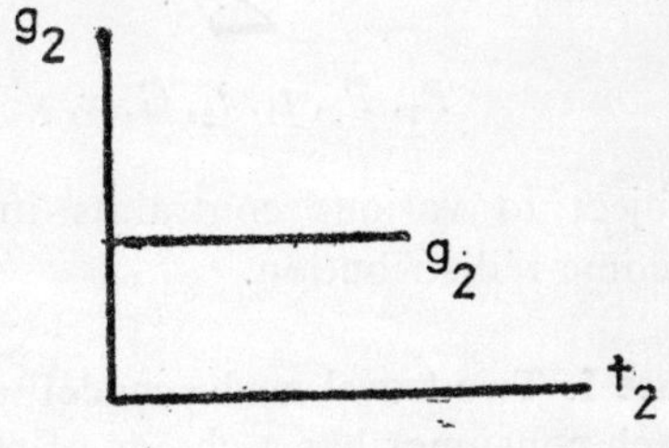

FIG. 16.2

will add to the traffic congestion. The vehicle will get in the way of other vehicles using the road and will cause their cost to increase as they waste more time in traffic jams and incur higher maintenance costs per mile in the dense traffic. This is why g_1 is upward sloping in Figure 16.1.

The total amount of resources used for travelling is G

(3) $G = g_1 t_1 + g_2 t_2$

G and X are related according to the following transformation function :

(4) $f(G, X) = 0$

The price of g in terms of X is denoted by. . . . With the price P per unit of t_i, X as numeraire, and y^i as the ith consumer's income, the budget constraint of the ith individual is

(5) $P_1 \; t_1^i + P_2 \; t_2^i + x^i = y^i$

From the first order conditions for maximization of (1) subject to (5), we obtain the following demand functions :

(6) $t_1^i = t_1^i \, (P_1, \; P_2, y^i)$

(7) $t_2^i = t_2^i \, (P_1, P_2, y^i)$

(8) $x^i = x^i \, (P_1, P_2, y^i)$

i.e., the demand functions are interdependent.

Now our task is to maximize social welfare—a linear function of individual utility functions with weights β^i. This is :

(6) $$\underset{P_1,\, P_2,\, t_1,\, t_2,\, G,\, x,\, y^i}{\text{Max}} \; Z = \sum \beta^i \; u^i \; (t_1^i, \; t_2^i, \; x^i)$$

subject to various contraints in order to find price levels and income redistribution.

Case I. Two travel modes model without special constraints

Each consumer has a choice of purchasing various combinations of t_1, t_2 and x. Our problem here is to find optimal levels of P_1 and P_2 in terms of the numeraire X and the optimal condition for income redistribution that will give the maximum social welfare. We can formulate our problem as follows :

(1) $$\underset{P_1,\, P_2,\, t_1,\, t_2,\, X,\, G,\, y^i}{\text{Max}} \; Z = \sum \beta^i \; u^i \; (t_1^i, \; t_2^i, \; x^i)$$

subject to

(2) $\sum t_1^i = t_1$ μ_β

(3) $\sum t_2^i = t_2$ μ_λ

(4) $g_1 \, t_1 + g_2 \, t_2 = G$ μ_r

(5) $\sum x^i = X$ μ_x

(6) $f(G, X) = 0$ μ_ϕ

where the Greek letters at the right denote the Lagrange multipliers associated with the constraints. The first order conditions for a maximum are :

$$(7)\qquad \sum \beta^{i} \lambda^{i} t_1^{i} - \mu_\beta \sum \frac{\partial t_1^{i}}{\partial P_1} - \mu_\lambda \sum \frac{\partial t_2^{i}}{\partial P_1} - \mu_x \sum \frac{\partial x^{i}}{\partial P_1} = 0$$

$$(8)\qquad \sum \beta^{i} \lambda^{i} t_2^{i} - \mu_\beta \sum \frac{\partial t_1^{i}}{\partial P_2} - \mu_\lambda \sum \frac{\partial t_2^{i}}{\partial P_2} - \mu_x \sum \frac{\partial x^{i}}{\partial P_2} = 0$$

$$(9)\qquad \mu_\beta - \mu_r \left\{ g_r + t_1 \frac{\partial g_1}{\partial t_1} \right\} = 0$$

$$(10)\qquad \mu_\lambda - \mu_r g_2 = 0$$

$$(11)\qquad \mu_r - \mu\phi \frac{\partial f}{\partial G} = 0$$

$$(12)\qquad \mu_x - \mu\phi \frac{\partial f}{\partial G} = 0$$

$$(13)\qquad \beta^{i} \lambda^{i} - \mu\beta \frac{\partial t_1^{i}}{\partial y^{i}} - \mu\lambda \frac{\partial t_2^{i}}{\partial y^{i}} - \mu_x \frac{\partial x^{i}}{\partial y^{i}} = 0$$

where λ is a Lagrange multiplier attached to the budget constraint (5)[6] on page 396. We use these first order conditions and the following relations (14), (15), (16), and (17)

$$S_{kj} = \sum_{i=1}^{n} \left(\frac{\partial t_k^{i}}{\partial P_j} - t_k^{i} \frac{\partial t_k^{i}}{\partial y^{i}} \right)$$

for $k=1, 2, 3$; $j=1, 2$

where S_{kj}'s are the Hicks-Slutsky pure substitution effect of the price change in P_j on t_k. Of course, when $k=3$, (14) is

$$(15)\qquad S_{3j} = \sum_{i=1}^{n} \left(\frac{\partial x^{i}}{\partial P_j} - X^{i} \frac{\partial x^{i}}{\partial y^{i}} \right) \qquad j=1, 2$$

$$(16)\qquad \frac{\mu r}{\mu x} = -\frac{dX}{dG} = \pi$$

where π is the price of g in terms of X. And also

(17) $\quad P_1S_{11}+P_2S_{21}+S_{31}=P_1S_{12}+P_2S_{22}+S_{32}=0$[2]

From these equations (identities) and the first order conditions we obtain finally[3]

$$(18)\quad \begin{bmatrix} S_{11} & S_{21} \\ S_{12} & S_{22} \end{bmatrix} \begin{bmatrix} \frac{\mu\beta}{\mu x}-P_1 \\ \frac{\mu\lambda}{\mu x}-P_2 \end{bmatrix}=0$$

where

$$(19)\quad \frac{\mu\beta}{\mu x}=\pi\left\{g_1+t_1\frac{\partial g_1}{\partial t_1}\right\}=MC_1$$

$$(20)\quad \frac{\mu\lambda}{\mu x}=\pi\left\{g_2\right\}=AC_2=MC_2{}^4$$

MC_1 is the marginal cost of the peak-period auto-trip. AC_2 is the average cost of off-peak auto trip. The first matrix on the left is positive.[5] We can conclude then that

(21) $\quad MC_1=P_1$ and $AC_2=MC_2=P_2$

and we can show that the condition for optimal redistribution of income is

(22) $\quad \beta^i\lambda^i=\beta^j\lambda^j$

where λ's and β's, respectively, represent the marginal utilities of income and their social weights. We obtain (22) only when $P_i=MC_i$. The relation (22) implies that an additional dollar of income spent by any consumer incurs a social cost exactly equal to unity, and that each consumer gets the same level of satisfaction from the additional dollar of income spent.

All of these results are expected—maximized social welfare, optimal distribution of resources, and optimal redistribution of income—in an ideal economy where price reflects marginal cost and perfect competition prevails. In the following cases we look into more realistic situations where price does not reflect marginal cost and/or price is required to deviate from marginal cost in order to render a higher social welfare.

Case II. The single price constraint

The most often criticized pricing practice of urban automobile traffic is the lack of price discrimination between the peak-period users and the off-peak period users. Our problem here is to find the optimal price level given an added constraint that the same price be charged in peak and off-peak periods.

We can formulate this problem as follows :

(1) $$\text{Max } Z=\sum \beta^{i} u^{i} (t^{i}, t_2^{i}, x^{i})$$

subject to

(2) $$\sum t_1^{i}= t_1 \qquad \mu\beta$$

(3) $$\sum t_2^{i}= t_2 \qquad \mu\lambda$$

(4) $$g_1t_1+g_2t_2=G \qquad \mu r$$

(5) $$\sum x^{i}=X \qquad \mu x$$

(6) $$f(G, X)=0 \qquad \mu\phi$$

(7) $$P_1-P_2=0 \qquad \mu\alpha$$

Proceeding in a fashion analogous to Case I, we obtain

(8) $$\begin{bmatrix} S_{11} & S_{21} \\ S_{12} & S_{22} \end{bmatrix} \begin{bmatrix} \frac{\mu\beta}{\mu x} -P_1 \\ \frac{\mu\lambda}{\mu x} -P_2 \end{bmatrix} = \frac{\mu\alpha}{\mu x} \begin{bmatrix} -1 \\ 1 \end{bmatrix}$$

where $\frac{\mu\beta}{\mu x}=MC_1$ and $\frac{\mu\lambda}{\mu x}=AC_2=MC_2$. We can rewrite (8) as

(9) $$\begin{bmatrix} MC_1 & -P_1 \\ AC_1 & -P_2 \end{bmatrix} = \frac{\mu x}{S\mu x} \begin{bmatrix} S_{22} & -S_{21} \\ -S_{12} & S_{11} \end{bmatrix} \begin{bmatrix} -1 \\ 1 \end{bmatrix}$$

where $S=S_{11}S_{22}-S_{12}S_{21}>0$.[6] Therefore we can write

(10) $$\frac{MC_1-P_1}{AC_2-P_2}=\frac{-S_{22}-S_{21}}{S_{12}+S_{11}}$$

But both S_{11} and S_{22} are negative, and S_{12} $(=S_{21})$ is positive because t_1 and t_2 are substitutes. The most likely signs for the ratios in (10) are positive, i.e.

(11) $$\frac{MC_1-P_1}{AC_2-P_2}>0 \text{ i.e.}$$

(12) $MC_1 - P_1 < 0$

and $AC_2 - P_2 < 0$[7]

and (13) $$\frac{-S_{22} - S_{21}}{S_{12} - S_{11}} > 0$$

i.e. (14) $-S_{22} - S_{12} < 0$

and $S_{12} + S_{11} < 0$[8]

But since $S_{12} = S_{21}$, we can have the following inequalities :

(15) $$-S_{11} > S_{12} > -S_{22}$$

which means that a decrease in the peak-period travel when the price of the peak period travel increases is greater than an increase in the peak period travel when the price of the off-peak travel increases, and that an increase in the peak-period travel when the price of the off-peak travel increases is greater than a decrease in the off-peak travel when the price of the off-peak travel increases.

From our current traffic situation, (15) is the most plausible situation. Therefore under (15), the condition (12) is satisfied, i.e.

$$MC_1 < P_1 \text{ and } AC_2 < P_2$$

That is, under the single price constraint the price of the peak-period travel is greater than marginal cost on the one hand, and the price of the off-peak period travel is greater than its average cost (=marginal cost).

The condition for the optimal income redistribution in this case is :

(14) $W^i \lambda^i = W^j \lambda^j$

where $$W^i = \frac{\beta^i}{\frac{\partial t_k^i}{\partial y^i}(MC_k - P_k) + 1}$$

where $k = 1$ and 2 ; 1 for the peak-period auto users and 2 for the off-peak-period auto users. The implication of this optimal condition is that income redistribution would favor the off-peak period users.

Case III. The peak period users are paying only average cost

In this situation the peak-period automobile users are paying only their private cost, i.e. average cost rather than marginal cost, ignoring the cost they are imposing on their fellow travelers and society. We can formulate our problems as follows :

(1) $$\text{Max } Z = \sum \overset{i}{\beta} \overset{i}{u} (\overset{i}{t_1}, \overset{i}{t_2}, \overset{i}{x})$$

subject to

(2) $$P_1 = \pi g_1 \qquad \mu a$$

(3) $$\sum \overset{i}{t_1} = t_1 \qquad \mu\beta$$

(4) $$\sum \overset{i}{t_2} = t_2 \qquad \mu\lambda$$

(5) $$g_1 t_1 + g_2 t_2 = G \qquad \mu r$$

(6) $$\sum \overset{i}{x} = X \qquad \mu x$$

(7) $$f(G, X) = 0 \qquad \mu\phi$$

Our problem is to find the optimal price level for P_2, i.e. the optimal price for the off-peak period users given the fact that the peak-period users are being charged only their average cost.

From the first order conditions we can derive

(8) $$\begin{bmatrix} S_{11} & S_{21} \\ S_{12} & S_{22} \end{bmatrix} \begin{bmatrix} \frac{\mu\beta}{\mu x} - P_1 \\ \frac{\mu\lambda}{\mu x} - P_2 \end{bmatrix} = \begin{bmatrix} -\frac{\mu a}{\mu x} \\ 0 \end{bmatrix}$$

or (9) $$\begin{bmatrix} \frac{\mu\beta}{\mu x} - P_1 \\ \frac{\mu\lambda}{\mu x} - P_2 \end{bmatrix} = \frac{1}{S} \begin{bmatrix} S_{22} & -S_{21} \\ -S_{12} & S_{11} \end{bmatrix} \begin{bmatrix} -\frac{\mu a}{\mu x} \\ 0 \end{bmatrix}$$

But

(10) $$\frac{\mu\beta}{\mu x} = MC_1 - \frac{\mu a}{\mu x} \pi \frac{\partial g_1}{\partial t_1}$$

(11) $$\frac{\mu\lambda}{\mu x} = AC_2 = MC_2 = \pi g_2$$

Therefore

(12) $$P_1 = MC_1 + \frac{\mu a}{\mu x} \left\{ \frac{S_{22}}{S} - \pi \frac{\partial g_1}{\partial t_1} \right\}$$

(13) $$P_2 = \pi g_2 - \frac{\mu a}{\mu x} \frac{S_{21}}{S}$$

From (12) and (13) we can derive by eliminating $\frac{\mu a}{\mu x}$

(14) $$P_2=\pi g_2-\frac{\frac{S_{21}}{S}}{\frac{S_{22}}{S}-\pi\frac{\partial g_1}{\partial t_1}}(P_1-MC_1)$$

But since $P_1=\pi g_1<MC_1$, the second term in (14) is positive. Hence

(15) $$P_2<\pi g_2$$

That is, the off-peak period users should be charged less than their average cost, when the peak-period users are paying only their average cost.

We obtain the same condition as Case II for the optimal income redistribution.

Case IV. The deficit constraint

In Case III the peak period users are paying only their average cost and the off-peak-period users are paying a price less than their average cost. Our analysis has shown that the situation there presents an optimal case, but one problem is that a government agency responsible for providing transportation facility will be in debt in such a situation. In case IV, therefore, we set a deficit limit. This constraint could very well be such as to require the agency to operate on a self-supporting basis.

We formulate this problem as follows :

(1) $$\underset{P_1,\, P_2,\, t_1,\, t_2,\, X,\, G,\, y^i}{\text{Max } Z=\sum}\ \overset{i}{\beta}\ \overset{i}{u}\,(\overset{i}{t_1},\ \overset{i}{t_2}.\ \overset{i}{x})$$

subject to

(2) $$\sum \overset{i}{t_1}= t_1 \qquad \mu\beta$$

(3) $$\sum \overset{i}{t_2}= t_2 \qquad \mu\lambda$$

(4) $$g_1t_1+g_2t_2=G \qquad \mu r$$

(5) $$\sum \overset{i}{x}=X \qquad \mu x$$

(6) $$f(G,\ X)=0 \qquad \mu a$$

(7) $$\pi g_1t_1+\pi g_2t_2=P_1t_1+P_2t_2+D \qquad \mu\phi$$

where D is the deficit limit.

From the first order conditions we derive

$$\begin{pmatrix} S_{11} & S_{21} \\ S_{12} & S_{22} \end{pmatrix} \begin{pmatrix} \frac{\mu\beta}{\mu x} - P_1 \\ \frac{\mu\lambda}{\mu x} - P_2 \end{pmatrix} = \frac{\mu a}{\mu x} \begin{pmatrix} t_1 \\ t_2 \end{pmatrix} \tag{8}$$

where

$$\frac{\mu\beta}{\mu x} = MC_1 - \frac{\mu a}{\mu x}(P_1 - MC_1) \tag{9}$$

and

$$\frac{\mu\lambda}{\mu x} = \pi g_2 - \frac{\mu a}{\mu x}(P_2 - \pi g_2) \tag{10}$$

Therefore we can show that

$$P_1 - MC_1 - \frac{\mu a}{\mu a + \mu x}\left[\frac{S_{22}t_1 - S_{21}t_2}{S}\right] \tag{11}$$

and

$$P_2 = \pi g_2 - \frac{\mu a}{\mu a + \mu x}\left[\frac{S_{11}t_2 - S_{12}t_1}{S}\right] \tag{12}$$

where, to repeat, $S = S_{11}S_{22} - S_{12}S_{21} > 0$. The Lagrange multipliers, μx and μa, can be interpreted as the rates at which welfare changes with increases, respectively, in the resource X and in the allowable deficit D. Therefore we can say that $\mu a > 0$ and $\mu x > 0$. Also we know that $S_{11} < 0$, $S_{22} < 0$, $S_{12} = S_{21} > 0$. Therefore the quantities in brackets in (11) and (12) are negative. Therefore we can conclude that

$$P_1 > MC_1 \tag{13}$$

and

$$P_2 > \pi g_2 = MC_2 = AC_2 \tag{14}$$

In order to recover some deficit, therefore, the prices are required to depart from their marginal costs.

We obtain the same condition as Case II for the optimal income redistribution.

Case V. Input tax and the optimal price for the off-peak auto travel
In this case the peak-period automobile users are paying their average cost as the previous cases. In case V, however, in order to recover a deficit input tax[9] is applied. Our problem then is to

find the optimal input tax and price for the off-peak period automobile users. We formulate this problem as follows :

(1) $$\underset{\pi;\ P_1,\ P_2,\ t_1,\ t_2,\ X,\ G,\ y^i}{\text{Max}}\ Z=\sum \beta^i u^i(t_1^i, t_2^i, x^i)$$

subject to

(2) $$P_1=\pi g_1 \qquad \mu\alpha$$

(3) $$\sum t_1^i = t_1 \qquad \mu\beta$$

(4) $$\sum t_2^i = t_2 \qquad \mu\lambda$$

(5) $$g_1t_1+g_2t_2=G \qquad \mu r$$

(6) $$\sum x^i = X \qquad \mu x$$

(7) $$f(G, X)=0 \qquad \mu\phi$$

Here we differentiate the above equations with respect to π also, in order to find the optimal input tax. Differentiation with respect to π will give $\mu\alpha=0$, which simplifies our calculation considerably.

From the first order conditions and identities, we obtain

(8) $$\begin{pmatrix} S_{11} & S_{21} \\ S_{12} & S_{22} \end{pmatrix} \begin{pmatrix} \dfrac{\mu\beta}{\mu x} - P_1 \\ \dfrac{\mu\lambda}{\mu x} - P_2 \end{pmatrix} = 0$$

where the first matrix on the left is nonsingular and

(9) $$\frac{\mu\beta}{\mu x} = \frac{\partial X}{\partial G}\left\{ g_1+t_1\frac{\partial g_1}{\partial t_1}\right\}$$

(10) $$\frac{\mu\lambda}{\mu x} = \frac{\partial X}{\partial G} g_2$$

Note that $\dfrac{\partial X}{\partial G} \neq \pi$ in Case V because of input tax. The optimal input tax and the price for the off-peak period users are therefore :

(11) $$\pi^* = \frac{\partial X}{\partial G}\left\{ 1+\frac{t_1}{g_1}\frac{\partial g_1}{\partial t_1}\right\}^{10}$$

(12) $$P_2 = \frac{\partial X}{\partial G} g_2$$

As you can see from (11), the peak-period users are now forced to pay their marginal cost by the use of input tax, i.e.

$$(13) \qquad P_1 = \pi^* g_1 = \frac{\partial X}{\partial G}\left\{g_1 + t_1 \frac{\partial g_1}{\partial t_1}\right\} = MC_1$$

Moreover the revenue from and the expenditure for the peak-period operation balance out. For the off-peak period operation we will have a positive profit, i.e.

$$(14) \qquad P_2 t_2 - \pi^* g_2 t_2 = \frac{\partial X}{\partial G} g_2 t_2 - \frac{\partial X}{\partial G}\left\{1 + \frac{t_1}{g_1} \cdot \frac{\partial g_1}{\partial t_1}\right\} g_2 t_2$$

$$= -\frac{\partial X}{\partial G} \cdot \frac{t_1}{g_1} \cdot \frac{\partial g_1}{\partial t_2} g_2 t_2$$

where $-\frac{\partial X}{\partial G}$ is the marginal rate of transformation of X for G under the scheme of input tax, i.e. the price of G in terms of X when input tax is imposed on G.

The same condition and interpretation as Case II holds for optimal income redistribution.

Case VI. The capacity constraint

Here we introduce the capacity constraint explicitly. The peak-period users are using roads to the limit of the capacity of the roads. In this case, as we will show below, the peak-period users are required to pay the expansion cost in addition to the usual marginal cost. We formulate this problem as follows :

$$(1) \qquad \text{Max } Z = \sum \beta^i u^i\left(t_1^i, t_2^i, x^i\right)$$

subject to

$$(2) \qquad \sum t_1^i = t_1 \qquad \mu\beta$$

$$(3) \qquad \sum t_2^i = t_2 \qquad \mu\lambda$$

$$(4) \qquad g_1 t_1 + g_2 t_2 = G \qquad \mu r$$

$$(5) \qquad t^1 = K \qquad \mu\psi$$

$$(6) \qquad \sum x^i = X \qquad \mu x$$

$$(7) \qquad E = E(K) \qquad \mu\varepsilon$$

$$(8) \qquad f(G, X, E) = 0 \qquad \mu\phi$$

where K is a constant representing the capacity of road. E

represents the amount of resources used for construction and expansion of roads.

$$g_1 = g_1(t_1, K) \text{ and } g_2 = g_2(t_2)$$

Under these conditions we derive from the first order conditions and other identities discussed before :

$$(9) \quad \begin{pmatrix} S_{11} & S_{12} \\ S_{12} & S_{22} \end{pmatrix} \begin{pmatrix} \frac{\mu\beta}{\mu x} - P_1 \\ \frac{\mu\lambda}{\mu x} - P_2 \end{pmatrix} = 0$$

Since the first matrix is nonsingular, we conclude that

$$(10) \quad P_1 = \frac{\mu\beta}{\mu x}$$

and $$(11) \quad P_2 = \frac{\mu\lambda}{\mu x}$$

But

$$(12) \quad \frac{\mu\lambda}{\mu x} = \pi \left\{ g_1 + t_1 \frac{\partial g_1}{\partial t_1} \right\} + \pi \left\{ t_1 \frac{\partial g_1}{\partial K} \right\} + \frac{\partial X}{\partial K}$$

$$(13) \quad \frac{\mu\lambda}{\mu x} \pi = \pi_2 = AC_2 = MC_2$$

Therefore from (11) and (13) we can say that $P_2 = MC_2$, *i.e.* P_2 is equal to its marginal cost, but from (10) and (12) P_1 is higher than MC_1 which is the first term of the right-hand side of (12). The second term is the cost-saving drived from capacity expansion $\left(\frac{\partial g_1}{\partial K} \text{ is negative}\right)$. The third term is the real cost of expansion. We can write therefore that

(14) P_1=the marginal cost of t_1+ the Cost of Expansion.

That is, the peak-period automobile users should be paying not only their marginal social cost but also the expansion cost. The expansion cost is however, lower than the real cost of expansion by the amount of reduced cost of congestion.

CONCLUDING REMARKS

In the above presentation we have discussed what optimal price levels should be for the peak and off-peak period users under today's pricing practice of urban automobile transportation. It was shown that under present pricing practice a strict adherence to marginal cost pricing principle would not yield Pareto-optimality. For the attainment of Pareto-optimality a systematic deviation from marginal cost is required. That is, we live in the area of the second best.[11] We are faced with a problem involving maximization of social welfare in the presence of many added constraints. Optimal prices discussed above are second best solutions in the current transportation practice.

As shown, when the peak-period users fail to pay their real cost, but also imposes as a form of congestion greater external economies the off-peak-period users are required to pay a price below their average cost.

What is not discussed in this paper is the presence of a substitute travel mode such as mass transit. Substitution exists not only between peak and off-peak use of automobiles, but also between automobile use and bus use. A more realistic and more preferable approach to the pricing policy of urban transportation would be to consider social welfare maximization in the presence of substitute travel modes in two periods, peak and off-peak. Also left out in this analysis is the case of increasing returns to scale, which will have a crucial bearing on the investment policy of transportation service.

FOOTNOTES

1. The input commodity, g, may include consumers' time as well. Then in order to preserve a single price we assume equal valuation of time by all consumers. More on this, see Sherman (9).
2. See (8, p. 105).
3. Detailed explanations on the derivation were given in (5, 6, 9).
4. AC_2 is constant. Thus $AD_2 = MC_2$.
5. See (8, p. 106). This is the second order condition for maximization.
6. S is a positive matrix. See footnote 5.
7. See footnote 8.
8. Of course, they could be all positive, but then the interpretation of results will be of no sense. In all we can have four cases : (1) $MC_1 > P$, $AC_2 > P$, (2) $MC_1 < P$, $AC_2 > P$, (3) $MC_1 > P$, $AC_2 < P$, and (4) $MC_1 < P$, $AC_2 < P$. Only the last case makes sense.
9. Input tax could be tax on gasoline, tire and/or vehicle.
10. Since $\frac{t_1}{g_1} \cdot \frac{\partial g_1}{\partial t_1}$ is cost elasticity of t_1, the higher cost elasticity is,

the higher is the optimal input tax level.

11. More on the second best, see (1, 4).

REFERENCES

1. Baumol, W. and Bradford, D., "Optimal Departures from Marginal Cost Pricing," in *The American Economic Review*, June, 1970, pp. 265-283.
2. Boiteux, M., "Peak-Load Pricing," in the *Journal of Business*, April, 1960, pp. 157-179.
3. Dreze, J.H., Some Postwar Contributions of French Economists to Theory and Public Policy with Special Emphasis on Problems of Resource Allocation," in *The American Economic Review*, June, 1964, pp. 1-64.
4. Lipsey, R.G. and Lancaster, R., "The General Theory of Second Best," in the *Review of Economic Studies*, 1956-1957, pp. 11-32.
5. Mohring, H., "The Peak Load Problem with Increasing Returns and Pricing Constraints," in *The American Economic Review*, September, 1970, pp. 693-705.
6. Marchand, M., "A Note on Optimal Tolls in an Imperfect Environment," in *Econometrica*, July-October, 1968, pp. 575-581.
7. Pressman, I., "A Mathematical Formulation of the Peak-Load Pricing Problem," in the *Bell Journal of Economic and Management Science*, Autumn, 1970, pp. 304-326.
8. Samuelson, P., *Foundations of Economic Analysis*; Harvard University Press, Cambridge, Massachusetts, 1948.
9. Sherman, R., "Congestion Interdependence and Urban Transit Fares," in *Econometrica*, May, 1971, pp. 565-576.
10. Steiner, P.O., "Peak Loads and Efficient Pricing," in the *Quarterly Journal of Economics*, November, 1957, pp. 585-610.
11. Steiner, P.O., "Peak Load Pricing Revisited," in H. Trebing ed., *Essays on Public Utility Pricing and Regulation*, Michigan State University Press, East Lansing, Michigan, 1971, pp. 3-22.
12. Strotz, R., "Urban Transportation Parables," in J. Margolis ed., *The Public Economy of Urban Community*, The Johns Hopkins Press, Baltimore, 1965, pp. 127-169.
13. Vickery, W.S., "Pricing in Urban and Suburban Transport," in *The American Economic Review*, May, 1963, pp. 452-465.
14. Walters, A., *The Economics of Road User Charges*, Johns Hopkins Press, Baltimore, Maryland, 1968.
15. Williamson, O.F., "Peak Load Pricing and Optimal Capacity," in *The American Economic Review*, September, 1966, pp. 810-827.

SEVENTEEN

MASATOSHI A. ABE, KUMARES C. SINHA

PRICING AND QUALITY OF SERVICE IN MASS TRANSPORTATION

INTRODUCTION

IT is now the general consensus that current pricing practices in urban transportation are irrational and conducive to congestion and waste. Two aspects which have been mentioned often as deficient in the area of urban transportation are the absence of adequate peak and off-peak period price differentials and the gross underpricing of an automobile trip relative to a mass transit trip.[8]

The purpose of this paper is first, to review briefly the pricing policy of public facilities such as transportation, and then to examine the optimal pricing strategy for mass transit under a situation in which an unfairly low price is charged for automobile trips. The present study shows that in such a situation mass transit users should be paid a subsidy.

Next, the pricing practices used by the privately operated bus transit company in the Milwaukee area is examined. It is observed that like virtually all mass transportation systems in the United States, the transit system in Milwaukee has been caught in an unending cycle—the continuing decline in patronage, the constantly rising cost of labor and equipment, and an almost periodic increase in bus fares. It is feared that this cycle will lead to the ultimate extinction of mass transit service in Milwaukee if it is allowed to continue unchecked.

This investigation indicates that a lowered bus fare together with improved service will substantially increase transit patronage, which will in turn reduce the cost of operating bus transit as a consequence of the existence of the economy of scale.

Lastly, the characteristics of urban mass transit users in this country are evaluated. Investigation indicates that the majority of the transit riders are captive riders in the sense that they do not have any choice in their mode of transportation. This finding substantiates the belief that mass transit fares should be significantly reduced not just for attracting automobile users to transit and thus limiting congestion, but also for increased social welfare resulting in improved equity.

PRICING STRATEGY

It is believed that the pricing policy of public facilities should be directed not only toward achieving an efficient allocation of scarce resources, but also toward promoting the social welfare. Pricing in urban transportation should then be used as a possible means of effecting a balance in the use of modes as well as toward achieving a redistribution of income. Therefore, in order to make a meaningful evaluation of the pricing policy of public facilities such as transportation, all three strands of economic disciplines, i.e. welfare economics, public finance, and regulatory institutions, should be considered simultaneously.

It is a well-known fact, that imbalance in the use of transportation modes results in congestion and that this is a direct consequence of an improper price mechanism : a too-low price is charged for automobile users so that an excessive number of automobile users are on the roads. This means an inefficient allocation of road users, for congestion results from too many automobile users and too few mass transit users.

If it is possible to persuade a sufficient number of automobile users to switch to mass transportation, the problem of congestion might be eased and a balance in urban transportation can be restored. This can be achieved by reversing the current practice of price mechanism—a relatively high price charged for automobile users and a relatively low price charged for mass transit users would accomplish the transformation of some of the automobile users into mass transit users. The proper use of the price mechanism in urban transportation may thus solve to some extent the problem of congestion or imbalanced transportation, but it will create another formidable problem—the problem of inequity. A higher price charged to automobile users might reduce congestion, but at the same time it would prevent the lower-income groups from using their automobiles. A situation is conceivable in which automobile use is limited only to higher-income groups. Lower-income individuals will be forced to give up the use of their automobiles and to use mass transit, thus increasing the number of captive riders. The transportation planners will face, therefore, a problem involving a choice of various combinations of efficiency and equity. What should be aimed at, then, is to set a price so as to maximize welfare (equity) and to achieve allocative efficiency.

Elsewhere,[1] in order to cope with this problem a general social welfare function was used to accomplish Pareto-optimality; evaluation was made on the basis of a linear function of individual utility functions with weights. The weights were included to reflect the fact that society does not value equally a dollar received by its members. This study has shown that under the current pricing practice in urban transportation where automobile users pay only average cost rather than marginal social cost, the mass transit riders should be given a subsidy. The same conclusion has been derived by Marchand[6] and Sherman.[7] The extent of optimal subsidy to the transit users explicitly taking into consideration congestion interdependence between the two travel modes, automobile and mass transit, has also been established.

PRICING AND QUALITY OF SERVICE OF BUS TRANSIT IN MILWAUKEE AREA : 1955-1970

Damand for transit service

The purpose of this section is to discover whether or not a relationship exists between the quality of service and the level of transit patronage in Milwaukee. Although the private firm, Milwaukee and Suburban Transport Corporation, which owns and operates the transit system in the area, has been rendering better than average service,[2] it has been in serious financial difficulty in recent years. To meet sharply rising costs of labor, equipment and materials, the company had to increase fares. Almost inevitably an increase in fares was followed by a reduction in patronage volumes, which led to a decrease in service, and this in turn led to a further reduction in transit ridership. Such service variables as the introduction of new equipment,[2] the age of transit vehicles, an extension of route miles, increase in transit vehicle speeds, and the frequency of service would, to an important degree, affect the level of transit use. Using time series data obtained from the Milwaukee and Suburban Transport Corporation for the period 1955-1970[3] the effect of transit patronage of some of the service variables have been estimated. The results of the regression equations are presented below with the *t*-values given in parentheses :

$$X_1 = 65.901 + \underset{(28.503)}{6.427}\, X_2 \; ; \; R^2 = 0.9831 \qquad \ldots(1)$$

$$X_1 = 47.162 + \underset{(35.431)}{62.083}\, X_3 \; ; \; R^2 = 0.9890 \qquad \ldots(2)$$

$$X_1 = 1136.259 - \underset{(-12.131)}{95.133}\, X_4 \; ; \; R^2 = 0.9131 \qquad \ldots(3)$$

$$X_1 = 162.099 - \underset{(-8.854)}{6.001}\, X_5 \; ; \; R^2 = 0.8485 \qquad \ldots(4)$$

in which X_1=the number of revenue passengers, in millions ; X_2=bus miles of route coverage, in millions ; X_3=bus hours of service, in milllons ; X_4=headway factor (This is another variable used to represent the quality of service and it is computed by dividing bus-miles by bus-hours. A higher headway factor would indicate lower quality of service ; with given number of buses and route-miles of coverage, as the hours of operation decrease, the headways among buses increase. An increased headway would have a negative effect on transit use.) ; and X_5=average fare, in cents.

In all cases significant results were obtained with high R^2 terms and correct signs, confirming that an increased bus fare and an increased headway have indeed reduced transit patronage, while increased bus coverage represented by bus miles and bus hours would have increased transit ridership.

In order to explore the collective rather than the individual effect of service variables, multiple regression equations were developed. The results are :

$$X_1 = 269.9913 + 4.7574\ X_2 - 26.7943\ X_4 - 0.07069\ X_5\ ;$$
$$(13.7160) \quad (-3.2663) \quad (-0.1543)$$

$$R^2 = 0.9948 \qquad \ldots(5)$$

$$X_1 = -0.3718 - 7.9200\ X_2 + 131.7730\ X_3 - 0.7470\ X_5\ ;$$
$$(-2.0875) \quad (3.5086) \quad (-2.3684)$$

$$R^2 = 0.9952 \qquad \ldots(6)$$

Note that the sign of X_2, bus miles, is negative in Eq. 6, this, however, is due to the fact that X_3, bus hours, another service variable representing transit coverage, was used in the same equation in addition to X_2, and that the effect of X_2 is overshadowed by X_3. The sign of X_5, average fare, is negative as it would be expected ; a negative sign of X_5 implies that higher bus fares have indeed discouraged transit use.

In summary, the implication of these results is obvious : the transit patronage in the Milwaukee area can be increased by reducing bus fare and improving transit coverage.

Supply of Transit Service : Economies of Scale—In this section the supply side of transit service is considered, and the effect of changes in the service variables on the cost of providing transit service are explained. The cost per unit service, cost per bus mile, may be critically dependent upon service variables which affect patronage volumes. The crucial point in this regard is the existence of economies (or diseconomies of scale in transit operation. If a deteriorating service and therefore, a reduction in transit patronage, should render a higher cost of providing transit service it indicates that the transit company is suffering from diseconomies of scale in transit operation.

By regressing the service variables on the cost per bus mile the following equations were obtained :

$$Y_1 = 7.5101 - 0.0032\ X_1\ ;\ R^2 = 0.0450 \qquad \ldots(7)$$
$$(-0.8123)$$

$$Y_1 = 7.6431 - 0.0177\ X_2\ ;\ R^2 = 0.0313 \qquad \ldots(8)$$
$$(-0.6735)$$

$$Y_1 = 7.5968 - 0.1730\ X_3\ ;\ R^2 = 0.0328 \qquad \ldots(9)$$
$$(-0.6895)$$

$$Y_1 = 1.7268 - 0.4998\ X_4\ ;\ R^2 = 0.1060 \qquad \ldots(10)$$
$$(1.2882)$$

$$Y_1 = 6.5787 + 0.0551\ X_5\ ;\ R^2 = 0.3004 \quad \ldots(11)$$
$$(2.4523)$$

The cost figure, Y_1,=adjusted operating cost per bus mile with adjustment being made by using BLS consumer price index of transportation. The notation of other variables is the same as before. In all cases the R^2 terms are very low, meaning that the individual effect of these variables is not significant. However, in order to find the collective effect of these variables, a multiple regression equation was applied and the following equation was obtained :

$$Y_1 = 2.7971 + 0.0572\ X_1 - 0.1565\ X_2 + 0.2581\ X_5\ ;$$
$$(3.9980) \quad (-1.9785) \quad (9.6860)$$
$$R^2 = 0.8990 \quad \ldots(12)$$

Note that the collective effect of the service variables on the unit cost of service is substantial. A negative coefficient of X_2 is important because it suggests the existence of scale economy in the operation of the transit system. If Y_1 and X_2 move in the opposite directions as a negative sign of X_2 would imply, the existence of scale economy is confirmed. Since X_1 and X_2 are positively correlated, in order to explore the existence of scale economy Y_1 was plotted against X_1. The resulting curve is shown in Fig. 17.1. The U-shaped curve in this figure infers that scale economy exists in bus transit operation. To confirm this further, the following regression equation was applied :

$$Y_1 = 13.7003 - 0.1362\ X_1 + 0.007\ X_2\ ;\ R^2 = 0.8351 \quad \ldots(13)$$
$$(-8.0427) \quad (7.8911)$$

Comparing Eq. 13 with Eq. 7, note that R^2 is considerably increased when a quadratic term, X_1^2, is added. This confirms that the unit operating cost of the bus transit company is U-shaped and thus there exists economy of scale. In other words, when the number of revenue passengers increases from 60,000,000 to 70,000,000 to 90,000,000 the average cost per bus mile decreases, but as the number of revenue passengers passes beyond, say 100,000,000 the average cost starts going up. Therefore, since around 1960, when the number of revenue ridership was 103,200,000 (in Fig. 17.1, it is about the bottom of the unit cost curve), the transit company in the Milwaukee area has been operating in the range of diseconomy of scale despite the fact that by increasing the number of revenue passengers the company could have taken the advantage of economy of scale. It can be argued, therefore, that the further reduction in the number of patronage will consequently raise the unit operating cost of transit operation.

IMPLICATIONS OF MILWAUKEE CASE STUDY

This investigation has shown that service variables are important determinants of the demand for and the supply of the bus transit in the Milwaukee area. Reduction in the quality of bus service, together with increased fares, have reduced patronage volume, which in turn has prevented the transit company from utilizing economy of scale. A simple diagrammatic explanation of this situation is presented in Fig. 17.2 where three demand curves and the average cost curve are shown. The slope of demand curve will measure the degree of responsiveness of the riders to a change in price. Considering the U-shaped cost curve of the transit company in Milwaukee, increased fares and deteriorating services have shifted the demand to the left from D_1 to D_2, thus raising the average cost of operating the system. Subsidies to the transit users or to the transit company, and other measures of improving transit service, would, as the present study has indicated, encourage transit use, shifting the demand curve from D_2 to D_1 and to D_3. This would increase the number of transit users and would consequently reduce the average cost of operating the transit system.

CHARACTERISTICS OF BUS TRANSIT USERS IN UNITED STATES

To examine the socioeconomic characteristics of the bus transit users an analysis was made on the basis of the nationwide data obtained from the 1960 census information.[8] In an attempt to find different characteristics among residents in urbanized areas of different sizes, three regression equations were applied : (1) For all urbanized areas containing at least one city which had

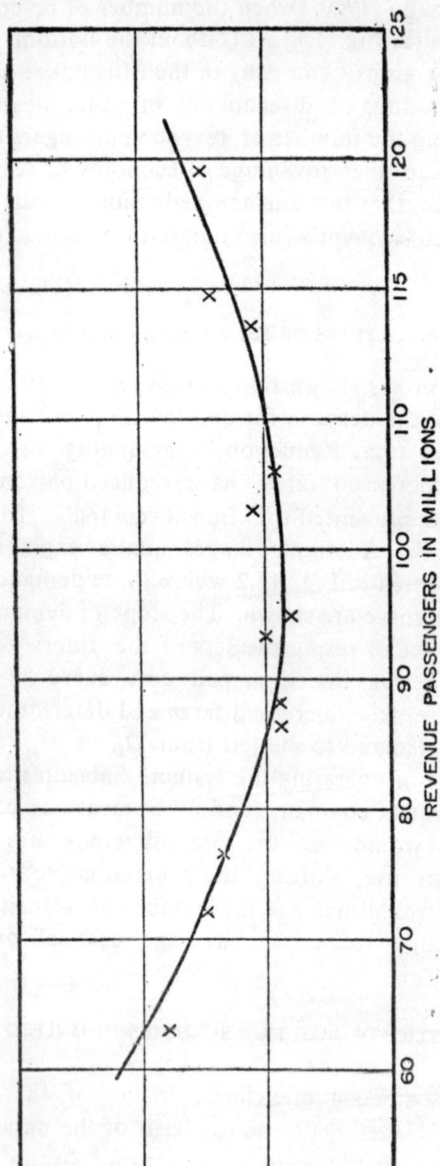

FIG. 17.1 : *Average unit cost of transit operation in Milwaukee ; 1955-1970*

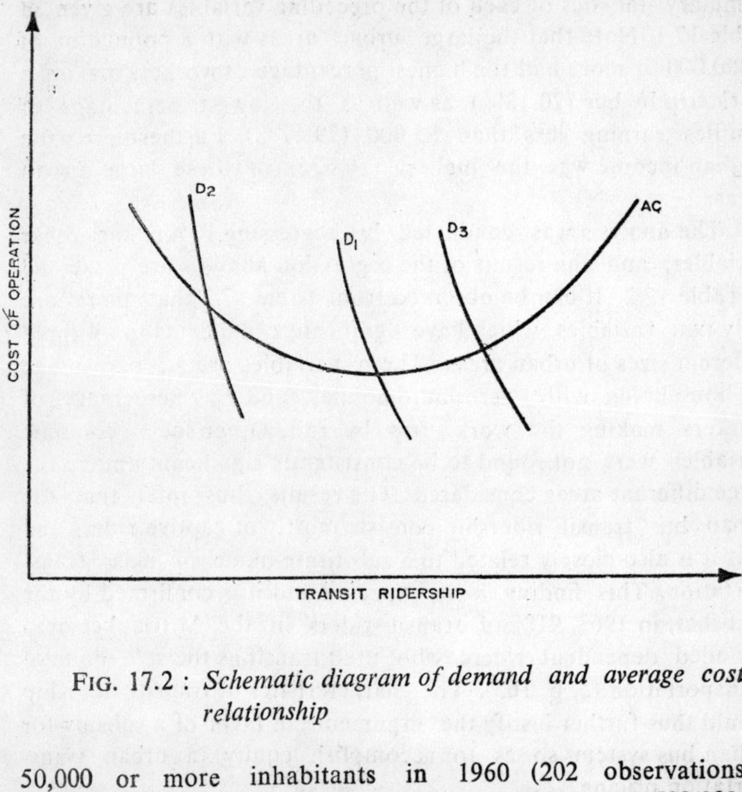

FIG. 17.2 : *Schematic diagram of demand and average cost relationship*

50,000 or more inhabitants in 1960 (202 observations); (2) Urbanized areas containing at least one city with 500,000 or more inhabitants (342 observations); and (3) Urbanized areas with a city population of 1,000,000 or more (156 observations). In the analysis the following socio-economic characteristics were considered :

1. Percentage of workers making work trip by bus, g_1.
2. Percentage of households with zero automobile, g_2.
3. Percentage of household with two automobiles, g_3.
4. Percentage of families earning less than \$5,000 per yr, g_4.
5. Percentage of workers in population, g_5.
6. Percentage of workers making work trip by rail, g_6.
7. Number of automobiles per household, g_7.
8. Median income per household, g_8.

Summary statistics of each of the preceding variables are given in Table 17.1. Note that the large urban areas with a population of 1,000,000 or more had the highest percentage of workers making a work trip by bus (20.18%), as well as the lowest percentage of families earning less than $5,000 (29.17%). Furthermore, the median income was the highest ($6,655) in these large urban areas.

The analysis was conducted by regressing g_1 on the other variables, and the results of the regression analysis are presented in Table 17.2. It can be observed from Table 17.2 that there are only two variables which have significant coefficients in all three different sizes of urban areas. These variables are g_2, percentage of households with zero automobile, and g_6, percentage of workers making the work trip by rail. Other socio-economic variables were not found to be consistently significant among the three different areas considered. The results thus infer that the urban bus transit ridership consists mostly of captive riders and that it is also closely related to a substitute mode of mass transportation. This finding is as expected and it is confirmed by the fact that, in 1963, 91% of transit riders in the Milwaukee area included dependent riders who used transit as the sole mode of transportation (5, p. 165). The characteristics of transit ridership would thus further justify the argument in favor of a subsidy for urban bus system so as to accomplish equity in urban transportation pricing.

CONCLUSIONS

The present modal imbalance in urban transportation is primarily due to the current pricing practice which has unduly favored the automobile users by charging less than what automobile transportation is supposed to pay. The automobile users are paying only their private cost, which involves average cost rather than marginal social cost, ignoring the cost they are imposing on their fellow travelers and society through increased congestion, pollution, and so on. In order to restore balance in urban transportation through improved efficiency as well as equity in pricing, the transit users should be provided with a subsidy in the form of a reduced fare. In this connection the recent experience of Atlanta, Ga. with transit fare reduction can be mentioned. The

TABLE 17.1 : Summary statistics of USER characteristics

Urban Areas with Population of	Parameters	g_1	g_2	g_3	g_4	g_5	g_6	g_7	g_8
50,000 and over	Average	11.79	20.85	19.69	38.06	37.41	.73	1.05	5,903
	Standard Deviation	6.85	6.45	5.82	10.44	3.52	3.49	.13	842
500,000 and over	Average	18.59	23.56	18.87	33.78	38.09	2.62	1.01	6,311
	Standard Deviation	6.63	6.30	5.08	8.09	2.47	7.65	.13	684
1,000,000 and over	Average	20.18	25.06	16.77	29.16	28.67	5.79	.98	6,655
	Standard Deviation	5.71	6.76	5.40	4.43	1.68	10.88	.14	394

TABLE 17.2 : **Results of regression analysis involving USER characteristics**

Urban Areas with Population of	Constant	g_2	g_3	g_4	g_5	g_6	g_7	g_8	R^2
50,000 and over	—29.565	.832*	.199	.189	—.142	.491*	—18.698	.007*	.6484
		(5.767)	(1.298)	(1.087)	(—1.429)	(—5.145)	(—1.773)	(3.061)	
500,000 and over	—45.703	1.315*	—.365	.051	—.080	—.697*	16.812	.003	.7765
		(3.765)	(—.826	(.112)	(.230)	(—6.069)	(.721)	(.617)	
1,000,000 and over	23.000	1.521*	—.645	—.738	—.656	—.621*	40.353	—.003	.8159
		(2.238)	(—.769)	(—.775)	(—.693)	(—3.477)	(.950)	(—.285)	

*Coefficients are significantly different from zero at the 5% level of significance.

transit fare in Atlanta was reduced from 40c with 5c transfer fee to 15c without any transfer charge, and in the first four months of operation the ridership went up an average of 23%.[4]

The privately operated bus transit system in Milwaukee, riddled with financial difficulties, had been following the practice of almost periodic fare increases and simultaneous reduction in service, thus losing the transit patronage, and thus it has been forced to operate in the range of diseconomy of scale. To rescue the transit system from further decline and to improve the quality of service it is imperative that a direct government subsidization e provided. The Milwaukee bus company falls in the category of a natural monopoly, and the existence of a natural monopoly, as is known from economics, would justify public participation in the production.

The government subsidies to transit users or to the transit companies would help establish mass transportation on an equal footing with automobile transportation. In addition to the reduction of fare, with improved quality of service in terms of expanded route and time coverage, decreased headways, and higher speed, the volume of transit ridership would no doubt increase. As a consequence of this the transit companies will be able to utilize the scale economy by reducing the per unit cost of operation. Realizing that most of the transit users are captive riders and that traffic congestion is due to a large number of automobile users, the actual cost of subsidy would be much less than social cost involved with the current pricing practice of urban transportation.

FOOTNOTES

1. Abe, M., "Urban Transportation : Congestion, Welfare and Optimal Pricing," presented at the 4th Annual Meeting of the Mid-Continent Section, Regional Science Association, Indiana University, Bloomington, Ind., March, 31, 1972.
2. "Analysis of Milwaukee's Transit Service," Barton-Aschman Associates, prepared for the Expressway and Transportation Commission, County of Milwaukee, 1970, pp. 5-17.
3. *Annual Report*, Milwaukee and Suburban Transport Corporation, each year from 1955 to 1970.
4. *Digest*, Special Issue, Institute of Rapid Transit, Annual Conference,

Washington, D.C., 1972, pp. 58-66.

5. "Land Use-Transportation Study : Inventory Findings, 1963," Southeastern Wiscons in Regional Planning Commission, *Planning Report No. 7*, Vol. 1, 1965.
6. Marchand, M., "A Note on Optimal Tolls in an Imperfect Environment," *Econometrica*, July-Oct., 1968, pp. 575-581.
7. Sherman, R., "Congestion Interdependance and Urban Transit Fares," *Econometrica*, May, 1971, pp. 565-576.
8. "Transportation Planning Data for Urbanized Areas Based on 1960 Census : A Summary," The U.S. Department of Transportation, Government Printing Office, Washington, D.C., 1971.
9. Vickery, W.S., "Pricing in Urban and Suburban Transport," *American Economic Review*, May, 1963, pp. 452-465.

INDEX